## About this book:

"Bob Avakian is a long distance runner in the freedom struggle against imperialism, racism and capitalism. His voice and witness are indispensable in our efforts to enhance the wretched of the earth. And his powerful story of commitment is timely."

> Cornel West, Class of 1943 University Professor of Religion, Princeton University

"A truly interesting account of Bob Avakian's life, a humanizing portrait of someone who is often seen only as a hard-line revolutionary. I can understand why Bob Avakian has drawn so many ardent supporters. He speaks to people's alienation from a warlike and capitalist society, and holds out the possibility for radical change."

> Howard Zinn, author of *A People's History of the United States*

## About other works by Bob Avakian:

**Revolution** (DVD):

"Avakian...lucidly explains concepts ranging from dialectical materialism to irony without condescending to his audience... He's no less sharp when he's answering questions than when he's outlining his revolutionary program."

> Jonathan Rosenbaum, *Chicago Reader*

"Recalling the vicious assaults on Claude Neal, Mary Turner and Emmett Till, Avakian provides a brutal and bloody outline of tragedy, and does it with a fervor that is far too uncommon coming from the mouth of a white man."

> Herb Boyd, *Amsterdam News*

"Bob Avakian, a thinker and activist of remarkable critical insights, sums up the lessons he has learned and ... termined during more than thirty years ... d guides present and future activists thro ... ls to the understanding of the imperative

> Dr. Juan Gomez Quiñon ... and writer, UCLA

"Just like landmark art work or historically seminal music, Bob Avakian's delivery and timing is truly inspiring. The only thing more inspiring is the vision and message he presents to us. Avakian is a revolutionary leader whose voice must be heard far and wide today."

Wil-Dog, Jiro and Uli from Ozomatli

### Preaching From a Pulpit of Bones:

"For this clergyman who has struggled with the relevance of the Biblical faith in the face of the crises in our society, the critique of Bob Avakian comes as an urgent challenge...There is insight and truth-speaking in this vital book which those of us of religious faith need to hear and to which we need to respond."

Reverend George W. Webber, President Emeritus,
New York Theological Seminary

"What is ethical thinking in a time of social fragmentation and imperialist globalization? Bob Avakian convincingly argues that morality has to be tied to a vision of a good society, a society free of exploitation and every form of domination. Even more does morality have to do with the struggle to create such a society. Avakian points the way toward what some doubt is possible, a materialist ethics. Like Mao's, this is a Marxism that aims at a social analysis that is clear and systematic but not 'cold'—a Marxism with heart."

Bill Martin, Associate Professor of Philosophy, DePaul
University, Chicago, author of *Humanism and Its Aftermath*

### Democracy: Can't We Do Better Than That?

"Avakian argues his position on the decisive limitations of democracy in such a way that careful readers are compelled to clarify and rethink their own views. Avakian has written a serious and demanding work of political philosophy and political practice."

Norman K. Gottwald, editor of *The Bible and Liberation:
Political and Social Hermeneutics*

"With marxist analysis Avakian takes apart the saints of liberal democratic theory: he guts Stuart Mill and shreds John Locke. To these ingredients he adds a dash of maoist seasoning—a *picante* dish!"

Ross Gandy, author of *Marx and History*

# From Ike to Mao and Beyond

## My Journey from Mainstream America to Revolutionary Communist

### A Memoir by Bob Avakian

Insight Press

Chicago

Front and back cover photos courtesy of the author.

Grateful acknowledgment is made for permission to quote from the following:
"Howl" from *Collected Poems 1947-1980*, by Allen Ginsberg.
Copyright © 1955 by Allen Ginsberg. Reprinted by permission of
HarperCollins Publishers Inc.
"The Times They Are A-Changin'." Copyright © 1963 by Warner Bros. Inc.
Copyright renewed 1991 by Special Rider Music. All rights reserved.
International copyright secured. Reprinted by permission.
"Bob Dylan's 115th Dream." Copyright © 1965 by Warner Bros. Inc. copyright
renewed 1993 by Special Rider Music. All rights reserved. International
copyright secured. Reprinted by permission.
"Restless Farewell." Copyright © 1964 by Warner Bros. Inc. Copyright
renewed 1992 by Special Rider Music. All rights reserved. International
copyright secured. Reprinted by permission.
"Subterranean Homesick Blues." Copyright © 1965 by Warner Bros. Inc.
Copyright renewed 1993 by Special Rider Music. All rights reserved.
International copyright secured. Reprinted by permission.

FIRST EDITION

Library of Congress Control Number: 2004116172

ISBN: 0-9760236-2-8

# Contents

Photo section follows page 242.

# Preface *(Summer 2004)*

A short time back, Cornel West, speaking to the important role Bob Avakian has played in the fight against white supremacy and in relation to the quest for a radically different world, suggested to Bob that he think about doing a memoir of his life so far. Bob raised the idea to me and a few other people. I thought it would be a good way to introduce this revolutionary leader and thinker to a new audience, and so I strongly urged him to take this on, as did others. He heard us out and agreed, and before too long a few of us got together with a tape recorder and he set about telling the story of his life.

I was not prepared for what I would learn.

I've known Bob for over 30 years, but there are sides to people that you only learn about when they start peeling back a lifetime of experience for recounting and examination. Three separate but interrelated stories began to unfold:

A white middle-class youngster who grows up somewhat sheltered in the '50s but begins to learn about things like segregation and discrimination and then goes to an integrated high school, where the larger forces in society play themselves out, in interconnection with his personal experiences, in everything from sports and dating to teenage bull sessions about Plato and agonizing over racism;

A college student who, after several years of battling a serious and nearly fatal disease, recovers and becomes involved in the upheavals of the 1960s, beginning with the Free Speech Movement in Berkeley, which leads him into close relationships with some key figures of the 1960s movement and eventually catapults him into being not only a dedicated activist but a leading theoretician within that movement;

And a man who decides to devote his life to communist revolution, beginning (but not ending) with building a new, revolutionary communist party in the U.S.

I found each of these stories very moving and quite fascinating as they emerged, and even more interesting in the way they related to each other.

Any reader can get a lot out of this book—it's not "for the specialist," or just for someone who is already committed to or interested in movements for fundamental change (although both historians and activists will get *a lot* out of it!). There is history, drama—with no small amount of tragedy—and plenty of humor over a life that spans more than 60 years. There is a panorama of characters who come vividly to life. There is biting commentary and deep feeling and thoughtful evaluation and re-evaluation of the epoch (and epic) that began when Marx and Engels first proclaimed the "Communist Manifesto." Let me put it this way: whatever you may expect in picking this book up—I guarantee you'll be surprised. (Look over the table of contents and you'll immediately get a sense of why I say this.) There is a breadth to this man. And if you thought that "communism is dead" or that all those who continue to uphold it conform to the stereotypes of "dogmatic totalitarianism," you are in for a real jolt!

Speaking as a communist revolutionary, as someone who considers Bob Avakian's insights and body of work to be on the level of a Lenin or a Mao, a continuation of what they represent but also containing and pointing to some bold new directions—and as someone who considers that to be a very good thing!—I found incredible value in meeting this leader in a very personal way. I saw the combination of the experiences and his own individual character and dynamism that gave rise to his particular orientation and outlook and accomplishments. I got a deeper sense of the method and approach that he applies to every sphere of life: from basketball to Black liberation, from family and love relationships to the problems of socialist transition and the whole experience of socialism.

Finally, for both the revolutionary activist and interested witness, there is something unprecedented in the way Bob Avakian walks you through, "up close and personal," his perspective on all that went into building the Revolutionary Communist Party, USA and maintaining it on a revolutionary course—long after many others from the same period either scaled down their dreams or retreated altogether from the challenge of fundamentally changing the world. Above all, Bob Avakian is someone who never gave up his dreams, while he has simultaneously continued to critically and unsparingly interrogate himself as well as the movement he is part of and has contributed so much to. Bob is someone who came out the other side of that process with the vision not only intact, but greatly deepened in complexity and tempered with what can only be called science—and, as he himself emphasizes, a living, critical, creative approach to that science and its application to changing the world.

\* \* \*

A word here on my own role. As I mentioned, I helped to interview Bob for this work, and we then corresponded on the editing of the material from the transcripts. I added a few footnotes to help contextualize things. Other than that, you're getting Avakian, straight-up and uncut.

And, as they used to say back in the day, it's gonna blow your mind.

*Lenny Wolff*
Summer 2004

# *Author's Note*

In attempting to write a memoir of a life which has already spanned more than six decades—and which has been enriched by a great diversity of people and experiences—it is difficult to decide which events, encounters and relationships are the most important and appropriate to mention. I have tried to select some which are particularly significant in terms of having a formative or major influence in shaping my life and my view of things. I have also included things that may seem of lesser significance but that I recall fondly and still find humorous or in some other way interesting—and this too may provide some insight into what I am like and what my life has been, and continues to be, all about. Although it is difficult to recall with complete accuracy all the people, events and circumstances which are mentioned here, I have done my best and I hope and believe that I have succeeded in this, at least with regard to the essentials.

In a number of instances, I have given only part of a person's name (a first name, nickname, etc.) or I have actually changed the name. In some cases, I have omitted reference to people who have been important in my life, or I have referred to them only indirectly (or anonymously). I have done this out of respect for their privacy, and out of concern that they not become the target of harassment, or worse, from the people and institutions I have spent my entire adult life struggling against—people and institutions which have repeatedly shown that they have no scruples or principles whatsoever, except to do whatever they feel is necessary to preserve the imperialist system, regardless of the cost in human suffering. Despite the limitations necessarily imposed by these considerations, I believe that I have been able to convey, at times indirectly and wherever possible directly, a sense of people who have been important in my life, on a personal level and in terms of shaping my view of the world and my values. For those who are not directly mentioned, but whom I hold in my heart, you know who you are. For the ways in which many people have played a positive role in helping me come to the understanding and commitment that has characterized, and will continue to characterize, my life and life's work, I am very grateful.

# Chapter One

# *Mom and Dad*

I was born on March 7, 1943 in Washington, D.C. My mother used to joke that I was almost born on the bridge over the Potomac River, because we lived in Virginia, but the hospital was in D.C. All of a sudden contractions had started but she was "holding me in" until we got to the hospital. So I was actually born in Washington, D.C. but lived my first three years in Arlington, Virginia, across the Potomac.

My mother, Ruth, was originally from Berkeley, and my dad, Spurgeon, was originally from Fresno, California. My father had become a lawyer by then, and had gotten a job working for the Justice Department as a tax evasion prosecutor. This was the time of World War 2, and he had wanted to join the navy but was too short, so he ended up working for the government as a civilian, and that's what we were doing in Washington, D.C. My older sister, Marjorie, was three years old at the time I was born.

## *Armenia to Fresno to Berkeley*

My dad went to Fresno State for his undergraduate college, and then to law school at Boalt Hall in Berkeley. He specialized in tax law and that's how he ended up working for the IRS. He'd gotten a lot of offers for jobs from private firms if he would change his name so it didn't sound Armenian, but he refused to do that—both out of pride and because it just seemed unprincipled and unjust for him to have to change his name and hide his family identity and nationality.

My dad's parents emigrated from Armenia, before the big massacre of a million and a half Armenians by the Turkish authorities in World War 1. Even before the war, the Turkish government had carried out and encouraged brutal pogroms against Armenians for many years. My grandmother's and grandfather's families had both suffered from that, and they had left Armenia and come to the U.S. when my grandparents were young, where they met each other and married. So my father was born in the U.S., in Fresno, where his parents' families had settled as farmers because the climate and the kind of crops you could grow were similar to Armenia.

By the time I was a kid my grandparents' farm was very small, and they sort of eked out an existence with that plus the income that my grandfather earned by washing windows. They grew grapes, walnuts, almonds, maybe a few orange trees, apricots—things like that. The grapes would have taken the most acreage, but the whole farm was only nine acres. My dad worked on the farm when he was growing up, as did his two brothers. Later, when he didn't have to do it for economic reasons any longer, the kind of things that he'd done as a farm kid became a sort of recreation for him.

My dad's older brother, Beecher, went to Stanford for a year, and I'm pretty sure it was on a scholarship because his family didn't have money. But Beecher only lasted one year at Stanford, and I think it was both because he felt a little bit guilty about being a burden on the family— even though he had a scholarship they still had to contribute to supporting him—and, from what my father told me, maybe Beecher was not all that comfortable at Stanford, which was a completely different environment for him. He came back to Fresno and opened a small business as an auto mechanic. And my father's younger brother, Herbie, never did go to college. So my father was the only one in his family who finished college. This was all during the Great Depression of the 1930s and nobody—at least nobody in my dad's circles—had a lot of money; he went to Fresno State because he could live at home, and then he went on to Berkeley for law school.

When I was growing up we would often go to Fresno to be with my father's relatives for Thanksgiving, and then we'd stay at home for Christmas, and a lot of my mom's relatives would come over for that. The main thing I remember about holidays with my dad's relatives, to be honest, is a lot of the food. I remember the smell of my grandfather barbecuing shish kebab on the farm. And there would be chickens running around, and sometimes my grandmother would disappear, and then come back a little bit later with a chicken for dinner. I guess she was very adept at wringing their necks, plucking the feathers, skinning them, and getting them all prepared—and we never saw it! I just knew that she made delicious chicken. They'd have Armenian pilaf, which was very rich with butter, and I would just pile the pilaf on top of this chicken and then I'd put my fork down through the pilaf, and the chicken was so tender it would just fall away from the bone when my fork got to it.

A lot of the relatives in Fresno spoke Armenian, at least among themselves, more than they spoke English. My father spoke Armenian, especially to his parents and to other Armenians, when they were in that cultural scene. I learned just a few phrases from being around my father, but neither I nor my two sisters really learned how to speak the language. Yet we did imbibe, so to speak, some of the culture just from being around. It wasn't just the food.

My grandparents were very good-hearted, generous people, and some of my other Armenian relatives were as well. But many of them were also petty property owners and proprietors, with the corresponding outlook. So it was a very contradictory kind of relationship. I was fond of them, because they were relatives and many of them were very kind on a personal level; but, at the same time, many were very narrow-minded and conservative, or even reactionary, on a lot of social and political issues. And from a very early age, because I was raised differently than that, there was a lot of tension, which sometimes broke out kind of sharply.

Fresno was an extremely segregated city, with a freeway through the center of town serving as a "great divide." On one side of the freeway lived all the white people—and essentially *only* white people lived there. Ironically, the Armenians, who were not actually European in origin, in the context of America were assimilated as white people, even though they faced some discrimination. By the time I was growing up, if you were Armenian you were accepted among the white people, by and large, somewhat the way other immigrants, like Italians, might have gone through some discrimination but finally got accepted as being white.

The Blacks and the Latinos and Asians lived on the other side of the freeway in Fresno, where the conditions were markedly and dramatically much worse. And none of my Fresno relatives ever ventured, at least if they could help it, across the freeway. So this was emblematic and representative of a lot of the conflict that came up. For these reasons, I have acutely contradictory feelings about Fresno and my Armenian relatives.

My dad was very aware of the discrimination against Armenians, and this had a big effect on how he looked at things more broadly. He ended up setting up his own practice, and practiced law with a couple of partners, partly because he couldn't get hired by these other firms, even though, as I said, many of them offered him jobs *if* he would change his name. I remember his telling a story about when he was on the college debating team. They were traveling to a debate in Oregon, I think, and they went to the house of one of the debating team members for dinner before the debate. So, as people do when they are being hospitable, the family was lavishing a lot of food on the team, and it got to a certain point where the debating team guys were saying, "No, we're full, thank you very much"; and the hosts were saying, "Come on, eat, eat, don't be a starving Armenian." Then all the members of the debating team got this look on their faces, and the parents realized they must have committed a faux pas, and then someone told them what the deal was with my dad. Those kinds of incidents stamped the question of discrimination very acutely into my father's consciousness. Besides learning about this directly from him, I've seen interviews that he's done, or speeches that he's given, where he has talked about the big impact this had on him and how it made him very acutely aware of the whole question of discrimination and the injustice of it. This would carry over importantly into his life, when the struggle around civil rights and the oppression of Black people broke open in American society in a big way in the 1950s and '60s.

I don't have many memories of my very early childhood. I remember running around what seemed like a huge courtyard when I was maybe two years old. I went back and saw it as a teenager and it turned out to be a tiny little space, but at the time it seemed pretty big to me. And I can remember watching my dad play softball. But one very strong memory I do have is when my dad got polio and was paralyzed. This was pretty traumatic for me—to see someone so strong in my life in such suffering. On top of this, a lot of the other parents didn't want their kids to play with me or my sister any more. My mother nursed my dad back to health while she was pregnant with my younger sister, and she had to keep two boisterous kids indoors because other parents didn't want to risk getting their kids exposed to polio—and she had to keep us quiet on top of that, since my dad couldn't take too much noise.

My dad was determined to regain his ability to walk and even to run and to play sports. He had always been a sports fanatic—he was really into tennis but he was a fanatic about sports in general—and I remember being told later that part of the reason he was so determined to walk again was to teach me how to play sports. I recall a story that my parents used to tell all the time, very fondly, about how one day he was doing these exercises where he was just trying to lift his leg a little bit off the bed, and my mom was in the other room, and he called her: "Ruthie, Ruthie, come here, come here—I lifted it, I lifted it!" She came running in and his leg was just microscopically off the bed, but he was so excited, because that was the first time, since he got polio, that he'd been able to lift his leg on his own. It took him quite a while to get back to walking but eventually, with a lot of determination and help from my mom, he got back all of his abilities to do things, though his stomach muscles were permanently weakened.

### Compassionate...and Determined

My mother was both very compassionate and generous on the one hand, and at the same time very determined if she made up her mind about something. And this was very important in my dad's recovery from polio. There was no other way for my father to recover, other than for her to essentially nurse him back to health and assist him with his exercises (what today would be called physical therapy). I don't remember exactly how long a period that was—it wasn't years, but it was months.

My parents were very fond of each other and very good to each other —they were married for over sixty years. But there was also this sort of classical post-World War 2 division of labor where mainly my mom took care of the kids and my dad worked. I can remember, for example, when my younger sister, Mary-Lou, was born, just before we left Washington, D.C., in 1946. My older sister and I both had the chicken pox while my mom was in the hospital having my sister. Then my dad had to go out of town for work, so they had to get a baby sitter. At that point, my sister and I were at the totally unmanageable stage of just getting over the chicken pox, and the baby sitter could only take a few hours of us before she was calling up my dad and threatening to quit right in the middle of all this. Eventually, as I recall, my dad prevailed on her to stay, but that gives you a feel for how it was in those days, with the classical post-WW2 division of labor.

My mother's family name was Welch, and she came from a long line of families from Great Britain, both her mother's and father's, and that's a very different background than my dad's. My mother was much more deeply religious than my father. But a lot of the religious side of her was this spirit of "Christian giving" and the golden rule and doing for the less fortunate. Even some of the things that could have been tokenistic were more than that with my mom. We used to have "sacrifice night" on Sundays during Lent, when instead of having a regular meal, we would have a very sparse meal, and not eat anything for the rest of the night. Then we would take the money that we would have spent on having a regular meal and contribute it to a church charity. There were two things that were supposed to be accomplished with this: one purpose was to send the money to the charity, but at least as importantly, especially to my mom, was that you were experiencing what it was like to not just be able to go to the cupboard and eat what you wanted to eat. Now, obviously, we weren't sharing the conditions of the oppressed or of the really impoverished people in the world. But to my mom it was more than just a tokenistic thing. To be honest, some of us kids kind of dreaded it, but it also had a good effect on us, even though it was in the context of "Christian charity" and so on.

That was my mom. She wasn't self-effacing, but she was very self-sacrificing and generous.

Now, my parents weren't just together for over sixty years, they were extremely fond of each other the whole time. This was something that I always recognized and appreciated, and in particular with my mom I always recognized and appreciated her compassion and generosity and self-sacrificing qualities. But growing up as a boy in the '40s and '50s, in the more middle class stratum that I was from, in a lot of ways I kind of took my mother for granted. You know, she was always there, she was always supportive, she was always helpful, she was always so compassionate and sympathetic, and she was always sacrificing for other people in the family or for other people beyond the family. But as an adult I actually learned a lot of things about my mother, and learned to appreciate her much more fully, than I did as a kid. For instance, when she was still pretty young, back in the 1930s, she drove her family across the country at one point, which was not that common for a woman to do then. Another time, when she was teaching high school, there was one student there who needed to get certain credits for college—in particular she needed to take Latin, but there was no Latin class there. So, just for this girl's benefit, my mom arranged to teach Latin. But even more than those incidents, I've come to see how I've taken many of her values and made them my own.

Also, my mother had a great love of the outdoors that she'd gotten from her family, in particular her father. She liked taking us to the mountains and out into nature, to all these beautiful places that I learned to love. One time, my younger sister Mary-Lou and myself and my parents had gone up into the mountains and on our way back home, we had to go through the little, dreary town of Merced, just a little ways from Fresno. It was getting to be about lunchtime, and Merced was about an hour away, and my mother was very determined that we were going to eat in the beautiful setting of the mountains. But the rest of us wanted to have ice cream or something, down in Merced. Finally after a long discussion we decided to have a vote, and my father ended up voting with us two kids to eat in Merced. This infuriated my mom and, looking back on it, with good reason. Of course, she had the right stand, yet she didn't win out. But in order to try to win, at one point, when we said we were ready to vote on it, she said: "Okay, let's have a vote now—who wants to eat lunch up in the mountains by a beautiful rippling stream" —she said this in a very lilting and appealing voice—"and," she continued, "who wants to eat in *hot old Merced!*" She said the latter with such disdain that you would've thought we were going to be eating in a garbage dump.

Unfortunately, even her way of stacking the argument didn't lead to her winning out in that case—although it did become a sort of family metaphor for indicating a strong preference while posing as neutral. She was completely right, of course, and now I would have no hesitation to side with her if she were here. But, that was my mom. It shows both her determination and her love for nature.

I took that in from her and it's been with me ever since. My dad grew up on a farm, and later on he very much loved a home that my parents had in the Santa Cruz mountains, but as far as roughing it, that wasn't really his thing so much. As I said, my dad grew up in very modest circumstances, so it wasn't that he was spoiled. But "roughing it in nature" wasn't his idea of an ideal vacation the way it was for my mom. She often prevailed in that, for which I was very glad.

My parents met in Berkeley. My mom was a student at Cal, which was also somewhat unusual for a woman at that time, and then because of the Depression and because my dad was still in law school, they couldn't afford to get married. So they were engaged for three years before they got married. And during that time, after she graduated from Cal and after a year of looking for work, my mom got a job teaching school in a small town a couple of hours from Berkeley—she taught high school there for two years. She could not say that she was engaged while she was teaching, because then they would think she would leave once she was married and would fire her. So she had to hide the fact that she was engaged, and a number of the guys who were teaching at the school were trying to ask her out. It was a very awkward thing. But after a couple of years, when my dad finished law school, my mom and dad got married.

While my parents were from different backgrounds, neither of their families resisted their marriage. Despite a lot of insularity among the Armenian relatives, my father's parents felt the important thing was what kind of person you marry, not whether they were an Armenian. My mother was pretty readily accepted both because of the attitude of my father's parents, but also because she was a very likeable person. And my mother learned how to cook some of the Armenian foods, and picked up some of the other cultural things. Beyond that, my father would not have put up with any crap! So the combination of all that meant that she got accepted pretty quickly. I'm not aware of friction from my mother's parents toward my dad. They were nice people generally, although they too were pretty conservative in a lot of ways, and also, to be honest, my father, having graduated from law school, was someone who had a certain amount of stature when my parents got married.

Despite the fairly conservative atmosphere in which she was raised, my mother was very far from being narrow and exclusive in how she related to people. If she came in contact with you, unless you did something to really turn her off or make her think that you were a bad person, she would welcome and embrace you. And that would last through a lifetime. Besides things like the Sunday "sacrifice night" meal, my parents, mostly on my mother's initiative, would do other "Christian charity" things, like in that Jack Nicholson movie, *About Schmidt*, where he "adopts" a kid from Africa and sends money. But they not only paid a certain amount of money, they took an active interest—they corresponded, they actually tried to go and visit some of the kids or even the people as grown-ups with whom they had had this kind of relationship. My mother had a very big heart and very big arms, if you want to put it that way. She embraced a lot of people in her lifetime. You really had to *do* something to get her not to like you. She was not the kind of person who would reject people out of hand or for superficial reasons.

I remember when I was about four or five years old and somehow from the kids that I was playing with, I'd picked up this racist variation on a nursery rhyme, so I was saying, "eeny, meeny, miny moe, catch a nigger by the toe." I didn't even know what "nigger" meant, I'd just heard other kids saying this. And she stopped me and said, "You know, that's not very nice, that's not a nice word." And she explained to me further, the way you could to a four- or five-year-old, why that wasn't a good thing to say. That's one of those things that stayed with me. I'm not sure exactly what the influences on my mom were in that way. But I do remember that very dramatically. It's one of those things that even as a kid makes you stop in your tracks. She didn't come down on me in a heavy way, she just calmly explained to me that this was not a nice thing to say, and why it wasn't a good thing to say. That was very typical of my mother and it obviously made a lasting impression on me.

One thing I learned from my mother is to look at people all-sidedly, to see their different qualities and not just dismiss them because of certain negative or superficial qualities. And I also learned from my mother what kind of person to be yourself—to try to be giving and outgoing and compassionate and generous, and not narrow and petty. I think that's one of the main influences my mother had on me.

## Chapter Two

# *One Nation Under God –*
# *A '50s Boyhood*

I had a sort of typical American boyhood for the 1950s—a lot of sports, a lot of good times (and bad) with my sisters, and a lot of cutting up in school. But that doesn't mean it was idyllic or somehow cut off from the world: there was the pervasive gender conditioning and there were ways in which the big issues of the "grownup world"—segregation, McCarthyism and conformism—were expressing themselves even in my boyhood.

We moved to Berkeley when I was three, and I have a few very sharp memories and some impressions from those days. I remember when I was told there was no Santa Claus, when I was five years old. We used to have Christmas presents on Christmas eve, and my father or one of my uncles would dress up as Santa Claus. After you get to be a little bit more of a thinking person, you realize that there's always someone missing every Christmas eve when you're passing out presents. So this Christmas eve, after "Santa" came and we passed around and opened up our presents, as I was going to bed my parents came into my room and told me, "I guess you've already figured this out, but you know there isn't really a Santa Claus." And I said, "yeah, I kind of figured that out." I remember that this led to some tension with some of the other kids in kindergarten because, of course, when you're a kid that age, you may not have that much awareness of or respect for how other kids' families are handling this. So you just start saying, "oh there's no Santa Claus," but some of the kids still believed there was.

To give you a sense of the kind of little kid I was, one time I got the idea that instead of going to school it would be fun to go off and do something else, and another kid and I just completely disappeared and never showed up for school. My parents were panicking, and in particular my mom was trying to find me, and eventually they found us somewhere—we just thought it would be fun to go off and do something else that day. Another time, some teenager in the area was trying to get me to jump out of a second-story window, promising to catch me. I was just about ready to do it, but my mother came along and just caught it in the nick of time—she stopped me just as I was swinging my legs over the window sill. She was furious. I remember little things like that, crazy things that happen but you somehow survive—or usually people survive them.

## Sports

Sports has been a big part of my life since I was very, very young. I think I started playing football and basketball and baseball when I was about five. True to his word when he had polio, my dad took me out and taught me how to play all these things. It was a very important part of his life: he loved sports, and he wanted me in particular to take this up —there was a whole thing about being the boy in the family at that time, frankly. It's not like my sisters were explicitly excluded from this, but this was more of a thing with me, being the boy.

My dad started taking me to Cal football games and basketball games from the time I was about four or five years old. I remember every year there'd be a parade through downtown Berkeley before the start of the football season, and this was one of the highlights of my year. The parade made it almost tolerable to have to go back to school. Our elementary school was small, but we did have organized teams in baseball, basketball and football. We played other schools and had city championships; we even had a young kids' team for first and second graders, and I played on that when I was six and seven.

Whenever he could take off from work, my dad would always come to my games from the time I was really little. You'd always see him with his little eight-millimeter camera taking pictures on the sidelines. When I got a little older and I'd throw a pass that was a pretty long pass for a fifth or sixth grader, you'd see my dad pacing down the sidelines trying to measure how many yards long the pass was. He'd say, "33 yards, that was a 33 yard pass for a touchdown." So he gave me a lot of encouragement. My dad had this friend—I think he was a lawyer who worked with him as a government lawyer when we were back in D.C.—and my dad used to write to him all the time in these deliberately exaggerated terms, bragging about my sports exploits. He'd write about it as though it were professional teams playing, sort of in a self-consciously exaggerated way, and then his friend would write back.

In her own way, my mom also shared in my enthusiasm for sports, but my dad in particular was just full of passion for it, and he had a lot of pride in whatever I was doing. But it wasn't that sort of disgusting thing where you put pressure on your kid and you have no appreciation for other kids. He wouldn't yell at me when things didn't go well, and when we lost the city elementary school championship game in football, my parents consoled me, they didn't act like I'd let them down. It was never that kind of thing.

I just loved sports, and whenever I got a chance I tried to play—I didn't care if the other kids playing were a lot older than me. So, from a very early age, around five or so, I started hanging around kids who were older, playing sports—even young teenagers, or ten- or eleven-year-old guys. And, of course, one of the big things when you get into sports, in this kind of society, is that there's this whole macho element to it, and one part of that is you swear a lot. So, one day, we were just playing catch with the family, and I think I dropped a ball or something, and I said "Oh, shit." Now my parents came from the kind of a background where you didn't say things like that, especially in public. They didn't get too angry, but they told me that what I had said wasn't a very good thing to say and I shouldn't do that. So after a little while I looked up at them and said, "Well, okay then, but is it all right to say 'hubba hubba'?"—which was another thing I'd heard hanging around the older kids playing sports.

So, as a young boy, I was just football, basketball, baseball all year around: from September until the end of November it was football; then from December until the spring it was basketball; then in the spring and through the summer it was baseball. My life was kind of seasonal in that way, and I loved all those sports in their turn, in their season.

When I was six we moved into a new house and it was about equidistant between two schools that were in the Berkeley hills. One of them was called Cragmont and the other one was called Oxford. I remember my parents telling me: "You can go to either school you want. We'll let you choose." I said "Okay, but I want to look at them." So, my dad drove me around and we looked at both schools, and I picked Oxford because, when we drove by it, I could see the basketball courts on the playground.

I was lucky enough to have a good coach when I was coming up. He was a student at Cal and took care of the playground in summer and on the weekends and after school. But he was also the coach of our teams. I remember him fairly fondly—he was a nice guy, not like a military drill sergeant. To give you the contrast between him and some of what you often see, we had an incident when I was in fourth grade where we were behind by a couple of points in a football game, and on the last play of the game, I threw a pass for a touchdown and we won the game. Or so we thought. Nobody had showed up to referee the game, so the coach of the other team was refereeing, and his own team was offsides on this play. He called offside on them, and then he came running up to the kid who was the captain of our team for that day, and said, "They were offside, you wanna take it? you wanna take it?" And the poor kid got confused, not knowing what "it" was. He was thinking this coach/ref was talking about the touchdown, so he said "Okay, we'll take it," and then this coach/ref insisted that "it" meant the offside penalty, so we were forced to run the play over again. We ran the play again, I threw the pass again, but this time it was incomplete and we lost the game. That coach/referee should not have put that kind of pressure on an eleven-year-old kid, he should not have tricked him in that way. There should not have been that kind of atmosphere, where winning was that important.

Our coach was not like that—he was actually a fairly decent guy as I remember, and he didn't make us feel like we'd failed the universe, or him, if we didn't win a game, or even a championship game.

But from the time I was nine or ten I was pretty regularly playing sports with teenage kids, and they inculcated in me the idea that you had to win, you had to win, you had to win—and that losing was a disgrace. They had had this drummed into them, and it's not so much that they sat me down and said, "this is the way it is," but it just kind of rubbed off on me, along with a lot of macho stuff and the bullshit that boys in general absorb in this kind of culture. It was generally very pronounced in the '50s, but especially boys who were deeply into sports got a heavy dose of this. Those are the kinds of things that more came from hanging around with older kids playing sports—that was kind of the negative side of it. There were a lot of positive things that came out of it because of the particular times and because of the opportunities that it presented to have a lot of experience with kids from completely different backgrounds and situations, particularly Black kids. That was very positive. At the same time, there was the negative side—the sort of macho, militaristic, win-at-any-cost kind of stuff. But I didn't get that from my own coach in grammar school, and I didn't get it from my parents.

## My Sisters

Overall I got along well with both of my sisters. But, it was kind of a classical situation where my sisters had to do things like iron clothes —they even had to iron *my* clothes. When I got into high school I had friends who were from poorer backgrounds who ironed their own clothes. But my sisters had to do all the stuff like ironing the clothes, even my clothes—there were all those "domestic" things they had to do, while I didn't have to do much of that—and generally I didn't have to do as many "chores" as they did.

I can even remember—at one time I had forgotten this, but my younger sister reminded me of it—that when I got to be driving age and got my license, my parents would let me use one of their two cars, and I would drive all over, but when Mary-Lou came along later and wanted to use the car, my attitude at that time was: "What do you need the car for? You're a girl, *I* need the car." So there was tension that resulted not just from being siblings, but also from the sort of gender socialization and male domination which I just grew up with—even though I loved my sister, I just assumed that driving the car is what a guy does. A girl gets a guy to drive her around in a car, girls don't drive cars. That's how I saw it then.

But even earlier, there was tension just because I was always kind of a prankster. For example, my father would quite often at dinnertime say, "okay gang" and then start telling us about the latest case he was involved in as a lawyer. And so we got a lot of that training. All of us got it, but one of the ways in which I used it—because, again, I was always sort of a prankster—was, just for the nasty fun of it, I'd get Mary-Lou, who had her favorite toys, to sign contracts that would turn over these toys and the ownership of these toys to me. Not because I wanted them, but just to trick her. She would naively sign these contracts, trusting me, and then I would say, "okay now, give me this toy or that toy." She'd say, "no, that's my toy"; and I'd reply, "yeah, but you just signed it over to me." Then she'd go running, crying to my dad who would then come down and look at the contract and invalidate it as having been achieved under fraudulent circumstances! Now Mary-Lou and I were very close in a lot of ways, so I don't want to give a one-sided impression, but these were pranks I liked to play, and then my dad would have to come down and invalidate them. And all my hard-earned trickery would be undone.

We used to play around the house together a lot. From the time I was about nine until into high school, I had this recurring "Sunday-night sickness." That is, when Sunday nights came around, I would not want to go to school the next day, so I would start calculatingly coughing about eight o'clock at night on Sunday; and after I went to bed, I'd wake myself up and have these "coughing spells" in the middle of the night. Then I'd wake up again at five or six in the morning and really start coughing, and after a little while my mother or my father would come and say, "Oh, you've been coughing all night," and I'd answer, "Yeah, I really don't feel well, I think I'm sick." Then there would be this little dialogue: "Well, do you think you're well enough to go to school?" "All you care about is whether I go to school or not—you don't care about whether I'm sick." So then I would get to stay home.

When my younger sister got a little older, I'd try to get her to do the same thing, and sometimes she would, and we had all kinds of games. We had a rollaway bed on wheels, and I used to tie a rope to the rollaway bed and tie the other end to a door handle, and we could pull ourselves around, and get rides on it and things like that. Or we'd make a fort, using blankets, bed covers. I also remember when I was about six, I guess, the big star football player at Cal was a guy named Jackie Jensen, so my dad and I were always playing catch and talking about Jackie Jensen. I remember Mary-Lou, she was just three, picked up a football and ran around the backyard saying "me Jackie Jensen, me Jackie Jensen," because she was trying to get in on things too, she didn't want to be left out.

My older sister Marjorie would be in charge of us when my parents would go out sometimes. So then there would be conflict between my older sister and the two others of us, and we'd get into a lot of fracases. But, while I'm talking about a lot of the conflicts we had, we were also really good friends. We would confide in each other a lot, the way kids do, and conspire against our parents, or complain about our parents, about what they wouldn't let us do, or what they made us do. I remember one time my parents went on a trip for a week and they left us in the charge of this college student who was a friend of the family's. He, of course, didn't know anything about how to raise kids anyway, and he particularly didn't know how to deal with us. And so we had all these grievances that had accumulated against this guy, who we thought was a tyrant. We would get together and conspire against him, and try to give him a hard time because we thought he was just absolutely unbearable. Of course, he was actually in an impossible position. But I remember we'd do a lot of conspiring together like that, or just getting together and talking about things, the way kids do.

So I was actually very close to my sisters. There was the usual tension between siblings, and then there was the tension that came from the larger societal roles that expressed themselves within our family. But within all that, we were still very good friends and very close.

Still, the gender conditioning went on from an early age and was pervasive. I would interact with girls in school—sometimes maybe we'd work on projects together—but as far as things you would do outside of school, at recess, or during your "own time," the girls pretty much played with the girls and the boys with the boys. There were the usual grammar school flirtations that went on, but friendships were not really developed that much across gender lines.

With my sisters, it was again a contradictory thing—I really loved my sisters a lot, we were very close in a lot of ways, and I did some things with them. In some ways, I was the good big brother, and in some ways I was the jerk big brother—or little brother, depending on which sister it was. But they would go to dance rather than sports, or they were Girl Scouts, or Campfire Girls, when I was in the Cub Scouts (I didn't go on to join the Boy Scouts—because it took too much time away from sports!). We were in different worlds a lot. When we got older, when we started really getting interested in the opposite sex, we'd talk about that with each other and get advice. So it was kind of contradictory like that. Our worlds overlapped, especially in the family context, but they were also very different.

And, again, this took place in a whole societal context. For instance, there were all kinds of ads on TV at that point and, in retrospect, you see that in addition to the products, they were selling ideology, too. You had

Lorraine Day, for instance, who was a spokesperson for Amana, which is a religious group that financed themselves through making household appliances. Lorraine Day was like an institution herself. She'd demonstrate a refrigerator and show you what a great freezer compartment it had, and so on. The Lorraine Day thing was directed toward women as housewives, all the latest appliances that they needed to have.

Although my mother was cast somewhat in the role of the classical wife and mother at that time, there was a lot more to her than that. She went back to teaching when we kids got a little older. She did a lot of substitute teaching, and sometimes her assignments turned into long term substitute teaching. A lot of the dinner table conversation was dominated by my father talking about his legal cases, but she would join in that and she would also talk about other things, and not just "waxy build-up on the floor."

## School

My whole neighborhood, the grammar school I went to—pretty much my entire universe—was very monochromatic: almost entirely white. There were a few Asian kids, and in the sports that I watched things were changing, so if you include those kinds of influences, the world I lived in was not entirely white. But the immediate neighborhood and the school I went to were just about entirely white. And so were the teachers and the principal and all that.

I liked school alright, but to be honest, if someone asked me what was your favorite part of school when you were a kid, I'd have to say *recess*, when we could go out and play. It's not like I never enjoyed anything in the classroom. But a lot of it, frankly, wasn't that interesting. Even for that time, a lot of my teachers seemed like fuddy-duddies— old-fashioned, strict, kind of narrow-minded people—and this was from the time I started first grade, back in 1949.

I remember when I started first grade, we had the alphabet up on a poster on the wall of the classroom, and we were supposed to learn how to write the alphabet—a lot of it was very uninspiring. You learned how to print the letters and how to write in script, which is necessary, but you can only do that for so many times until it starts getting to be a bit boring. And we literally read those books with Dick and Jane and their dog Spot—"see Spot run."

Mainly, a lot of what I learned, even reading, was from reading the sports page. From the time I was very young, I used to read the box scores of the baseball games and the results of the football and basketball games. I remember, even before that, around the time I was just starting first grade, a friend of my father's was visiting and my dad starting bragging about what a bright kid I was or something. And so the guy asked me, "Okay, how do you spell cat?" And I said, "I don't know." (I don't remember if I really didn't know, or if I just didn't feel like going along with this.) But then my dad said, "Just wait a minute, wait a minute, tell him what's 7 times 7." And I answered, "I don't know 7 times 7." My dad answered, "Sure you do, what's 7 touchdowns all converted?" And I immediately replied, "Oh, 49." That's a lot of how I learned as a young kid. When I got a little older, maybe in second, third grade, I started reading other things, like the Hardy Boys mystery stories, but the way I got my introduction to arithmetic and reading was through the sports pages.

Just to give an example of how mechanical teaching was, in California at that time you could start school not only in September, but also in February. Then your school year would run from February to February, and you'd graduate in February rather than in June. So, because of that, and because the school I went to was small, when I went into the fourth grade, there were also the kids who'd been in the fourth grade for a half year already, who were in the same class. And I remember this fourth grade teacher had all the kids write the multiplication tables on cards. Then she'd call on someone and they'd have to stand up, and the teacher would say, "Jenny, do your 6's"; and Jenny would get up and go 6×1 is 6, 6×2 is 12, 6×3 is 18, like that. I was just about one week in this class, having come in at the mid-term, and I already knew my multiplication tables. But I didn't know that you were supposed to have cards with these tables written down on them. A little later my turn came—the teacher called on me and said do your 8's. In anticipation of this, I had taken a piece of paper and just scribbled some things on it, and folded it up so it looked like I had my multiplication tables written on it; I got up and I looked at this card that just had scribble on it, and I went 8×1 is 8, 8×2 is 16, 8×3 is 24, 8×4 is 32, 8×5 is 40, and so on. The teacher nodded approvingly, and I sat down with a great sigh of relief. But this girl sitting behind me raised her hand and said, "Mrs. so-and-so, he wasn't really reading from a card, he didn't have anything written on his card at all." But the teacher couldn't really do anything, because after all I had gotten them right. Still, you can see how mechanical the whole approach was.

By the time I got into junior high, and even before that, I was notorious for playing pranks in school, and I drove a lot of teachers crazy, including maybe some who didn't deserve it. Nonetheless, my friends and I were always playing jokes on each other and pulling other pranks, disrupting the classroom—like doing something, then making the teacher think it was the other one who did it. I got sent down to the principal's office fairly often, and fairly often I would hear this lecture about how I came from a "good family," and I was a good student, so why was I so ill-behaved?

## Froggy the Gremlin

We got a television when I was fairly young. Saturday mornings I used to like to watch "The Andy Devine Show, brought to you by Buster Brown Shoes." Andy Devine was this old, somewhat over-the-hill actor, and he had this kids' show; they used to advertise Buster Brown Shoes and some other things. But the main thing I remember about it was a puppet named Froggy the Gremlin. The highlight of that show was when Andy Devine would say to the audience, "Okay, kids, it's time now." And all the kids would get excited and start cheering, because they knew what was coming. Then he'd say, "Okay, pluck your magic twanger, Froggy," and there'd be this little puff of smoke and then this little miniature puppet of a frog would appear: "boing, boing, boing." He had this low-pitched sort of frog voice and he'd go, "Hiya kids, hiya, hiya hiya," and the kids would come back, in their high-pitched voices, "Hi Froggy." Froggy was an imp and they'd bring on guests who were shills for him. There would be Mrs. Pillsbury, say, who'd give a lecture about how to bake cookies. She'd go "Now, kids, you take the flour and you put it in a bowl, and then you put in some eggs and milk, and you stir it up and…" Then Froggy the Gremlin would say, in this low, insinuating, mischievous voice, "And you pour it on your head." Then Mrs. Pillsbury would say, "That's right, you pour it on your head"—and she'd pour it all over her head. Then, when she realized what she'd done, she'd yell, "Oh Froggy!" and he'd go "Haw, haw, haw." You had to be there as a nine-year-old kid at the time, I guess, but to me it was hilarious. I looked forward to that every Saturday morning. Every kid—at least the ones I knew—wanted to be like Froggy the Gremlin. But I think I actually carried that more into practice than some other kids.

When I got into junior high school, I developed this unique voice of my own, which was kind of like the Froggy the Gremlin voice but a little different, and I would cut up in class and disrupt the class in this voice whenever the teacher would turn his or her back. Then I taught a friend of mine to do the voice. At one point we were taking a test, and he did that voice. He was sitting two seats behind me in the same row and ironically the teacher made *me* stay after school in detention, because she was convinced that only I could do this, and no one else. I tried to just tell her I didn't do it—I wasn't going to rat out my friend, but I kept insisting, "I didn't do it, I didn't do it, somebody else did it." She wouldn't believe me, of course. But I got a lot of inspiration from Froggy the Gremlin.

### One Nation Under God

Since my father was religious and my mother was very religious, Sunday school and church were required—there might be certain special events we could miss it for, but generally we had to go to Sunday school, or at least to church on Sundays.

To me it was another occasion where you would have friends and you'd see other kids. We'd kind of cut up in Sunday school the way we did in regular school, but going to church was another matter. My mother was really into music and she'd given us a lot of that love for music, so some of the hymns I didn't actually mind singing, even as a kid. But listening to the prayers and then sitting through the sermon was just something you did until you could get out of there and go enjoy the rest of your Sunday, before you had to go back to school the next day. It's not that I wasn't religious, or didn't believe in those things—I more or less did. I'd never really been challenged on that, or challenged it myself. I believed in it, because that's the way I'd been raised. But on the other hand, I wasn't the kind of person who looked forward to going to church or Sunday school or wanted to sit in church all day. A lot of times we'd go out to eat Sunday dinner, after church. So I remember sitting in church, thinking about the shrimp cocktail I'd be eating when the church service got over, or how I was going to be able to go home and watch some sports with my friends in the afternoon, or just go out and play.

I didn't know anybody who was an atheist, or who openly expressed even agnostic views. Those were times when if you were in the United

States, in the middle class and white, then you went to church, and that's just the way it was. I know that there were exceptions to that. But in the world that I was in, and overwhelmingly among that section of the people, that's the way it was. And you weren't really encountering a lot of people who questioned it. I did in high school, especially, and maybe a little bit beginning in junior high. In high school, given the nature of the high school I went to, Berkeley High, there were a lot of people whose parents were intellectuals and academics, and they were agnostics or outright atheists, and some were even communists, I now realize more fully than I did then. But that was more in high school, and mainly, in the social setting of my childhood, people were just religious.

When I was 13 or 14, my father took me on a trip to L.A. One day he had to go off to a meeting or something, so I went downtown to an area modeled after Hyde Park in London—I think they even called it Hyde Park. People gathered around giving talks, up on little soap boxes. Anybody could get up and talk, and some people were giving talks refuting the existence of god and putting forward atheism. I think that's the first time I heard somebody put forward a coherent atheist position publicly like that, and even though the people were adults, I got up and argued in refutation, or attempted refutation, of their atheism. That's one of the first public speeches I remember giving. I wasn't one of these religious fundamentalist reactionaries, but I *was* raised to be fairly strongly and fervently religious. And while it wasn't a big deal to me on a day-to-day basis, when it was hit at, I would hit back, because the things I'd been raised to believe deeply were being hit at, and this was like hitting me.

One time, when I was about 12, I met a Jewish kid while I was taking swimming classes. This was the first time I talked with a Jewish person about what we believed and didn't believe. And I remember saying very ingenuously—naively, and not with any malice, but just being shocked—when it finally dawned on me as he was telling me what he believed, "You mean you don't believe in Jesus Christ?" He very calmly and patiently explained to me that he didn't, and why. That was a shock to me. That was the first time that I'd heard someone put forward, face to face, in a personal conversation, that they didn't believe in the Christian religion that I'd been raised with. I wasn't outraged, I was just taken aback, I just sort of didn't believe it.

In elementary school we used to say the pledge of allegiance, and I didn't question it. I actually remember, when I was something like nine or ten years old, literally thinking to myself—I didn't physically do it, but I thought it—that I should get down on my knees and thank god for living in this great country that we live in, and I should be grateful that I don't live in one of those awful countries that so many people seem to have had the misfortune to be born in. This is literally what I was saying to myself. And talk about being religious, I remember I used to tempt god—I would say things like "fuck" to myself to see what god would do, then I'd pray for forgiveness because I'd said something awful. But I couldn't resist doing it again. A few minutes later, or the next day, I'd say "shit," because I'd already heard all these words from the older kids I was playing sports with. So, yes, it was very patriotic, very strait-laced —it was middle class America in the '50s.

It went along with the whole anti-communist thing, the drills to duck under your desk to save you from a nuclear bomb, to get people into the psychology of maybe we're going to have a nuclear war with the Soviet Union—though I don't know how ducking under a desk was going to save you from a nuclear bomb.

### Traffic Boy

We not only had the whole usual patriotic drill, but we literally were drilled in the fourth, fifth and sixth grades as traffic boys. We didn't have adult traffic guards at Oxford elementary school, it was the kids themselves—the boys, again—who were organized into squads who would get to school early and go out before school, then at the beginning of lunch, at the end of lunch and at the end of school, when kids might be coming or going. We would go and actually perform these duties, stopping traffic. In our school, this was very serious. We had a cop who came from the Berkeley police force, who was assigned to train us. We had this whole routine where we had the traffic signs we'd hold, and we had whistles. You were supposed to march out when the whistle blew and stand at attention, and you'd hold your sign out to the front and side; and when the whistle blew again you'd twirl your sign and pull it back in, then march back to the sidewalk.

They used to have parents' nights, when we would go through these marching formations. Oh, we wore uniforms and caps, and we'd go through these marching routines. I remember that when I was in the fourth grade, they had a drilling contest. There were maybe forty traffic boys. The cop would put us through our paces: left face, right face, forward march, attention, about face, to the right march. And if you did the wrong command or if you didn't do it at the right time, then you got eliminated. That time it got down to three of us. I was so proud, because my parents were there, and I was in the fourth grade, first year as a traffic boy, and I'd hung in there all the way to the end, me and two "upper class" guys, fifth and sixth graders. Then the cop ran all these commands on us, trying to get one of us to mess up, so he could finish the thing. And we all kept doing it right. So then, finally, he eliminated me because, even though I was standing at attention the way I was supposed to, he said my feet weren't quite together the way they were supposed to be. I was determined to win this contest, as a fourth grader, because that would have really been a big deal, so I was bitterly disappointed. This is the kind of stuff you got indoctrinated with.

Then there was what they called the "top sergeant," the head traffic boy, who ran all the squads of traffic boys, under the direction of the school officials, of course. It was always a sixth grader — the boys in the fifth grade would vote for who should be the top sergeant the next year. I remember one time that the kid who was voted to be the top sergeant had to be put through the paces before they would officially allow him to be it. So, during school, we all got on our uniforms, and we went out in the yard, and the cop who was assigned to us from the Berkeley police was there, and then he turned us over to the kid who was supposed to be top sergeant. This kid was marching us around and doing pretty well. And then, all of a sudden, a girl came down from the principal's office to tell this kid who was going to be the top sergeant that his mother was very sick. Now he was an eleven-year-old kid, so he just took off running to the principal's office to find out more about his mom. And they reprimanded him severely, because he hadn't put his troops in proper order before he'd gone running off. And his mother wasn't even sick! They'd lied to him. That was the really sick thing. They lied to this kid to see how he would react under pressure. An eleven-year-old kid!

I've reflected on that a lot of times, how similar it is to the bourgeois military. The principal, this cop from the Berkeley police force, and the fifth grade teacher who ran the traffic boys — they were all part of this conspiracy. And it all seemed like this prim and proper and righteous stuff — the "good guys," as they like to call themselves. But look at the vicious essence that came to the fore: they severely reprimanded this kid, after they had traumatized him in this way, and they never apologized to him as far as I know.

When my turn came, even though that had disgusted me, I still wanted to be top sergeant, because it was an honor. I won the popularity contest and got to be top sergeant, but it was very clear that the teacher who was in charge of the traffic boys, the principal, and this cop all thought that I was not fit material for top sergeant. I was too much of a cut-up and too mischievous, too much of a kid who was always on the verge of being in trouble. They had to go along with the vote, but they were continually looking for ways to say I was messing up.

In particular, I remember that year when I was top sergeant, my friend Ray, who was in the same grade with me and lived about a five-minute walk from the school, found this stray puppy, which he named "Mutt." He really fell in love with this puppy, and so did I, and we used to go every day after school and during lunch time to play with "Mutt," and then we'd come back before school started again. Because I was the top sergeant of the traffic boys, I had to leave class a little early, and get all the traffic squads out, and then wait until about ten after twelve when they all came back in and turned in their equipment, and then I ran up to Ray's house. We'd play with the puppy, and then I had to get back about a quarter to one so I could get all the squads out. I did this day after day, and there were never any problems, until one time, I was coming back from outside the school about twenty minutes to one, and the principal and the teacher who was in charge of the traffic boys saw me coming in. They demanded to know: "Where have you been?" I said, "I've been at my friend Ray's house." And they replied, pretty much in unison, "What do you mean you've been at your friend Ray's house? You can't leave school during lunch hour." And I asked, "Why not?" They replied, "Because you're in charge of the traffic boys." I looked at them and said "Yeah?" And one of them came up with this: "Well, a captain doesn't leave his ship." And I came back with, "He does when it's docked at the harbor." That was my father's training in particular—they weren't going to get away with that one. They just had to shut up and walk off with a chagrined look, but the fact was that they just really didn't like me as top sergeant.

## *I Liked Ike*

I first started getting interested in the presidential elections and all that in 1952, when I was nine years old. My parents were going to support Eisenhower that year instead of Stevenson. They usually voted for Democrats, but they decided to support Eisenhower, who had promised to go to Korea and end the Korean War. I remember that on occasion, after church service, usually the adults—mainly it was the men, but not only them—would stand around and talk about all these things going on in the world. This was especially the circle that my dad was most involved in at the church. And one time, I think it was the same year, 1952, I was listening to them talk about the Korean War and what do we do, and then at the end of the conversation I came up with my plan for how the Korean War should be ended. They all turned and looked at me, and said, "Oh well, okay." So I remember starting to get really interested in these things at that time.

I don't really remember my plan, although I'm sure it was totally unrealistic.

By the time the Republican and then the Democratic conventions came around that year, my parents had quit supporting Eisenhower when Eisenhower refused to denounce and dissociate himself from McCarthy.[1] But I was nine years old and they had already gotten me into supporting Eisenhower, so I stuck with Eisenhower, even though my parents went over to Stevenson. The Republican convention came on in one month and then the Democratic convention the next month, and for those weeks I would not budge from the house. I was glued in front of the TV all day and all evening, watching these political conventions. You know, "Mr. Chairman, the great state of Ohio casts twenty-seven votes

---

1. Joe McCarthy was a senator from Wisconsin who acted as the spear point of the domestic anti-communist crusade of the late '40s and early '50s in the U.S. During this period hundreds of people were imprisoned and tens of thousands were harassed and deprived of their jobs on suspicion of being communist. McCarthy was notorious both for the recklessness of his accusations and his calls to purge ruling class institutions like the State Department and Army. However, this recklessness ran him into serious trouble when he began to target the army, and McCarthy himself was discredited and lost most of his power as a result.

This overall anti-communist crusade occurred in the context where the World War 2 alliance between the U.S. and the then-socialist Soviet Union had given way to open antagonism between the two countries.

for whomever"—all this fascinated me.

Now, usually during the summers when I was young, every day I would get up in the morning and leave the house by nine o'clock, go down to my grammar school where there was a playground, and just stay down there all day, playing ball, mostly baseball. Six days a week, I'd be down there just playing baseball or sometimes football, all day long. My parents usually had to drive down there about six or six thirty and pull me off the playground to come home and eat dinner. That was what I did. But during those political conventions my friends would ring the doorbell, I'd come to the door, and the dialogue would go like this:

"Aren't you going to come down to the playground?"

"No, no, I'm gonna stay in."

"What are you doing?"

"I'm watching television."

"What are you watching on television?"

"I'm watching the Republican convention."

"The *what*?!"

Then after that week was over, I went back to the playground, the way I had before. But there was just something about the conventions that fascinated me.

My parents would discuss the paper, or the evening news when it was on television. Around these elections in '52 and again in '56—because I was still an Eisenhower supporter in '56, though as I remember I didn't like Nixon even at that time—I used to read the newspaper when the campaigns were going on, the political conventions, and stuff like that. I was fascinated with aspects of it, but I didn't really understand the issues very deeply, although I was beginning to think about things like the Korean War. I had a loyalty to Eisenhower that I'd developed, and I just stuck with it, you know. I couldn't give you then or now any kind of deep analysis of what I thought was good about Eisenhower. It was just that my parents had liked him and, even though they changed their mind because of McCarthy and I became familiar with some of the issues bound up with McCarthyism, it wasn't enough to make me stop supporting Eisenhower.

## *"Have You No Decency?"*

I was recently watching *Angels in America* where that phrase from the McCarthy hearings came up: "At long last, sir, have you no decency?" I watched a good part of the McCarthy hearings with my parents, and I actually saw that incident live, with McCarthy asking these questions the way he did, and Welch, the lawyer for this guy in the army, very dramatically saying: "At long last, sir, have you no decency?"

My parents regarded McCarthyism as a witch-hunt. I remember there was this Black woman who was brought up before the McCarthy hearings, and they ruined her life. She wasn't even the person that they were supposedly going after, she just had a similar name. They hauled her before the committee and ruined her life—and they had the wrong person! Leaving aside the fact that whenever they had the "right person" it was just a witch-hunt anyway.

In my house and among the people that I knew, to be a communist was a bad thing. But, as we saw it then, McCarthy was falsely accusing a lot of people, ruining them and persecuting them, conducting witch-hunts, spreading the net way too widely, and getting people to testify, even falsely, against other people, in order to get out of trouble themselves. That was the whole thing that disturbed my parents and the circles that they were part of, and that's what I kind of picked up. McCarthy only really got into trouble when he started going after the people in the army. Then the powers-that-be joined ranks and said, "No, no, you can't do that," and they pretty much put him down.

Jumping ahead a few years to when I was in high school, Edward Teller's[2] son was in one of my classes—that was the ugly side of Berkeley, because of the Livermore Lab and research to serve nuclear weapons development and that kind of thing. In grammar school, while I don't have a recollection of going around feeling scared all the time that a bomb was going to be dropped, I'm sure it had an effect on us kids psychologically in a lot of ways to be continually put through drills that were said to be part of preparing for a possible nuclear war. Still, I don't remember my childhood having a heavy mushroom cloud over it.

The time that I do remember really feeling that, and I think everybody did, was the time of the Cuban missile crisis.[3] But by then I was in college already. At that time I really thought the world was going to end, or that there was a good chance of it—and that fear was not unfounded.

---

2. Edward Teller was "the father of the hydrogen bomb" and a right-wing ideologue who played a very active role in the anti-communist witch-hunts.

3. See Chapter Five.

But I don't remember feeling that as a young kid, and in fact I think back on my childhood as being a time when there wasn't a lot of heavy weight like that.

Even in Berkeley, though, the atmosphere was very heavily repressive and any kind of protests didn't really break through until the late '50s. Even after McCarthy got slapped down, things were still pretty repressive; not that you felt like your door was going to be kicked in by the secret police or something, but more like you didn't protest, you didn't step out of line, you didn't call attention to yourself in that kind of a way.

During that time, when I was in the last years of grammar school and the first years of junior high school, in the mid-1950s, there was also a lot of "keeping up with the Joneses"—all this consumerism that came off the victory of the U.S. in World War 2. More generally, you didn't step out of line, you didn't get yourself branded. It was *very* repressive in that kind of way, for girls in particular. So I don't remember a lot of protests, even in Berkeley. There may even have been some, I just don't remember. But I do remember a lot of debate about the Korean War, and there would be different occasions when I'd hear adults in particular debating social and political issues.

## Becoming Aware of Segregation

When I was nine years old or so, I began to become aware of segregation. Around that time, my parents got me a membership at the YMCA. The YMCA in Berkeley was very unusual, especially for that time, in that it was integrated—there were a number of Black people, including kids, who belonged to "the Y." I went to "Y camp" for about five years, beginning when I was nine, and the main thing I remember about the camp is that it was integrated. Not only was the camp in general integrated, but we stayed in cabins, maybe a dozen kids, and the cabins were integrated.

Each year the same kids would tend to come back, so there were about three or four Black kids that were in the same cabin I was in, year after year. And, yes, I had some conflicts with them: they thought, not without any justification, that I was sort of a spoiled rich white kid from the Berkeley hills. But I also learned a lot from them. I remember one time, for example, we were going on a hike—we were hiking up the side of a hill that seemed to me very steep and high at the time, though I'm sure it wasn't really. I got halfway up and I got stuck—one of those situations where, if you try to go ahead, you can't get secure footing and you can't go back. I was just stuck there. These two Black kids, who I think were a year older than me, had already made it to the top; they came charging back down to save me, because it was clear I was stuck and I was getting more and more freaked out. They did this even though they really didn't like me very much. I also remember one time I was homesick and I knew some of these kids didn't like me, and I just broke down crying on my bunk. Well, one of these Black kids came in and started talking to me and told me that I wasn't so bad after all, and comforted me.

There were a lot of experiences like this, pretty early in my childhood, and it's to my parents' credit that they had me join "the Y" in Berkeley and go to "Y camp." It was a contradictory experience, because I was still coming from where I was coming from and these kids picked up on that and there was a lot of tension, but on the other hand I learned a lot out of it, and not just in some academic sense—these experiences touched me and made a deep impression. So I was beginning to become aware of some larger social issues. As I was only nine or ten years old, I wasn't very deeply aware of these things, but I knew these Black kids came from a different part of town than me, and that their lives were different from mine in many ways.

Toward the end of the week the camp would have these talent shows. And there was a kid, Fritz, who used to be able to do this thing they called the hambone, where he would slap his thighs and then his chest, pop his mouth and make noise with it—he was really good at it. I've seen adults do it, and maybe it's my distortion from being a nine- or ten-year-old, but I don't remember seeing anybody do it as well as Fritz. Fritz absolutely *owned* the camp because he was so good at this. All week long, he was never short of candy bars or whatever goodies there were in the camp, and other kids were making his bed for him, because they'd say, "Fritz, do the hambone!"—and he'd answer, "Oh well, I don't know...." So they'd keep going: "C'mon Fritz, I'll make your bed for you." It was that kind of thing.

I'm sure there was racism at the YMCA camp. But on the surface and in their principles, the camp wasn't run on a segregated basis. They made a point of that. They had some counselors who were Black, they had a lot of staff who were Black, though I don't think there were as many Black counselors as staff. Some of the high school kids who were paid staff would also come out and play ping pong, or tether ball or stuff like that. You got to see some of these Black guys who were a little older and they had a little different perspective, so you learned. I remember one guy, I think his name was James, who was about 17 and worked in the kitchen staff. All the kids really loved it when he came out and played tetherball with us, because he was a really nice guy, but he was also hilarious. He'd stand by the tetherball and say, "Okay, you ready?" as if he were going to go one direction—then he'd hit the ball in the other direction. He'd let you hit the ball for a while, like you're almost going to wrap it around the pole, and then he'd grab the pole and start shaking it, so you couldn't hit it. And I remember being really endeared to someone like that, like an older brother. But while there wasn't a lot of overt segregation, I'm sure if I'd been a little older and talked to those guys like James, they could have told me a lot of stories. But I didn't perceive a lot of it, because what I was aware of—not only things like the dining hall, but the cabins—were integrated. The people who ran the camp were consciously trying to do something against segregation.

The way I lived in the regular school year was segregated, so you didn't notice the segregation as much, if you were white. However, once again because of sports, from about the fourth grade, we'd play basketball, football, and baseball against other grammar schools in the city. We went to west Berkeley and south Berkeley and played against the Black kids who went to schools like Columbus, Washington, and Lincoln. I remember one guy named Earl, who played basketball for Washington —he was about 10 years old and really a great dribbler. I used to pride myself on being able to really dribble the ball well, so there was very intense competition between us when we played Washington. When you'd go to these schools to play against these kids, you'd see this school was not of the quality of your school, and the playground was not of the quality of your playground. And you could see signs that the lives of the kids were harder. But it was only later that I put some of these things together more consciously.

I remember my parents talking about discrimination from the time I was very young. They were opposed to segregation in housing and in the schools. It didn't depend on my asking them, they were already talking about this, so I was aware of these things. But it was like snippets, what I'd hear from them, what I'd see when I'd go to play a basketball game at one of these schools in west Berkeley or south Berkeley, or one of the kids would come up to our playground and maybe you'd talk to him a little bit. Or you'd go to "Y camp" and you'd get some sense of people's lives from when you'd sit around and talk at night by the campfire or back in your cabin. The things that the kids from west and south Berkeley would talk about were often very different. In some ways they were the same, kids do a lot of the same things, but in some ways they were very different in their experiences and how they saw certain things. But what I was learning was in pieces.

Our family would have dinner table conversations, where we'd talk about segregation and how it was wrong. The neighborhoods we lived in and the school we went to were virtually all white; but, at the same time, it's not like my parents wanted it to remain that way. And it's not just that they talked about it—they became involved and very active in things like the Fair Housing Act and desegregating the schools.

At that time, the public schools in Berkeley were very segregated— until you got to Berkeley High. This was one of the great things about it —there was only one high school. At one point there was talk about splitting the city and having two high schools. I remember all my friends in high school and I were very vehemently opposed to this, for two reasons. One, and I will say it was the main thing, we knew it was a move to segregate the high schools. And two, it would undermine the strength of our sports teams! On the first ground mainly, but also on the second ground, we were vehemently opposed to this.

But there was, of course, "even in Berkeley," plenty of racism. When I went to junior high school, I think there were about twenty-five Black kids, and there were some Mexicans and Chicanos and some Asians, but it was overwhelmingly white. Still, everybody knew we were going to Berkeley High, which was essentially half Black. There were three junior highs at the time. The one I went to, Garfield, was mainly white; another, Willard, was about half Black; and the other junior high, Burbank, was overwhelmingly Black with some Latino and Asian students and a very few white kids, mainly working class. We interacted with them in sports and in other school programs, and the anticipation of going to Berkeley High was a big deal. Everybody talked about what was it going to mean when you went to Berkeley High. There were a lot of episodes and incidents where things would break out between the different junior high schools, or they'd have programs where the ninth graders would all go to the high school for a one-day orientation, to get them ready for next year, and there'd almost always be a fight. Everybody would be talking about it. A lot of racist shit came out, especially in that context. Among the boys it was often put in terms of "how you gonna fight with the niggers" when you get to Berkeley High—there was a lot of that kind of talk. Not so much among my circle of friends, but more broadly there was a lot of that.

## Family Vacations

I also loved to travel when I was a kid. When I was three, when we moved to Berkeley, we took a long car ride across the country and I liked that a lot. Then when I was around eleven, we were visiting relatives in Fresno, staying with my grandmother (my grandfather had died a little while before that). And, at the end of the trip, even though we'd driven down in the family car, I really wanted to take the train back, because I loved riding on trains. I guess my parents weighed it and decided I was old enough, because they let me take the train back. But they made a point of talking to the conductor and some of the other people who worked on the train and asked them to keep an eye on me. It was interesting, there was this kid whose father was a porter on the train, this Black kid named Lynn, and we struck up a friendship during the train ride. We ran all up and down the train, causing havoc, and he got free food because his father worked on the train. It was just a natural thing that kids do—we were about the same age, we were traveling on the train, we struck up a conversation, and pretty soon we were running all up and down the train having all kinds of fun. Then the train pulled into Berkeley and my parents were there. That was a big deal to me, to be able to ride on the train, and the whole experience.

When I was around nine, we went in the summer to Ensenada in Mexico and spent a week or two there at a hotel on the beach. There was this kid named Francisco who lived in the town but used to come down to the beach every day and play, so he and I struck up a friendship. I didn't speak any Spanish at the time, except for maybe a few words, but somehow we managed—he spoke a little English, and he taught me a few Spanish words—and by the end of the vacation we'd become really good friends. I would go down to the beach and wait every day for him to come, and he would show up every day. I don't know what we did for the whole day, we just hung out together. The water was warm and you could go way, way out; it was great for kids, you could go something like a quarter mile out and it would still only be up to a little over your waist. So we'd swim and come back and build sand castles, and just manage to communicate whatever way we did.

Another time, we took a trip to Reno—my dad was doing some work there—and we got put up in the hotel owned by his client. We got these seats for the show in the main restaurant/theater of the hotel right down in the front, really great seats. The show wasn't that much, but there was this comedian and it was like a typical nightclub act: he told these jokes that were really more appropriate for adults, but I laughed anyway—some of them I understood, some of them I didn't. I used to love to chew a whole bunch of pieces of gum all at the same time, and by the time this guy came on to do his act, I think I had something like 10 pieces of gum going in my mouth at the time. Then he got to this part in his act when he was going to do this ventriloquist routine. So he looks around and he says, "Let me get a volunteer to come up here and be the dummy to sit on my lap." Since I was the only kid there, he says, "You, you come on up."

So I go on up there and he says, "What's your name?" and I answered "Bobby." He asked, "How old are you?" and I dutifully replied, "Nine." He asked me some more questions of that type: "Do you go to school?" "Yes." "What do you want to be when you grow up?" I thought for a while and then I said, "I want to be a basketball player like Bob Matheny," who played for Cal at that time. He came back: "Don't you want to be a comedian, like me?" I was actually taking this all seriously, so I stopped for minute and reflected, and then said, "No," and the whole crowd just cracked up. Then he got down to business: "Okay, I'll tell you what you're going to do now." Meanwhile, my mom is furiously signaling me from our table right in front to take my gum out of my mouth. So I take the gum out of my mouth, but there's nowhere to put it. I'm looking around desperately for a place to put it while he's talking to me, but I can't find any place, so I stick it in my pants pocket. Then he says "Okay, now, you're gonna sit on my knee and when I squeeze the back of your neck, you just chomp real hard on your gum and it'll look like you're talking." When he said "chomp real hard on your gum," I realized I didn't have my gum in my mouth anymore, so I reached down into my pocket to get the gum out, and of course there's this big wad of gum that's stuck to my pocket. I'm pulling at it, but it's stuck to my pocket and I can't get it out, and everybody's just cracking up. Finally I get the gum freed from my pocket and I stick it back in my mouth. He does this whole routine, whenever he squeezes on my neck I chomp on my gum. Then, when we finish, he runs off the stage, and I run off behind him; he comes back on stage and takes a bow, and I come back and take a bow. Then I go back to my seat.

The next day we were skiing, and I could see these two women were looking at me. They kept eyeing me, and I looked around, wondering if I'd done something wrong. Finally, one of them came up to me and asked, "Is your name Bobby?" I said, "Yeah." Then she asked if I were at the show at the hotel last night. And I answered "yeah" again. She said, "You weren't really just a kid in the audience, you're actually part of the show regularly, right?" And I said, "No, no, I'm not." "Oh," she explained, "I bet my friend that you were really part of the show regularly."

### The Movies

I didn't really do that much reading outside of school until I got to high school. Before that I read things like the Hardy Boys mysteries and some sports fiction, and sometimes I read the Collier's Encyclopedias we had in the house. But I went to the movies all the time as a kid. There used to be a theater in Berkeley where they had kids' movies on Saturday afternoons—and it would always be double features. I would often go to those, especially when the weather wasn't so good. You could sit there for hours. I didn't care where in the movie I went in: The movie could be two thirds over and I'd go in and watch the end of that movie, then I'd stay through the next movie and I'd stay through the first movie again until it got back to the point where I came in. These were typical kids' action movies, a lot of westerns.

One of the movies that made an impression on me, when I was maybe 13, was this movie about Cochise. That movie made a big impression on me at that time because it presented Indians in a very different way than the whole "cowboys and Indians" stereotype that was all over the TV and movies. Even though, looking back on it now, what this movie showed Cochise doing was actually conciliating with the white expansionists, what struck me then was that it presented Cochise as a dignified person who wasn't just doing all this really crude stereotypical stuff they had the Indians doing in the average "cowboy and Indian" movies.

## The Baseball Hat

There was always stuff "I had to have"—nothing really fancy, just toys, sports equipment, stuff like that. And when I got a little older I'd sometimes want clothes. There'd be certain kinds of clothes you had to have if you were cool—like when I was in junior high school it was really cool to have a Pendleton shirt. So, I had to save up money to get a Pendleton. I think my parents went in half with me: if I did a few odd jobs and saved money, they'd pay for half of the Pendleton shirt and I'd pay for the other half.

One time, my mother gave me a baseball hat. When I was a younger kid, they didn't have any major league teams yet in the Bay Area. They came when I was in high school, the Dodgers and the Giants came to L.A. and San Francisco. But in the Bay Area they had minor league Triple-A baseball teams—Triple-A was the rung just below the major leagues. They had the Oakland A's (short for Acorns) and the San Francisco Seals. I used to go to Oakland A's baseball games all the time —if you were a kid and you sat way out in the bleachers in center field, where you could hardly see anything, you could get in for nine cents in those days. So I used to go and sit in the nine-cent seats on Saturday a lot—and more often during the summer months—I'd go with my parents, or sometimes just with my friends. I was a big Oakland A's fan.

One year for Christmas my mom gave me a baseball hat, but she got confused and gave me a baseball hat for the San Francisco Seals, which was a big rival of the Oakland A's. So I traded that hat with one of my relatives or friends for something else. And then a day or so later, my dad came and told me, "You know, your mom is really upset because you traded away the present she gave you." I said, "But it's the wrong team, it's the Seals, not the Oakland A's." And I'll never forget his response: "Yeah, but she put a lot of thought into buying you this hat, and she's pretty upset and kind of heartbroken that you traded it away." So I went and got it back, and since that time I have never, ever traded away a present, because it tore me up that my mother was so upset. When I traded it, I didn't think of how she felt, I was just thinking: it's the wrong team, I'll trade it for something else I'd rather have. But my mom didn't get hurt that often or that easily, so it really made a big impression on me when my dad told me how upset she was. Not only did I get that present back, but after that, whether I liked a present or not, if someone got me a present, I kept it, because the whole incident with my mother was strongly, indelibly burned into my consciousness. I learned to see things more from someone else's perspective, to think more about *their* feelings.

\*   \*   \*

Berkeley and all, I was still pretty typical of the mainstream middle class in my outlook during my childhood. In high school, I became more socially and politically conscious—a lot of things were breaking out into the open much more, the civil rights movement, things in the intellectual sphere, civil liberties things. In high school, I was very much conscious of that, and proud of being from Berkeley—the sort of place that wasn't typical. But not in grammar school, or even in the first years of junior high. Really, insofar as I thought about it, I probably just thought of myself as an American. And very lucky and privileged to be one.

# Chapter Three

# *The World Begins to Open*

Junior high school was a big transition for me. I went from a small school to this junior high school which had about fifteen hundred students in three grades — seventh, eighth, and ninth grade. It was not just a change in size, but it was an open campus, almost like a high school. You could come and go during lunch, for example. Instead of being with one teacher the whole time you went from class to class like in high school.

## Testing

And then there's this whole thing—at least in the '50s, and from what I know it still goes on—when you're a guy and a new kid, you're almost forced to fight your way through some situations. I don't want to exaggerate, because it wasn't anything like being in jail in an overall sense, but in this particular dimension it's almost a modified form of going to jail—you're new, and people are going to test you out. I remember when I first got to junior high, older guys would pick on you and you'd have to stand up for yourself, so you got in fights. And even people who used to be your friends would pick fights with you to prove themselves to their new friends.

Earlier I mentioned Ray, who was a very close friend of mine during most of my grammar school years. He lived down the street and we used to spend a lot of time at each other's houses. Then his mom had a stroke when he was still in grammar school and, while she didn't die, she also never recovered from it. So his life became very, very difficult and I think that's maybe why this stray dog he found was so important to him. But when we went to junior high school, at one point I ended up getting in a fight with him because we kind of went into different worlds and he was in a crowd that didn't like the crowd that I was in—that kind of stuff.

It was just a whole bigger world, and you had to deal with a whole new set of conflicts and contradictions that you didn't have to deal with in the grammar school that I went to in the Berkeley hills. At the junior high I went to, to a large degree there were the same kind of people, from the same strata and groups in society, as at my grammar school—out of fifteen hundred kids at that junior high, there were maybe twenty-five or thirty Black kids, maybe an equal number of Chicanos, and maybe a few Asians. It was still overwhelmingly white, although some of the kids were from more working class families. One of the Black kids in my class became my best friend at one point, but that didn't happen until ninth grade. Yet overall it was a different dynamic—you were swimming in a much bigger pool and it felt like there were more dangerous fish in the water. So it wasn't quite so innocent or so safe, even though things weren't as "raw" as in the other junior highs in the city. It was a big change. And there was a lot of social pressure to start acting like a "man," to prove you're tough.

For example, I spent eighth grade carrying a switchblade knife around with me. Fortunately, I never really had to do anything with it, because I didn't really know what to do with it exactly, and really I didn't want to do anything with it. But I carried it around, and I suppose I could have gotten into a situation where the logic of it could have taken over, and I would have been forced to do something terrible, or have something terrible done to me. There was a lot of posturing—and that was what you were expected to do in a certain way. It was almost like a ritual, a rite of passage that you were going through, to prove that you were tough, that you could handle yourself. You developed a certain swagger, you know, you tried to convey a certain image of yourself. Inside, you were very conflicted, and not all that happy about it. It was a very difficult time—I felt alienated from things, but I couldn't quite exactly say why, even to myself. It wasn't all negative. I did make a lot of new friends. But I was still going through a lot of changes at that time. I never got in any really serious trouble. I had a few brushes with the police, but nothing serious—the social stratum that I came from meant that I didn't get in the same kind of trouble as somebody else would have. But I had a lot of run-ins and "friction" with teachers and other school authorities. I had a certain kind of posture and a lot of the parents didn't like the influence I was having on their kids—or that they imagined I would have on their kids. Sometimes these parents didn't know what their own kids were into—or if they did, they wanted to blame somebody other than their own kids or themselves.

Anyway, the word would get around. I don't know how the grapevine of the parents worked, but they knew about me. I was not into big trouble, but always on the border of big trouble, always on the brink of getting into something bad. So a lot of parents didn't want their kids hanging around me, and when my thirteenth birthday came, nobody came for my party or anything. I was all by myself on my birthday—which was, of course, very upsetting to me.

### Tournament of Champions

But one good thing that came out of that was when my father said, "You know, there's this high school basketball tournament going on at Cal, the Tournament of Champions. Why don't you go down there? Since you don't have anything to do, maybe you'll have a good time with that."

So he gave me a ride and dropped me off. And this was the most wonderful thing I'd ever seen. All these high school teams were playing one game after the other, and the place was crammed with high school students from all these different schools, along with a lot of other people. I had missed a great game the night before, where El Cerrito beat McClymonds by one point at the buzzer. McClymonds was this school in west Oakland that always had these great teams—a little later they won sixty-eight games in a row, and they won this Tournament of Champions something like six years in a row. I'd missed that game with El Cerrito, but then I came the next night and there was McClymonds, playing for third place in the tournament, and they had all these players on their team that I still remember. They had Cleveland "Pete" McKinney, who could really shoot the ball outside and considered himself open for a shot as soon as he crossed half court. ("Pete" McKinney had a younger brother, Charles "Cha Cha" McKinney, who was a star player for McClymonds a couple of years later and kind of a legend around the playgrounds—I was thrilled when, during my high school years, "Cha Cha" came over to Live Oak Park and I ended up playing on his squad quite a few times in pick-up games.) Another legendary player for McClymonds that year was Joe Gardere, who was only about 5'9", but was a tremendous leaper—he could just about jump out of the gym. And all these schools would bring their rooting sections to the Tournament of Champions. So all of a sudden, here you had a whole lot of students from McClymonds in the Cal gym.

There would also be these all-white schools from the suburbs, there would be Catholic schools which were almost all white at that time, and then there would be schools like Richmond High, which was a real proletarian high school. When I was going to Berkeley High, they used to jokingly say that "even the white kids are tough at Richmond High." Later, when I was in high school, we were in the same athletic league with Richmond High, and over the years if Berkeley High didn't make it to the Tournament of Champions, Richmond High usually did.

But that first year I went to the TOC was a completely new and different experience for me. After that, as long as I lived in the Bay Area, I was sure to be at the Tournament of Champions (and, after moving away from the Bay Area, in the early 1970s, I would try to get back to see the TOC whenever I could). It was a three-day tournament, Thursday, Friday and Saturday, early in March every year, and the first game used to start at 4:30 on Thursday. I would always be one of the first three or four people to be there when they'd open the doors for the 4:30 game, and I would always stay until the very end every night. This was just a wonderful thing—not just the athletics, but the whole social experience. Going to the TOC completely turned things around for me on my thirteenth birthday—and became an important part of my life from then on.

## Cutting Up

I had all kinds of friction with my parents in eighth grade. Usually I got good grades and, while I might cut up in class and be kind of a prankster and cause all kinds of chaos, I didn't get in *big* trouble, with the police or with the school authorities. So that would generally keep my parents feeling good about me. But in eighth grade I was going through all these changes, and for a good part of one semester in particular, I let my grades go. I had this one English teacher and we just clashed all the time. I was cutting up in class, and she was new to teaching. She didn't even dislike me — in fact she met with my parents several times and said, "Look, I really like him, but I just can't teach with him in my class."

I'll give this teacher credit for not being completely uptight. For example, we were reading a Dickens novel (I believe it was *Tale of Two Cities*) and I fell way behind. At one point, she gave us a test, and as part of it we had to identify a character named Pryor Edwards. I didn't know who "Pryor" Edwards was, so I gave as an answer: "so named because he had the habit of always being *early*." This was a four-point question, and she gave me two points for creativity. (Early on, I got from my father in particular this propensity for telling puns and doing word play and, to some people's great dismay, I've continued this throughout my life.)

This eighth grade English teacher was also the "victim" of this very unusual "froggy" type voice I had developed. Whenever she would turn her back on the class and say, "Now who knows what happens at this point in the book?," I'd go into my voice and say, "Nobody does." That kind of stuff, and other things I did, would really disrupt her class. She tried everything. She kept me after class, so I'd have detention after detention, and I wanted to be at the playground or off with my friends. Finally, I wrote this manifesto, some five- or six-page thing declaring this dictatorial system of detention and the teacher's word being law to be totally unjust. I showed it to a bunch of my friends, including the ones who were in detention with me, and they all said, "Great, this is like our Declaration of Independence, let's go present this to the teacher or the principal." But somehow it never happened, it kind of faded away.

Like I said, she wasn't really a bad person, but she was new to teaching, and I was going through this difficult period, so we just locked horns all the time. And that started getting me into real conflict with my parents. She would keep me in detention, but that wouldn't stop me. So she called in my parents, and they were at their wits' end.

Finally, they got me to "behave" or sort of pull in my horns and get through this semester because of a track meet coming up. My dad had taken me to my first track meet at Cal earlier that year, 1956. On the Cal track team was this great Black sprinter named Leamon King, who had this beautiful running style, which I really just fell in love with. He was running in the Olympic trials, which were being held at Cal. My parents told me that if they didn't get a "seal of approval" from this teacher, saying that I was straightening out in class, they would not let me go to these Olympic trials. I had my heart set on this, so I agonized, literally spending sleepless nights over whether it was worth it to keep cutting up in class, and I finally decided, okay, I'll make a tactical retreat. I started studying more, and I got my grades back up, and my parents backed off a bit, because at least in the outward manifestations of these things, I smoothed out the rough edges.

## Arbitrary Authority

Even though I did this whole traffic boy thing in grammar school, I had also at a very early age internalized the idea that arbitrary authority wasn't deserving of respect. I had gotten from my parents a strong sense that you should not have to follow people who required unthinking obedience—the drill sergeant or the military dictator being the embodiment of that. I don't know if they ever articulated it exactly that way, but that was sort of a general value or outlook that I got.

I remember we had this math teacher in junior high who kept three of us after class one time, because we were joking around in class. He started reading us the riot act, and one of the kids started laughing out of nervousness. The teacher yelled, "You think that's funny?" He grabbed the kid by the throat and started choking him and almost pushed him out this second story window. So that kind of arbitrary, dictatorial authority was something that I hated from early on. It was against everything that I thought was worth anything and should be respected.

I had also internalized from my parents and from my father in particular that the Constitution provided you with certain rights, and you should stand up for them. If people tried to take away your rights, you should resist that. So, in my own mind, with a lot of these teachers, that's what I was doing. They were exercising arbitrary authority, insisting on their way in the classroom, and not willing to be flexible or to bend. That's overwhelmingly the way the teachers taught in the '50s, so I had a lot of conflict with them.

But one time, when I was thirteen, I applied what I had learned from my dad—and got in big trouble with my parents for doing so. I had been down at the park and I was coming home, riding my bike. I took a shortcut that ran by my old grammar school. It wasn't actually on the school property, it was a public sidewalk, or a kind of a paved path between two streets, right next to the school. A couple of my friends were hanging around my old grammar school, so I stopped and started messing around with them. One of the things we liked to do was to climb up on the roof of the cafeteria of the grammar school. But we knew that you weren't supposed to do that, that you'd get chased off of it. So we took our shoes off and threw them up on the roof, and then climbed up—ostensibly to retrieve our shoes. It was about five o'clock and the only person there was the janitor. Understandably, as I look back on it now, he was freaked out that we were up on the roof. First of all we could get hurt, and second he could be held liable. So, he's yelling at us to get off the roof, and we're saying we have to get our shoes, because somebody threw our shoes up here! But he kept insisting we come down. The more he insisted that we come down, the more we refused to come down. Finally he said, "I'm gonna call the police if you don't come down right away," and at that point we did come down off the roof.

Well, he *had* called the cops and a cop showed up. By that time my friends had split, but I had decided to stand my ground. I was standing on this pathway, which was adjacent to the school grounds but was not technically school property. So the cop comes and he starts giving me all this trouble. He says, "You know you can't be up on the roof." And I answered, "Well, I got down off the roof. I had to go get my shoes, but I got down off the roof." Then he noticed that I didn't have my shoes on, and he said, "What's the matter with you, you don't even wear shoes?" —and he started insulting me and told me to go home. But I said, "You can't tell me to go home. You can tell me to get off the school property, but you can't tell me to go home, this is public property, I can do what I want, you can't make me go home." He argued with me a while longer and then got in his car and took off.

At that point I started riding my bike home. I was about halfway home when I see my dad driving down toward me. And he sees me and pulls over. I get off my bike and I go running up to the car, and I say, "Dad, dad, a cop can't make me go home if I'm on public property, he can't tell me what to do, can he?" "You better get on your bike and go home," said my dad. So then I knew I was in big shit. I go home and we go through the whole story, and I'm insisting, "Okay, I shouldn't have been on the roof, but I got off the roof, and I was on public property, and I was standing up for my rights, and this cop had no right to tell me to go home."

And then it turned out that the worst part of this is that what really bothered my parents was that they were embarrassed in front of all the neighbors in their nice neat middle class neighborhood—a policeman had come to their door to tell them their son was doing something wrong. And all the neighbors must have figured out that something like that was happening. Here was my dad, with his stature as a lawyer, having a policeman come to his door to tell him his son was doing something wrong. On top of that, this cop tells him, "Well, you know, we're used to getting this kind of attitude from kids in west Berkeley"—in other words, in the ghetto—"but we're not used to seeing that from kids around here."

Instead of standing up for me, my parents were embarrassed and actually coerced me into writing a letter of apology to this cop. I held out and held out, but it was gonna be hell for me in the house if I didn't. So they finally made me write this letter of apology. And here what I was doing was standing up. At that point I frankly had pride in being associated with kids from west Berkeley, because I felt that they must know how to stand up for their rights then—I felt like I was being cast into good company. But, at the time, my parents were just horrified. That really made me feel terrible, and lowered them in my estimation, because I felt like: "What hypocrites!" They taught me all this stuff—how did I know to stand up for my rights? How did I know to tell this cop that I had a constitutional right to go where I wanted, and he could tell me not to be on school property but he couldn't tell me I had to go home when I was on public property? I knew that from my parents, and in particular my dad, all the legal training that I'd gotten, just by listening to him tell stories, but also talking with him about the constitution and everything. And here they were turning on me when I stood up for this. So that was kind of a traumatic experience. On the other hand, it was an experience that stood me in good stead for the rest of my life, really.

As I said, for a while this really dropped my parents in my estimation. But I will give them credit that later on they recognized they were wrong and criticized themselves. My dad, with great chagrin but also with a certain amount of pride in having learned better, would always tell this story from the point of view of how screwed up he was in taking this position. It was years before they finally recognized that I was right and they were wrong, but they did finally recognize it.

## Live Oak Park

Around this time I also started going to this park in Berkeley called Live Oak Park. They had built a new rec center just a little while before I started hanging out there, and a debate had come up as to whether they were going to build indoor basketball courts at the rec center (they already had outdoor courts). My dad told me that the people around there were afraid that if they built an indoor gym it would attract a lot of the Black people from the ghettos of the city and from Oakland and they didn't want that—so they didn't build a new gym. Nonetheless, kids from other parts of Berkeley started coming and Black kids who went to El Cerrito High School, which was between Berkeley and Richmond, started coming over there to Live Oak Park around the time when I was in eighth grade.

These kids came to play basketball and hang out on the playground. I'd get out of junior high school around three o'clock, and I would go and hang out at Live Oak from say three thirty until my parents came and found me or I got hungry and went home. Later in the spring and summer, when it would be light in the evening, I would go back and hang out in the evening. So I was starting to have a lot of new experiences and different influences on me, and I was starting to develop different interests, too.

By that time basketball was my favorite sport—I played it all the time—even later when I played on the football team in high school, I still played basketball on the weekends, and I played it all year round. Partly I loved the game itself, but it was also the social atmosphere of hanging around the playground, playing ball and then bullshitting with the people who were there.

Live Oak Park was still mainly white, but it was changing—they started summer basketball leagues and Bill Russell, when he was a big basketball star at the University of San Francisco, played there. Teams formed up from McClymonds, Richmond and these other schools and would come over and play in the summer leagues. Big changes were beginning to happen, and of course there was a lot of tension. I remember one summer, a team from McClymonds was in a summer league at Live Oak—and they were playing "shirts and skins" (one team wore shirts and the other team went without shirts). The McClymonds team was "skins" that night—and they were playing an all white team. Well, someone, a white guy who I guess was trying not to be "insensitive" (or maybe he was just out of it) asked: "Which team is the one from McClymonds?" And a guy from McClymonds who was sitting in the stands—his name was Fritz Pointer, and he later played basketball for McClymonds himself—answered: "They're the ones in the brown uppers." For a brief moment nobody said anything, then kind of cautiously people acknowledged the joke with a ripple of laughter, and the tension eased.

## White Port and Lemon Juice

There were a lot of things that were going on like that. My older sister, Marjorie, for example, went to the same junior high school I did, three years ahead of me. They had a yearbook they put out, and they had all these things like favorite movie, favorite song, favorite food, and so on. The year she graduated from junior high, their favorite song was a rhythm-and-blues/doo-wop number called "WPLJ," which stood for "White Port and Lemon Juice." It was really improbable for this song to be the favorite song of this kind of a junior high, but that just showed how this culture was beginning to make its way into the larger society. KWBR was the rhythm-and-blues station in Oakland at that time, and my older sister started telling me when I was 13 or so: "If you want to hear some good music, quit listening to that stuff you're into, listen to KWBR." And that was a big thing in opening up a whole other world for me.

I'd always liked music a lot. My mom played the piano and liked to sing and she got us all involved in music in one way or another. I played the clarinet from age nine until I was fourteen, when it began to take too much time from other things I wanted to do. I wished that I'd kept going with it and branched out and learned to play the saxophone, but I never did. Nevertheless, I liked listening to music, and I loved singing—all that I got mainly from my mother.

As a young kid, I listened to all the corny mainstream music. We used to watch this TV show, *The Hit Parade*. They had a regular stable of singers who would sing these mainstream, white-bread type of songs, and they'd count down the hits to number one. I actually enjoyed singing some religious music, and I even went caroling at Christmas a few times, when I was a teenager. About the only part of church that I could stand was singing hymns, just because I liked to sing.

But now, as I was introduced to R&B, it was like a curtain lifting on a whole new world for me. Some friends of mine and I made this "pilgrimage" to KWBR. It was just an old warehouse-type building in Oakland, but we'd heard all these disc jockeys on the radio, so to us it was this magical place. We went down there and walked through the studio and listened to them on the air, and we almost felt as if we were in some holy presence.

There was this record store that advertised on KWBR—Reid's Records—on Sacramento Street in Berkeley, which was kind of like the center of the ghetto of Berkeley. I remember getting on the bus one time when I was about thirteen or fourteen and making another pilgrimage down to Reid's Records, to just go in there and buy a 45 of R&B music. A lot of things were just getting turned very sharply upside down for me, and I loved it. There was the basketball, and there was the music.

There were all these vocal doo-wop groups who were on the radio and had records out. There were the Heartbeats (with James "Shep" Shepherd singing lead), "Pooky" Hudson and the Spaniels, Earl "Speedoo" Carroll and the Cadillacs, and on and on. And, among the "girl groups," I especially remember the Chantels, whose lead singer, Arlene Smith, was only about thirteen or fourteen at the time, but she could really sing with a lot of power and beauty. Then, of course, there was a proliferation of singing groups in high school. Along with the doo-wop vocal groups, there was the broader genre of music that was generally called Rhythm and Blues. I used to really like Jimmy Reed, a blues singer who had this very characteristic beat—he played the harmonica as well as the guitar. There were songs like "Guided Missiles," which was a reflection of the larger world out there. It was a love song, but it was using this metaphor about how your love is like a guided missile which shot me down. Sometimes there were groups that had just one song that would become really big in the doo-wop/R&B circles—and sometimes it "crossed over" to become a big hit in "popular music" as a whole, that is, among a white audience—but then you wouldn't hear that much from them again, or they wouldn't have a hit on the same level (and a lot of times white groups would do a watered-down "cover" of an R&B song, and that would be promoted as the big "hit version"). But it wasn't just one particular doo-wop group or R&B artist that I liked, it was the whole thing.

When I was thirteen or fourteen, Marjorie took me to San Francisco to see Chuck Berry in concert. She told my parents that she was taking me to this concert, but then she dropped me off and snuck out with her boyfriend, and came back and picked me up when the concert was over. That was a big deal, seeing Chuck Berry perform live. Once my older sister kind of lifted this veil from me and turned me on to what was playing on KWBR, everything about my tastes in music very radically and dramatically changed. Given what was happening in society, I was sort of ripe for that. It also struck a chord with my own feeling of alienation and my shifting values.

In ninth grade, my best friend John, one of the few Black kids in the school, got together with me and another white kid to form a doo-wop group for a talent show. We did a Coasters song, "What is the Secret of Your Success?" Now John, even though he was only fourteen or fifteen, had this very low bass voice. This Coasters song was kind of a novelty song. I sang the lead, and John came in with the bass part, and this guy Randy—the other white kid—did back-up singing on it. But when we got to high school, there was this flowering of singing groups on a whole other level, and I'm sure this was also happening at the other junior highs in the city which had a large percentage of Black students.

## James Dean Generation

As I spoke to earlier, my sisters and I had these contradictory relationships, mainly because of the larger societal relations which figured into our family—the way they had to do a lot of things that girls traditionally had to do, and some of the privileges I had being a boy. On the positive side, we were close, an example being Marjorie turning me on to this music. It wasn't just somebody telling me about music, it was more intimate—like she was sharing with me something important that she had discovered.

But when she was about fifteen, my older sister really started butting heads with my parents. As I've looked back on this, I've seen it this way: she was part of the rebel-without-a-cause, James Dean generation, kids who were starting to come into conflict with a lot of the very strict social conventions and mores that were being imposed from their parents' generation onto them. Especially as this applied to the girls, it was very acute—they were restricted in a lot of ways, a "proper girl" didn't do this and that. It was very constraining and limiting and suffocating for them.

My parents were part of that 1930s Depression/WW2 generation, and while they were very sweet and compassionate and generous people, they were also pretty strait-laced at that point. So Marjorie came into a lot of "rebel-without-a-cause" conflict with them. Of course, there were causes, there were reasons, but it hadn't really formed itself into a conscious rebellion—it was against certain things, but not very consciously. So it would take a lot of different forms and some of the things she did were kind of stupid, frankly. Nevertheless, stepping back and looking at it with perspective, you can see the larger thing that was going on, regardless of particular forms it took with her.

For example, one time my dad walked into my room, when I was about twelve or thirteen, and said, "You're not smoking, are you?" I wasn't, and I had no interest in smoking, so I said no. And he came back, in a gruff way that was unusual for him: "Well, you better not!" And he walked out of the room. I couldn't figure out what the hell that was about. It turned out that my older sister was smoking. My parents were down on smoking, but not just because it was unhealthy—the whole thing about cigarettes and cancer was really just being discovered. It was more like it wasn't proper to be smoking, especially if you were a kid, and more especially if you were a girl. This was the grinding of gears of different social forces and generations in conflict, so to speak. So there was a lot of that kind of conflict, and it became pretty acute at that time. That's why Marjorie would do things like volunteer to take me to a concert so she could sneak off and see her boyfriend, because she *had* to do things like that—she couldn't just tell my parents she was taking the car and going somewhere with her boyfriend.

Stepping back to get some perspective on this, I think you can see that it wasn't just a matter of my parents as individuals and my older sister as an individual, but the larger social forces underlying these things —the tectonic plates in society were moving and changing and coming into conflict with each other. Marjorie, my older sister, was caught up in that. The difference between the two of us was kind of like the difference between "Rebel Without a Cause" and Bob Dylan's "The Times They Are A-Changin'": Later on, when I rebelled against my parents, it was a more conscious rejecting of a whole set of social and political ideas that was the negative side of what they believed, their acceptance of a lot of mainstream American values from the prevailing institutions. But with my older sister it was more inchoate, more formless, more beginning, and it didn't really have a clearcut stance exactly, except butting up against the constraints and the restraints and the suffocation.

Later on Marjorie was sympathetic to a lot of those social causes and struggles that did arise, at least up to a certain point in a pretty general way. But she got married young and that put a limit on her activity. Still, what was involved was kind of a generational difference—and when I say generational here, I'm not talking about the general difference all of us kids had with our parents, I'm talking about a very compressed difference, with my sister's age-group just three years older than me. This difference just between her "generation" and mine gives you a sense of just how rapidly things were changing. The civil rights struggle broke out in the mid-'50s, but it really became a big phenomenon and had an impact on the whole country in a sustained way by the late '50s and early '60s. That was more *my* coming of age time, whereas my older sister was a little bit ahead of that time. But she was sympathetic with those changes, and that's reflected in the music that she turned me on to and things like that.

### Umpire

In junior high I stopped playing baseball and, although I would still go to baseball games sometimes, I didn't have the same enthusiasm for it that I did as a younger kid. I just didn't think it was as exciting as basketball and football and track. But I remember very starkly a story involving a baseball game which has a larger social significance.

Even in seventh grade, I was known to kids in my school, including older kids, as being really knowledgeable about sports. And one day there was a ninth grade baseball game between my junior high, Garfield, and Burbank Junior High, which was overwhelmingly Black, with some Latinos. The Burbank team showed up for the game after school, all ready to play, but there was no umpire so it looked like they would have to cancel the game. Some of the guys from the ninth grade Garfield team came up to me and said, "Hey, we want to play this game, but there's no umpire—will you umpire the game?" And I foolishly said okay.

So I was the only umpire. Usually, even in these junior high school games, you had at least two or three umpires. But I was all by myself: I had to stand behind the pitcher and call all the balls and strikes from there and I had to cover all the bases too. I stood behind the pitcher and called balls and strikes, then the ball would be hit and the runner would run toward first, and I had to go over there and say "safe" or "out." Then if somebody was running the bases, I had to run around with them and say safe or out.

Well, the game came down to the last inning and the Garfield team was ahead by two runs. The Burbank team got two guys on base, the next Burbank batter came up and it was one of those dramatic moments: two outs, the last inning and two guys on base for Burbank. The batter hit the ball to left field, way past the fielder, and these Burbank guys started running around the bases. One guy scored, another guy scored, and then there was a question whether the guy who hit the ball was going to get all the way around to home. I'm running around the bases next to him. The Garfield outfielder finally catches up with the ball, throws it in to an infielder, and the infielder then turns around and throws it to the catcher at home plate. The Burbank guy runs in and slides. There's this cloud of dust coming up from the dirt as he slides, the game is literally in the balance, I'm standing there and there's like a little delay—and everybody looks up at me. I yell, "Safe!" And all these guys from my school were furious at me.

But I made the right call, because if you're in doubt or it's a tie, you're supposed to say safe, and there was so much dust and everything that I couldn't really see, and it was really close. So I made the call that I thought was the honest call, which was safe. But, of course, all these kids in my junior high accused me of being intimidated by these guys from Burbank, and none of them would talk to me for a long time.

## Marques Haynes Style

I played basketball in the seventh, eighth, and ninth grades. We played Burbank and the other junior high school, Willard, which was about half Black. These games were not only a lot of fun but also formative experiences, especially given everything that was going on in the larger society. Schools in Berkeley, up through junior high, were still very segregated, as I've been describing. Usually when we would go play Burbank, we'd go down there in a bus; every year there would be a fight, every year the kids from Garfield would run from the gym onto the bus to try to get away, and every year some of them would get their asses kicked trying to run away after the game at Burbank. It was like a ritual and an institution, and from the time you were in seventh grade you knew this was going to happen.

When I was in eighth grade, some friends of mine and their parents had taken me to go see the Harlem Globetrotters. I was really taken with the Globetrotters—not so much all the comedy routines, but more this one player (I believe it was Marques Haynes) who was a really great dribbler. He could dribble behind his back, in between his legs, he could lie on the floor and roll over and dribble the ball, and I just thought this was unbelievably great. So I practiced and practiced and practiced, learning how to do these things.

Then Burbank came up to play us at Garfield when I was in ninth grade. It was really close, going right down toward the end of the game. There was less than a minute to go when we finally pulled ahead by about eight points. I'd been practicing and practicing and practicing my dribbling and thinking about the Globetrotters. So when the game got down to about forty seconds and we were just trying to hang on to the ball, I started dribbling and all of a sudden I went down on one knee, and then went on my back while still dribbling. And at first everybody thought it was just a mistake, like I'd fallen down. So I got up, dribbled around for a few more seconds and then did it again. And then, of course, everybody knew I was doing it on purpose. At that point, the coach of our team called time out. There were only about thirty seconds left in the game, but he took me out of the game and told this other guy, Randy (who was in the singing group I talked about), "Go in for Avakian." Randy says, "I don't want to go in now." "Go in for him *now!*" So I come out and the coach takes me aside and he says, "**WE** don't do that here."

By that time, my eyes had been opened enough that I knew exactly what he meant. I was being influenced by a lot of Black culture. My best friend, John, was Black and I was becoming, as they say, sensitized to these things. So, I knew exactly what the coach meant, I knew exactly what he was saying, and of course, that pissed me off all the more. But then, on the other hand, I took an "I don't give a fuck" attitude because we'd won the game and I got to do my thing.

The irony was that I was doing this out of admiration for Marques Haynes—I had modeled myself after him and his ability to dribble. It wasn't really that I wanted to show up the Burbank kids, it could have been anybody we were playing against. I just couldn't resist the chance to do this. The Burbank kids of course took it as an insult, and as an affront and as a challenge, and that carried over to when we went down to the game in their gym. They had this one guy who assigned himself to guard me—his name was Langston Tabor, and he became a friend of mine in high school. But this was still our last year of junior high, and all the way down the court he would not only stick right with me, but he would push me and bump me; and, three or four times in the first few minutes of the game, the game was stopped because there were these shoving matches and fights started to break out.

Going into the game, a number of us had decided that we were not going to have this thing happen that had happened every year, where you'd be chased out of the gym. Now that decision was a mixed bag. With some kids, there may have been some racism in it, but actually for some of us in a certain way it was the opposite of that. We saw it as condescending and racist to run away. So it was all this mixed bag of different feelings. But anyway they were angry at us not just because we'd beaten them in our gym, but because of what I'd done, because they took it as showing them up—and I guess there was a certain point they had, even though that wasn't my intention. So there was this very tense atmosphere.

Finally, one of the officials from their school came down out of the stands and said, "Either you guys are gonna play this game or you're not. The next fight that breaks out, I'm calling off the game, that's it." So then we proceeded to go through the rest of the game without a fight, but with a lot of tension. We ended up winning the game, and after the game we didn't run—and there was no fight.

### First Love

When I was fourteen, I started really getting interested in girls and I had my first real girlfriend, Nancy. At that time, you didn't see this phenomenon that's interesting to observe now, where you have boys and girls just being friends and hanging around in a group together as friends. There was some of that, but not too much. Mainly it would take the form where sometimes, if you were interested in a girl, maybe you would actually develop a friendship with her friends, because if they liked you they would help you get together. And so, on that level, you'd kind of become friends and share some intimate secrets about your feelings and things like that. But it didn't go much beyond that.

Nancy and I really felt like we were in love. We went together for more than a year. My parents didn't like this so much—they felt I was spending way too much time with her. They may have had a point, but there was no way they were going to break us up. In fact, they tried to limit how much time I could spend with her, but I found ways to get around that. For example, Nancy lived about exactly a mile from my house—if you knew how to take shortcuts, which of course I did. So, especially in the spring, summer and early fall, when the weather was nice, and all the kids in my neighborhood would be out playing in the evening, I would tell my parents I was going out to hang out with the other kids, and then after a little while I would take off running the mile to my girlfriend's house. Then, after a few hours at her house, I would run the mile back to my neighborhood, and then go in my house. I got to where I could run that mile each way in six minutes.

## Teacher's Trial

There was one thing that I was really proud of in graduating from junior high. In our yearbook, besides things like favorite movie, favorite song, favorite food, etc., they also had categories like "most likely to succeed," "most popular," and so on. And I got voted "teacher's trial," which meant the kid who gave the most trouble to the teachers. That was one of my proudest achievements and honors. So even though I had to make certain compromises and pull in my horns somewhat in the eighth grade to not get completely knocked down from things I wanted to do, I didn't strategically give in on my basic orientation of challenging authority, particularly where I felt it was unjustly or arbitrarily exercised. A lot of teachers regarded themselves as unchallengeable authority that had to be unquestioningly followed, and that just really rubbed me the wrong way. And, to be honest, I took a lot of delight in finding ways to disrupt the classroom and challenge them. Ironically, I think a lot of my teachers actually liked me. But there was a lot of tension because I didn't like their exercise of arbitrary authority and I enjoyed disrupting that.

In my last year in junior high I ran for election to this "entertainment coordinator" type post. You had to put up posters and things like that to get people to vote for you. I had a few friends who were helping me, but I also wanted to get some help from my family. So I asked my older sister if she would help me come up with some slogans and make some posters, because she was pretty good at that kind of stuff.

By this time Marjorie was already married and had been out of the house and had a very young baby. But her husband was in the navy, he was at sea somewhere. That poor guy used to come over to our house and he'd have to put up with a lot of my antics; for example, I'd get ahold of his sailor's hat and do "magic tricks" with it—which weren't really magic tricks at all, so he'd end up with orange soda in his hat, and things like that. Anyway, they got married and at this time she was living back in my parents' house. So Marjorie made a deal with me that she would help me come up with slogans and make posters if I would get up at night and feed her baby a couple of times during the week. It seemed like a good deal to me, but I found out it was harder work than I thought. But we did make that deal and carried it out, and she came up with a number of slogans. The one I remember the most was: "Don't be a crustacean, vote for Avakian." So I made posters with that slogan, and put them up all over the halls of the junior high school. But although I won the election, the much bigger charge was when John and Randy and I, with our little group, were the big hit of the talent show that year.

# Chapter Four

# *High School*

I started high school at the beginning of 1958, just a few months after federal troops were called out in Little Rock, Arkansas to protect nine Black teenagers who enrolled in a previously segregated all-white high school.[4] Berkeley might seem to be on the opposite end of the spectrum from Little Rock, and in many ways it was. But Berkeley was nonetheless still part of America, and the same issues would play themselves out—in different ways—in my high school years. I, of course, didn't understand it in quite that way when I started high school —I was mostly just a 14-year-old kid trying to figure out where I fit in.

## Orientation

I remember two things from my first day at Berkeley High. First, my friend John and I had arranged that we would see each other. We were starting in February, so there was only a one-week break, at the end of

---

4. In 1954, the Supreme Court ruled that segregated schools were illegal. In the fall of 1957, nine Black students attempted to enroll in Little Rock's Central High School. On September 4, the Arkansas National Guard with drawn bayonets forced one of the nine away from the school entrance and back into an angry mob of white racists that threatened to lynch her. Day after day, the mobs howled and attacked students and their supporters, but it took a full three weeks for Eisenhower, the president at the time, to order troops in to protect the students. A year later, the governor of Arkansas, Orville Faubus, closed all the schools in Little Rock for a full year in order to resist integration.

January, between junior high and high school. We'd agreed that the first day of school we'd hook up and kind of go through the experience together and continue to be tight as friends. But then when I got there, I looked all around for him and he wasn't there. He wasn't there all that week, or the next week, or the next month; and then I found out he'd been busted and been sent to juvenile hall. So that was kind of a jolt for me.

The second thing I remember is the orientation assembly for all the kids who'd just come into the tenth grade. (The school was a three-year school, tenth, eleventh and twelfth grades.) The February group was a smaller class than the one that started in September, but still they had a program for all the new kids who'd come from the three junior highs, Willard, Burbank, and Garfield. This was the first time we all got thrown together this way. I was walking around, trying to find a place to sit because I got there a little late, and a lot of the seats were taken. There was this one Black kid who was leaning against the wall with his feet sticking out a little bit, just looking around. As I went by him I very consciously made a point of walking around him so I wouldn't bump into him or anything, because I was uptight—everybody in my junior high had always buzzed about how this was a big deal when you went to Berkeley High and how you were going to have to deal with all this stuff, and maybe get in fights. So I was stepping very carefully. As I walked all the way around him, all of a sudden he turns toward me and says, "Hey man, you stepped on my dogs." "No, I didn't." "Yeah you did, man, you stepped on my dogs." Now by the time I was a senior in high school, this guy, whose name was Odell, was part of a singing group that I was also part of. This was how things went through changes. On that first day, though, he was just messing with me as part of the general thing that was going on. So that was my orientation: I don't remember anything the principal or teachers said; but I remember Odell.

My earlier experiences didn't really count for much in this setting. Even though John had been my best friend in junior high, he wasn't there, and in any case that was a somewhat more limited experience. Although he went to the same school I did, he lived in a different part of town. We didn't go to each other's houses—outside of school, our contact was just mainly on the phone. And my earlier experience at YMCA camp was as a younger kid.

This was a *BIG* change. All of a sudden you were going to a school that was about half Black, where there was a lot of cohesion among the Black students as well, so they had a big influence. Plus there was a lot going on in the world, things were changing. Black people were becoming much more self-assertive—proud of being Black and not putting up with shit any more. As I said, there were battles about desegregating the schools beginning to go on all over the country at that time—even in Berkeley, where the schools had been segregated. During the time I was in high school my father got on the school board and was playing a leading role in the fight to desegregate the schools. So this was the larger context at that time, and this definitely had an effect where I was. I was quite nervous—I didn't react in the way I know some of the kids from Garfield did, with pretty traditional straight-up racist kind of garbage, but I was still very uptight about the whole thing because I didn't know what was going to happen.

### *"You Don't Know How Lucky You Are!"*

Now I learned to love this very quickly! But when you're first stepping into it, it's like WHOA. Especially in my second semester in high school, though, because that was football season, I started having closer interconnections and relations with people of all different races, or nationalities, including a lot of Black people. But some things happened even in my first semester that started taking me down a certain path, you might say.

I'd already started to make friends with people that I knew were going to be on the football team, including people who'd gone to Burbank or Willard that I played against in sports. We were now in gym class together—all the guys who played a sport were put in the same gym classes—and so we started to break down some of these barriers. I got to know and started becoming friends with Langston Tabor, with whom I'd been in these shoving matches and near-fights during that basketball game at Burbank.

One day, when our gym class "instruction" was in swimming, I was at the edge of the pool and Langston was just kind of hanging out nearby. All of a sudden, I looked up and there was this guy kind of looming over me. He looked down at me and said, "Is your name Bob Avakian?" And I answered, "Yeah." He went on: "Did you go to Garfield?" "Yeah." Next, he asked: "Did you play basketball for Garfield, did you play against Burbank?" Again, I said "yeah"—and now I'm trying to figure out where all this is going. And then came the punch line: "Did you *foul* me?" Now I really didn't know what was going on, but I just gave him a straightforward answer, because I was sort of naive. I said, "I might have, I can't remember something like that." So then this big grin came over his face, almost like a leer or a smirk—he just kept that look for what seemed like minutes to me, but was probably only 10 or 15 seconds. Then he slowly turned and walked away.

I was still trying to figure out what the hell was going on, and Langston comes up and says, "Man, you don't know how lucky you are! That's Jack McRay, he's one of the baddest dudes in the whole school." I said, "Yeah?" and Langston went on: "He was getting ready to fire on you, he was going to punch you out." I said, "What are you talking about, man? He was *smiling!*" Langston laughed: "Yeah, but when he gets that smile on his face, that's when he's getting ready to unload on somebody." This made a big impression on me.

I learned about Jack McRay a little bit more in high school and after high school. I even played basketball against him again, at a rec center in southwest Berkeley—it was all cool. I believe he's still sort of a legendary figure in the Sacramento Street section of Berkeley. But this was a very dramatic experience for me, and afterwards Langston kind of joked around with me about it and schooled me in how I might handle this kind of situation better. But he was getting a good laugh out of the fact that probably to Jack I just seemed so out of it that he decided, "I'll just let this white boy slide."

There were a lot of encounters like this, it wasn't just with me. This was a time when Black people were fighting for justice and equality in the civil rights movement, and more generally, even in their personal interactions with people, they were asserting themselves more. This was going on all throughout the school and in the larger society. As part of this there was a lot of testing—to see how you are going to react, to see what kind of person you are.

## Segregation Within Integration

While Berkeley High was integrated, in the sense that kids from all over the city went there, within the school it was very segregated. There was tracking, and the classes were largely segregated—not entirely, but to a large degree. The lunchroom was very segregated and there would tend to be segregation even within the gym classes, where Black and white students were mixed together. Generally people did not hang out together socially, and things were segregated on that level too.

As I started to make more friends among the Black kids in school, and to hang out with them, many of my white friends—or former friends—were not accepting of that. Not only were things still pretty segregated within the school, the school was very stratified and very cliquish. Among the white students you had these social clubs, which were basically junior versions of sororities and fraternities. The clubs were exclusively white, with the exception of one Black female social club, and they were completely segregated—there were no integrated social clubs. Except for the Black sorority, they were preserves of privilege and bastions of segregation in the school; they exerted a lot of influence, and they were generally hated by everyone who wasn't in them. The Black kids especially, with very good reason, hated these social clubs. And a number of kids I had known in junior high, including some of my friends, joined these social clubs.

I wasn't into that, I was making friends with all kinds of kids—including a lot of Black kids—and the general attitude coming from the white kids that I'd known in junior high school was: "What are you doing?" In fact, there was one guy from junior high named Gary who came up to me and said, "I want to ask you something." I looked at him as if to say "yeah?" Then he blurted out, "Why don't you stick with your own kind?" I looked him in the face and said: "You mean like *you*." And that was the end of that conversation, and of any friendship between us.

I don't think that making new friends, especially with Black kids, was any kind of conscious "statement," or anything like that. I didn't really think about it in what you might call "social" or "political" terms, except in situations like the time this guy Gary challenged me in this straight-up racist way. More it was a matter of what I wanted to do. I started making friends with people I liked, and that was it. I hung out with a lot of different groups of people. For a couple of semesters, I regularly sat with this group of Japanese-American kids, mainly girls, during lunch and they would talk about things that I hadn't really had much experience with or understanding of before that. I really liked them—they were very interesting, very intellectual, but they weren't snobbish or stuck up.

Then there was my friend Kayo, who was a white kid that I'd known ever since grammar school, even though he didn't go to the same grammar school as me. He was a real sports nut like me, but he also had a lot of other things going on. He was a couple of years ahead of me in school —I think he was only there for one semester when I was at Berkeley High, and then he graduated. But we often ate lunch together during that one semester. One day during school, he didn't show up for lunch, which was unusual. So after school, that evening, I called him up to ask him where he'd been. He said: "First fuckin' day of the fuckin' baseball season." The Giants had just moved from New York to San Francisco. I said, "Oh really, you went to the game?" "Fuckin' A man, great game, fuckin' great game." I asked what was so great about it. "Fuckin' Willie Mays, unfuckin' believable. First fuckin' pitch, fuckin' line drive over the fuckin' fence. Fuckin' home run. Unfuckin' believable." I said, "Kayo, do you realize how many times you've said 'fuck' in the last 10 seconds?" "No, how many?" I said, "probably about a dozen." "Oh fuck."

I remember one day at lunch he came in and he had this little drawing on a piece of paper, and I asked, "What's that?" He said, "You know, I've been thinking about infinity." I said, "Really, what about infinity?" "Yeah," he says, "see, I don't really think it's boundless in space, but I think it kind of winds back on itself." And he had this piece of paper with a drawing on it, one of those things where it would wind back on itself, like a moebius strip, or something like that. He said, "This is how I think infinity is." So then we started discussing infinity. This was completely out of nowhere, but he'd been thinking about infinity. On the one hand, he'd take off from school to go to the baseball game. Then another day he comes in talking about infinity, with this diagram to illustrate how he thought infinity was.

From the time I was thirteen, his family—Kayo, his two brothers, and his father—would go to track meets with me and my dad. As I said, we used to really love this sprinter at Cal, Leamon King. He was a world class sprinter, but he was one of these guys who didn't like to practice. He'd run down the track a few times in these old gym shoes, practice a few starts, and that was it. We'd go to the Cal track where he was "practicing," and we'd talk to him—ask him how he felt about the upcoming meets and things like that. They used to have this track meet called the West Coast Relays in Fresno every spring. We would get in our car, Kayo's family and my family, or at least my dad and his dad and his brothers, Kayo and me. We'd all pile in and go down to Fresno. We'd go to watch Leamon King run, and sometimes we had banners on our car saying things like "Leamon, King of Fresno."

## Clarence, Lonnie...and Larger Forces

I remember these two Black guys named Clarence and Lonnie. They were known by everybody in the school—I mean Black, white, whatever—as being the kind of guys who were always causing shit. For example, when you would come out of the showers in gym class, they'd stand there and snap people with their towels, especially all the white guys, and they had this whole routine they did. One day I came out of the shower and one of them snapped me in the butt with a towel. So I went up to Clarence and I said, "Hey, Clarence man, why'd you snap me in the butt with a towel?" He insisted, "That wasn't me, man, that was Lonnie." Then I go up to Lonnie and I say, "Lonnie, why'd you snap me in the butt with a towel, man?" "That wasn't me, man, that was Clarence." So they had this whole Lonnie-and-Clarence routine they did all the time. I think even there it had a little bit of a social meaning to it —reflecting what was going on in society on a larger scale. They didn't just snap everybody's butt, it was mainly the white guys.

Now we had an open campus, where you could go out at lunchtime and get snacks or go up to the stores a few blocks away, and there was one main street where people walked up and down and hung out. One day some guys from the football team, who were also part of this whole social club scene, were walking down the street, and on the other side of the street were Clarence and Lonnie and some of their friends. And either Clarence or Lonnie threw an ice cream cone and hit this white guy named John in the face. John was wearing his social club jacket, so he was like a walking provocation.

John crossed the street with some of his friends and went up to Clarence and said, "Clarence, was that you that threw that ice cream cone at me?" And Clarence said, "No man, that wasn't me, that was Lonnie." So then John says, "Lonnie, you threw that ice cream cone at me?" And Lonnie says, "No man, fuck you," and then starts yelling at him. Then Clarence starts pretending he's gonna restrain Lonnie, "Aw c'mon man..."—and all of a sudden he wheels and punches John in the face. The whole street immediately broke out into these opposing lines fighting up and down the street, Blacks against whites, as if it were choreographed. I was hanging out with some kids, Black and white, and we didn't get into it. But the fight went on for a while, it became a big deal in the school, and we all got the usual lectures about it. The football team got lectures about how we all hang together, and blah, blah, blah—as if there were no racism even in the football team.

A few days later, when I came out of gym at the end of the school day, there was this long line of Black guys who'd come from different schools around Oakland, as well as our school. And they kind of formed a gauntlet. (The reason I know they were from different schools is that I came out from gym with a couple of friends of mine, and they knew some of these guys—they had family connections or just social connections—and they told me: "That guy is from McClymonds, that guy is from Castlemont," and so on.) So I'm walking out and I'm trying to figure out what I'm going to do, because every white guy coming out there in the aftermath of this fight is getting kicked and punched. I didn't particularly want to be kicked or punched, and as I'm getting ready to enter into this gauntlet, I see two or three guys that I know. So I said, "Hey so-and-so, how's it going?" and I held my breath and started walking. They nodded at me or said something back, and I managed to make it all the way through the gauntlet without being kicked and punched. Then I noticed once I was through there were some other guys who came behind me and the kicking and punching started again. But this was bigger than anything having to do with me, this was coming from the larger contradictions of society and the larger racist relations and racist ideas that were being challenged, and this was breaking out in a lot of ways. I mean Lonnie and Clarence weren't politically conscious activists, and they had their own particular characters and things they did. But even though you could say Lonnie and Clarence started it by throwing the ice cream cone, this whole social club thing was a standing—and in this case a walking—provocation: these guys wearing their social club jackets, going down the street, were making a statement, and people resented this for good reason. *That* was the provocation that led to this.

People have these idealist visions of Berkeley as some place that's always been the way it became through the '60s. But there was a lot of open segregation and overt racism in Berkeley at that time. A couple of years after I left Berkeley High, in the early '60s, a really ugly racist incident took place. There was this area called the slope, where people would eat lunch outside. There were certain areas where the white kids ate, and Black kids better not come over and eat there or there'd be a fight. If you were a white kid you could go eat where the Black kids were, and some of us did. But if you were Black you did not go in these other areas. Finally, this came to a very overt and very ugly head during my younger sister's senior year. One night some white kid from the south, named Jeff, and some of his friends drew a line on the slope and wrote on it "Mason-Dixon Line." When the segregationist content became overt like that, fights broke out in the school and then the lines were very clear. But things were beginning to change, and this guy Jeff and his friends were more isolated than they would have been even when I was in high school. I remember my friend Billy—who I'll talk about later and who was in the same class as my sister—Billy put out the word when this happened that he was looking for this kid Jeff. And Jeff didn't show up at school for some time after this.

But even in this earlier incident, with Lonnie and Clarence, though it didn't have the same overt, clearcut social content, we sensed and knew that this had something to do with these larger things going on in society. To one degree or another, many people, including myself, understood that, even if we didn't feel like getting into this particular fight. And that was true for some Black friends of mine who also didn't feel like getting into it, because it was kind of like, "Aw man, that's Lonnie and Clarence." Yet everybody understood it was a bigger thing at the same time.

### Basketball, Football...and Larger Forces

At that time, the basketball coach at Berkeley High, Sid Scott, was a Christian fundamentalist. He was always lecturing the players about religion. He was also a big racist. Every year when I was in high school, and even before I got there, the starting team would always be three Black players and two white. My friends and I used to always talk and argue about why this was, because while sometimes there were white guys who should have been on the starting five, a lot of times you could easily see there were five Black players who should have started, or at least four. I thought that this coach's thinking went along the lines that if he had four Black players and one white on the floor, the four Black players would freeze out the white guy, so then they wouldn't all play together—even though, of course, this was ridiculous. And if he had five Black guys out there, he figured all the discipline on the team would break and it would just be an undisciplined mess—also ridiculous. And he couldn't have less than three Black players because it would be so outrageous, given who was on the team and how good different players were. This is how I used to analyze this.

But when I would discuss this with a lot of my Black friends, including ones on the basketball team, they would explain to me very patiently, "Look, man, it's not just Sid Scott, it's the alumni and all that kind of shit from the school, people who have more authority around the school, they don't want an all-Black team out there. So this coach, yeah, he's a racist dog and all that, but it's not just him." And then I would argue, "No it's him, he's a racist dog." And, of course, they were much more right than I was.

My friends and I would go to each other's houses, stay overnight at each other's houses, and we'd talk about this kind of stuff all the time—especially the more the civil rights movement was picking up and the more this carried over into all kinds of ways in which people were saying what had been on their minds for a long time but were now expressing much more openly and assertively. One time, when I was a senior in high school, our school got to play in a night football game. Now, we didn't get to play many night games. They would always be afraid there'd be a riot at the game, because of the "nature of our student body." I think this was the only night game we ever played. We went on a bus trip to Vallejo, which is maybe 20, 25 miles from Berkeley, and the bus ride took about an hour.

During that time and on the way back after the game I was sitting with some Black friends of mine on the football team, and we got into this whole deep conversation about why is there so much racism in this country, why is there so much prejudice and where does it come from, and can it ever change, and how could it change? This was mainly them talking and me listening. And I remember that very, very deeply—I learned a lot more in that one hour than I learned in hours of classroom time, even from some of the better teachers. Things like that discussion went on all the time, on one level or another, but this bus ride was kind of a concentrated opportunity to get into all this. A lot of times when we were riding to games we'd just talk about bullshit, the way kids do. But sometimes, it would get into heavy things like this, and there was something about this being a special occasion, this night game—we were traveling through the dark, and somehow this lent itself to more serious conversation.

## Dating...and Larger Forces

I was not part of the social life that a lot of people with whom I'd gone to junior high were part of. There were girls who actually liked me, but they would say things like, "You know I like you but I can't go out with you because you hang around with all these Black people," and things like that. And that instantly made me not want to go out with them anyway. There were things that were explicitly said like that, and then sometimes you could just tell the deal by the way people acted. And all this was being shaped by the larger things going on in society and the world. Whom you were even attracted to and whom you were interested in going out with, whom you were interested in as a girlfriend, and whom you wanted to be friends with—this was being shaped, or heavily influenced, by these larger things going on.

There were taboos. You didn't date "interracially." You didn't do that. There were a few kids in my class who did, and they took a lot of shit for it. In my senior year, there was one girl that I was very fond of, who was in glee club with me, and we went out for a little while. She was actually the head of the one Black social club in the school. Now it was a rule that every social club had to invite at least the president of every other social club to whatever function they had. So she was invited to a New Year's Eve dance sponsored by one of these white social clubs, and she asked me to be her date for that. I said sure, 'cause we liked each other. So we went, along with another couple, two Black friends of hers. Of course, there's this whole tradition that on New Year's Eve you give your date a big kiss when it strikes midnight. So, at the dance there was all this tension because we were there and we were dancing together the whole night, and hanging out together, just like any other couple would. Except...I could tell as it got to be 11:00, 11:15, closer and closer to midnight, this palpable tension was in the air: "What's gonna happen when midnight comes?" When midnight came, she and I gave each other the biggest imaginable kiss—both because we really liked each other, but we also really wanted to make these people eat it. So we had a great time doing that! But it was a big deal. The tension there was very real.

Of course, I got called things like "nigger lover" and I didn't get invited to join these social clubs—which was nothing, because I wouldn't have wanted to do that anyway. But whatever ways in which I was "ostracized" and "outcast" among the mainstream whites was really nothing compared to what my Black friends went through. From the time I was a junior in high school, there were four of us who hung out together: Matthew, Joel, Hemby, and me—two of us white, two of us Black. We were always hanging out together. One time Matthew, who was Black, really had a crush on this one white girl; he wanted to ask her out and finally he worked up his courage and asked her out. And she told him, "Well, you know, I'd like to go out with you, but my parents and my friends..." and all this kind of shit. That was *much* more painful than anything that happened to me—it was very painful for me, being his friend, and it was the kind of thing that I know left a deep scar in Matthew. It was just horrible and excruciating, and the scars of that were much deeper than anything that happened to me.

## Street Corner Symphonies

I had this friend Sam. Actually I knew him before high school, because I went to a church in Berkeley where his father worked as the custodian and he would come around and help his father sometimes. Then, when I went to high school, he was a little bit ahead of me but we became friends and then we became part of a singing group.

Sam had this one characteristic: when he was eating, he didn't want anybody to say anything to him. It was just leave him alone and let him eat. I don't care who it was or what the circumstances were. That was just Sam, you just knew you should stay away from him then, because he didn't want to talk, he wanted to eat. So one day, I had forgotten to bring my lunch money, and I was really hungry by lunch. I couldn't pay for anything in the cafeteria or the snack shack, or anything. I was walking all around looking for some friend to loan me some money. So first I went over to Sam and I knew that I was violating his big rule, but I couldn't help it. I went over and I said, "Sam." "Leave me alone, man, leave me alone." I said "Sam, I'm really hungry." "Leave me alone, I'm eating lunch." So I just finally gave up there, but I started walking all around looking for someone to loan me some money or give me something to eat or something.

Finally, I saw this guy who had a plateful of food. What particularly stuck out to me was that he had two pieces of cornbread on his tray. And that just seemed so unfair, because I was so hungry and he had not one, but two pieces of cornbread! I just sat down at the table, across from him, and stared for a long time at his plate. He kept looking at me, like "what's this motherfucker staring at me for?" I just kept staring at his tray. And finally I said, "Hey man, can I have one of your pieces of corn-bread?" "No, man, get the fuck out of here." I said, "Please man, I'm real-ly hungry, I forgot my lunch money. Can I please have a piece of corn-bread?" "No man, get the fuck out of here." I don't know what came over me—maybe it was just the hunger—but without thinking, I reached over and grabbed one of the pieces of cornbread. He kicked his chair back, jumped up and got ready to fight. So I didn't have any choice, I jumped up too. He stared at me for a long time—a *long* time. And then he finally said, "Aw man, go ahead." So I took the piece of cornbread. Then after that, Sam, who had looked up from his eating long enough to see all this, came over to me—again it was one of these things—and he said, "Man, that was Leo Wofford, you don't know what you just got away with." But I was just so hungry, and I guess Leo figured, "oh this crazy white boy, he must really be hungry," so he just let it go.

Sam lived in East Oakland, but he went to school in Berkeley. A few times I went out to his house—he lived right where East Oakland abutted against San Leandro, and it was like in the south. There was this creek and a fence right outside of 98th Avenue in East Oakland, and if you were Black you did not go on the other side of the fence into San Leandro or these racist mobs would come after you. Sam lived right at the border there.

A few times Sam took me to places and events out in East Oakland. One time we went to this housing project which was kind of laid out in concentric circles, with a row of apartments, arranged in a circle, and then another circle inside that, and then another one. And at the very center was the playground, where there was a basketball court. When we got there, there were some guys getting ready to play ball—I recognized a couple of them who ran track for Castlemont High—so I went over and got in the game. Well, at a certain point, one of these track guys and I got into a face-off—we had been guarding each other, and sometimes bumping and pushing each other, and then it just about got to the point of a fight. Everybody else stood back and gave us room, but after we stared at each other for a while, it didn't go any further, and we just got back to the game. But, as this was happening, I noticed that Sam, who had been watching at the edge of the court, was turning and walking away.

Another time, Sam and I went to a basketball game between Castlemont and Berkeley High. The game was at Castlemont, but I didn't have any sense, so I kept yelling shit at the Castlemont players. Their star player was a guy named Fred "Sweetie" Davis, and at one point he got knocked to the floor by a guy on our team. So, I stood up and yelled, "How does it feel to be the one on the floor, Sweetie?" Sam had been trying to get me to stop acting the fool and shut up, and when this happened, he just got up and walked away, like "I don't know this crazy white boy." So, sometimes, without meaning to, I put Sam in some very difficult situations.

Sam was a really good singer. So one day I went to him and I asked: "Hey, Sam, you want to start a group?" He thought about it for a while, and then he got back to me and said, "Yeah, let's do it." Sam had a cousin named George who played piano, and George could also sing. So Sam said, "Let's get George in the group." And there was this other guy, Felton, who was one of the few Black kids who had gone to junior high school where I did. So I went and asked him if he wanted to be part of it, and Felton said "Yeah." And then I asked Randy, this white kid who'd been part of this impromptu singing group with John and me in our last year in junior high school.

So the five of us—three Black, two white—formed a group. We figured out pretty quickly that Sam should sing lead, at least on most of the songs, and then the others of us took our parts. You have to have a bass, and that was Felton. We had to have a baritone, and that was Randy. Then you had to have a second tenor, which was the lower-range tenor, and that was George. And the first tenor was me. We had this whole thing worked out. Sometimes we practiced at George's house, because he had a piano in his house, and sometimes we'd go to my house, because we also had a piano. We'd spend three or four hours a lot of days just practicing, working on our music. And we'd sing anywhere we could get together to sing—this was part of a whole thing where people would get together, sometimes in formal groups and sometimes just with whoever was around at the time, and sing everywhere: in the locker rooms before and after gym class, in the hallways and stairways at school, and out on the street corners.

Eventually, Randy left the group and then Odell—Odell who claimed I'd "stepped on his dogs" way back on our first day of school—replaced him. When Odell replaced Randy I reminded him of that run-in we had, and he didn't even remember it. But he did get a big laugh out of my telling the story. Odell used to write songs—I'd see him out in the hallway: "Hey, Odell, what are you doing, how come you're not in class?" "I'm writing some songs, man." We'd practice and we'd try to get gigs, wanting to get paid and get known a little bit.

We had to come up with a name for the group. There was already the Cadillacs, and the Impalas, so we became the Continentals. Now we'd also been rehearsing at the rec center at Live Oak, because they had a piano in there. The director of the rec center heard us and said, "Hey, I like your sound, would you guys be willing to play for this dance we're having?" We answered, "Yeah, are you gonna pay us?" And he said, "Well, we have a tight budget, but I could pay you something." So then we all got together and said, "How about a hundred bucks?" He came back with, "How about 25?" We looked at each other and said, "Okay." 'Cause any money was good then.

We rehearsed a lot for this, and we came there that night ready to do this Heartbeats' song, "You're a Thousand Miles Away," and some other tunes. As we were about to go in the rec center, this friend of Sam's who had been playing basketball was coming over to get a drink of water. And he said, "Sam, what are you doing here?" Sam said, "We're gonna sing for this dance." "You can't sing, Sam." "Yeah I can, man." So before we could go in to perform for the dance, we had to have a sing-off between Sam and his friend—they both did a Spaniels song, and after a couple of verses the other guy threw in the towel, because Sam could *really* sing.

Another time my younger sister got us a gig performing at their ninth-grade dance. The other guys in the group said, "Okay man, this is your sister's thing," so they let me sing lead on one song—I think it was called "Oh Happy Day." And that was a lot of fun.

Some of the white parents just couldn't relate to this music at all. And with some there was a whole racist element in it, because it was the influence of Black culture working its way "into the mainstream." But a lot of the white youth were taking it up and were really into it, as exemplified by my older sister's junior high school class voting "WPLJ" as their favorite song. I think Richard Pryor made this point in one of his routines—when it's just Black people doing something, then maybe they can contain it, but when it starts spilling over among the white youth, then "Oh dear, everything's getting out of control." So there was that sort of shit, and there was a general thing among the racist and backward white kids, where listening to this music and getting into this culture was part of a whole package of "things you didn't do." They would give you shit for that, but it was just part of a whole package of everything they were down on, and all the things they'd give you shit for.

Besides singing doo-wop, I was in the glee club in school. When I was a senior, the glee club teacher talked me and three other guys — two of us Black, two of us white — into doing a barbershop quartet song for the talent show. And we did it — with our own little touch to it. Another time, when I was sixteen or seventeen, I went to a Giants baseball game. Right before the game starts they always have the national anthem, and I was still somewhat patriotic — I wasn't super-patriotic, but I still thought this was a good country overall, even though I was very angry about discrimination and segregation and racism and all that. So we all stood up for the anthem and, for whatever reason, I started singing along. The song finished and this woman in front of me turned around and said, "You know, you have a beautiful voice." I've often thought back on the irony of that.

But it wasn't very long before I quit singing that. Later, when I would go to ball games and they would play the national anthem, I would stand up and sing, as loudly as I could, a version that someone I knew had made up: "Oh, oh Un-cle Sam, get out of Vietnam. Get out, get out, get out of Vietnam . . ."

### Family Clashes

We had these Armenian relatives in L.A. They were relatives of my father, but they were unlike my father — they were very provincial, very snobbish, very big supporters of Billy Graham and big-time racists. One time my younger sister Mary-Lou and I were staying in their house and we got in an argument about all this kind of stuff. My dad's uncle — ironically his name was Sam, and we called him Uncle Sam — started this argument, and at one point he said to me, "Well, Bobby, what would you say about it and how would you feel if your younger sister, Mary-Lou, started dating a Negro, or even married a Negro?" And I answered: "Well, that's up to her, if she wants to do that it's fine with me." So then we got into a big roaring argument. And here you see not only the racism but also the patriarchy. He didn't ask *her* how she'd feel about it — and she was sitting right there. But it was as if she were invisible.

Within our broader family circles, there was a lot of that kind of shit. As I mentioned earlier, Fresno was very segregated at that time, a lot of backward, reactionary stuff was concentrated there, and my relatives were, again, sort of narrow, provincial and into a lot of this backward, reactionary and racist stuff. When I was maybe eighteen or nineteen we were visiting down there on one of the holidays, and they asked me to do a dramatic reading of something that was being circulated in their circles. I didn't know what it was, so I agreed. When I started reading it, it turned out to be this racist parody about John Kennedy's son marrying Martin Luther King's daughter—all this racist garbage. When I realized what they were having me read, I just stopped and I got furious, and they must have regretted ever having given this to me to read. Because I just launched into a tirade against them and their segregated Fresno: "You don't know anything about Black people. You refuse to go anywhere where they are, you avoid them, you with your freeway through the middle of town and all the segregation," and so on. I don't even remember everything I said, but it went on for about five minutes and they all just sat there, frozen. Then I just threw the thing down and stalked out of the room, and it became, of course, a big episode in family relations. But they deserved it, and I didn't feel the least bit sorry about it.

Now, I do have to say that, when I was in high school I drove to Fresno with some friends of mine, Black and white, to go to the West Coast Relays, and my Auntie Bit and Uncle Beecher put us up in their house and were very warm and welcoming. Given the general atmosphere they were a part of, that spoke to how they were very kind and generous people, on a personal level. Still, the racism among my relatives in Fresno was very pervasive.

Actually, while my dad and my mom were very different from this—they were liberals—they were at the time sort of "typical liberals." They were against discrimination, segregation and racism, especially in any kind of overt form. But at the time they weren't completely free of some of the more "subtle" forms of this.

I remember, for example, that in the same general time frame as that incident when we were visiting in Fresno (this was in the early '60s), a discussion came up when my parents, myself and my younger sister, Mary-Lou, were on a trip. My friend Matthew had started flirting with Mary-Lou—writing her poems, calling her up and talking with her on the phone, and all that. I wasn't sure how much this was a situation where he was actually infatuated with my sister, and how much it was a matter of his testing us—testing me and testing my parents—to see what we would do. I think it was probably a little of both. Anyway, somehow this led to a discussion during this trip about interracial dating and marriage, and I was surprised, and frankly shocked, to hear my parents bringing up all the "difficulties" that would be involved in this, emphasizing this especially to my sister. After listening to this for a while, I got involved and things got pretty heated. Finally, I had had enough, and I told my parents in no uncertain terms: "I can't believe what I'm hearing—if you don't say that you wouldn't have a problem with Mary-Lou going out with or marrying somebody Black, then I'm leaving this family right now!" Well, that kind of brought the argument to a crashing end. A kind of irony in all this is that some years later my sister did marry somebody Black—her boyfriend from high school, Buddy—and by that time, in the late '60s, my parents had gone through a lot of changes and genuinely welcomed Buddy into the family.

## Plato in the Park

To the degree that I ever was a jock, I kind of grew out of it, because of a lot of different influences that had a lot to do with the nature of the city I grew up in. I never "grew out" of being a sports fanatic, but you can be a sports fanatic without being a "jock." A lot of the kids I knew who played sports in high school were also into other things. Some of them came from more academic or intellectual families, but also the people I was close with during my junior and senior years in high school—me, Matthew, Hemby, Joel, and some others—used to read Plato and Aristotle, John Stuart Mill and Shakespeare, and things like that. If we were hanging out having a hamburger, or if we'd be on the playground during a break between games, we'd start talking about all these different things we were reading and we'd have debates. Some guys would make fun of us, but some others would join in.

I remember having this one discussion with several people, and there was this question, I think it might have come from Descartes, about how god could draw a triangle without using a pencil. I said: "How can that be? How can he draw a triangle without using any kind of an instrument?" And my friend Matthew said, "Just by saying: there's a triangle." That was like one little sliver of the kind of conversations we had. It wasn't necessarily about god most of the time; sometimes it was about John Stuart Mill's views on liberty, or John Locke and the rights of individuals and how the different rights of individuals conflicted with each other, or about democracy—and of course we talked about slavery too.

Before I got to a certain point in high school, I did my school work and I read what I was assigned to read, but that was it—then all of a sudden, when I was sixteen or so, I became really fascinated with all this discussion and wrangling over different ideas. This kind of thing may have been going on in other places, but I suspect it was more of a phenomenon in Berkeley because of the particular and almost peculiar mix of Berkeley—you have people coming out of the ghetto and you have a lot of people who were related to the university. Like I said, even a reactionary asshole like Edward Teller's son was in one of my classes—we got into a debate where he was justifying the hydrogen bomb. So you had all these different kinds of things. My friend Matthew actually lived in Oakland, but he wanted to go to Berkeley High—he was a great athlete, and so they wanted him at the school, but he also wanted to go there because he and his parents thought it was better academically. So he came to our school, and he was very interested in and fascinated by all these big debates. It wasn't just the kids whose parents were professors or something—Matthew's father was a longshoreman and his mother worked as a domestic worker. So it was a unique kind of mix.

Matthew was a really good football player, and one day he called me up: "Guess where I am?" "Where?" "At the Air Force Academy." I exclaimed, "What the fuck are you doing at the Air Force Academy?!" He said, "I'm thinking about going here, they're trying to recruit me." All I could say right then was something like "Oh fuck"—because I'd grown up hating the military and all that kind of military discipline. So I really went after him when he got back. I said, "You want to eat meals where every bite you gotta lift it up and make a square before it gets to your mouth?" and "You want to march in formation all over the fucking place?" I just kept after him and after him, until finally he said "Okay, man, okay, I won't go to the Air Force Academy."

## Spring Thaw

There was a guy in my Spanish class named David, who knew all these obscure facts about all these great literary figures from Latin America and Spain. I was tremendously impressed by this guy, but he wasn't really a friend of mine—he kept to himself a lot. But he seemed to be really very cosmopolitan, sort of a Renaissance man and when you could draw him out in a conversation—which wasn't so easy to do—he was fascinating.

David was part of a big thing in 1960. The House Unamerican Activities Committee (HUAC) was going around the country with their anti-communist crusade and they came to San Francisco. Before then, there had been people who testified before HUAC who had been defiant. But now a lot of people, more than a thousand I believe, demonstrated against HUAC in San Francisco. This was a massive outpouring, the first time that people stood up against HUAC in a mass public way.

I was an aspiring poet and that day I'd gone off to a conference of high school poets around northern California. But I'd gotten back in time for Spanish class and I'd noticed that David wasn't there. So the next day I asked him where he'd been. He explained that he was at the demonstration against HUAC. He and a number of other kids from my school who went to the demonstration talked about how they'd been attacked by the police, how fire hoses were used to drive them down the steps of the courthouse, and how it was a big outrage. It became a big deal politically in the society as a whole, and they were all very proud they'd been part of this. I was really envious of them—I felt like I'd really missed out on something important, and I asked them a lot of questions about it.

So, it was kind of a spring thaw, a lot of things were busting loose, a lot of intellectual and cultural ferment was going on. The Beats were breaking out—they had started up in Greenwich Village in Manhattan and had come out to North Beach in San Francisco. I remember William Buckley came to debate some liberal about the first amendment, loyalty oaths, and all that kind of stuff, and Buckley started these disgusting antics to distract the audience while the liberal was talking. At the time, I was of course still strongly opposed to communism and accepted all the conventional wisdom, or "un-wisdom," about communism and how horrible it was. I remember asking David, "Well, are you a communist?" after he told me about the HUAC demonstration. He said, "No, but I hate HUAC" and then he explained why he hated it and everything it stood for. So this was a very exciting time.

A lot of the girls I knew were influencing me at the time, including the Japanese-American girls that I ate lunch with who were interested in a lot of different artistic and intellectual questions. Just as a side point, I remember one of them telling a story about Marlon Brando. She was talking about how her grandmother, who had come from Japan and lived with their family and spoke no English, was watching a movie about Japan. Brando was in it and at one point he spoke Japanese, and this girl told me that her grandmother said that if she closed her eyes when Brando was speaking, she couldn't tell he wasn't Japanese. For some reason that story stuck with me. I later came to really like Marlon Brando for a lot of other reasons and actually met him at the time of a rally in support of the Black Panther Party in Oakland.

There were other girls I knew from my classes who had an impact on me—one of them even said something to me to the effect of, "You know, when you were in junior high school you were a real jerk, but now you're a much better person." So there was a kind of mutual, or reciprocal thing there, where we influenced each other. They played an important part in getting me interested in poetry, in philosophy and a lot of the general intellectual ferment that was going on. Of course, it wasn't only girls. This kind of ferment was going on pretty broadly among a number of my friends and people I knew, both boys and girls. But it was significant, and kind of a new thing for me, that I developed close relationships with a number of girls, not as girlfriends, but just as friends who happened to be girls. And that was also a lesson for me, because I had had more of a traditional view of girlfriends before then and I really didn't have very many friends who were girls.

I remember a few teachers very fondly from that time. Ms. Bentley was an English teacher who had us read a lot of Shakespeare, and I remember one time I deliberately set out to write a paper about Macbeth to prove a thesis that I didn't actually believe. For some reason I just thought it would be fun and provocative to do this, but she got so furious at me that she wrote on the bottom of the paper, "You have too good a mind to be an intellectual ambulance chaser." I was really angry with her at the time, but she had a point—she didn't want to see whatever abilities I was developing misused for what she saw as paltry purposes. But she encouraged me to write, as well as opening me up to reading a lot of different things, and seeing the value of that.

I also learned a lot from Ms. Rodriguez, my senior year history teacher. Later on, she quit teaching and after I heard about this I wrote her a letter trying to argue with her to stay on, because she was such a good teacher. She left anyway, but people like her had an influence on me, broadening my vistas about a lot of things.

On the other hand, when I was either a sophomore or junior, we had this real "old school" history teacher. One day we got into class and she said, "Today we're going to see a movie about "isms," and we saw this movie that was the equivalent of "Reefer Madness" about communism and socialism. Of course, there was nothing about *individual*-ism or *capital*-ism, it was just about *social*-ism and *commun*-ism. It was like a melodrama, with a vile-looking guy who was selling bottles of poison— but instead of having "X" on them for poison it said "social-ism" or "commun-ism." So a lot of that, even in Berkeley, was still being drilled into the students at that time. Nonetheless, history was one of my favorite subjects.

### Getting Free of Religion

About that time I was becoming an atheist. Ironically, one of the influences that convinced me not to believe in god was Freud, who actually put forward and reinforced some reactionary notions, including in regard to women, but whose critique of religion I found compelling. He tied religion in with the tradition of the powerful father figure, and that influenced me to recognize that religion was a human invention and a human device. At that time, most of my friends were still religious, and in fact, the four of us who hung together all the time—me, Matthew, Hemby, and Joel—all still nominally went to the same church. Mainly that was because we were playing on the church-league basketball team together and so we sort of had to put in our time in order to legitimately "represent" the church. Also, I was still living with my parents, still under their aegis so to speak, and they wanted me to go to church and I still went, even after I started not believing, which was obviously a source of tension. But the intellectual ferment—getting into philosophy, starting to study history as well as literature, and so on—led me to see from a lot of different directions that religion and the idea of god were human inventions. All these different cultures had different ideas of god that conflicted with and contradicted each other. We studied Greek mythology with Ms. Bentley and you could see that different people in different ages believed in all different kinds of gods, and that some of these had passed out of convention and weren't widely believed in any more.

To tell the truth, "losing my religion" was more emancipating than upsetting. I talked earlier about how when I was a kid I used to "tempt god" by saying "fuck," then wondering if god would punish me and if I should atone for my sins and pray for forgiveness. I know some people say that "faith in god" gives them a system of beliefs to live by and to do good things in the world—even some very progressive people say this—but I found belief in god to be very intimidating, very oppressive and repressive. The Christian religion is full of fear—as is Islam—over what's going to happen to you if you somehow displease god. So, while there may have been a time when giving up that set of fairly strong beliefs that I'd been raised with shook me up, I increasingly found it emancipating to throw that off, to more look at the world the way it is, and to not have that feeling that something was going to happen to you if you said "fuck," or in one way or another "displeased god."

I still believed that there was right and wrong; I don't know exactly what I thought it was rooted in, but I just believed that certain things were right and certain things were wrong. Racism was wrong, for instance. You didn't need religion to tell you what was right and wrong, and you didn't need the fear of god to make you do what was right. There were just some things that were right and some things that were wrong, and you acted accordingly. That might have been somewhat naive, and obviously it's not deeply enough rooted to carry you a long, long way; but at that time it was very emancipating for me. I just didn't feel the need for god.

My parents were aware of this, especially once I got out of high school and became more intellectually emancipated as well as practically emancipated in a lot of ways. I just started voicing my view more, and this was the source of a lot of conflict and tension, and we got into big arguments about it.

As for my friends, today there's all this nonsense about how Black people are just inherently religious—and that's a whole thing that gets me pissed off, it's just bullshit. These are socially conditioned things. A lot of my Black friends and a lot of people who influenced me later in life, like the Panthers, were going through the same thing I'd gone through, and recognized that these religious ideas and institutions are human inventions—and not very good ones. So some of my friends were still religious, but many of them were going through the same general kind of emancipating experience that I was in casting off religion.

## Anne Frank

I was in the senior play in high school, "The Diary of Anne Frank." I played Peter Van Dam, Anne Frank's boyfriend. I never sat down and memorized my lines. I just went to rehearsal all the time and by the time the play was actually put on, I knew everybody's lines from beginning to end, without ever studying any of them. If you'd plug me in anywhere in the play, and give me the first word, I could just go forward from there through the whole play.

But I don't think the full heaviness of that story really hit me until a few years later. Obviously, I understood it on a certain level, and even though this was just a senior play in high school, I actually did try to get inside of the play and understand my character and the other characters as well, and really give some expression to it. But still, I was a seventeen-year-old kid, I hadn't lived through an experience like that.

I knew about the Holocaust, but I didn't really have a deep understanding of it. I got that later, when I went to college and I had more Jewish friends and learned about it more. It wasn't just that I had never experienced anything like that, but I'd also never had relationships with friends whose family had gone through that, or who knew people very closely who'd gone through that. That happened a little bit later. So, although at the time of this senior play in high school I knew about the Holocaust and I was somewhat familiar with the very gripping story of Anne Frank, as I grew and developed my understanding of it got deepened.

## Football

Playing on the high school football team was very important to me in a lot of ways. I spoke earlier about how the integrated setting of the team ended up teaching me more than any class that I had. But it was also just important to me as football. And, on the level of football itself, in my senior year things didn't go so well. We usually had a really good team, but that year I think we only won four out of the nine games we played, so that was kind of frustrating. People kept getting injured, people were quitting the team, and the coach was using all these old-fashioned formations which weren't really working, so he kept shifting them. From week to week everybody had to learn new assignments, which was part of why we didn't have such a successful season.

Still, even though we were losing games, it was a lot of fun. We traveled 50 miles to play against a school in Stockton in my junior year, for instance. The socializing was a lot of fun in general, and there would be some occasions like that Vallejo game with the bus ride, where we had that deep talk about racism and discrimination, *and* we ended up winning that game, and I had a good game that night—so that particular experience was a very positive one. There were other, more frustrating experiences, but overall I have very positive and fond remembrances of this whole experience. Interestingly, when I went to college at Berkeley, and I was starting to practice for the freshman football team, I already started to get the sense that in college it was going to be much more of a serious affair, like a business, and not nearly so much fun as in high school. In high school, whether we won or lost, we had a lot of fun. You lost a game on Friday and on Monday you'd be back at practice with your friends and you'd get ready for the next game. If you had a good game, you'd get written up in the paper for having a good game and if you had a bad game, you had to put up with being written about for having a lousy game, but it was all part of the fun.

At the same time, there is a lot of militarism, a lot of macho, a lot of downright misogynistic shit that goes along with sports in this society —that whole dominant sports culture. And that could have had a very negative influence overall if it weren't for the larger things happening in society and in particular the whole thing breaking loose around Black people, which mainly made this a positive experience and a positive influence on me, even though a contradictory one.

I played quarterback, and when you're sort of leading a team that's not doing that well, it can be a pretty sharply mixed experience. But I had always been encouraged to play sports by my parents, with my father directly teaching me how to do things and my mother more generally being very supportive, so I had a lot of confidence. I wasn't intimidated by being quarterback, but I also didn't really think of it that much as being a "leader." I just thought of it as a position I want to play, largely because I loved to pass in football and I developed a pretty good ability to pass. I remember one game when I was playing on the junior varsity, we came from behind to tie the game, and I completed five or six passes in a row and then we scored a touchdown and that felt really good. But I never thought of myself as the "field general," I just thought okay, I'll call the plays, and I sort of led the team in a general sense—but more it was that I liked this position because I loved to pass the ball. I thought that passing, if you could really do it well, was a beautiful art—that's the way I looked at it.

I also loved track, and our school always had really good track teams. In my younger sister's class, there was a guy named Jerry Williams, who was a great sprinter—he broke all kinds of records and had a beautiful running style. My friend Matthew was on the track team as well as the football team, and he won the state meet one year in the shot-put. Later on, he didn't like his college shot-put coach, so he asked me to coach him! I didn't know that much about it, so I had to go read up on it. Anyway, I really loved track and basketball, and I went to almost every one of our school's basketball games and almost all the track meets.

During my senior year there was a league track meet, leading toward the state championship meet. I really wanted to go to this track meet, but it started at something like 2 p.m. on a school day and was an hour drive away. I was able to get my parents' car for that day—of course, I didn't tell them what my plan was. I don't like to come into sporting events after they start—I wanted to see the meet from the very beginning, but it started at two and I didn't get out of school until three, and if I left then it would be almost four o'clock and I'd miss more than half the meet. So I devised a plan where I got a friend of mine, who had a very deep bass voice, to call up the school attendance office during lunch break and pretend to be my father: "This is Spurgeon Avakian, I'll be coming in today at one to pick up my son to take him to a dentist's appointment." So I was sitting in my Spanish class, and they sent me a note saying you're supposed to meet your father outside at one to go to a dentist appointment. Of course, I went out and got in the car and drove to the track meet. A vice principal in the school, who also was an assistant coach on the football team, saw me at the track meet early, but since he sort of liked me and knew me from the football team, he just came up to me a few days later and asked, "Wasn't that you at the track meet about 2:15?" I said, "Are you sure you saw me there?" and he just kind of let it slide. But, then a couple of days later, the attendance office called me in and they asked me, "What's this about how you were supposed to go to a dental appointment and instead you showed up at the track meet?" I don't know if it was this vice principal or someone else who told, but I said, "Well, it's not my fault, you sent me a note saying I was supposed to meet my father to go to the dentist." I think I got away with it mainly because I was a good student.

After the football season in my sophomore year, I went out for basketball, and the coach tried to tell me that I was too short to play on the basketball team. So I just walked off. I'd played with a lot of the guys on the team at the playgrounds, so I knew I could play with them, I knew I was good enough to be on the squad. But I just got pissed off when he told me I was too short. Then, a couple of years later, the basketball coach was my gym teacher, and we used to play basketball in gym class. Finally, one day he comes up to me and he says, "How come you never came out for the basketball team?" I just looked at him, and then I told him, "'cause you said I was too short." He just got a funny look and walked away—I guess he'd forgotten.

### Keeping the "Rep"

I still prided myself on my reputation as "teacher's trial." For example, I always tried to get my homework done in study hall—partly because I didn't want to be burdened with homework, and partly because I was trying to cultivate this reputation of someone who was both a wild kind of guy, but also a surprisingly good student who never had to study. Part of that whole image was never carrying books home after school. So I really worked hard in study class, and only rarely did I take books home to study—only if I had to write a paper or maybe study for a test.

But sometimes I'd get bored in study class, and I'd think up antics and pranks. There was a teacher in one study class who was this nasty disciplinarian, and everybody hated her. Now, if you were in study class and had to do a make-up test or something, you could be excused from study class to go do it. So I had a friend of mine write a note saying that I had to go take a Spanish test during this study class, and my friend signed the note with the name of my Spanish teacher. I then walked up to this study class teacher whom everybody hated and presented her this note. She counter-signed it—at which point I tore it up and threw it in the wastebasket. I said, "I just wanted to see if I could fool you." She got so furious that she took the note out of the wastepaper basket and meticulously scotch-taped it back together, and then sent it down to the vice principal in charge of discipline for students. So I got called into the vice principal's office the next day, and my defense was, "Look, I was just having fun, I didn't actually cut study class. I was just trying to see if I could actually fool her, and once I fooled her, I just tore the note up and threw it away. You can see she had to put it back together, so I wasn't really trying to cut class." Once again I got away with it, because I was a "good student," and let's face it, also because I came from a "good home" and "good family."

I also had a physics class as a sophomore, and I think the teacher's name was Mr. Nelson. He was a lively teacher, and a pretty good teacher, but he also had this strict thing about no talking out of order in class. You were not allowed to talk unless you're called on by Mr. Nelson himself. This is a rule I found very hard to go along with. He would take points off every time you spoke out of turn in class, and that would take away from your grade average. Even knowing that, there were times when I couldn't resist. One time he was talking about measurements in physics, one named after Isaac Newton, called the Newton, and the other called the Dyne. He asked, "Does anybody know what the equivalency is between Newtons and Dynes?" I wasn't sure I'd get called on, so without raising my hand, I just spoke up and said, "I think down at the corner store, you can get two fig newtons for a dyne." Mr. Nelson said, "Very funny," and then docked me ten points. But to me a good pun is worth ten points any time.

## Wild Times and Hairy Situations

My love for basketball and music sometimes drew me into some wild situations.

My first semester in Berkeley High our school won our league and therefore qualified to go to the Tournament of Champions (TOC). We ended up losing in the final to McClymonds—it was a good game, but they had a better team. This was bitterly disappointing to me, as I was all excited about how we were gonna win the TOC. But even before our game on the first day of the TOC, I went with a couple of friends who'd come up to Berkeley High from Garfield Junior High with me—Jim, who was sort of a prankster, and Phil, who was one of the tough kids at Garfield. We were sitting in the front row right under one basket, and Poly High was playing, a school from the Fillmore ghetto of San Francisco. They had a good team, but they were behind at half time. (The Fillmore district of San Francisco has since been "gentrified," and thousands of Black people who lived there have been driven out through this process. Poly High no longer exists.)

Poly High had this really good player named John Lewis, and we were watching him all during the game. He had a real bad act on the court (though it probably wasn't just an act). Every time he'd line up on the free throw line, he would intimidate everybody around him. At the end of the first half in this game, when Poly was still behind, the ball rolled off the court and right to where we were sitting. There were only a few seconds left until halftime, and the ball rolls right to me. John Lewis comes running up, he's trying to get the ball in play so they can score before halftime, and he says to me, "Give me the ball man, give me the ball man!" So I pick up the ball and I try to hand it back to him, but Jim sticks his hand underneath the ball where you can't see it, and when I try to give it to John Lewis, Jim pulls the ball back. So Lewis thinks I'm playing a trick on him. Then the buzzer sounds, and John Lewis looks at me with this really penetrating glare and goes, "Aw shit, man." Then, fortunately, his team went off the court and he turned and ran off with them. But Jim and Phil both said, "I'm getting the fuck out of here," and they went and sat way, way up high in the gym, as far away from the court as they could get. But I loved basketball, and the whole scene by the court, too much to just move away like that.

When John Lewis was maybe a senior in high school or just out of high school, he was arrested for pulling an armed robbery of a store in San Francisco. The reason they were able to arrest him was that during the robbery he pulled out his gun and said to the store owner: "Give me all your money, give me all your money!" And the guy apparently was taking too long, so finally John Lewis says to him: "Hurry up man, hurry up, don't you know who I am? I'm John Lewis, I'm all-TOC!"

Just after I graduated from high school, a carload of me and my friends, many of whom were still in high school, went down to see Oakland City College play against San Francisco City College. This guy, Charles, who had gone to our high school was playing for San Francisco City College, and they won the game. Afterward, he was standing in the doorway leading down to the locker room and bragging about how he had held down this player named Howard Foster, who had played for McClymonds and was now playing for Oakland City College. He was bragging about how "Howard Foster ain't shit, I held him to 8 points, he ain't shit," and all this kind of stuff. Suddenly this guy who ran track for Oakland City College stepped out of the crowd and said to Charles, who was still bragging, "You ain't shit either"—and boom, he hit him.

Charles was standing against the wall and he was knocked out on his feet—he went sliding down the wall.

Then, of course, the whole place was ready to go up, and all of my friends were saying, "We gotta get out of here, man, we gotta get out of here"; but I'm saying, "Oh let's wait and see what happens," and they were coming back with, "Are you crazy, let's get out of here, let's get out of here now." Of course, they understood the potential there for big trouble much better than I did! So they were trying to get me out of there, and on our way out, we passed this woman that I'd always seen at McClymonds games at the TOC—she was maybe in her thirties or early forties, and she always wore this McClymonds sweater. She had it on that time, and as we walked by someone turned to her and said, "Aren't you a little worried about what's gonna happen here?" She opened her purse and said, "No I'm not worried, 'cause I always got my friend with me," and pointed to her gun. Then all my friends were saying, "Man we *really* gotta get out of here now," and they finally succeeded in prevailing on me to get us out of there.

Another time, Joel, Matthew, Hemby and I had been hanging out on a Saturday night. There was this place called Bobo's, a hamburger joint in west Berkeley, and we decided we wanted to get a hamburger. So we pulled into Bobo's, and as we come up to make our order, we see there's this crowd gathered around. There's this real buffed-up, bulky white guy holding a bench. And there's this other guy I knew from high school named Wazell, with a knife, and the two of them are in a stand-off, going back and forth and threatening each other. Finally Wazell's girlfriend— this was a ritual that I'd seen Wazell do, he kind of allowed his girlfriend to talk him out of a fight—his girlfriend says, "C'mon Wazell, c'mon Wazell, let's go, let's go." They start heading toward their car and all of a sudden this white guy who's been holding the bench feels emboldened and says, "Yeah, next time, motherfucker, you pull a knife on me, I'll wrap this bench around your head." So Wazell says, "Oh yeah motherfucker? Oh yeah?" and he comes out of his car with a paper bag and pulls the biggest knife that I'd ever seen out of that bag. And everybody, including the guy with the bench, takes off running, saying, "Hey, they called the cops, they called the cops," because naturally the people working at Bobo's saw something had to be done about this. So everybody left but the four of us. We calmly went and put in our order and got it, and we were sitting in the car with our hamburgers and shakes when the cops pull up. We're the only people left in the parking lot, and so a cop comes up, knocks on my window, and I open it a little bit and say, "Yeah?" He says, "I heard there was some kind of a fight around here." I just kind of shrugged my shoulders, so he says, "Do you know anything about it?" "Naw." He goes on: "And I suppose you don't know who was involved or what happened, huh?" And I said, "Naw," again, so he turned to the others in the car and said: "What about the rest of you?" "Naw." Then he got all pissed off and drove away. My friends and I, we wanted our hamburgers, and this wasn't a big thing to us—Wazell was just this kind of character, always getting into this kind of shit. On the other hand, we weren't going to cooperate with these cops either.

Another time Matthew and I went to the Oakland Auditorium to see a concert with James Brown and the Famous Flames, the Drifters, and I think maybe Hank Ballard and the Midnighters—it was a big show. But it wasn't just a concert, it was also a dance. So part of the floor was cleared and people would stand and also would dance, even before the acts came on—they played music before the show started and in between the sets. The scene was already a little bit tense, because you had all these rivalries, with people from different schools and different cliques and everything, all there in this Auditorium. Since Matthew was from Oakland, he knew a lot of people there, and he was going around talking to them. Then he and I went and sat down. For a while during the evening, when the acts would come on, and people were dancing, fights would break out. Then they'd cool it out, the fights would stop, and the acts would start up again—and then the same thing would happen.

This happened two or three times, and finally Matthew said, "Man, I don't want to get caught up in all this, let's go upstairs," because there was a balcony and we could see the whole thing from up there. So we were sitting in the balcony, and again one of the acts started up, and now this really big fight broke out, much bigger than any of the previous fights. People were fighting all over the floor, and all of a sudden the main door into the auditorium flies open, and this phalanx of Oakland cops—who were known to be particularly brutal and racist—comes in, pulling out their clubs and swinging on people. And from where we were sitting in the balcony, we could see all the people down on the floor just rotate and form a kind of phalanx of their own to fight the cops. It was some of the most beautiful choreography I've ever seen—they stopped fighting each other, swung around 90 degrees, got into formation and started fighting the cops. This was all spontaneous, there was no plan or leadership, but it was very impressive.

### *"He Walks in the Classroom, Cool and Slow..."*

I mentioned earlier the Pendleton shirt that was considered really cool when I was in junior high, and how I saved up and paid for part of that. I also saved up and bought myself a cashmere sweater when I was thirteen because, for whatever reason, that was considered to be the height of cool in the crowd that I was in at that time. But when I got to high school, again things changed for all the reasons I've been talking about, and my sense of cool changed completely as well. I have to confess that one of the things I prided myself on was what was then called "the mack," which was how cool you walked. Of course, you can see the contradictory nature of it because "mack" is another word for pimp, and this was sort of imitating the supposedly cool walk of the pimp. Now the guys who were into this, most of them didn't have any interest in being a pimp, but how slowly you walked and how you moved your body when you walked was a barometer of cool. And I used to really pride myself on having a really good mack.

When I was a senior, I worked in this school office where I would sometimes take messages to different classrooms. And there was one math class in particular where the math teacher was kind of a wild, crazy guy anyway. So I was coming to deliver this message to his class, and I just happened to walk in through the back door. When I opened the back door, everyone looked up to see what was happening, and I think I literally took forty seconds to walk the forty feet to the front of the room to deliver the message. The whole class started cracking up because I was really putting on my mack. After that, there were a number of times during that semester when I would have messages for that class, and every time I would open the back door, all of the students would look up and as soon as they saw me, they would begin clapping their hands and snapping their fingers rhythmically. Even the teacher would join in sometimes. This became sort of an institution—it happened maybe ten times during this class, and I could always tell that the students in the class were glad when I opened the back door and they saw it was me because they knew there was going to be a diversion, a little entertainment, a break in the routine.

Then, when I was a senior in high school, we had an awards assembly. A number of us on the football team decided informally to have a contest to see who could have the baddest mack walking up to get our football letter, and as part of that, who could take the longest from the time their name was called until the time they actually were handed their award. So that was the kind of thing that was a matter of style and cool, even though it obviously had a negative aspect, the whole thing associated with the mack. But it was a much broader phenomenon—you didn't think of yourself as a pimp, you just thought it was cool.

### "A Little Guy...Brimming With Confidence"

I would say I graduated from high school at a very optimistic time. A lot of things were changing—there were a lot of challenges, but there was a feel in the air that things could change for the better. A lot of Black people, a lot of people like those who went to the anti-HUAC demonstrations, a lot of people generally felt a certain optimism. And the fact that I came from the kind of family and the kind of middle class background that I did, that can give you a certain sense of confidence too, frankly. But even for people who weren't white or middle class, there was in the air a feeling of a positive wind blowing, and optimism about social change for the better and getting out of years and centuries of oppression. All that was part of the swirl of the times, if you want to put it that way.

That was how I felt about things, and about myself. I remember even though our football team didn't do very well, I felt good about playing football. My younger sister, Mary-Lou, used to always kid me because at one time this local sports reporter wrote an article that featured me and at one point he referred to me as "Bobby, a little guy...but brimming with confidence"—that was a phrase that was in the article. Mary-Lou had a friend who read this article, and every time she'd see my sister, she would repeat that phrase, "Bobby, a little guy...but brimming with confidence." So my sister would kid me about this, but this did sort of capture something about me, personally, but also how I felt about the times.

There was also, from sports and a lot of the influences on me, this whole bearing I had of being kind of "bad." And speaking of my younger sister, there was this guy Buddy, whom she went out with in high school and later married. But my first encounter with Buddy was when I was a senior in high school and he was a sophomore. Some of my friends and I were driving around in Oakland looking for something to do on a

Saturday night, stopping at different friends' houses and asking if anything were going on, and finally somebody said they knew something about a party in East Oakland. Even though Buddy lived in Berkeley, he had some relatives in East Oakland with a bigger house, so he was having a party out there. Of course, I didn't know him at this time. But we got out of our car and went walking up to the door, rang the doorbell, and when Buddy opened the door we could tell there were all these people inside—the place was packed. We said we had come for the party. Buddy looked at us, and said, "I'm really sorry, but I just can't let anybody else in." So we were pissed off—it was getting late and we'd driven way out there to East Oakland to go to this party. As Buddy was going back into the house, I turned to my friends, and I said, "Let's turn this punk out." And they all said to me, "Naw, naw, man, calm down, c'mon, we can't do that. Look at the house, man, it's full of people, you can't blame him, c'mon, cool out." So that's what prevailed, we just went on and did something else.

But part of the whole culture that I had taken up as my own was that you had to be cool and you had to be kind of bad. Later, Buddy and I laughed about this when I told him this story—he remembered the incident in a general way, but once we became really close and became family, then it had a whole different meaning, obviously, and we laughed about it. Later on, after they were married for a few years, my sister and Buddy broke up, but even though that was painful, she remained fond of him, and I liked him a lot too. By then Buddy was a revolutionary-minded guy. A number of his relatives were among the first members of the Black Panther Party. But Buddy, tragically, died in a car accident not too long after he and my sister broke up.

At the time I graduated from high school, I didn't have any clear idea what I wanted to do with the rest of my life in the big sense. But I definitely knew what I was going to do next: I was going to go to Cal and play football. I was interested in English literature and history and politics. So I was going to major in one of those, or some combination of those, and maybe I'd end up in law, or maybe not, I didn't know. Maybe I was going to end up being a lawyer, maybe I was going to write poetry, maybe I was going to... I didn't know what I was gonna do for sure. But I *knew* I was going to Cal.

## The Truck Barn and the Office

I graduated from Berkeley High in January 1961, and my parents suggested that I work for the eight months or so until September, and then start college. Coming from this middle class, professional family, we had enough money that I didn't have to work. But they thought it would be good experience for me to do some work, and I could save some money, so I got two part-time jobs. One was working in an office in the morning. And in the afternoon and evening I worked in a truck barn, where the trucking companies leave their trucks at the end of the day. I had to make sure the trucks had enough gas, that the motors were oiled, that what they called the fifth wheel, which connects to the trailer, was greased so everything would fit together right, and things related to that. That was my job in the afternoon and evening. I could come in during the afternoon, whenever I wanted more or less, and work in the evening until I finished—I just had to get the job done. And, at the end of the week, I could work either Friday or come in Saturday morning, because they didn't run on the weekends, so I just had to get the trucks ready for Monday.

The office job was the first time I'd worked in that kind of situation, and the people were very narrow and petty. But interestingly enough, I went back and worked there for a little while about four years later, when the Vietnam War and the protests against it were beginning to become really big, and some of the people working there had really broadened their outlook. I even saw some of these people at anti-war demonstrations—people you could never have imagined being at something like that four years earlier.

I worked at those jobs right up until the end of August in 1961, and it was a very good mix and a very good experience—working two different jobs with two very different situations and kinds of people.

One day at the truck barn, for example, a tanker truck came in to fill up the underground tank with gas for the gas pumps at the truck barn. The guy put the hose down into the tank, and then he went off into the office to do something. But he hadn't put the hose in very well, and so the hose started slipping out of the tank in the ground and gasoline was spraying everywhere. Like a fool, because I wasn't very experienced, I went running up to try to grab the hose and shove it back in. And, of course, I got this geyser, this torrent of gas, shooting into my face and into my eyes. Not only did it sting, but I was temporarily blinded. And even more upsetting, I wasn't sure if the blinding was only temporary. So I went running into the area where the mechanics worked, screaming to a mechanic, an older guy who had worked many years as a mechanic. I quickly told him what happened and desperately asked him, "Am I gonna be blind, am I gonna be blind?!" He said, "No, no, no, don't worry about it. Just run some water and wash it out." And I said, "Has this ever happened to you?" He laughed: "It's happened to me a dozen times." Those kinds of experience were new for me, and taught me a lot.

Even though I was working these two part-time jobs, I still tried to have my social life. After I finished work in the truck barn, I would go hang out with my friends. One night I had arranged with my friend Hemby to go to a party after work. But he'd forgotten about it and fallen asleep. So, when I came over about eleven o'clock at night and knocked on the window of his bedroom, he woke up, not knowing what the hell was going on, and he said, "Yeah, who is it?" I said, "It's me." "Who's me?" "It's me, Hemby, it's me." Then he says, "Well, listen 'me,' I got something for your ass." So then I had to quickly explain to him who it was and remind him we were going to a party—which we then did. But it was a little nerve-wracking there for a second.

I still loved the TOC, but now I had a problem because the TOC ran from Thursday through Saturday. Thursday it started at 4:30 and Friday it started at 4:30, and the last game started at nine, so the schedule conflicted with my work. What was I gonna do? Somebody got me a pass to the TOC that let me go in and out every time I wanted to, without having to pay each time. So that took care of part of the problem. Then I schemed to get to the games and miss as little as possible. McClymonds was playing in the first game on Thursday and I really wanted to see that game. And in the nine o'clock game Richmond High was playing, and I really wanted to see that game too. So, I figured okay, I could miss the other two games on Thursday if I had to.

I showed up at the TOC on Thursday at my customary time, about five minutes after four when they opened the doors. I strategically parked my car and watched the McClymonds game, which ended a little before six. Then I went sprinting out, got in my car—I won't say how fast I drove, but I drove the five or six miles to my job as fast as I could, went ripping through the job at the truck barn, finished up about 8:40, got back in my car, went ripping back up to the gym (again, I won't say how fast I went) parked the car, got my pass out, ran in and got there just in time for the tip-off of the Richmond game. Then, Friday it wasn't a problem, because I could put the work off until Saturday morning, so I went to all the games on Friday. I only missed two games that year.

Everybody was waiting to see Richmond and McClymonds play in the final of the TOC that year. In the first game of the year that season, Richmond had broken McClymonds' sixty-eight-game winning streak, but McClymonds hadn't lost another game all year, and they'd won the TOC five years in a row. Richmond and McClymonds were in separate brackets in the TOC, so they were supposed to meet in the final. Richmond had this great player named Leroy Walker, who later played for the Globetrotters—he's the one who really made the difference in beating McClymonds earlier in the season. But when they got to the TOC, for some reason, he had an off game—I think he only made five out of twenty-three shots that day—and Richmond lost unexpectedly. So McClymonds and Richmond didn't have a rematch, but nevertheless there were a number of great games, including the final, which McClymonds won once again. All the effort I went through that year to see as much of the TOC as I could was definitely worth it.

## Camping in Yosemite...and Then

My friend Matthew graduated from high school before me, and he had gone off to the University of Illinois on a football scholarship. He only stayed there one year before he got disgusted by the racism in the school and in the football program, so he came back to go to Cal. But he was gone much of that year, 1961.

A couple of weeks before school started in the fall that year, I quit the two part-time jobs. But, before I started college, some friends of mine and I, including Matthew, who was home for the summer, decided to go for a camping trip to Yosemite. I borrowed my family's car and the four of us went up to Yosemite. We were having a great time, but then something happened that changed all that.

Matthew wanted to learn how to drive, but his father was kind of a tyrannical patriarch, who always liked to have something over him. We'd go to a movie and Matthew would want to borrow some money from his dad, and his dad would basically make him beg for the money, even though his dad had a relatively good job as a longshoreman and could afford a few dollars for a movie. As part of this whole "lord of the house" bullshit, he wouldn't let Matthew get a driver's license. So Matthew was always after me, even though he didn't have a driver's license, to let him learn how to drive by driving the car that I had. But the car that I had at that point was my parents' car, so that made me especially reluctant. We got up in Yosemite and he kept after me, "Let me drive, let me drive, let me drive." I held out and held out and held out. But finally one day we decided that two of us would hike up this mountain in Yosemite and the other friend who *did* have a driver's license and was an experienced driver would go with Matthew and Matthew would drive the car—not just on the flat... I don't know what we were thinking...but up this winding mountain road!

So the two of us hiked up to the top, and we expected to find the other two up there waiting for us, because obviously you could drive up faster than you could hike it. But they weren't there. We looked all over the parking lot—we looked and we looked and we looked—and all of a sudden this car pulled up. I still remember, it had Alabama license plates—it struck me as an irony, because they were these white people from Alabama and the driver said to us, "You have a friend named Matthew?" My heart just sunk right down to my knees, and I answered, "Yeah." And he said, "Well, they've had an accident, and they're okay, but the car looks like it's totaled."

We got a ride down to the site of the accident, and luckily Matthew and the other guy had only really minor injuries, basically just scrapes and bruises. But when I looked at the scene of the accident, they could easily have been killed. They'd gone off a mountain road on a turn— they sailed over a pile of rocks, between two trees, and landed on an upside-down fallen tree which acted as a brake and brought them to a stop, nudged right up against another giant tree. And, even though they escaped serious injury, it was obvious that the two of them *could* have been *killed*. These were friends of mine, and Matthew was one of my very closest friends.

Of course, I felt terrible. I felt responsible, and then I had to call my parents and tell them that their car had been totaled. They were away somewhere and got a third-hand garbled message, so they thought that I'd been in an accident. When they found out what had actually happened, they were relieved that I hadn't been in an accident and that nobody had been badly hurt or killed, but of course they were angry about my really bad judgment in letting Matthew drive the car. And I felt responsible, not only for their car being wrecked, but for allowing a situation in which he and the other guy could have been killed. So this put a negative shadow over the end of that vacation. But then I was getting ready to go to Cal, so I turned my thoughts toward that.

I'd always wanted to go to Cal ever since I was a kid growing up in Berkeley. I knew Cal was a good school academically, and I was interested in the academics, but it had also always been a dream of mine to play football at Cal. I was looking forward to playing on the freshman football team, even though I knew I could never be a starter—it turned out that the quarterback in my freshman class was a guy named Craig Morton, who ended up playing for many years in the NFL. But I still wanted to be on the team, and at least maybe get a chance to play. So it was both things, academics and sports.

I was also excited about all the intellectual and artistic ferment going on. In my senior year in high school we used to go to jazz clubs, and then at the end of the night, we might stay up all night talking—I can remember arguing one time with people, late into the night, about the writings of St. Augustine, for example. They had a room in the library at Cal where, even if you weren't a student at the university, you could sit and listen to different recordings. There was a recording of Allen Ginsberg reading his poem "Howl," and I used to put those headphones on and go into a whole different world, listening to this hypnotic recording. I remember the poem's indictment of American society, as Moloch, which spoke to feelings of alienation I was beginning to experience—it moved me in a way that a political manifesto would not have at that time:

> "Moloch whose mind is pure machinery ! Moloch whose blood is
> running money ! Moloch whose fingers are ten armies !
> Moloch whose breast is a cannibal dynamo ! Moloch whose
> ear is a smoking tomb !"

The opening line of that poem also made a deep impression on me: "I saw the best minds of my generation destroyed by madness..."

I couldn't wait to get started at Cal.

# Chapter Five

# *Life Interrupted*

I enrolled at Cal the week before classes formally started, and we began football practice for the freshman team at that time. Even though I was really looking forward to it and excited about it, they had already given us big play books and I could tell the whole thing was going to be more like a job and a business. In high school you had to learn plays and you had to practice, but it wasn't all so serious. There was a camaraderie about it and there was a particular social experience that went along with it in a school like Berkeley High at that time. It was also just fun. But I could already tell this was going to be a much different atmosphere. Nevertheless, both because I loved football and because it was sort of a thing I'd always dreamed of doing, I still wanted to play football for Cal.

## *"Uh Oh, That's Not Good"...Hospitalized*

But during that week I started feeling sick. I would be throwing up a lot. I noticed that while I hadn't changed my diet or anything, I was gaining weight really quickly. Even though a lot of different things indicated that something was wrong, I thought that maybe I just had a little bit of the flu. But this persisted for that whole week, and I kept vomiting all the time. It's one thing if you do that a couple of times in one day, or for a couple of days. But this went on all week. Every time I would do anything and exert myself, I'd feel alright for a little while, and then I'd feel terrible. Or I'd be hungry and eat food, but as soon as I ate I felt terrible. I was staying that semester with my parents, and finally I talked to them and said, "I really think I better go to the student clinic and see what's wrong, whether I have a bad case of the flu or whatever." So my dad drove me down to the student clinic, and I still remember the last words he said as I got out of the car and headed for the clinic: "Well, don't let them keep you."

So I went into the clinic, and I described my symptoms, and they gave me a urine test and some blood tests. Pretty soon they came back and said, "We have to admit you to the hospital. You've got kidney casts in your urine and you've got albumen, protein in your urine, and that means there's something wrong with your kidney function." So I was put in a room, and as I mentioned I had been inexplicably gaining weight, so they said, "Don't give him anything to eat, but let him drink as much water as he wants." They wanted to see what would happen—and between that afternoon and evening I gained five pounds, because my kidneys were basically shutting down and I was retaining all the water that I was drinking.

At this point my parents called a friend of theirs who was a doctor and asked him to go check and see what was happening. When they told him what the urine tests had showed, he said, "Uh oh, that's not good," and explained to them that it could mean there was a serious problem with my kidneys. I was in this room with three other people, and all of them were having visitors; they were all laughing and joking, and this doctor friend of my parents came in—and he didn't have the best style —he just yelled at everybody in the room: "Be quiet, settle down, don't you realize that this patient here," pointing at me, "is very sick?" And that was the first time that I knew that I was very sick. I knew from what they said about the tests that something wasn't right, and the fact that I was gaining this weight meant something. But this was news to me in a very bad way: "this patient is very sick." Right after that, they moved me into a room by myself.

This all happened very quickly. The next day, the head of the medical staff at the student health clinic, who became my doctor—his name was Mort Meyer and he was a really great guy—came in and took over my case, because he recognized it was very serious and he told me, frankly, that I was very sick. And for a couple of months I was in the hospital, in a bad way, because my kidneys just completely shut down.

But it's kind of funny. They were telling me I was very sick and, obviously, the way they were saying it meant they were serious. You could follow that logically and know that you might die. But, for whatever reason, I didn't really think about dying. I just knew I was very sick and the question was how to get well, that was what was in my mind. My parents, I know, got the point that I was very sick, and the implications of that. After all, there were no transplants at that time. They could put you on dialysis—where they basically take your blood out and filter it and put it back into your body, because your kidneys are supposed to do that but they're not functioning—and they almost did that with me. But you couldn't stay on dialysis indefinitely, and dialysis then wasn't even as good as it is now. I know that my parents understood right away the seriousness of the situation. Although my father was very affectionate and wasn't one of these fathers who wouldn't show emotions, he didn't cry a lot in front of other people. And I was told by my mother and my younger sister, later on, that he went into a closet and just wept, because he understood what this meant.

To save my life, I became kind of like a test tube. They would come in every morning and take a bunch of blood tests to see what the chemicals in my blood were. Since my kidneys weren't functioning, I wasn't allowed to eat anything for about a month. I could drink around five hundred milliliters of water and an additional amount of water equal to whatever I was able to urinate for the day—which was often very, very little, because it's your kidneys that release the urine. So all this uremic poisoning was backing up in my body, because I couldn't urinate—the doctor used to come in, look at my eyes and see that I had uremic poisoning in my eyes.

They would come in the morning and take these tests, and if my potassium were too low they would give me potassium during the day, in pills; and if my potassium were too high, they would give me something to counter-balance that. So I felt as if I were a test tube and they were chemically adjusting what was going on in my body to keep me alive, especially during the acute phase, which lasted more than a month. That's why I couldn't eat anything, because they didn't want anything to complicate things further—every time you eat, it affects the chemical balance of everything in your body.

Even when I wasn't eating, I used to vomit three or four times a day. Vomiting became a function like blowing your nose. It was unpleasant, but I got so used to it that when people would visit me and I got nau-

seous, I'd say, "Could you excuse me for a second? I have to vomit."
Despite that, one thing that was hard was that I'd get very hungry every
day. There was a guy across the hall from me who had hepatitis. And,
because that weakens the body, they had him on a 5,000-calorie-a-day
diet. He would describe to me how he had two or three milkshakes a day,
and I would get really jealous. You know, in the hospital, one of the
things people look forward to, if they're not too sick, is meal time—it
breaks up the monotony and you get something to eat. I used to lie there
and listen to the dishes clinking on the trays, but I could never eat. I was
hungry, but if I had eaten I would have felt even worse. I can still
remember when, finally, they let me have something to eat—it was a
peach. I remember how grateful I was, and how I profusely thanked the
orderly in the hospital who went out and got that peach and gave it to
me with some fanfare.

Of course, there were a lot of ways in which this whole thing was
very difficult. The treatment wasn't as bad as the sickness, but sometimes you kind of wondered, because they'd have to get potassium in me
by one means or another. So one time they gave me these great big horse
capsules that were full of potassium, and I'd have to take something like
fifteen of them at a time. I'd take so many and then I'd throw them up,
so then I'd have to take them again. Or they'd give me this potassium in
liquid form. One day after I'd passed the most acute stage of this, they
brought in this glass of orange juice, and they said here's some orange
juice with just a little bit of medicine in it. I said okay and I started
drinking. I took one swig, and I can't even describe the taste, it just made
my body shiver, it was such an awful taste. I went, "Yucch, what is *that*?"
"That's potassium, but there's only a teaspoon in there." I said, "I don't
care—please, the next time you bring me potassium, bring me the
potassium separately, and then give me the orange juice on the side—
I'll take the potassium down and then I'll have the orange juice to wash
away the taste." Since then I've used this as a metaphor sometimes—the
one teaspoon of potassium that ruins a whole glass of orange juice.

But that was not as bad as what I had to go through earlier, when I
couldn't orally take in the potassium because I'd throw it up. Then they
decided that the only way they could keep it in me was to give it to me
by enema. So I'd have to have an eight-hour drip of potassium coming
in by that means. It didn't hurt, but there was a pressure build-up, the
way it is with IV drips. If a nurse doesn't come around to check it every

so often, then the drip will start going a little faster. The nurses can get very busy and preoccupied with something else, and it starts going faster and faster—and the more it goes, the more the pressure builds up. One time I was something like seven hours and forty-five minutes into the eight-hour potassium enema: the pressure is building more and more, and I'm furiously pushing on the buzzer to get the nurses to come and turn it down, but before they could get there everything just came back out! And I had to start it all over again. These are the kinds of things you had to put up with in order to overcome this disease, especially in its acute phase.

All this was very difficult psychologically as well as physically. For example, one of the ways that my parents knew I was really sick, and even I recognized it, was one Saturday they were visiting me and there was a Cal football game on the radio, and my dad said to me, "Do you want me to put the football game on?" I was lying in bed and I could barely work up the energy to answer, "No, I'm too tired, I don't feel up to listening to it." And they knew that if I were too sick to even feel up to listening to a football game, then it was very serious.

There was also a time when a doctor other than Dr. Meyer was on rounds at the hospital, and he came in to check on me. He asked, "How are you feeling?" I said, "Not very good." So we started talking, and then I told him: "Here's what bothers me. Sometimes when I stand up, like to go to the bathroom or something, if I feel up to that, pretty soon I feel weak and bad, but then if that's the case I can sit down; and then when I'm sitting down and I feel really bad and really weak, I can lie down; but what about the times when I'm lying down and I feel really weak and really bad—what do I do then?" And the doctor looked at me and said, "Just try to rest." It only dawned on me later that clearly I was very close to dying—that was really what my question reflected—and the doctor, of course, knew it, but what could he say?

I never had the attitude that "I'm dying, I'm just gonna let go." I had the attitude: "I'm sick, I'm gonna get over this." I would always ask the doctor, "When am I gonna be well, when am I gonna be over this?" Because I was young, and even though this hit me completely out of the blue and really knocked me down, I felt like "I'm going to overcome this, I'm going to conquer this, I'm going to get back on my feet, I'm going to do what I did before." But, of course, it is very difficult when you feel the way a lot of youth do—invulnerable and optimistic and enthusiastic and very confident about life—and all of a sudden everything's knocked out from underneath you, you're just barely hanging on to life, and you feel completely vulnerable in a way you never did before.

## Friends

My friends were a big part of giving me the support and strength to keep going, as well as my father, my mother and my sisters. My friends would take time away from other things to be with me. When you're eighteen years old, nineteen years old, you want to be doing a lot of things, but they would spend hours with me, when they were allowed to visit in the hospital, they would come and do all kinds of things to try to keep my spirits up and keep me in the orientation of fighting this, rather than giving in.

I was in the hospital for a couple of months in this sort of acute phase. Then they let me go home for Thanksgiving. After that I went back into the hospital to get a biopsy of my kidneys. The biopsy was actually somewhat encouraging, because it showed that there was damage to the tubes of my kidneys, but not to what's called the glomeruli, which are the actual filtering units. So that meant there was a reasonable chance that I would recover, whereas if I'd had serious damage to the filtering units, the glomeruli in the kidneys, I would have had a much worse prognosis.

They decided they'd start me on these cortisone steroid treatments. They put me back in the hospital to start these treatments because I was very weak and also because they wanted to monitor me. Cortisone is a very, very powerful drug, and they were giving me very high dosages to begin with. So I went back into the hospital for several weeks.

The cortisone had all kinds of physical side effects. It can also have very serious psychological side effects, which fortunately I never had. But physically, you get what is called Cushing Syndrome, where all of the fat in your body gets mobilized into your trunk, your neck gets really thick, your face swells out, while your arms and your legs become very thin and your muscles tend to get broken down. And I couldn't do any exercise to counter that. So this had a very distorting effect on the way I looked. You look very swollen and sort of disfigured, especially when you're taking high dosages of cortisone. Within a month or so I began to experience those kinds of symptoms.

I responded well to the treatments on one level. And I was actually in relatively good spirits. I remember there was this guy who was a cook in the hospital where I was then; he used to be on the basketball team at Berkeley High—his name was Lavon "Cookie" Patton—he had been a year or two ahead of me in high school. And when he found out I was in the hospital, during his off hours or "down time" he'd come up and visit with me for a while. That meant a lot to me, it was good for my spirits.

I didn't really realize then that I still had a long-term battle ahead. I was hoping that I would get this steroid treatment, this cortisone, and I'd get well in a few months, then I'd be back to what I was before. But actually it was three years before that happened, and a lot went on during that time. I got sick right at the beginning of September in 1961, and I wasn't able to go back to school, even on a limited basis, until the next fall. So there was a whole year when I was basically recuperating, and at the beginning of that, after I got out of the hospital and was just getting going with the cortisone treatments, I had to spend a lot of time at home, because I was very weak and I was only really beginning to overcome the acute phase.

### Re-thinking

During those years, while it would be an exaggeration to say that I literally didn't recognize myself when I looked in the mirror, in all but the most literal sense that was true. I just looked completely different to myself, really disfigured. I was altered very significantly in my physical appearance, and not in a good way, and I was also very sickly. I grew up in this society and came of age in the '50s, with all the conventional and superficial ways in which people are conditioned to think about relations between boys and girls, men and women; and I, obviously, was conditioned myself by all that. For example, I mentioned that among my good friends in high school were girls who were intellectuals and whom I respected for their minds and their thinking. On the other hand, while I didn't go for the classical separation—where there are some girls who are smart, and they're friends, and there are other ones who are pretty or sexy or whatever, and they're the ones you are interested in romantically—a girl did have to be good-looking, in the conventional sense, for me to get romantically interested.

But when everything's knocked out from underneath you and your whole life changes and even your looks change in this way, your outlook begins to change too. It wasn't as if this were an epiphany, and my whole viewpoint changed completely, all at once, but it did start me thinking in a different way and more deeply about what's really important in people, and in particular women, both as friends and even as people in whom you might be romantically interested. But this was only the beginning and part of a longer term process through which I underwent some real changes—it wasn't an overnight dramatic thing, where I woke up one morning, looked at myself in the mirror and said, "Well, look what happened to you, so why bother to think any more about how people look?" That would be an exaggeration and a silly distortion. But it did cause me to start thinking more deeply about what really matters in people, what are the important qualities in people.

Also, my friends were coming to visit me when I was able to go home from the hospital but couldn't get out of the house for a while. My friends would spend their weekends with me, and this meant a tremendous amount to me. They could have been—and probably, on one level, would have liked to be—out doing a whole bunch of other things. But they cared about me and it was important to them to be with me and give me support, and this kind of thing also makes you think differently and more deeply about things, or at least begin to.

I wouldn't necessarily have described myself as "popular" in high school. I was controversial. I was popular with some people and very unpopular with other people, including people who were "popular" in the classical and conventional sense. But I did think of myself as a guy who's "got something going for him," and I more or less expected people to like me. As for those who didn't like me, fuck 'em—it was for good reasons they didn't like me, it was because I was doing things that I believed in and things that I wanted to do that are important and right. So if they don't like me for that reason, to hell with them—there are other people who will like me. That was all part of the whole "brimming with confidence" thing, which also partly comes from the background that I came out of, where the world seems like it's open to you. Then all of a sudden you are knocked down, with this serious illness and all its side effects, and you don't have everything going for you.

Of course, I still had a lot of people and resources to support me. My parents still had money for my health, and my mother spent a couple of years basically revolving her life around helping me recuperate, down to the level of paying very minute attention to my diet, which was very restricted. For example, I could only have very, very limited amounts of sodium every day. I used to write up menus, going through books calibrating the milligrams of sodium in different things, then my mom would find the right foods and prepare the meals that fit that diet. She had to weigh everything, she had to shop at special stores, at a time when they didn't have the whole broad array of health food stores and different kinds of health foods that they have now. So this took up a big part of her life, for a couple of years, besides giving me other kinds of practical and emotional support.

At a time when I was beginning to go out on my own, all of a sudden I was forced not only to live at home for a couple of years, but to be very dependent on my family. My older sister, Marjorie, was out of the house at that point. My younger sister, Mary-Lou, was in high school. She was very supportive, but she also had her own life, and while my parents also cared about her and her life and paid attention to that, they frankly devoted a lot of time to my needs, and my mother in particular did this on almost an hour-by-hour basis, especially in the early stages, to help me survive and recover. Of course, I had tremendous appreciation and gratitude for my mom and for everything that she was doing for me. I always was very fond of my mom, but this made it much deeper.

## *"And No Birds Sing..."*

There was also a more intangible part of this whole experience that was extremely difficult emotionally. Taking all this medicine all the time, and the side effects it had, including the physical disfigurement, and not being able to go out and do the things that I loved, all took a heavy toll. Certain things became very important to me. For instance, my family had a recording of Harry Belafonte, whom I really liked, and I used to play that record over and over again, because somehow it lifted my spirits and made me feel better. Also, by this time I had started to get really interested in poetry—this started during my last years in high school. I really got into the English romantic poets, Keats in particular. While I was recuperating at home, I used to read Keats, and sometimes late at night I would stay up and constantly play this recording of this English actor, Ralph Richardson, reading some of Keats' poems, because it seemed to suit my mood and my orientation at the time. I liked the beginning of Keats' poem "Endymion," which has that famous line about how "A thing of beauty is a joy for ever." I liked the classical Keats

"Ode" poems—especially "Ode to a Nightingale" and "Ode on a Grecian Urn," which ended with: "beauty is truth, truth beauty, that is all ye know on earth and all ye need to know." It's funny, not too long ago I was watching a movie where they quoted a line from a Keats poem without attributing it. There was this scene by some water and one of the characters in the movie says, "the sedge is withered from the lake." And as I was watching this, I said to myself the next line of the poem: "and no birds sing." I still remember lines from Keats poems that are very evocative and seemed to be especially speaking to me at that time.

But, with all the pain and difficulties, I still had this attitude that "I'm gonna get my health back, I'm gonna get back everything that's been taken away, I'm gonna get back to what I was and where I was, I'm gonna resume my life." But also, society was changing at this time in dramatic ways, and because of the influence of these larger things, which I was still very passionately interested in, I just didn't think very much about giving up. Of course, there would be moments of despair when I'd really feel down. But I'd rebound from that, because I still felt that I was going to overcome this.

As soon as I was able, I tried to throw myself into things that could give my life some meaning within the severe limitations that it had. At the beginning, the doctors had been worried that any kind of exposure to infection could just kill me. But within a few months they said, "Well, now you're past that phase, even though you still have to be careful." And as soon as I was able, I wanted to get back out, I wanted to go and watch sports, I wanted to go to musical concerts, I wanted to go to poetry readings, I wanted to go listen to jazz, and I wanted to follow what was going on in the world.

At the same time, because of the way I felt about being acutely physically disfigured, I was very reluctant to go out and even see anybody that I knew. One thing that my friends and I were later able to laugh about, but at the time was very painful for me, was that my friends would come over and visit me and say, "Look, you know you gotta get out of the house, you gotta get out and do things, you can't just sit here all day—the doctors say you can do it now, let's go, let's go do a few things," and I would be tempted but I'd answer, "Naw, I don't want to, I'm not ready to do it." It wasn't because I didn't feel physically up to it, although I would get tired very quickly, but because I didn't want to face people that I'd known before looking the way I looked now. My friends worked on me for literally two or three weeks: "C'mon, let's go out, we'll go down to the library, you can read a few books down there, and we'll just hang out." They wore me down—I finally gave in.

So a couple of friends drove me down to the library to meet this other friend of mine, Art. Art hadn't seen me since I'd gotten sick, but these other friends of mine had been visiting me all the time, so they knew what the deal was and what I looked like. They helped me into the library, and there I was in the entryway to the library, and they said, "Okay, we're gonna go get Art." Now, Art wasn't always known for having the most tact anyway. But they brought him out to where I was, and he looked around, not recognizing me. So they pointed to me: "That's him there." Art stared at me for a second, and then he exclaimed, "God, what happened to you?!" I just turned around and walked out of the library, went back to the car, and refused to go out of the house again for the better part of a month.

But finally I got over that, because there were things happening in the world, there were things I cared about, and there were things I wanted to do. I started doing things that I *could* do. I started going again to basketball games. I went to some of the Cal games, but actually I was more interested in high school sports, and I mainly went to Berkeley High and other high school games.

Right before I first got sick, when I had just come back from Yosemite, a good friend of mine from high school, Jeff, had died from tetanus. His family was one of many Black families that had recently come up from the south, and he didn't have any tetanus shots. He had been working around some construction, they were tearing down some things, and there were all these boards with nails. It was this horrible thing where, after he stepped on a nail, he waited a couple of days to go to the hospital, and by the time he did go it was too late. So this had a big effect on me too.

Soon after I had gotten sick, my old high school had a football game and they dedicated the game to Jeff and to me. So a lot of my friends thought I was dead. I remember a guy who was a year behind me in school, Melvin, who was very tight with Jeff but was also a friend of mine, said to me some months later: "You know, they told me that Jeff died, then they told me that you died too, and"—I remember his words to this day—"and I just looked at the ground." A little later Melvin had a breakdown and became very mentally ill. So, these are the kinds of heavy things that were going on.

Anyway, I finally started getting out, and besides sports events I would go to some of the clubs that I could go to, that would admit people under twenty-one. Then I started looking for things to do that I thought would be useful, that would mean something. I started tutoring people at my old high school, particularly some of the guys who were into athletics, but also other students, because that was something that I could do and it made me feel as if I were doing something worthwhile.

### *"Now Give Me My Milkshake!"*

I referred earlier to this guy who was in my sister's class in high school named Jerry Williams, who was this really great sprinter with a beautiful style of running. He had a lively personality and his own approach to *how* he ran. When I went back to do tutoring at my old high school, sometimes I'd help officiate at track meets and I'd see him run. And I still vividly remember different things that gave a sense of his style.

One time, there was a meet at Castlemont in East Oakland, and I went out there to see the meet in general and specifically to see Jerry run, because it was always a great thing to see. Castlemont had these two sprinters who were supposed to be pretty good. But Jerry won the 100, and then it came to the 220 (at that time races were measured in yards, not meters). They came off the curve and Jerry was ahead by a few yards, and he lengthened his lead, so he was ahead by more than five yards. He got down to about 20 yards from the finish line and you could see him just ease up, and then he went through the tape and won by a couple of yards. Jerry, as you might imagine, had kind of an entourage of people on the track team and others who'd follow all of his exploits. So, immediately, this entourage comes running up to him and they're congratulating him, and one of them says: "Jerry, Jerry, why'd you slow down at the end, man?" And Jerry coolly answered: "I looked over my left shoulder, and I saw that cat wasn't doin' shit; then I looked over my right shoulder and saw that dude wasn't doin' shit either; so I just *styled* on in."

Now Jerry was really fast in the 100, and at least as good in the 220, and because he was so good in the 220, one time I asked the track coach, "Do you think Jerry could break the high school record in the 220 if he'd quit drinking wine?" And the coach replied: "Well, the wine is one thing, but if he quit smoking cigarettes, he'd really be fast." But the guys on the track team didn't like the coach that much. He was always trying to get them to do more and to train harder. Jerry had great speed and great style, but training hard was not that much of his thing, let's just put it that way.

One day the coach comes up to Jerry, and he wants him to run the 440, because he figures he's so good at the 220, he'd really be good in the 440. There were these two guys who ran the 880 (half mile), and they'd just finished their workout about 15 minutes before that. They were pretty fast in the 440 too. Now, the coach thinks he's gonna hustle Jerry, so he says to him: "Jerry, I'll bet you can't beat those two guys in the 440." Jerry says, "You bet me what?" "I'll bet you a milkshake." Jerry says alright, and they line up for the race, Jerry and these other two guys, and the coach fires the starter gun. The coach has got his watch out, doing what they call "timing splits"; they start off running and when they get to the first split, the first 110 yards, Jerry is ahead by about 15 yards, and his time is under 12 seconds, which means his pace is under 48 seconds for the 440, which is a very good time, especially for a high school runner who hasn't even trained for the 440. So the coach is getting all excited, and they get around to the 220 mark, the halfway mark, and Jerry is ahead by about 30 yards and his time is under 24 seconds, keeping up the same pace. The coach is getting more excited. Then they get to the 330 mark, 3/4 of the way through, and Jerry's ahead by about 50 yards and his time's under 36 seconds—he's keeping up the pace—and the coach is *really* excited now. And then, as Jerry comes off the final turn, he's ahead by about 60 yards—and he just slows down and starts loping, and wins by about 20 yards. The coach comes running up and exclaims, "Jerry, Jerry, what are you doing?! You had perfect splits, you were gonna come in under 48 seconds, what'd you slow down for?" Jerry turns and says: "Shit. I knew if I came in with a fast time, under 48 seconds, you were gonna make me run the 440. Now give me my milkshake!"

## *Most Courageous Athlete—Until...*

Around 1963 or 1964, after I'd been doing tutoring and helping out in other ways at my old high school, especially with the athletes, some friends of mine got together with some officials of the school, raised some money and established an award in my name—an award to be given out every year to "the most courageous athlete." The first year this was given out, my friends who had been involved in this just told me that we had to go down to Berkeley High because there was something important happening there. It turned out that it was a school assembly where they were introducing and giving out this award. This was the first I had heard of it, so I was very surprised and, of course, moved. The interesting thing, though, is that after I became somewhat notorious in that area as a radical activist, the award was discontinued.

For the first year after I got sick, I was still taking very high dosages of the cortisone. I had all these side effects from that—and I had to take other medicines to counteract the side effects—so I felt as if I were a walking pharmacy. I had to take my pills with me everywhere I went. I did my best to make that part of my routine, and I'd try to get out and do things that I thought were worthwhile, like tutoring. But realistically, I wasn't really able to get back into doing very much for the better part of a year. Even if I could tutor or officiate at track meets, it was very, very limited what I could do. I would get very weak, I'd get very tired very quickly, and I had to be very careful not to get injured or get an infection.

And then things would throw me back. It wasn't just this one incident with Art, but for a couple of years, when I would go places—say, to a bookstore, or just walking down the street—I would frequently have this terrible experience where I'd see somebody that I'd gone to school with for years, and I would instantly recognize them, but they would not recognize me. Then they would start looking at me, the way people do sometimes when they wonder, "Do I know that person?" And I would always want to go and hide—sometimes I would actually *try* to hide, or quickly walk out of the bookstore to get away, because I didn't want to go through the excruciating experience where they would finally realize who I was, and then would react to how different I looked. Even when they did it in a really good and kind way, I just wanted to avoid it.

One time I was with one of my close friends who'd been hanging out with me all this time and we ran into somebody else that we knew. This person asked my friend, "So how's Bobby doing?"—and I'm standing right there. I told him who I was, of course, but that kind of thing was very painful, and I wanted to avoid those situations. On the other hand, I remember one time when I went to watch a practice of my old high school basketball team, this one guy on the team, my friend Billy, came right up and talked to me very naturally, as if nothing had really changed. That meant a tremendous amount to me, in a way *because* it was a small thing. Here was this guy who, because of his life conditions, had one foot into the criminal life, even in high school, but who had the sensitivity to know that it was important to me for him to see me as still the same person and who recognized that the superficialities of how my looks had changed didn't matter. He was able to convey that just by coming up and saying, "Hey, how you doin'?" in the way that he did.

There were times when the whole thing with the illness would be very discouraging. Taking the cortisone went through cycles: they were trying to get to where they could stabilize me on a low dosage of the medicine and then eventually get me off of it. So they'd knock it down five milligrams, and then after a couple of weeks they'd knock it down five more milligrams, and so on. All this time I had to go in the doctor's office twice a week and have tests to see how my kidneys were reacting to the lowering of the dose. Near the end of the first year, they'd gotten it down pretty low, and I actually felt a little better, because the medicine took a lot out of me. But then the tests started to show that my kidneys were losing function again. So they had to raise the dosage way back up again and then start again slowly trying to reduce it. I would reach those points where I'd start thinking, "Okay, the dosage is getting down and next week I'll be almost down to nothing, and then after that I won't need any medicine, I'll be back to the way I was." And, boom, I'd have a setback, and I had to start over again. The cycle would take the better part of a year, and this happened to me twice—two cycles over the better part of two years, where we'd get down low in the dosage, and then, boom, the symptoms would start showing up again, so they'd have to raise it back up.

## Coaching

When I got a little bit stronger—even though I was still taking a lot of medicine for my kidneys, and other medicine to counteract the effects of *that* medicine—I started doing more tutoring and things like officiating at track meets. And one summer, I got together, organized and coached in a summer league the players who were going to be on the varsity next year at Berkeley High. Berkeley High hadn't won the TOC in a long, long time and I wanted to make it happen that year. So I was tutoring some of these guys, along with other people, and then I was coaching them in the summer league. It was a way I could interact with people that I cared about. That was in the second year of my illness, after the first acute phase of a couple of months and the really bad year where I was very weak and it was still kind of touch-and-go in a very real way, even though I was past the most acute phase.

So I was coaching in the summer league. And one of the side effects from this medicine was susceptibility to really bad throat infections. Sometimes I'd lose my voice for as much as a couple of weeks. This happened during the time I was coaching this summer league team, but I was determined to keep on coaching, and my dad helped me out. I managed by sign language or writing things down to indicate to my dad that I wanted him to go down to the playground where they had the summer league and be my assistant coach, or my voice. So we went there together, and I had a clipboard, and whenever anything would happen in the game and I wanted to make a substitution or tell somebody something about what to do in the game, I'd write it down on the paper on the clipboard, and then my dad would be my "translator" and verbalize it to the players.

As it happened, those guys that I coached—and I also tutored some of them—won the league championship that year and qualified for the TOC. They got all the way to the final of the TOC, and lost in the final to McClymonds, by one point in overtime. What made it particularly hard to take is that there was a crucial point, right near the end of the game, where Berkeley High was ahead of McClymonds by three points, and they were putting on a full-court press. This guy from McClymonds threw a pass downcourt, and my friend Billy, who was a tremendous leaper, went way up in the air and stole the pass; and then he went down and dunked. They would have been up by five points, with less than two minutes to go. But they called him for walking, because they said he shuffled his feet in order to get his steps right to dunk the ball. So that was doubly heart-breaking for me, and of course even more so for Billy. I remember going to a basketball game with him years later, and these kids in front of us were talking about: "Billy Carr, you remember that time in the TOC when he took steps and Berkeley High lost." So he had to live with that for years.

But, as I said, this loss was heartbreaking for me too—it took me a couple of weeks to get over it. I remember I was at the playground, just hanging out, back at Live Oak Park, and there was this guy named George who was from Oakland—he started getting in my face about how McClymonds had beaten Berkeley High, and I just couldn't take it. So, sick as I was and as dangerous as it was for me, I actually tried to challenge him to a fight, but he had a big enough heart that he just sort of grabbed me and turned this hold he had on me into an embrace until I calmed down.

## Back to Cal and Engaged in the World

At the end of that first year of illness, I wanted to go back to Cal. I talked to the doctor, and he said, "You know, it could take too much of a toll on you, that kind of a schedule might be just the kind of thing that would cause you to have a whole relapse." But I kept at him and at him and at him, and he finally said, "Okay, I'll write something to the school administration explaining that you can only take a reduced load." I found out later that he separately talked to my parents and told them: "Well, he wants to go, and we might as well let him because this might be his last chance."

So I went back to Cal on a reduced schedule, and then I started being able to get into things a little more than I had before. I still had to live at home, because I had to have a special diet and I had to take all this medicine and I had all these side effects from the medicine. My poor mom was basically 24/7 doing this above anything else. But I needed that kind of assistance, or I couldn't have made it.

In 1963, when I started to get a little bit better, my father had to go on a trip to Washington and New York, and I had gotten stabilized medically to a point where I could travel and do a few things. So we went to DC, and we saw the Congress building and went in, and even though I had some criticisms of the government, I still looked upon these government buildings and the people in them with a certain amount of not only respect but awe. Congress was in session, and I remember walking in and being really struck that there was nobody in there. Here I had this vision from the history books of this place where they had these great debates, and yet this Congressman was up there giving a speech and there were only three or four people in the whole hall, most of them reading newspapers and paying no attention, and one guy was spitting on the floor while he was reading the newspaper—and I'm thinking, is *this* the way the government is supposed to be run? Then, all of a sudden, a bell rings, and all these Congressmen come running in and raise their hands for a vote—then the vote's over and they all leave, and once again some guy gets up to give a speech that nobody's listening to. This really stuck with me a long time. Of course, I was young at the time, but there were these congressmen I'd heard of, and when I saw some of them, close up, they looked not just old, but decrepit. I asked myself: how can *these guys* be the people running the country?

As part of the same trip we went to New York City. At that time in New York City the drinking age was eighteen, and I was twenty, so every night I would leave the hotel that my dad and I were staying in, get on the subway and go down to the Village, walk around and then go to the Café Wha? I thought it was the greatest scene—they had a Jamaican steel drum band, different comedians, and some other acts, and it was a very vibrant scene there in the Café Wha? and in the Village as a whole. Of course, I found out later that my dad would hold his breath every night until I got back at one or two in the morning, after having been in the Village all that time.

During that period, even though I was still very limited in what I could do, I started to get involved, in the ways I could, in some of the bigger issues that were going on. People may not think of Berkeley in this way, but this was at a time when there was still a lot of open, overt segregation in the schools and in housing, and there was a big struggle about ending that. A lot of these issues were being battled out during that time. There was this ballot initiative to pass a fair housing law in Berkeley, which was narrowly voted down. Now, of course, since then these things have been changed. But that gives you a sense of what things were like *then*.

I was very much into that battle, even though I could only be involved from a distance, so to speak. For example, there was this talk show host, Les Crane, who was memorialized in a Phil Ochs song, "Love Me, I'm a Liberal." Les Crane *was* a liberal, and as such he obviously had his limitations. But he was supporting the right side of this fair housing law. And he had these people on his program, one who was supporting the fair housing ordinance, and then this small property owning, narrow-minded conservative type who was opposing the fair housing law. I was listening and getting more and more angry and passionate as this debate was going on, getting infuriated by the arguments of this conservative guy. He kept saying things like, "I'm not a racist, it's not that I want to discriminate on the basis of race, I just don't want the government to tell me what I can do with my own house, and who I can and can't sell it to. The government shouldn't be able to tell you what you can do with your own home."

So I called up the *Les Crane Show* and got on the air—my parents knew Les Crane and had his private number so I didn't have to go through the screener—and I said, "I want to talk to this guy who's opposing this fair housing thing, I want to ask this guy a question: Are you opposed to the fire regulations that apply to housing in the city of Berkeley?" "Well, what do you mean?" "For example, there are regulations that tell you that you can't have electrical outlets anywhere you want, they have to be separated by so many feet, because there'd be a fire danger otherwise—are you opposed to those things?" "Well, no, nobody's opposed to that, you have to have those regulations," he answered. "So," I said, "you're not opposed to the government regulating what you can do in your house, you just don't want them telling you that you can't refuse to sell your house to Black people."

This was one outlet I had for my passion that was being stirred by what was happening. I was still very much concerned with what was going on in the larger world beyond me, even though I was severely restricted in being able to be actively involved in anything.

## The Cuban Missile Crisis: World in the Balance

During the acute period of the Cuban Missile Crisis, in 1962, those events, and their implications, loomed much larger, even in my own mind, than my own situation of being sick. Everybody sensed to one degree or another—certainly anybody who was paying any attention, and most people were, they couldn't help it—that the world could literally end at any time. I still remember feeling very, very deeply, right down into my bones, that the whole world could come to an end. At that time, I was back on a restricted schedule in school, but I followed this whole thing very intensely.

Of course, they always give you only the U.S. imperialist side of the picture, and that's what people get drummed into them. I remember this dramatic incident that they still like to replay from time to time, when Adlai Stevenson, who was the U.S. representative to the United Nations, gave this speech where he showed these photos of the Soviet missiles that had been brought into Cuba. And then he turned to the Soviet ambassador and said, "Are those or are those not Soviet missiles in Cuba? I can wait here till hell freezes over, Mr. Ambassador." The Soviet ambassador wouldn't answer, and Stevenson just kept saying, "Are they or aren't they, Mr. Ambassador"—on and on like that, putting him on the spot. But they never show how a year before that, at the beginning of the Kennedy administration, Adlai Stevenson got up and vehemently denied in the United Nations that the U.S. had anything to do with the Bay of Pigs invasion of Cuba—which, of course, was a blatant lie. So they like to show the one thing on TV as a highlight from history, but not the other thing where Stevenson was overtly lying in front of the whole world.

At the time of the Cuban Missile Crisis, Kennedy put a naval block-ade around Cuba, and said that if any Soviet ship tried to break that blockade that would be an act of war, and the U.S. would respond. Kennedy tried to justify this—and I remember this very clearly—by claiming that the Soviet Union had violated the UN Charter by putting missiles in Cuba. Now even though I had a lot of suspicions about the government already at that time, and even though I was very angry about a lot of injustices in American society, and especially the oppres-sion of Black people, I still wanted to believe in my government. I still wanted to believe the government could at least be brought around to doing the right thing. And I didn't want to believe that on something where literally the fate of the world was involved, they would just open-ly lie to everybody. But I felt strongly, with the fate of the world up for grabs and hanging by a thread, that "I have to know the truth here."

So I went to the university library and I dug out the UN Charter, remembering that Kennedy said it was a violation of the UN Charter for the Soviet Union to have missiles in Cuba. I read the whole charter through, and I naively expected I would find a statement in the Charter that would say, "It is a violation of this Charter for the Soviet Union to have missiles in Cuba." Of course, I didn't find anything of the kind. So then I started looking into it further: "Well, does it say it's a violation for one country to put missiles into another country?" Of course, there wasn't anything like that in the Charter either and, as I later found out, the U.S. had missiles all over the place, including in Turkey, and even though the ones in Turkey were older generation missiles, they were still missiles that could set off nuclear devices. These missiles in Turkey were closer to the Soviet border than Cuba was to the U.S. border, but they weren't talking about that either in the U.S. media. I kept looking for *anything* in this UN Charter that would justify what Kennedy was saying about how this was a violation of the Charter. I read that Charter over and over, and I couldn't find anything.

Kennedy was just lying. He was really saying, "We can do whatever we want, and nobody can do anything we don't want 'em to do." That was the logic he was using then, and that's the logic that, right up to Bush, they use now. Some of my favorite lines from Bob Dylan are in the song where he talks about trying to get in a nuclear fallout shelter and the owner says, "Get out of here, I'll tear you limb from limb." Then the next lines are: "I said, 'You know, they refused Jesus too.' He said: 'You're not him.'" The way of thinking, or not thinking, that Dylan captured there—the inability or unwillingness to engage in abstract thought, and to abstract from one situation to another, the refusal to be consistent in applying a principle (what applies to you doesn't apply to me; I can do what I want, and you can't do it if I don't want you to)—that same sort of "you're not him," or "you're not me," logic was being applied by Kennedy. And this was a big shock to me. I knew some things about injustices in American society, but lying on this level, lying before the world with the fate of the world literally at stake, was more than I expected. It may have been unusual to actually go and pore through the UN Charter, but there was so much at stake that I felt like, "I have to know the truth, and just because it's the leader of my country, I can't accept what he says when something this big is at stake."

Of course, this didn't immediately cause me to become a communist —I was still against communism, as much as I understood it, which was very little. But it shook me up a lot and kept circulating in my mind as other events, like Vietnam a little later, unfolded. The Cuban missile crisis and things like the fair housing struggle contributed to my feeling that there were important things in the world and I should do something about those things, I should do something important with my life when I got my life back. I still had the passion that I had for sports and things like that, but that was something you do for entertainment and fun—I mean your life *could* be about that, and I always thought that if I hadn't ended up being a communist, maybe I would have been a high school basketball coach—but I was feeling that my life should be about something more than sports, as much as I still had real passion about that. I felt that there were so many big things going on in the world, I wanted to do something with my life that would mean something or, to use the phrase of the time, be relevant and not just be a personal passion for me.

## A Scientific Approach

Being sick didn't "turn me back to god." I no longer believed that god existed, and being sick didn't make me feel any more like I should believe that god existed. I didn't think "god" had anything to do with this. I didn't yet have a communist, dialectical materialist approach to things, but I did have a sort of basic scientific approach. I would always ask my doctor, over and over again, why this happened. And he'd say, simply, "I don't know." But the fact that he didn't know, the fact that there are things we don't know at any time, is not a reason to start inventing imaginary causes and forces to explain things. That just gets in the way of actually learning more about the reality of things.

I really loved this doctor, Dr. Meyer. He never charged us a single thing for the intensive care, and then the years of ongoing medical treatment, because he took a liking to our family and to me. And it wasn't just us. He died recently, and when I read his obituary I learned even more what a great guy he was, and how this had been a part of his whole approach to medicine, to give people the medical care they needed, even if they couldn't pay for it. He'd finally quit practicing medicine late in his life because these HMO's would not let him really give people the kind of medical care that they needed. All during the time I was sick, he'd let me come into his office at any time and have the tests done that I needed, and whenever I'd go into his office I would see people who could not afford the medical care he was giving them—he was giving it to them free, or letting them pay what they could, and charging other people who *could* afford it in order to keep his practice going. So whenever I'd ask him why did this happen, or what was the cause of this, he'd answer—and I still remember the way he'd say this to me, in his inimitable style and voice—"I don't know." He never was able to say what caused this reaction in my body. But I never thought it was punishment from "god," or that "god" had anything to do with it. This was a medical condition, it came on because of "natural causes," real-world things, even if the precise causes couldn't be known. Just because the doctor was honest enough to simply say, "I don't know" and couldn't tell me exactly why this happened, didn't mean that I started looking to supposed supernatural causes for this.

As I said, I felt that casting off belief in all that stuff was an emancipation for me, and I felt absolutely no pull toward wanting to go back to believing in what I frankly regarded as superstition. There are many things we obviously still don't understand, but there are many things the people thousands of years ago didn't understand that we do understand now. They made up myths and stories to explain things they couldn't explain otherwise, and then the ruling classes down through the ages have found it convenient to keep people believing in these kinds of things. But I had gotten free of that, and there was no attraction to me to go back into believing in that stuff. This was a real-world thing that had happened to me, and there was a real-world way that I was going to get over it, by putting up with all this medicine and struggling to regain my health. That was my part of the struggle: I put up with the medicine, and all the side effects and everything else, and even when the medicine itself knocked me down, I'd get up and keep going, because that's the way I felt this was going to be dealt with, not by praying or turning back to some religious views that I'd come to understand didn't really represent the truth about the way the world is and the way things are.

## *Turning the Corner*

After a year of going to Cal on a limited schedule, by 1963 I was feeling better and able to take a more regular load. This was a time when important changes were starting to take place around Vietnam. In fact, one day I was walking on the campus and all these people started running down toward the gym. I didn't know what this was about. But even though I couldn't really run at that time, I was walking as fast as I could to try to keep up, and I asked somebody, "What's going on?" They said that Madame Nhu had been invited by the university to speak in the gym. Madame Nhu was the wife of the brother of the president, so-called, of South Vietnam, the U.S. puppet, Diem, and her husband was the head of the secret police. She was there speaking on behalf of the U.S. puppet government and the U.S. intervention in Vietnam, and people were protesting even then.

People were running to try to get into the auditorium to protest Madame Nhu's appearance at the university. This was just before Kennedy and the CIA decided that Messrs. Nhu and Diem had become a liability and had them assassinated—and just before Kennedy himself was assassinated. But, anyway, there were things like that going on that seemed to come out of the blue. At the same time, my health was slowly recovering, though it wasn't in a straight line—it was kind of one step backward and a couple of steps forward, and then two steps backward sometimes.

The thing that kind of turned the corner for me, ironically, actually started when was I was lying in bed one morning—I think it was in the summer of '63—and I started getting this really severe stomach pain, like I'd never experienced before, as if someone took a two-by-four and hit you in the stomach as hard as they possibly could when you were not expecting it. This pain just kept getting worse and worse, and I was literally doubling over, so finally I woke up my parents; at first they didn't realize how serious it was, but as soon as they did they called the doctor, and the doctor said, "He's got a perforated ulcer"—which means it had broken open and was bleeding into the stomach. (The cortisone I was taking, among other things, can give you an ulcer.)

So I had to be rushed to the hospital and they put a tube—but it felt like a hose—through my nose down into my stomach to drain the stomach. They severely restricted my diet. They decided that I was too vulnerable and fragile to undergo surgery. But, because of the ulcer, they stopped the cortisone treatments, and there was a question of what was going to happen as a result of that. Surprisingly to both me and the doctors, my body didn't respond too badly to not having the cortisone. I didn't get well, but I didn't get really, really sick either. So then my doctor came to me and said: "Look, I've been doing some reading on this and there's this treatment that they first used in Italy with these cortical steroids where, instead of giving you a fairly high dose every day, they give you a fairly high dose for part of the week, and then discontinue it for the rest of the week." The theory was that it was like giving a jolt to the body, almost like a kick-start to get the body to recover. He told me: "We want to try this on you, since you seem to have tolerated fairly well these couple of weeks when you weren't taking any cortisone." So they started with this treatment, and as it turned out this was like turning a corner for me.

Just before this I'd gone through my second long cycle of going down, down, down in the dosage of the medicine and then just when I thought *maybe* I was going to be through with this and get off the medicine, I went in on a Friday, when the doctor was out of town, and the nurses did the tests and discovered that some of the symptoms—in particular the protein in the urine—had begun to reappear. So I got really down. But, when I went back and saw the doctor on Monday he said,

"You idiot, that's just a little setback, we'll deal with it." That was always his attitude, and it helped get my spirits up, even though I still had to up the dosage of the medicine again. But then, not long after that, I had this ulcer perforate and, after seeing that I did pretty well without any cortisone for a few weeks, they decided to try this new approach.

Generally when you have to take all these steroids it has a lot of different effects on you, and I'd feel really weakened and tired a lot of the time. But now it was a completely different experience, and eventually it evolved to where I would take the steroids on Thursday, Friday and Saturday—pretty high doses—and then nothing Sunday, Monday, Tuesday and Wednesday. I was carrying pretty much a regular load at the university at that point and trying to do other things. But then I had to adjust my week to the rhythm of this treatment. I'd start in on Thursday taking the steroids, and by Thursday night I was flying—cortisone is actually an extract from the adrenal gland, so it's like a jolt of adrenaline, and by the time it kicked in on Thursday night, man, I was *going*. And Friday and Saturday I was going. Then on Sunday I would stop the medicine, and by Sunday afternoon it was almost like withdrawal symptoms. My nose would start running, my stomach would get sick, I'd feel just completely sapped of energy, and I couldn't hardly do anything. On Monday I felt really draggy, then by Tuesday, Wednesday I'd sort of feel leveled off and okay, and by Thursday night I was back on the steroids and flying again.

This went on for the better part of a year, but it turned out that either my body was just ready to respond and/or this different treatment actually did work better. But, for whatever reason, I started noticing real improvement in how I felt, and my body was responding well, so that by the summer of 1964—more or less a year later—they finally took me off the medicine altogether. My doctor told me: "Well, it looks like you might make it now. We're gonna have to keep monitoring you very carefully for a while"—and for years they did—"but it looks like you might make it, you might be through this." And I never had to go back to the cortisone after three years of taking it.

In 1964, when I was just starting to feel better and on my way to recovery, though not fully recovered yet from all the sickness, I turned twenty-one. So I could go to bars and things like that. I wasn't a big drinker at that time, but I liked to go to clubs and see different acts. One time the Coasters were performing at a club in North Oakland, and I really wanted to go see them. I couldn't find anybody to go with me that time, so I just went by myself. Around that time the Coasters had out this song called "'Taint Nothin' To Me"—sort of a novelty song, which was characteristic of the Coasters, a whole funny song that I really liked. And I liked a lot of the other Coasters classics, so I really wanted to go see them. So I went, but the show didn't start until pretty late, and when you sit in a bar you have to drink, so I had a couple of drinks. Then the Coasters came on and they did the first set—they did "'Taint Nothin' To Me," and some other songs—but then they said, "Okay, we're gonna take a break now, we'll do a second set in a little while." I'm thinking, "Oh man, I really wanna hear more, so I'm gonna stick around for the second set." But then I had to drink more. I'm sitting at the bar, I order another drink, and I start drinking the drink, and then I set it down— and the next thing I know somebody's tapping me kind of forcefully on the shoulder. I look up, realizing that I've fallen asleep, and I'm staring into the face of the bartender. And he says, "You can't fall asleep in here —you gotta stay awake or you gotta leave." You know, I wonder what the other people in the bar thought, what the bartender thought—but here I was, the only white guy in this bar, a little bit embarrassed that I'd fallen asleep and had to be awakened by the bartender. Some people later told me that this sounded like a scary experience, but I just thought the whole thing was great!

# Chapter Six

# *"Your Sons and Your Daughters..."*

$M$y family and all my friends and I were still holding our breath, because you don't know—twice before I'd been through a situation where things were going well with low dosages of cortisone, and then the symptoms of kidney disease would reappear. So there was the possibility of a relapse now that I was completely off the cortisone. But that summer brought a lot of big changes in my life.

I had been nominated by some of my English professors to be part of an undergraduate honors seminar on John Milton, the English poet who wrote *Paradise Lost* (and *Paradise Regained*), over the summer. There were about ten of us in the seminar, which was taught by Stanley Fish, a big Milton hotshot who was only a few years older than we were —I think he was 24 at the time. He's now a big figure in academic and intellectual circles more generally in the U.S., and I've written a few things recently commenting on some of his books. At that time, I hadn't heard of him but I was into English literature, I was still trying to write poetry, and this sounded like an exciting thing to do. So when they asked me, I said sure.

We met for a number of weeks, five days a week for several hours, and it turned out to be a fun seminar. One time Professor Fish brought in this guest lecturer who talked about a certain aspect of Milton's work, and I was wearing my dark glasses in the classroom. While he was talking he kept pausing and looking at me, and finally he just couldn't take it any longer—he turned to me and said, "Why is it that you're wearing shades in this class?" And I don't know why, but for some reason I had an answer ready, and I responded without even hesitating: "Plato has written that the eyes are the window to the soul, and I don't want anybody peering into my soul." Even that guest lecturer couldn't help cracking up at that point.

### Opening Up

I met Liz in this seminar, and she had a big influence on me. I was already anxious to be more involved in political affairs, and she came from a progressive family—her parents had been sympathizers of the old Communist Party. She told stories about how people she knew had to bury their Marxist books during the McCarthy period. She had a radicalizing effect on me, to put it that way—for instance, I was drawn to the Free Speech Movement (FSM) when it broke out that fall, but she had a big influence in getting me more deeply involved in it.

I was going through a lot of changes in a kind of a telescoped way, the way you do when big, world events happen one after the other. There had been the Cuban Missile Crisis in 1962, and then a couple of years after that the Chinese exploded an atomic bomb. I remember walking with somebody after we'd gone to a civil rights demonstration in the Bay Area against one of these local businesses that wouldn't hire Black people, and there was this BIG headline in the local newspaper: "Chinese Explode Atomic Bomb." I turned to the person next to me, who was more radical than me at that time, and I said, "Man, that's scary, that's bad." And he said, "No, I think it's a good thing." I said: "Why? That Mao, he's crazy, it's not good for him to have the atomic bomb." And he answered, "No, it's a good thing, because it could mean the U.S. won't be able to fuck with China so easily." I still was not by any means a communist and, as reflected in the comment I made about Mao at that time, I still accepted a lot of the anti-communist propaganda and bullshit. But I was open. The prejudices I had were clashing up against somebody else who had a different understanding and was challenging me—that kind of thing was repeatedly happening. So, when he said this, it wasn't like I just dismissed it. I didn't say, "Oh I see" and just agree with him, but on the other hand, it became one of those things circulating in your mind.

This was when the U.S. was escalating the war in Vietnam, in the period of 1964 and '65. I hadn't yet made up my mind about Vietnam, even at that point. In fact, during the Free Speech Movement there were some people in leadership of that movement, including Mario Savio, who were making statements against the Vietnam War. And I wasn't sure that I liked that—I was still wrestling with questions about the Vietnam War, and I felt this should not be a dividing line, or a necessary point of unity, in the FSM. But all these things are clashing in your mind in times like that.

### Torn by Kennedy and the Democrats

Just to backtrack for a minute, the Kennedy assassination was a perfect example of the contradictoriness of my thinking. I came to class at the university that day and everybody was stunned and saddened that Kennedy had been assassinated—they were all openly grieving. And I remember one of the women in one of my classes got mad at me because I was sort of aloof and not expressing any emotion. But then, as it sunk in, believe it or not, I actually wrote a poem memorializing Kennedy a few weeks after that. I sort of felt like Phil Ochs at that time, who talked about his Marxist friends being unable to understand how he could write a positive song about Kennedy—and about how that's why he couldn't be a Marxist. And that kind of speaks to where I was at, at the time.

My father was part of the Democratic Party. Toward the end of his life, he became more alienated from the whole system and more outraged about the injustices in the U.S. and what the U.S. is doing around the world—but for much of his life he was a real liberal Democrat. In fact, he had been offered a position in the Kennedy administration, but he turned it down because I was in the Bay Area and too sick to move, and he didn't want to be separated from me while I was sick. My parents, of course, were very upset about the Kennedy assassination, and in fact I think my dad went to a meeting and read this poem that I wrote memorializing Kennedy.

This kind of contradictory thinking that characterized my parents, and myself, at that time, is fairly common among progressive people. You see a lot of the injustices and what we sometimes call the "running sores" of the whole society and the way in which it grinds up people, and you see ways in which the people presiding over the society are responsible for this. But you still carry along the illusion and have the hope that they can be brought to their senses, that they can be made to see that this is wrong, and—since they're in a position to do something about it—you want to believe that they *will* do something about it, if they can just somehow be made to see what's wrong. That's an illusion that is often difficult to shed; it takes a lot for people to fully cast that off, and that was true for me too.

## Into the Student Life

At this point, in 1964, I was finally able to leave home. Since I had been cut off from a lot of social experiences, I wanted to go live in the dorms, even though I was by then in my third year of classes. But there was still a question of whether my health requirements would allow that. Among other things, I had this very strict diet, where literally every day I was calculating how many milligrams of sodium I could eat, and things like that. Finally I had a discussion with my doctor and he said, "You know you're probably at the point where if you're just careful about what you eat, if you don't eat salty foods and don't add any salt to anything, you'll probably be all right in the dorms." That was the big hang-up about living in the dorms at that time: I had enough strength, but there was also the question of diet, because something that threw my system off could give me a severe setback.

This friend of mine from high school named Tom was living in the dorms, and we got it arranged so that he and I could be roommates, which made it easier for me. That was a very important step for me at that time, given how dependent I'd been forced to be. Even though I loved my family, I wanted to be taking steps to be on my own more.

While the dorms, obviously, have their limitations, this was a positive experience for me under the circumstances. Mainly people go in the dorm when they first come into the university, and then move on—but since I hadn't been able to do that, I actually enjoyed it quite a bit for the short time that I was there. Tom, my roommate, was a progressive guy and also a big sports fanatic like me. This was a time when even life in the dorms was beginning to be affected by the big changes sweeping through society and the world. That kind of ferment was finding expression throughout university life.

At that time I still physically bore the scars of being sick and I was also struggling to overcome them psychologically. My friends used to talk me into going to parties, and my love for singing provided a way for me to sort of break out of my shell socially. I'm not exactly even sure why or how I got the nerve to do this, but when I'd go to the parties—and I didn't have to get drunk or high to do this, either—often at a break I would just start singing. I would sing R&B songs or Motown or whatever. I even did this in the dorms. We had four dorms together in a group where everyone ate at the same cafeteria, and at the big meal on Sunday they used to have a microphone for people to make announcements. So one Sunday at the urging and daring of my friends, and somewhat on my own initiative as well, I actually got up and just took hold of the mike and started singing this Mary Wells song that I loved, "Bye, Bye Baby"—and the whole place just responded. So that became a Sunday institution during the time I was in the dorm.

### Dylan and "Beatlemania"

I remember also when the Beatles first came to the U.S. It was a big deal. They were on one of those shows like *The Ed Sullivan Show*, and everybody in the dorms gathered around the TV to watch the Beatles—except for me and Tom, who really didn't like or care about the Beatles that much and were also making a statement that we had other kinds of music we were into and we weren't going to get caught up with the herd. In retrospect, I've sometimes said, in explaining how I really didn't get Jimi Hendrix at the time, that some of the influences I had from high school—the friends I had, and the musical interests—had given me almost a "narrow nationalist" view: "Jimi Hendrix, what's he doing playing all this psychedelic white hippie stuff?" I've since come to understand how narrow that was, how I failed to appreciate something that was new and breaking with some conventions and molds, and I've tried to learn from that, not just about music but more generally.

But even recognizing that narrowness, there was something that I still think was valid in how Tom and I were making a statement: "What's the big deal about these English white boys coming here and singing rhythm-and-blues?" I remember a friend of mine telling a story about a track meet in L.A. that took place during this time, and how Mick Jagger was staying in the same hotel as some of the athletes in the meet. At one point a number of them surrounded Mick Jagger and said, "Oh, you're supposed to be a big singer," and they started singing all these different doo-wop and rhythm-and-blues songs, and challenging him: "Let's hear you sing this one, let's hear you sing that one." And I cracked up when I heard that—I thought it was a great story. So, in sort of the same spirit,

Tom and I were not gonna become part of Beatlemania. Later on, I came to appreciate especially John Lennon *a lot*, in a different way—especially for his political and social views, but even musically. But back then, we were not gonna get swept up in "Beatlemania."

Bob Dylan was another story altogether. There was this one guy at Cal who used to sing the whole repertoire of Bob Dylan music, and he had the Bob Dylan look as well. I'm sure there was this kind of phenomenon all over the country, and I'm also sure that this kind of "imitation" was exactly the kind of thing Bob Dylan didn't like, but this guy had the harmonica and the guitar and everything, and that's actually where I first started hearing some Dylan songs. Then, as I got more political, I really got into Dylan. I remember in particular the album *The Times They Are A-Changin'*. They *were* changing, and this brought a lot of generational conflicts.

One time, when we were together with my parents somewhere, Liz and I put that song on the record player and played it very loudly, sort of right up in their face: "Come mothers and fathers throughout the land, and don't criticize what you can't understand..." So, even though I didn't want to have anything to do with the Beatles, there was a way in which Bob Dylan spoke for the whole social and political upheaval that was occurring, especially for a lot of youth out of the middle class, but not only for them. A lot of his early songs had to do with the civil rights struggle, outrages like the one captured so powerfully in "The Lonesome Death of Hattie Carroll," about the killing of a Black maid by this rich young white planter in Baltimore. And the poetry of Dylan also captured me—because I was into poetry, and the poetry of his songs just really drew me. I didn't see him as a white boy who was just mimicking other people's music. I looked at him as a poet-musician and somewhat a voice of a generation who was speaking to a lot of things at a point where "The Times They Are A-Changin'."

## New People, New Influences

I only stayed in the dorms for a short time, and then Tom and I and a couple of other people got an apartment. One of my good friends in the dorm, who later moved into an apartment with me and Tom, was from India. His name was Sidhartha Burman, but it got shortened to Sid, and especially some of my Jewish friends liked to joke with him, "Sid Berman, good Jewish boy from India." But his name was really a classical Indian name, Sidhartha Burman, and he was from a very wealthy bourgeois family. We had a lot of struggle with him. He was a really good-hearted guy, but he used to recount to us, for example, that when he was back in India, he was awakened every morning by being given a massage by servants. Then he would walk from his house to his father's business in Calcutta, where he lived, and he acknowledged to us that every day he would step over the dead bodies of the poor people who had starved to death on the streets of Calcutta the night before. We struggled with him and struggled with him, and we finally got him for a little while to become kind of a hippie, but that's as far as we could get with him. On the other hand, he did share with us a lot of experiences and open us up to an understanding, or at least a glimpse, of a whole different part of the world and different cultures and customs.

Politically at that time—in the period before the Free Speech Movement—there was mainly civil rights activity among students. In fact, the right to organize for civil rights activities on the campus was the focal point of what became the Free Speech Movement. It may sound unbelievable now, but in those days, the Cal administration had a rule that you could organize things like student clubs, but you could not carry on political activity on campus for "off-campus political causes," such as civil rights. You were not allowed to organize on campus for, say, a civil rights protest or demonstration against a company that wouldn't hire Black people—it was against the rules and you could be expelled for it. That gave the spark to the whole Free Speech Movement (FSM). The FSM not only radically changed the Berkeley campus, but was a major impetus for a wave of changes on campuses all across the country. When the FSM was going on, people, young people in particular, came to Berkeley from all parts of the country.

For example, one day I walked on campus and there was this guy from New York who'd come to Berkeley specifically because he recognized the significance of the gathering Free Speech Movement. He told me stories about having visited Italy, where the Communist Party was looked at very differently than in the U.S.—it was a mainstream political party there. He also told this vivid story about being in a courtroom in New York City when they brought in this prisoner to appear before the judge, and the prisoner had obviously been brutally beaten by the cops. It was so bad that the judge sort of lost control for a moment and blurted out, "god, what happened?!" Then he described how the judge regained his "composure" and went on with the ordinary business of the court as if nothing were wrong. When I put things like that together with things I knew and was learning, from my own personal experience, and especially the experience of many of my friends, it had a kind of cumulative effect.

## Malcolm X

As I described earlier, even when I was in high school some of the gathering momentum of the civil rights movement carried over in various ways and found various expressions among the students and within the school, among the Black students in particular. So I knew about Malcolm X by the time I graduated from high school. And I remember a year or so later, when I was in the hospital starting up the cortisone treatments, I saw a Sunday afternoon political discussion/debate program on TV. They had different people talking about Malcolm X and the Black Muslims, with people on different sides of the argument, though they were all white—arguing about whether the Black Muslims were just as bad as the Ku Klux Klan and the white supremacists. I remember one guy making the argument, "No, they're not, because the Ku Klux Klan and the white supremacists are defending and upholding oppression, whereas whatever you think about the Black Muslims they're on the side of opposing that oppression." That immediately struck me as true and important—I agreed with that right away. It was in line with everything I already felt, but it also put something together for me.

I remember listening to Malcolm X's speeches and seeing him on television, and always being riveted and, increasingly, inspired by him. I agreed with Malcolm X when he said "freedom, by any means necessary." I had never agreed with the pacifist view. It's one thing if you want to say there should be pacifist *tactics* in a particular situation, like a demonstration, but I never agreed with pacifism as a *principle*—that Black people, for example, should always turn the other cheek. When I heard about the Deacons for Defense in the south, who organized and took up arms to defend the Black community from the KKK and all the racist sheriffs, I thought that was right—it was necessary and important. So when Malcolm X articulated "by any means necessary," I felt that was right, and I didn't agree with the idea that you should confine the people to turning the other cheek or just to passively accepting, for whatever supposedly loftier purpose, being brutalized.

I loved to listen to Malcolm X speeches. At one point, I got a record-ing of "The Ballot or the Bullet," and I listened to that over and over. Later, when I started making speeches myself, I drew a lot from Malcolm X, especially the way in which he exposed profound injustices and con-tradictions of the system so sharply. (I also drew from Richard Pryor, particularly the ways in which he used humor to bring to light things in society that were covered up, or that somehow you weren't supposed to talk about.)

## Straddling Two Worlds

My friend Matthew came back to Cal, and he had a circle of friends who were mainly Black that I also got to know and became friends with. And when I went back to Berkeley High to do tutoring and officiating at track meets and coaching summer league basketball teams and things like that, I maintained contact with my old friends and that milieu, so to speak. While I didn't think of it that way at the time, looking back on it now, I feel like I was straddling two worlds, but to me they were both part of my life, they were both part of my world. And the same kind of shit that I ran into in high school came up again —for example, there were people at Cal who would straight up tell me that they would not be friends with me because I hung out in the Student Union and around campus with Black students. As I said, I was sort of straddling two worlds, but to me this was all part of what I was about. I wasn't trying to make a "statement"—these were just my friends, these were the peo-ple and things I was interested in and cared about, these were just the different parts that made up the whole of my life. I wasn't saying to myself, "Oh, I'm straddling two worlds," but objectively I was.

In a lot of ways, culturally, I was drawn more to things that were from my earlier years, especially my high school years, than I was to the university. But then politically, and in terms of intellectual ferment, there were things about the university that were increasingly drawing me. There was the Dylan music, the poetry, even the Milton seminar. I took courses in Shakespeare and Chaucer, and I'm one of the few people that I know of who has actually read the entire "Faerie Queene" by Edmund Spenser!—which is a classical epic poem, hundreds and hundreds of pages long, written at more or less the same time as Shakespeare. I read that—I actually took a course on this poem—mainly because I knew Spenser was a big influence on Keats and I was really into Keats. All that was one part of my life, too.

I also had a goal of learning five or six languages. I took Italian and I took some Spanish, but I didn't ever fulfill my goal—other things intervened which became more important to me. But by taking Italian I got interested in some of the Italian romantic poets from more or less the same period as Keats and the other English romantic poets. My favorite Italian professor was very progressive, and I used to have talks with him about what was going on in the world—as much as I could, I would talk with him in Italian about all this.

But, once again, I was straddling different worlds. You know, most of the people who were big into athletics—let's put it this way, they were not among the vanguard of the progressive and radical forces on the campus. There were some friends of mine, like Kayo and my roommate Tom, who were sports fanatics and who also had strong progressive views and radical tendencies, but that was more the exception than the rule. So, in that way you could say there was a certain conflict in terms of things that I was passionate about. But by this time, around 1964, I was finally getting back on my feet physically and feeling like I dared to do some things. So when the summer gave way to the fall and the Free Speech Movement arose, and in addition with the influence of Liz—with whom I was starting to fall in love—I was ready to throw myself into that.

## The Free Speech Movement

Despite the administration's rule that you couldn't do "on-campus organizing for off-campus issues," people at Cal were organizing on the campus to protest against local businesses which they identified as practicing racial discrimination in their hiring, such as the *Oakland Tribune* and this drive-in restaurant called Mel's Diner. Everybody on campus was aware of this, it was becoming more and more of an issue that people were debating and talking about and getting involved in—or not getting involved in and opposing, because there was polarization. To jump ahead for a second in order to give a sense of this, at a later point in the FSM, during one of the nights when people were sitting in around a police car, 500 fraternity boys came to throw things at the people sitting in and shout insults at them. I've often said that in the '60s even fraternity boys grew brains, but that was later in the '60s—at the time of the FSM they didn't have them yet.

So the administration sent the campus police to put a stop to this on-campus organizing for "off-campus issues." A guy named Jack Weinberg was sitting at a table organizing for this and he refused to fold up the table. They arrested him, put him in a police car to drive him off, and then a bunch of students came and surrounded the police car. While this sit-in was going on, I was at a reception that the Chancellor, Chancellor Strong, was having for honor students at the university. At that reception, one of the students asked him what was going on with the sit-in, and the Chancellor basically said: "Well, the area in which they were originally organizing wasn't the area where the police car incident took place, but where they were originally organizing, we thought that was actually city property, because it was right at the entrance to the campus. But then we looked into it and found out that it *was* university property, so we decided we should put a stop to it." And why did they look into it? Well, he went on to tell us, because of pressure from the *Oakland Tribune*, which was owned by William F. Knowland, who was a well-known reactionary.[5] The *Tribune* called up, the Chancellor told us, complaining about the organizing of civil rights demonstrations against the *Tribune* for discriminatory hiring practices. "So," Chancellor Strong concluded, "we cracked down on that organizing."

I was just stunned. I was shocked, first of all, that this was actually how this came about and, second, that he was just saying this so baldly as if everybody would accept it. As I've said elsewhere,[6] I guess his idea was this: since we had good grades, we must be "grade-grubbers," in training to become money-grubbers, and we wouldn't find anything objectionable in what he told us. But a lot of people there *did* find this very objectionable, including myself. I immediately went over to the sit-in around the police car and got in line to speak—the police car had been surrounded by the protesters and transformed into a speaking platform while Jack Weinberg was still sitting inside. It was really great! So

5. William F. Knowland was nicknamed William "Formosa" Knowland because of his big-time support for Chiang Kai-shek, who had ruled China with the backing of the U.S. and other imperialist powers but had been driven from power in 1949 by the Chinese revolution, led by Mao Tsetung, and forced to retreat to the island of Taiwan, which was formerly called Formosa.

6. For more on the author's views on the Free Speech Movement, see "FSM Reflections—On Becoming a Revolutionary," by Bob Avakian, *Revolutionary Worker*, #882, November 17, 1996, available at rwor.org.

when my turn came, I got up on the police car and told this story and explained how it led me to support this whole thing, and I donated my $100 honorarium for being an honor student to the FSM. And that's how I first got directly involved.

Stepping back, I think the FSM expressed the general feeling that students wanted to be treated as adults and citizens, they wanted to have the same rights as other people. Phil Ochs had this song where the refrain went something like, I've got something to say, sir, and I'm going to say it now. And as it was in that song, so it was in reality with students and youth at that time. But, beyond that, there were a lot of big things going on in the world. Vietnam was already beginning to heat up in the fall of '64, and there was the civil rights movement. People wanted to be actively involved in or debating about these things, they wanted to be part of the larger world—they didn't want to be treated like little children just because they were students. So all this was going on and mixing together: the general resistance against treating college students as if they didn't have any minds, against the whole bureaucratization of the university and the functioning of the university as machinery to serve the corporate world and the military, and against the depersonalizing effects of all that on the students, on the one hand, as well as the big things going on in society and the world, like the civil rights and anti-Vietnam War movements, that people wanted to be involved in. It was all that together.

The university tried to claim that it was all being fomented by "outside agitators." There *were* some people who weren't students who were involved—and they were welcomed, it was good that they were involved. But it was overwhelmingly students who were involved. This came out, for example, when people were arrested in the big sit-in at the University Administration building. In the aftermath of these arrests, this claim was made: "Oh, these are just ne'er-do-wells, these are just disgruntled students and non-students." But the records showed that overwhelmingly those arrested were students. Then, since they couldn't deny that most of those arrested *were* students, they claimed that they were students who were failing or getting poor grades anyway, so they were just being troublemakers. In response to this, the FSM committee took a survey of the people who'd been arrested, and among other things asked the grade point average of the students who were arrested. This survey revealed and confirmed that the students who were arrested had *higher* grade point averages than students in the university overall, and were generally *not* failing or getting poor grades.

At this time Liz was more politically aware and more of an activist and radical than I was. She had a family background of people who'd been involved with the Communist Party, and even though that ultimately meant revisionism—reformism in the name of communism—it still gave her a broader political outlook than I had at that time. And she had a big influence on me. It was partly the political discussions we had and partly, to be honest, the fact that I was interested in her romantically and she wanted to be very active in the Free Speech Movement, that led me to be so consistently involved.

When we went into Sproul Hall for the big sit-in, and as the sit-in went on, I was trying to help keep the morale up. At one point I went from floor to floor organizing singing to keep the spirits up. But, at the same time, this sit-in lasted several days and I was still a serious student, so I was also trying to keep up with my schoolwork during the sit-in—until at one point I just decided, "Oh, the hell with it," and threw my homework away. I literally took my homework and threw it down the hall. But this also had a larger symbolic meaning, even though I myself wasn't fully aware of it yet.

Another one of those ironies of "straddling two worlds" happened to me at the end of the sit-in, when people were arrested in almost an assembly line fashion. As they were arrested, a lot of people were thrown down the stairs, and the women in particular were grabbed by the hair and thrown down the stairs. I was on the top floor and saw many people brutalized like that and, of course, this was only a few months after I had finally recovered from being sick. So besides being outraged generally, I was also a little worried about what would happen to me if I got thrown down the stairs or otherwise brutalized, especially if I got hit in the area of my kidneys. And as my turn came to be busted, I recognized the cop who was arresting me as someone who had played basketball for a local college. I saw his nameplate said Gray, so I said, "Aren't you the 'Gray' who played basketball for St. Mary's?" And I kind of shrugged my shoulders as if to say, "So what you gonna do?" And he replied, "Sorry, can't do nothin' for you"—and off I went.

Of course, I was very happy to be arrested, to put it that way. I wanted to be part of this, and there was a great camaraderie. When I did this thing with this cop Gray, I wasn't trying to not get arrested, I just didn't want to get thrown down the stairs or hit in my kidneys. But I was very happy to be part of this.

At the same time, my whole involvement in the Free Speech Movement came shortly after my dad was appointed as a judge by the same governor, Edmund G. "Pat" Brown, who sent the police in to arrest us in Sproul Hall. So that kind of captures a sharp contradiction. My dad was saying to me and also to my younger sister, "Look, I just got appointed..." In effect, he was saying: "Don't do anything to screw up my getting established as judge." My sister and I both had the attitude: "Well, we're not gonna go out of our way to make trouble for you, but we're also not gonna hold back from doing the things we think are right or important."

When I did get arrested, it was another case where both of my parents agreed with the principles of free speech, and even agreed generally with what the students were fighting for, but I think were made very nervous, not only in a personal sense but in a larger sense, by the whole turmoil that was being created—the shutting down of the university, in effect, and people getting busted and all that kind of thing, as well as the personal dimension of how this might affect my dad's standing as a judge. On the other hand, as soon as they learned that I got arrested, my parents called up my doctor, since I had just gotten over this very serious illness, and I was still in a precarious position. And my doctor, who I later learned was sympathetic to protests like this, told my parents: "This could be very dangerous for him. Even if he spends just one night on a cold floor, it could kick back in his whole kidney disease." Actually, my doctor felt so strongly about this that he insisted that my dad get me out that night, so that I wouldn't have to spend the night on a cold floor under jail conditions. So I was surprised to get out a little earlier than some of the other people did, though most everybody was out by the next morning or the next day sometime.

## Mario Savio

Mario Savio, who led the FSM, had a big effect on me, though I didn't really know him personally. I was active and involved in FSM pretty much all the way through, from the beginning; I went to all the rallies and heard Mario and others speak. Like everyone else who was involved, or who heard his speeches, I was very moved by them and felt they spoke very penetratingly to how we saw things and what was motivating us. But while in general I was very moved by his speeches, I remember one time right before we all got busted in Sproul Hall, Mario gave a speech. I think this was just when we found out that the governor, Pat Brown, was sending the troopers to bust us, and Mario talked about the duplicity and the double-dealing of the university administration and the governor and so on—that they hadn't negotiated in good faith and that they'd done these back-handed things—but then he said, "And this is just like what our government is doing in Vietnam." This was in early December of 1964, and I was actively looking into the Vietnam War and trying to figure out what stand to take on it, but I hadn't made up my mind yet.

As I referred to earlier, I was troubled by Mario's saying this at that point, because I felt like we had a certain level of unity in the Free Speech Movement, but it didn't include opposing the Vietnam War. You didn't have to be opposed to the Vietnam War to be actively and enthusiastically involved in the Free Speech Movement, though probably if you took a survey, the overwhelming majority would have been opposed to the Vietnam War. And, within a short time after this, I myself became convinced that it needed to be very actively and strongly opposed. But at that time I was still in the process of wrangling with this—debating and studying and trying to learn enough to make up my mind about it. So this was a little troubling to me—although, as I've said before, as I was trying to make up my mind and come to a decision about Vietnam, the things that were said by people like Mario Savio, for whom I had great respect in general, obviously had a big influence and played a role in convincing me to oppose what the U.S. was doing in Vietnam. So it was that kind of contradictory thing.

## The Assassination of Malcolm X

Shortly after this, in February of 1965, Malcolm X was assassinated. This hit me as a devastating loss for Black people, and also for people generally fighting against injustice, not just in the U.S., but throughout the world. I knew Malcolm X was seeking to link up with people in other parts of the world who were fighting against injustices and oppression. And I never believed that it was just Elijah Muhammed and the Nation of Islam who were involved in Malcolm's assassination. Whether or not they were involved in some way, I knew that the U.S. government was somehow behind this. I knew enough to know that.

So this was another thing further radicalizing me. First, I saw Kennedy blatantly lying, before the whole world with the fate of the world literally hanging in the balance around the Cuban Missile Crisis, then you see something like this, the assassination of Malcolm X, and you know that somehow the U.S. government was involved in this. I hadn't studied the issue, and a lot of the exposure of how they were involved hadn't come out yet, obviously. But I just sensed this—I knew they hated Malcolm X and saw him as very dangerous to them—and it made me really sad but very angry too.

I had been aware of the transformations Malcolm was going through. A lot of my friends and I were following this very closely. People were debating about the split between Elijah Muhammed and Malcolm X, and most everybody I knew sided with Malcolm X. We saw him as more radical, more willing to take on the powers that be, more willing to stand up in the face of any threat against Black people and against their oppression. So I was following that very closely, and all that was an important part of what was causing me to undergo a lot of changes in how I was seeing things and what I felt needed to be done.

I don't remember exactly where I was when I heard the news about Malcolm's assassination, but I do know how I felt immediately upon hearing this. My friends and I were just devastated by it. There's that Phil Ochs song that I mentioned before, "Love Me, I'm a Liberal." It is done in the persona of a liberal—it is a biting exposure of the contradictoriness and hypocrisy in liberals—it starts out with how sad this liberal was when Kennedy got killed, and even what a tragedy it was when the civil rights leader Medgar Evers was murdered, but then this liberal says that Malcolm X got what he had coming. That was a fairly widespread view among a lot of liberals, and Phil Ochs captured that with rather brilliant and biting irony. So there were a lot of very sharp arguments with some people that I knew, because I vehemently disagreed with that view.

## Deciding About Vietnam

All these things were influencing me in making up my mind about Vietnam. Obviously Malcolm X was not only against what the U.S. was doing in Vietnam, but was giving these speeches like "The Ballot or the Bullet," where he sided with the Vietnamese people and talked about how great it was that these poor people who didn't have a lot of technology were standing up and giving battle and delivering blows to this mighty, powerful, white power in the world, as he saw it—"the great hypocrite America." So this was having a big influence on me.

Then there were a lot of debates that were sharpening up on the campus and in activist circles. One thing I remember in particular was a lot of argument about who was responsible for violating the Geneva Agreements that had been made in 1954 about Vietnam, which were to provide for the reunification of Vietnam and elections in 1956.[7] France was getting out of Vietnam—they'd been forced out by the struggle of the Vietnamese people, having suffered this devastating defeat at Dien Bien Phu. In fact, Malcolm X talked about that—about how the Vietnamese sent the French running. As I looked into these arguments, and when I went to the university library and read the initial Agreement and most of the reports of the commission it set up, I found that their reports overwhelmingly demonstrated that the U.S. was systematically sabotaging this Agreement. I learned that Eisenhower, who was then President of the U.S., recognized that Ho Chi Minh would have been overwhelmingly elected to head any government of a reunified Vietnam. So the U.S. set up a puppet government in the southern part of Vietnam, the Republic of South Vietnam, as a separate state and refused to allow the elections for reunification in 1956. I was reading all the pamphlets and articles about this and listening to the debates, trying to figure out the real truth in all this, just like I'd done at the time of the Cuban Missile Crisis. And I discovered that it was unmistakably true that the U.S. had sabotaged this Geneva Agreement and prevented the reunification of Vietnam, because they knew that things wouldn't go their way if this Agreement were implemented.

All this was percolating within me, and I still remember very clear-

---

7. The 1954 Geneva Agreements came out of a conference that included China and the Soviet Union, which were then both socialist, as well as the U.S., France, Britain and other lesser powers. This conference occurred in a situation where liberation forces in Vietnam, headed by Ho Chi Minh, had delivered a devastating defeat at Dien Bien Phu to the French colonialists who were attempting to maintain their domination of Vietnam—and in doing so were receiving major backing and aid from the U.S. The Agreements set up a commission to oversee the reunification of Vietnam, which was temporarily divided into north and south along the 17th parallel; the Agreements called for elections in 1956 throughout Vietnam to establish a single government for the country as a whole.

ly when I got up one morning in early 1965 and got the newspaper, and there were big banner headlines about the brutal attack in Selma, Alabama on civil rights marchers. I said to myself: "How in the world could the U.S. government be over there in Vietnam fighting for the freedom of the Vietnamese people, as they claim to be, when this is happening to Black people right here in the U.S. and the U.S. government is doing nothing about the freedom of Black people right in this country, and in fact it is allowing freedom fighters here in this country to be savagely attacked by these KKK and the racist sheriffs and the authorities in the south?" So that was the final straw for me. I knew they could not be fighting for freedom in Vietnam. That was the thing that led me to be firmly convinced that I had to become actively involved in opposing the Vietnam War too.

There was still a lot of division, even in the city of Berkeley itself, on these issues, however. As I've described several times, I grew up in a pretty well-off middle class family. And among people coming from that part of society, there were very strong generational divisions developing. And there were also political divisions in line with larger economic and social divisions in society as a whole. Many Black people I knew in Berkeley and Oakland were much more inclined to oppose the Vietnam War because of the basic understanding that I'd come to by reading about Selma—they kind of knew, "Look these people are not up to any good, I don't care what they say, whether it's Vietnam or here." I don't mean to say that they necessarily had a developed understanding of all the "ins and outs" of the issue, or had read all the Geneva Convention reports, and things like that, but they had a basic understanding of the truth: "these people are up to no good in Vietnam." They had a lot of experience to draw on that told them that. So there were those kinds of divisions as well.

The '60s were a time when the universities were opened up to broader sections of society. Previously, they were much more restricted to the elite strata. But it was still largely the middle class whose kids went to college, and largely white students who came to a university like Cal at that time. Among the students, there was tremendous conflict developing with their parents over a whole host of issues, including Vietnam. That was a big phenomenon of the time. For example, my parents were troubled by the Vietnam War, but they were still supporting it.

I used to argue all the time with my parents about this, and one time in particular I had this pamphlet written by Bob Scheer, who now works for the *L.A. Times* and is more or less a liberal, but at that time was more radical. He'd written this pamphlet making very strong and cogent, very well-documented arguments about the Vietnam War and what the U.S. had done and why it was wrong, and I was using this pamphlet to argue with my parents. And my dad started making what I regarded as nit-picking arguments. Some people might refer to this kind of nitpicking as being "lawyerly," but I had a lot of respect for the way my dad used logic in his legal arguments—and I'd learned a lot from the dinner table training that he'd given our whole family when he'd sit down and say, "Okay gang, here's a case, here's what happened, what do you think?" I respected that and enjoyed it. But I didn't appreciate this sort of nitpicking way in which he was approaching the question of Vietnam—a way in which things would be argued to actually get away from the truth. I got very frustrated with this, and I took this Bob Scheer pamphlet and threw it across the hall and stomped out of my parents' house.

There was that kind of very sharp conflict, and I remember at one point my parents said, "Okay, look, if you feel this strongly, write our congressman"—our congressman was Jeffrey Cohalen, my parents were friends of his and worked on his campaigns—"and give him your arguments." So I wrote a several-page letter laying out my arguments about what the U.S. was doing in Vietnam and why it was wrong. He sent me back what was pretty much a form letter—and I probably only got that because he knew my parents and didn't want to insult them. He just ran out the standard government propaganda about what the U.S. is doing and why it's good for the Vietnamese people, and he quoted something from this professor, Robert Scalapino, at Berkeley, whom I, and many others, simply regarded as a State Department professor. That just infuriated me more and convinced me even more deeply that (a) what the U.S. government was doing in Vietnam was wrong; and (b) they weren't going to listen to people who had real arguments about why it was wrong.

## Getting In Deeper

At the time there were students who were aggressively supporting the war, like the Young Republicans. But other students, even kind of liberal students, were still not really sure or maybe wanted to cling to the belief that the U.S. was doing something good in Vietnam, perhaps because it was Democratic administrations—first under Kennedy and then Lyndon Johnson—which were carrying out the war at that time. So there would be debates with these liberal students as well. And then there were people who would come from off campus and seek us out to debate. The anti-war organization on the Berkeley campus was called the Vietnam Day Committee, because they'd organized a big teach-in called "Vietnam Day" in the spring of 1965. People from off-campus would seek out the Vietnam Day Committee table—and this included many soldiers who would do a one-year tour of duty in Vietnam and, if they didn't volunteer to be sent back again, would then come back and do the rest of their time in the military somewhere in the U.S. Or they'd come on leave, on their way back from Vietnam before going to somewhere like Germany. They would often seek us out to argue—sometimes they'd be in their uniforms, sometimes in "civilian clothes," but they would identify themselves as soldiers and talk about how they'd been in Vietnam and how we didn't know what we were talking about.

Many of these soldiers would try to hold sway by acting as if they knew all about Vietnam, because they'd gone there to conquer it and occupy the country and oppress the people. They would give us the standard military line. This was before massive rebellion hit in the military. A few years later, there would be many, many soldiers and veterans of the Vietnam War with a very different viewpoint, but this was earlier, in 1965 and '66, and the soldiers were still mainly defending what they were doing. A lot of times it would go from the level of all this bullshit about fighting for freedom to talking about their buddies. That was the last line with which the government and the military brass could keep the grunts fighting: "Look what happened to your buddy, your buddy got killed by these 'gooks'"—as they would call them, along with other racist terms—"so therefore, you have to hate them and fight against them all the harder." A lot of times the arguments would break down pretty quickly to that—what happened to "my buddies." But first they would try to give us more lofty-sounding arguments about freedom, in terms of what was happening in Vietnam—the same kind of bullshit the U.S. uses about Iraq now. At that time, it was "we're there to liberate the people from the communist tyrants."

And so we'd get in these big arguments and, after a while, when people would challenge them and show that what they were saying about the history of things and so on wasn't true, they'd fall back on, "Well, I was there and I know." They'd demand: "Have you ever been to Vietnam?" I'd say, "No," and they thought that was the end of the argument. But then I would ask *them*, "Well, look, you've been saying all this stuff about communism and the Soviet Union and China and all that, have you ever been to the Soviet Union or China?" "Well, no." "Then what do you have to say about all *that*, if you're gonna put the argument on that level? According to your logic, you can't say anything about the Soviet Union, or China, or communism, because you've never been to those places, you've never been to a 'communist country.'" Then they'd sort of hem and haw and we'd get back to the substance of the issues, once we got rid of that ridiculous line of argument. Besides being actively involved in demonstrations, what I loved most was being in all these vibrant discussions and arguments. Knots of people would form around the table and then they'd break up and another knot would form, and more people would come to the table and new discussions and debates would break out, over these tremendously important issues.

Sometimes the arguments got pretty heated, even with people that you would expect would be on your side. The hippie thing was generally cool, as far as I was concerned, even though that wasn't really what I was "into," as we used to say. But I didn't have any patience for some of the "hippie/dippy" stuff about "everybody do your own thing," without regard to what "your thing" was. One time I was at the office of the *Berkeley Barb* newspaper, which was kind of an alternative newspaper that was pretty radical at the time. And there was this kind of hippie-biker type in there. I was talking to some other people in the *Barb* office about the Vietnam War, denouncing it and exposing different things that were going on. And I was really ripping into Lyndon Johnson, what a mass murderer he was—everybody hated Lyndon Johnson, because he was both the symbol of continuing and escalating the war and the president who was actually doing it. This hippie-biker type was listening for a while, and finally he pipes up and says, "Hey man, you know, like, maybe the Vietnam War is just like Johnson's thing, maybe he's just doing his thing." I got really angry and turned to him and said: "Well, what if my thing is just punching you in the mouth right now?" And he went, "Oh, okay, man, okay—I get it man."

During this period, Liz and I had continued to become closer, and then to become lovers. In 1965 we got married. For some reason I had decided that I wanted to become a doctor. I'd switched my major from

English to pre-med. I was an activist and wanted to remain an activist, but I was thinking about what I wanted to do as my life's work, so to speak. I didn't want to become a doctor so I could go to the golf course. I wanted to become a doctor so I could give people medical care who didn't have medical care. But my pre-med studies lasted less than a semester. I remember having to go to chemistry lab several afternoons a week, and every time about two o'clock or so I'd think: why am I not at the Vietnam Day Committee table, or why am I not helping to organize a demonstration? So that didn't last very long. I went to the university administration and asked if I could withdraw from school that semester. Because I had a good standing as a student, they allowed me to withdraw that semester "without prejudice," and I became much more of a full-time activist.

Liz's parents had an interesting reaction to that. Remember, they had a whole history of being political activists and communists perhaps, or at least radical people who were communist sympathizers. They weren't so upset when we became active in the Free Speech Movement or even opposing the Vietnam War. But when I took this step of withdrawing from school to become involved full-time in anti-war activity, as well as civil rights and things like that, they got very upset. They lived back in New York, and I remember one time her father was talking to me on the phone, and he said, "Look, this is very serious what you're doing. I know what you're doing—you're becoming a full-time revolutionist, and pretty soon you'll be meeting together with other people who are revolutionists and making plans for a revolution." I argued vigorously with him that this wasn't true, because at the time I didn't think that was where I was headed. But ironically he, who had had some experience with things like this, could see it more clearly than I could—and of course, in retrospect, he was right. I mean, it wasn't bound to turn out that way, but he recognized the trajectory that I was heading off on.

## Chapter Seven

# *"...Are Beyond Your Command"*

I was now a full-time activist in the Vietnam Day Committee. We had rallies on campus, but we would also organize marches and demonstrations in the broader community—against politicians when they'd come into town, or against shipments that were being sent off to the Vietnam War, and other things like that. I often spoke at these rallies and demonstrations, and then I signed up to be on the speakers bureau, and would go speak at everything from junior high schools to Rotary Clubs, or I'd debate the Young Republicans or the Young Americans for Freedom, which was another right-wing student organization.

I did go back to Cal for one more semester as a student, even while I remained very active in the political movement. But then I finally dropped out of college altogether, about a year's credits away from graduating, in 1966. And that caused tensions and conflict with my own family and also with Liz's family. From the conversation I previously described with her father, you could tell they were worried, very worried, about the direction I was taking. When I went back to school maybe they were temporarily relieved, but then when I dropped out altogether and didn't even talk about going back any more, they were really upset, as were *my* parents.

## Ramparts

Bob Scheer, who I mentioned earlier, had come out from New York to the Bay Area, and he was part of what was then generally called the "new left," which was trying to develop a movement that was different from and more radical than the old Communist Party. Besides reading things he wrote and listening to speeches he gave, I talked to Bob Scheer a lot. He had a big influence on me at that time and generally a positive one in radicalizing me.

Scheer went on to *Ramparts* magazine, which had originally been founded as kind of a liberal Catholic journal; as things got more radical in the '60s, the magazine drew more radical people into it and it became an important voice opposing the Vietnam War, supporting Black people's struggles, and so on. It was still within a certain framework, but it was an important radical voice at that time. Scheer asked me if I wanted to come work there, doing research and helping to prepare different articles. That sounded like a good way for me to combine earning a living with doing something worthwhile, and it also gave me a job where I didn't have to do the 9-to-5 thing. I would get my research assignments done, but I also had a lot of freedom to be involved in the things that I thought were most important.

One of the important stories we did at *Ramparts* concerned Donald Duncan. One day some people from the Berkeley anti-war movement came to me and said that they were talking to this guy who was a soldier who was questioning the Vietnam War very seriously and deeply. They wanted me to talk to him because I had done a lot of public speaking and study around the war. So I spent quite a bit of time over at their house talking to this guy, who turned out to be Donald Duncan.

Duncan had been a soldier in Vietnam—he was at the rank of master sergeant when he left Vietnam. He'd come back very disaffected by and very bothered by the war—questioning it and thinking it wasn't right, but not that clear on a lot of things about it, understandably. I asked him a lot about his experiences in Vietnam and did what I could to help him come to a clearer understanding of the nature of the war and what was wrong with it. And at a certain point, I suggested to both the *Ramparts* editors and to Donald Duncan himself that they do an article in which he would tell his story and come out and denounce the war. This ended up being a front cover article, with a picture of Duncan in uniform and the headline "I quit!" At that time, there weren't that many soldiers who'd been in the war itself and come out and publicly denounced it. *Ramparts* had a circulation of a couple hundred thousand or so, and this article had an impact even beyond the readers of *Ramparts*.

While I had argued with soldiers that the mere fact that they had been in Vietnam didn't mean that they were right about the war, there *is* a truth that if you've "paid your dues" fighting there and then you come to say that it's wrong, that has a big impact on many people—including for the reason that people who are more backward or conservative can't say, "Oh, that's just those disgruntled hippies who are cowards, who are draft dodgers, and all that." As a matter of fact, I would, and did, uphold those people who dodged the draft as doing something truly heroic— not George W. Bush, but people who dodged the draft because they opposed the war, not just to save their own ass. People who evaded the draft, or outright refused to be drafted, or refused to go to Vietnam once they were in the military—people who did these things because they opposed the war—they were doing heroic things, definitely more heroic things than U.S. soldiers who, with all their destructive technology, were massacring and slaughtering the Vietnamese people. Nevertheless, for the U.S. population broadly, for someone who'd been in that war to speak out against it had a very big impact.

I also worked on an article about discrimination in professional sports. This was right up my alley, combining my love for sports with being able to do something to expose injustice. So I interviewed some professional athletes—and I tried to interview Bill Russell, who had been a big hero of mine when I was a kid. I described the article and the magazine to Russell, and he refused—I'm not sure exactly why.

But Jim Brown, one of the great running backs in football history, did agree to be interviewed, and this was interesting. This was around the time when I first met Eldridge Cleaver, who had gotten out of prison on parole. As a condition of parole, he had to have a job. *Ramparts* had given him a job as a writer, and I'd met him in that context. He and I went to L.A. together to interview Jim Brown, who had these programs that were supposed to improve the lives of Black people, with small businesses and things like this. At one point in the interview things got very sharp because I asked, "Well, what are these programs actually going to do for the average Black person in Hough?" (Hough referred to a street in the center of the ghetto in Cleveland, where Jim Brown had played professional football and where his programs were centered at that time.) And, let's put it this way, he didn't like that question—he got very indignant and gave me some answer which I don't remember in all its details, but which didn't really answer the question.

But the article did end up being mainly a positive one, focusing largely on Jim Brown—which partly reflected where people at *Ramparts*, including myself, were at then, and partly the fact that Jim Brown was in certain limited ways standing up against the Establishment at that time, although the main aspect of what he was doing was very well within the system. And that came through as well in the interview.

Eldridge in particular was very acutely aware of this. When we were leaving, after interviewing Jim Brown, Eldridge told me, "This guy's just bullshit, man. This is just bullshit what he's running. This has got nothing to do with ending the oppression of Black people." That verdict from Eldridge obviously made an impression on me, even though the article ended up being mainly positive in its presentation of Jim Brown.

## Getting with Eldridge, Huey and Bobby

Eldridge Cleaver was much more radical than people that I'd known before. When I first met him, he was talking about how, when Malcolm X had been assassinated, Malcolm had been trying to get together this organization that he called the "Organization of Afro-American Unity," inspired by the Organization of African Unity,[8] and Eldridge was talking about trying to revive that organization. Then he ran into Huey and Bobby and decided that the Black Panther Party was really much more the way to go. But generally he was very radical, and through him I met people who were associated with SNCC[9] and things like that. All this obviously had a big effect on me.

---

8. The Organization of African Unity (OAU) was formed in 1963 by newly independent governments of Africa.

9. SNCC, or the Student Non-Violent Co-ordinating Committee, grew out of the civil rights sit-ins and voter registration drives in the South during the early 1960s. SNCC became increasingly radicalized and nationalist as the decade developed: in 1966 Stokely Carmichael (Kwame Ture) assumed leadership and declared its goal to be "Black Power," rather than integration; in 1967, Rap Brown (Jamillah Al-Amin) became leader and the whole organization assumed a more revolutionary and anti-imperialist stance.

One time through Eldridge I got this issue of the SNCC newspaper and they had this cartoon portraying Nasser, who was the head of the government of Egypt at that time, going up against Israel, and the cartoon drew a parallel with how Black people had to deal with Jews who were exploiting them in the ghetto in America.[10] This really bothered me. I was already learning about imperialism, partly from Eldridge, so I said to him: "Look, this is not right. The common enemy here is imperialism. What's wrong with Israel is not the Jewish character of it; it's the fact that it's an instrument of imperialism. And the common cause of Black people in the U.S. and people in Egypt is that they're going up against imperialism." Eldridge said, "Well, why don't you write them a letter?" So I did. I made these arguments and I made the point in writing the letter that I was a strong supporter of SNCC and of Black liberation, but this bothered me because it wasn't the right way to look at the problem and to analyze friends and enemies, and so on. So they wrote back and said, "We take you at your word that you're a supporter of Black liberation and let us make clear that we are not anti-Semitic and we don't see Jews as the enemy."

I had already met Bobby Seale and Huey Newton separately from Eldridge, and then after I had known Eldridge for a while and he started becoming part of the early beginnings of the Black Panther Party, I got to know Huey and Bobby more deeply and in a more directly political way in *that* context. Before that I had met them through some old high school friends of mine. One night at a rec center in Berkeley, my friend Billy introduced me to this guy who was nicknamed Weasel, who was going to the community college in Oakland—he had formerly gone to McClymonds and played on the team that beat Berkeley High in overtime in the 1963 TOC—and he told me about this African-American cultural program that was being held by a group on the community college campus called the Soul Students Advisory Council. And that's

---

10. In 1967, Israel launched a surprise attack on Egypt, Syria and Jordan, and seized the Gaza Strip, the West Bank, and the Golan Heights, further dispossessing the Palestinian people, who had already been turned into refugees by the 1948 war which created the Israeli settler state. This was the so-called "six-day war." The U.S. left as a whole not only did not take a clear stand against this, but many actually supported the Israeli attack. SNCC stood out at the time for taking a stand against the Israeli aggression, and lost quite a bit of financial and political support as a result.

where I met Huey for the first time.[11] I had actually seen Bobby Seale before that on Telegraph Avenue in Berkeley reading this poem called "Uncle Sammy Call Me Full of Lucifer"—which, as I recall, may have had some macho bullshit in it but was mainly a stinging political indictment of the U.S. and what it was doing in Africa and around the world as well as to Black people in the U.S.

So I'd seen Bobby before, but then I met Huey at that cultural program and we actually got into a conversation when he came up to me and said, "Who are you, Socrates?" There weren't very many white people at this program, and I guess he thought I looked sort of philosophical! I laughed and said no, and then we got into a philosophical and political discussion. He asked me, "Are you in the CP?" I said I wasn't. And then he said, "Well, that's good 'cuz they're not radical at all. They're just counter-revolutionary. Are you in PL (Progressive Labor Party)?" "No," I said. He went on: "They're not radical at all. They pretend to be radical, but they're not radical either. They're not really for overthrowing the government or anything like that." So we had this whole discussion.

Bobby Seale was actually the emcee of this Soul Students cultural program, and there were a lot of different performances that night. But what I remember most was Bobby Seale—both because he was very effective at this and also he was hilarious. I found out from him later that he'd actually been a comedian for a while after he got out of the Air Force. He would do really great impressions of everybody from Kennedy to Bill Cosby and was just really hilarious as well as being very penetrating with some of his satire and the ways he was going after the government.

Huey, Bobby and Eldridge saw themselves as the heirs to Malcolm X, taking up what Malcolm X was doing when he was assassinated and carrying it forward. In my eyes, they were taking it and becoming even more radical with it. They had this revolutionary stance, they were indicting the whole system—that's what they got from Malcolm X—but they were calling for revolution, too. At the same time, they were open to

---

11. Bob Avakian has written a number of pamphlets and articles on the Black Panther Party, including "Huey Newton and the Panthers...The Early Years...and What's Up Today"—a four-part interview conducted in May 1989 immediately after Newton's death, which touched on his relationship with Newton and Newton's strengths and weaknesses as a revolutionary leader and the tragedy of his life. Excerpts from the interview are available at rwor.org. See also the book by Bob Avakian *A Horrible End – or An End to the Horror?*

talking and debating and struggling over things. That struck me as well.

I remember one time I was down at the same community college and there was this other Black nationalist group meeting in a classroom and the door was open, and this guy was giving an agitational speech about the blue-eyed devils, and so on. I couldn't help it, I was interested and I was drawn to listening. He was denouncing the honkies and the blue-eyed devils, and he looked up at one point and he saw me and he said, "And that goes for you, too, honky!" So, I just said, "Okay," and walked off. But what struck me about Bobby Seale and Huey Newton and Eldridge was that their indictment of the system was more powerful and more profound than this, but along with that they were open to anybody else who was opposed to the system and they would try to push you to become more radical. That was a lot of the influence that Eldridge and Bobby and Huey had on me, pushing me to become more radical, to move more toward a revolutionary position, because they were taking up things that I felt very passionately about and they were doing it in a way that I saw as being very uncompromising—and at the same time they were willing to argue and debate and struggle with you. So all this had a tremendous impact on me in the context of everything that was happening in the U.S. and in the world at that time, and everything I'd learned up to that point.

## The Conservative Communist Party, USA

I should probably elaborate here on how we saw the old Communist Party, USA—the CP. People who were radicalized during the 1960s, in the context of everything going on in society and the world, were overwhelmingly disgusted with the CP. The CP claimed to be for socialism and ultimately communism and a whole different kind of world, but the people who were in the CP were very conservative to our eyes—always trying to appeal to the mainstream and to the lowest common denominator—and the CP as a whole was always opposing and denouncing the most radical things that were coming forward.

In the anti-war movement, you'd say "U.S. out of Vietnam" and they would want to reduce it down to "Negotiations." Or you'd say, "Ho, Ho, Ho Chi Minh, the NLF is gonna win—let's support the National Liberation Front, support the Vietnamese people in driving the U.S. out" —and they'd say, "No, no, no, no, no, let's talk about 'Bring the boys home' and let's make the focal point what's happening to the U.S. soldiers, or let's sweeten the pot by talking about how the Vietnam War is bringing a heavy economic cost for the people in the U.S." Not that these issues were totally illegitimate, but they wanted to bring those to the forefront in order to take anything radical out of it and make things "palatable." However much the movement advanced and become more radical, they were always trying to drag it back down to the lowest common denominator.

Within the Black liberation struggle they wanted to support only things that they could present in the context and the confines of civil rights, and especially someone like Malcolm X was way too radical for them. When he tried to make it an issue of human rights and put it in the context of the whole international struggle against the U.S. and against imperialism, they didn't want any part of that. They denounced him as an advocate of violence the same way the bourgeoisie did.

When the Black Panther Party emerged, the CP had dual tactics toward it. At the same time as they had their leading Black spokespeople openly denounce the Black Panther Party, they also infiltrated Black members of the CP into the Black Panther Party to try to take it in a more reformist direction. So they were actually working to destroy it from both directions: denouncing it from the outside while infiltrating it and trying to cut the revolutionary heart out of it.

### Family Conflicts

Huey and Bobby formed the Black Panther Party for Self-Defense in 1966, and shortly after that Eldridge joined up with them. I've written about this elsewhere, but it may be hard today to realize just how radical and, yes, shocking the Panthers were when they came onto the scene. Here you had Black youth, dressed in uniforms of black leather jackets and berets; carrying guns not to use in "gang warfare" but to defend the masses against police violence; and attempting to apply Mao's Red Book[12] to making revolution in America. This took everything to a whole other level. There was nothing remotely like this on the scene in terms of the specter it raised and the impact it had, and I'll get more into this in the next chapter. But here I want to speak to the impact that my relations with the Panthers had on my relations with my family.

A little while after the Black Panther Party formed, I began working

---

12. *Quotations from Chairman Mao Tsetung* (Peking: Foreign Language Press, 1966).

with and supporting them, and even writing articles for their paper. And with that, I really crossed a line with both my family and Liz's family—and Liz herself. I remember there was something almost like a "summit meeting" where both sets of parents came over to our apartment and basically read me the riot act for what was I doing.

Liz's father, who was the most political, actually tried to engage me on an ideological level, criticizing the Black Panther Party for speaking in the name of the "lumpen proletariat" as if that were the most revolutionary force. The Panthers were really talking about sections of Black people who were largely proletarians, in and out of jobs, especially a lot of youth—while the "lumpen proletariat" actually refers more to people whose whole life is centered around crime. Now there aren't hard and fast divisions there, especially when you're talking about an oppressed people, but really the people the Panthers were rallying were a lot of proletarian youth by and large. Some of them had been in jail, because that was the situation for huge numbers of Black people, especially youth, at that time (and it is even more the case now). And they were constantly harassed by the police. But a lot of them were also in and out of jobs and actually had a more proletarian position.

Anyway, Liz's father was arguing with me: "The lumpen proletariat is not a revolutionary force. You're making a big mistake here." He tried to argue with me ideologically and politically as to why the Panthers were wrong and why I was wrong to be uniting and working closely with them. It ran the whole gamut, though. All of the parents were arguing that I was wrecking everybody's future—my future, Liz's future, everybody's future was being dragged down by what I was doing. So this was very intense and emotional.

My relationship with Liz was going through changes as well. As I said, when we first met Liz was more politically experienced, more politically advanced, more politically active than I was, and she had a very positive influence on me in that kind of way. But at a certain point—and I'll try to get into some of the complexity of it—she began to pull back from more radical positions, and especially to pull back from political activism. Now, part of the basis for that was that the women's movement was beginning to develop, feminist ideas were beginning to be brought forward more forcefully within the movement and also more broadly in society, even though this was the beginning stages of that, the mid to late 1960s. She was beginning to examine her own life and her own role in things, and she also had criticisms of our relationship because there were aspects of it that were more traditional, even though we shared a lot of intellectual interests and political beliefs. She was upset, for example, that when I dropped out of school, she was working while I was being a political activist and she felt like this is the traditional way in which things have always been done—a woman working to support a guy while he pursues his interests—although that situation did change once I got a job at *Ramparts* and we were both earning money.

But there were a lot of different aspects to this. Women were examining their position and role in society—and they were demanding changes in their personal relations. Liz was part of that in an overall sense, but one aspect of this was that she began to see things more in personal terms, to more and more turn inward, and to pull back from involvement in political struggles. As I was coming to see the problem as the whole system and starting to consider the question of communism, I remember at one point we had an argument where she was reading this book and she said, "Listen to this. Listen to this." And she read from this book where one of the characters says: "One nurse holding one bedpan in one hospital one night has done more good for humanity than all the communists in the world." Liz was reading this in a way that made clear that she agreed with it. And I said, "You know, that's exactly wrong. That's exactly upside down."

This kind of captured the different directions our lives were taking. I was struggling with her, "Look, we've got to become more radical, more revolutionary." As part of this, I was talking about moving from Berkeley—where we were living—to Richmond, which, as I mentioned before, is a more proletarian town. "We've got to go and integrate with the proletariat and take radical politics to the proletariat." So we were having a lot of struggle because she was resisting that. She was still progressive, she still had enlightened views on all these questions, she was still sympathetic to these struggles; but, partly out of feminist concerns and partly out of the fact that, as exemplified by this passage she read from that book, she didn't see how you could change things on a big scale in society, she was turning away from efforts to do that. She thought that the enemy was too powerful, that what you were up against was too great, or that in any case this wasn't the right way to go about changing things. More, the idea that started gaining currency with her was that you should change people individually or one at a time—people should seek change "within" and that would ultimately lead to change in society. So we were going in very different directions at that time, and it was a very emotionally difficult thing because we still shared a lot in common, but we had these fundamental differences about the direction of our lives and our priorities were becoming very different.

## Meeting – and Rejecting – PL

At this time I didn't yet consider myself a communist, but I was exploring a lot of different political tendencies and groups with different political programs and lines, as we say. I was open to a lot of things, I was in a lot of flux at that time, 1966 and into '67. I remember, for example, when the Cultural Revolution in China was in high gear, around 1966, PL (Progressive Labor Party) was sort of known as the Maoists in the movement. Just about everybody who considered herself or himself even sympathetic to communism thought PL was the most radical version of communism. In fact, I remember one time I was with somebody I knew from Berkeley, we were talking about what we were going to do on the weekend, and he said: "There's a party, but I don't want to go to that party, 'cuz there are going to be a lot of people from PL at the party, and if I go, I'm going to have to spend the whole night justifying why I'm not in PL." That's why Huey was talking about PL the first time I met him—they were supposed to be the most radical communists and even pro-Mao.

But I was confused about the Cultural Revolution. I was taken in by a lot of the bourgeois propaganda that this was just a lot of chaos and madness and Mao had gone nuts and was just making the whole society go crazy. So one time I went up to one of these PLers, and I said, "What's all this shit about the Cultural Revolution? What the hell is going on in China anyway?" And he said: "Don't ask me! I'm not a defender of the Cultural Revolution!" He just backed off entirely from defending or explaining the Cultural Revolution, or even trying to analyze it. That turned me off more to PL than to the Cultural Revolution because, although I still had my questions and ways in which I was confused and being influenced by the bourgeois slander about it, I knew better than that. I knew you had to learn about things like this and do your best to analyze what was going on, and this guy's backing off just made me lose respect for him much more than it turned me off to the Cultural Revolution and Mao.

## Running for Office

The only time I ever voted for president—except when I supported Eldridge Cleaver for president in 1968—was in 1964 when I voted for Lyndon Johnson, the first time I was eligible to vote. There were huge debates in the movement in Berkeley about whether you should vote for Johnson. A lot of my more radical friends were insisting that you shouldn't vote for Johnson, that it was all the same thing, but I have to admit that I did actually vote for Johnson because Goldwater was so terrible. Goldwater was going to escalate the Vietnam War. Well, lo and behold, look what Johnson did, after he was re-elected.[13] That was a real lesson for me.

By 1967, I was turned off to the bourgeois political parties and the whole bourgeois electoral process and all that machinery of deception and lies. But one part of me was still drawn toward reform. So in the spring of '67, if I recall the year correctly, I was actually part of a slate of candidates—I think it was called the "New Politics Slate"—that ran as sort of a radical reform slate for city council in Berkeley.

When I ran for office, a number of candidates came before this New Politics Group to ask for its endorsement. One of them was a Black candidate who got up and basically gave a riff about how, if this group really was opposed to racism, they should endorse and work for his candidacy. I was sitting next to Eldridge Cleaver who'd come to this meeting, and he got up and said to this candidate: "Well look here, you haven't told these people anything about what you stand for, you just run all this riff about 'if you're against racism, you have to support me'; but you haven't given them any basis to know whether they should support you or not, you haven't told them where you stand on anything, there's no content to it. If you don't tell them that, then you're just asking these people to go for a pig in the poke." This candidate was taken aback, and he kind of feebly replied, "I hope you're not talking about me, brother." And Eldridge Cleaver shot back, "Yes, I'm talking about you."

This made a deep impression on me—no matter who gets up and fronts off, and no matter what they might say is your obligation, you

---

13. At the time of Johnson's (re)election as a "peace candidate" in 1964, there were 25,000 U.S. troops in Vietnam. Shortly after the election Johnson began pouring approximately 20,000 troops a month into Vietnam, and by 1967 there were half a million U.S. soldiers there.

have to look for the content of what they stand for, that's the most important thing.

Our reform slate had a program of taking over Pacific Gas & Electric and making it publicly owned. And, of course, supporting civil rights and opposing the Vietnam War was part of our platform too.

As part of our campaign we managed to raise some money to have a few billboards around the city of Berkeley listing the candidates and several slogans. One of the slogans was "Oppose the War." But when the billboard company put up the billboards, they actually blotted out the slogan "Oppose the War." In Berkeley, in 1967! At Bob Scheer's suggestion, I got a ladder and then called the press and climbed up on the ladder and painted back in the slogan "Oppose the War." Then we actually went to court because the billboard company had the nerve to sue us for damaging their billboard property! They didn't get anywhere with that suit, and all this controversy around the billboard turned from a bad thing into a good thing in a certain way.

This whole experience gives both a flavor of the times and a sense that, even though I was learning about imperialism and becoming very radical in many ways, I still hadn't completely broken with the idea of reform on a local basis by running radical reform candidates for office. By the way, we didn't win, although our slate did get about 30 percent of the vote. But after this election was over, Eldridge said to me: "Well, now, you've got that all out of your system. You had your last fling with reform politics. So now you should get all the way into revolution."

## The Summer of Love

At that time, change was coming from a lot of different directions. You had people organizing for "Stop the Draft Week" and you had the "Summer of Love" going on at the same time. These, of course, were very different phenomena, even if they were both in a broad sense part of the same developing opposition to the way things were. "Stop the Draft Week" was planned as a week of active, militant demonstrations aimed at shutting down, or causing real disruption to, the draft process, while the "Summer of Love" was kind of a mass migration of youth to the Bay Area who were sort of "dropping out of the system" and trying to develop a whole new culture based on everyone loving each other.

I was not opposed to the whole hippie phenomenon and the "Summer of Love." I didn't mind the slogan "Make Love, not War" and

I certainly wasn't opposed to the underlying sentiment, but when it got articulated as a way you were going to change the world, then I couldn't agree with that. I could see that wasn't going to work. You were up against powerful forces that weren't going to be changed by your loving them or trying to teach them to love. Nor was it possible to change things by somehow creating a powerful wave of love that would sweep away unjust war and other injustices. So I went to some of those love-ins and all that kind of stuff just for the vibe, if you want to put it that way—to be part of all that. That wasn't my thing, but in a larger sense it was part of the thing that I was part of, too.

Of course, there was a huge cultural dimension to the hippie thing. At that time, I was listening to R&B and Motown and things like that, on the one hand, and I was also listening to Bob Dylan, although the crowd I was in were all very, very disappointed when he came out with *Nashville Skyline*. We said, "What the fuck is that all about?—'Lay, Lady, Lay' and all that kind of bullshit!" It was one thing when Dylan did "My Back Pages" and in effect denounced his association with radical and even revolutionary political groups, but as long as he was still doing other things that were giving inspiration to the youth rebellion and things like that, we were still pretty deeply into him. But when he came out with *Nashville Skyline* and that whole direction, that was too much.

But I listened to some of the music that was associated with the youth culture of the time, like Jefferson Airplane or the Grateful Dead or things like that, although that wasn't really my favorite kind of music and I had kind of conflicted feelings about that. I appreciated it on one level, but I didn't really get into it deeply, even after the Jefferson Airplane came out with music that actually had an unmistakably radical content. I mentioned earlier how I really didn't get Jimi Hendrix, even in his positive aspect, at that time because to me it seemed like psychedelic hippie music that I wasn't really into, and "Why is this Black guy playing this psychedelic hippie shit?" I later drew some lessons from this, about not just jumping to oppose things that are new and different, and learning to appreciate things that are coming at the world from new and different angles, not just in music but more broadly. But at that time I was not that inspired by it, and even turned off in some ways by it.

Take, for example, the Fillmore West Auditorium in San Francisco. When you say "Fillmore" to me, my first association is with the Fillmore district in San Francisco, which was one of the main Black ghetto areas in San Francisco, and I associate the Fillmore Auditorium with *that,* and with acts like James Brown, the Drifters, and Hank Ballard and the Midnighters. Then later it became an arena where these other groups like the Jefferson Airplane or Janis Joplin played, and I looked at it somewhat negatively as a hippie haven.

In fact, there's a funny story which kind of highlights some of the points I've been making. I talked earlier about how I had started getting up in the dorm cafeteria on Sunday and singing. After that had gone on for a while, some of the people in the dorm who were organizing a dance asked me if, during one of the breaks in the dance, I would sing a few songs. So I came there and when the group that was playing took a break, I got up and I sang some old doo-wop and Motown songs. I was getting into it and people were appreciating it—but then one of the members of the band that was performing at the dance came up to me and said, "Okay, dude, that's enough." They had finished their break and were ready to play again. Well, an ironic footnote to this is that the band that was playing there was Big Brother and the Holding Company, with Janis Joplin as their singer.

But there was still a feeling of solidarity there, between the hippies and the people, like myself, who were more into going up against the way things were in a more directly political way. When I was working at *Ramparts* I had a press pass authorized by the San Francisco police, and one time I was driving through the Haight-Ashbury area and I saw all these police cars around—they were clearly busting some people in this house. I stopped and I went up to the house and I saw it was some kind of drug bust, and they had all these people who looked like I did sitting on the floor handcuffed. So I showed my press pass, and I went in. But even though I was working for *Ramparts* and had a press pass, to the police and to the "straight people" I was dressed like a bum. I was wearing an old navy pea coat and old jeans and my hair was not cut the way it's supposed to be cut if you're a journalist. I looked "unkempt."

I looked around. I asked the cops a few questions, and they didn't answer much of anything. Then I walked by the people who were being busted, and I said some words of encouragement to them, like "Hang in there." The head cop there heard me doing that and he barked: "Who are you?" I showed him my press pass, and he said, "Well, you look just like one of them. How do I know you're really with the press?" And I said, "Well, check out my press pass." So he took my press pass, but then he wouldn't give it back to me and he kicked me out of there.

I went down to the police station a day or two later and went up to the desk and said, "I want to get a warrant for a citizen's arrest because someone has stolen some of my property." The cop starting taking down my information and then he asked, "Well, do you know who this was?" And I said, "No, I don't know exactly who they are, but you probably can find out easily, because they work for the San Francisco police department." And he said, "Wait a minute. You mean you're trying to do a citizen's arrest against a cop? You can't do that!" And I replied, "Well, he stole my press pass."

So that kind of gives a flavor for how even though the hippie thing wasn't my thing, you felt an affinity, that you were all part of the same sort of opposition to the establishment or the power structure or the "straight world"—however people saw it.

## Stop the Draft Week – "From Protest to Resistance"

"Stop the Draft Week" came later in 1967, in October, right around the same time as when Huey Newton ended up arrested and charged with murdering an Oakland cop and a massive struggle developed around that.[14] During that time there were people, including myself, who felt that the opposition to the Vietnam War needed to become more active and militant—and that it should appeal more directly to the soldiers and the people being drafted and more directly oppose the machinery that was carrying out the war. We came up with the idea that we would shut down the Oakland Induction Center, which was one of the major centers where they inducted people into the Army.

I myself at one point was actually called in for induction, but I had a letter from my doctor which explained why I couldn't serve in the military, given the whole history of my illness. But I also went there and passed out a leaflet exposing and denouncing the war and I was prepared, if I hadn't gotten the medical deferment, to refuse to go into the military. So I had that personal experience at the induction center. But

---

14. Huey Newton was accused of murder after a shootout in Oakland in which Newton himself was wounded and later handcuffed to his hospital bed during surgery. The Panthers led people to very aggressively take up Huey's defense with the demand to "Free Huey," and this campaign helped catapult them to national prominence. This is spoken to more in the next chapter.

the idea here was to go and *shut down* the induction center by having a massive sit-in at all the doors.

We got there—more than a thousand people—and there were just massive phalanxes of Oakland pigs all around. One of the things that was so heroic in what the Panthers were doing was going up against the Oakland police. Those cops were notorious for being especially brutal toward Black people in particular and toward anybody whom they saw as an enemy of the status quo. In fact, one of our early anti-Vietnam demonstrations (in 1965, I think) was supposed to go through Berkeley and Oakland; the Berkeley authorities gave it a permit but the Oakland authorities refused and then had large numbers of police out to prevent the march from going into Oakland. They stopped it at the Berkeley-Oakland border. There was a whole court battle before the Oakland authorities had to back down and allow a march to go into Oakland. So, the Oakland police were notorious in this kind of way.

As people got there that day with the aim of shutting down the induction center, the Oakland police were just everywhere in formation and obviously prepared for battle. And as soon as the first group of people sat down in front of one of the doors of the induction center, the police viciously descended on them and brutally attacked them. They attacked people from the media to prevent them from covering this, and they even attacked bystanders as well as people who were there to demonstrate, and not just the people sitting in around the doors.

Speaking of the media, a reporter for one of the local TV stations was knocked unconscious by the police and was in a very bad way, and some other demonstrators and I picked him up and carried him away from the scene and got him some medical attention. There was a real irony here, in that the media generally were slandering every demonstration and all the political activity we were involved in, but we ended up carrying this guy away before the Oakland police would have maybe even killed him, because they were just going viciously after anybody. And for some time afterward, whenever we wanted to get something into the media, we would contact that reporter, and he would actually try to get it on the air.

That day at the induction center was kind of a setback, but people learned a lot from it. We went back to the campuses and other places, and I remember there was heated controversy about whether to go back again, in the face of this, to the induction center. I think this demonstration had been on a Tuesday, and on Wednesday and Thursday there were rallies and debates about what to do. I remember one rally on the Cal campus, where a professor who had been a supporter of the Free Speech Movement and opposed the Vietnam War, and was a progressive guy in general, got up and gave this impassioned speech about how if we go back down and have another confrontation with the Oakland police —and I still remember his words—then we were going to lead to the destruction of "the thin membrane which protects the campus from the barbarism outside."

Well, that argument didn't win out. We rallied many people to go back. And when we came back, we came padded up and ready, with football helmets and other protective gear. I'd gone to a construction site and bought a construction helmet. So then when the police attacked, which they did as soon as we started rallying again there, it didn't have the same effect. That day they had these county sheriffs and highway patrol and Oakland police, and I remember it was almost comical in the midst of this very intense situation as these pigs would take their nightsticks and smash you on the top of the head with it—and it would just bounce off and you would keep on going because you had a helmet on. I remember more than one pig looking at his nightstick in bewilderment, almost as if to say, "What's wrong with my nightstick? What's happened here? It's lost its magic; it's lost its power." So that ended up being a very militant demonstration where traffic got blocked and cars got pulled out into the street; and although the original idea of doing these sit-ins around the induction center didn't succeed and they were still able to draft people that day, this actually became a much bigger thing, and it had a very powerful impact in terms of rallying opposition to the Vietnam war and raising the opposition to a more serious level. In fact, the famous demonstration to surround the Pentagon took place literally the day after, and someone who was involved in that told me how, the night before the Pentagon action, a bunch of people who were going were simply ecstatic and inspired from reading the Associated Press account of "Stop the Draft Week" in Oakland.

There were arrests off it, obviously, and a political defense and legal defense had to be mounted, and this happened more or less in the same time frame as the Huey Newton case. So then there was political work done by myself and others to link these things and to build support, particularly among people who'd been active in the "Stop the Draft Week," for Huey Newton and for the Black Panther Party. There was a whole swirl of things that were objectively interconnected, but there also had to be struggle to enable people to see the ties between different battles going on against the system and to link things up in a more conscious and powerful way.

As part of the whole swirl of activity in those days, a core of us were going all over. We went to anti-war rallies in the Bay Area and also in L.A. I went to the Century City anti-war demonstration that was viciously attacked by the L.A. police, and I remember going to a rally a little later in L.A. where, after he'd refused to go into the Army, Muhammad Ali came and signed autographs and generally expressed support for the demonstration.

Speaking of Muhammad Ali, I remember a convention of CORE—the Congress of Racial Equality, one of these reformist civil rights groups—that was held in San Francisco. They invited all these different groups to come speak there, and Eldridge told me that Huey had refused to go there because they had just formed the Black Panther Party—I believe it was still called the Black Panther Party for Self-Defense, which was its original name, but they'd formed it as a political revolutionary party—but CORE didn't invite them to have a speaker. Instead they said the Panthers could come and do security. So Huey told them to go get fucked. He said, "We're a political party, not a goon squad."

But Eldridge said to me, "Why don't you go down there and check it out and see what's going on at the CORE convention?" I remember Ron Karenga was there speaking—and of course people reputed to be members of Ron Karenga's organization US were responsible for murdering two Black Panthers later, John Huggins and Bunchy Carter, whom I knew—but this was before that happened. The Panthers were already in a lot of political conflict with Ron Karenga because they saw him as being just a reformist and basically a bourgeois nationalist. All these kinds of conflicts were going on within the movement, but they weren't just personality disputes, or "ego conflicts"; they were conflicts about what kind of program, what kind of politics and ideology were necessary to really end all this oppression, and what were you up against. As we say now, what is the problem and what is the solution.

So Eldridge urged me to go to this CORE convention and check it out. I did, and at one point during a break in the meetings, I went into this room with some people that I knew there—and, all of a sudden, in came Muhammad Ali. We're all sort of sitting there and he's not saying too much and, for whatever reason, at one point all the other people in the room got up and left. So there it was—just me and Muhammad Ali sitting in this room. I sat there quietly and he sat there quietly, it was sort of an awkward moment, and I said to myself: "I'm never going to forgive myself if I don't say something to Muhammad Ali." But I couldn't think of what to say, until finally I recalled that when I was back in the dorms at Cal and he'd fought Sonny Liston, nobody thought he could win, but I was sure he was going to win so I scrounged up all the money I had, I think it was something like $33, and I bet it on him to win. I told him this story, and he smiled and said, "Well, you must have had a lot of faith in me." And that was my encounter with Muhammad Ali.

## New Politics...And Old

Also around that time—the summer of '67—there was kind of a loose grouping of people who were trying to do radical reform politics in the electoral arena that got together and had this New Politics convention in Chicago. So some of us went there, mainly to build support for the Black Panther Party. We passed out this leaflet that said that if people there wanted to do something good, they should support the Black Panther Party and raise money to help the Black Panther Party buy weapons so that they could carry out their patrols for self-defense against the police. As you could imagine, that was kind of controversial —and one of the funniest things about it, looking back on it now, is that a couple of us not only signed the leaflet but actually put our address on it! Anyway, that created a stir at that convention.

More than a thousand people came to that convention, mainly people from the middle class, mainly white, who were undergoing some of the radicalization of the time, but still trying to work within the electoral arena. One of the big issues that was up there was whether to work within the Democratic Party or break out of that framework and try to build independent candidacies and run independent campaigns that would be opposed to the Democratic Party, as well as to the Republican Party. The Communist Party had some people there. As I've described, they were always trying to keep things within the framework of bourgeois politics and reformism, and even when they'd run their own candidate for an office, at the same time they'd support the Democrat for whatever electoral office was being contested. They were very much opposed to this New Politics thing breaking out of the framework and the confines of the mainstream electoral process, and breaking with the Democratic Party in particular. But if they'd opposed that straight up at that convention, they wouldn't have won.

So the CP—or the Black members of the CP who were there—got together with one of the bigger street gangs in Chicago at the time, the Blackstone Rangers (which later became the P Stone Nation), along with various nationalist groups, and formed a "Black Caucus." This Black Caucus met separately, and at a certain point they set down a bunch of demands on this New Politics Convention. Well, some of them were legitimate, taking up the fight against racism and discrimination, and some of them were ridiculous—for example, that white people should form "white civilizing committees" to go into the white community and civilize white people. Now I and the people I was with were there supporting the Black Panther Party—and some of us were preparing to move to Richmond because we were taking up the call of SNCC and other radical Black forces that if white people really wanted to do something good, they should go organize poor white people around radical politics, including the fight against racism. So we were all for that, but this idea of "white civilizing committees" was something else. I got up and argued against this. I said: "Look, I'm not going to go knock on the door of some white person and say, 'Hi, I'm from the white civilizing committee and I'm here to civilize you.' This is not going to go. I'm taking up the call to take radical politics to white people, in particular poor white people, I'm all for that, but this is not the way to do it."

So there were some ridiculous things like that as well as some more valid and important demands they made. But the net effect was to grind things to a halt, and the *real* thing that was going on there was that the CP was maneuvering to divert things and prevent this convention from taking a clear stand of breaking with the Democratic Party and out of this whole Democrat-Republican framework. While there were other forces with other agendas within this Black Caucus, the CP manipulated and maneuvered to get it to move on this convention in a certain way so that it ended up disrupting the whole thing of breaking with the Democratic Party and took things off into a whole other place. In the guise of radical, militant politics, they were actually maneuvering to keep these people from the middle class who were becoming radicalized from breaking with the bourgeois electoral framework, or at least with the two-party, Republican and Democratic, confines of it.

At the end of this New Politics convention, as we were leaving Chicago to head back to the Bay Area, we walked out to our car and we noticed what was obviously an unmarked police car parked right behind our car, with a guy inside who was obviously from either the Chicago police "red squad" or the FBI, writing things down. We walked up to him and asked him what he was doing, but he refused to answer. So we started marching around his car chanting, "No more FBI, no more FBI..."—and, after a little while, he tore out of there.

Then, as we were driving back from Chicago to the Bay Area—we were kind of crazy youth, and we didn't have much money, so we just took turns driving and didn't stay anywhere overnight—I ate a sandwich that had been sitting in the car, exposed to the sun for about 24 hours. And, of course, I got very sick, so that by the time we reached the mountains in Utah, we were having to stop the car every few minutes so I could throw up. Finally, we stopped in Winnemucca, Nevada and found the cheapest motel we could. In the middle of the night in that motel, I went down the hall to go to the bathroom, and after I finished, I was getting ready to head back to our room, and suddenly I felt a powerful blow against my cheek—I had passed out and hit the edge of the toilet. I managed to get myself up and barely made my way back to our room, nearly passing out again. I opened the door to the room, turned on the light, aimed myself at the bed and let myself fall straight forward onto the bed. As I passed out again, I heard one of the other guys yell: "Goddamnit, Avakian, turn out the light!"

The next day, as we started out again for the Bay Area, I called my doctor, Dr. Meyer, and told him what had happened and asked anxiously if this could cause me to have a relapse of my kidney disease. He gave me some advice on how to recover from this bout of food poisoning and told me to come see him when I got back to the Bay Area, but he also said that he thought I wouldn't suffer a relapse. Which I didn't.

## Restless Farewell

As I said, about the time of this New Politics convention, I was getting ready to make the move to Richmond, with my friend Kayo. After Kayo had gotten out of high school I'd lost contact with him, and when I got back in touch with him, he was working in some dead-end job and his life was kind of dreary. In fact, he was living with some other guys, one of whom worked for the FBI. And I said, "Man, you gotta get the fuck out of this situation!" I was still in college at that time, and I prevailed on him to get out of there and he decided he wanted to go back to college, which in those circumstances represented a break from the dead end his life had gone into. Then he also became very active politically—and here we were, going to sporting events and then going to political demonstrations all the time. These were our passions, and at a certain point, he and I became very active in supporting the Panthers and the Black liberation struggle, so we decided to take up this call of going to the poor whites, taking radical politics to them. Actually, we ended up working with poor whites and Blacks and Latinos and Native Americans after we started doing work in Richmond. But our original mission was to take radical politics to poor whites, and this was one area, in Richmond and San Pablo next door to Richmond, where there were actually a lot of poor white proletarians. We knew this was something we had to do.

So we were on the threshold of making this move, but it was a very wrenching thing, a real change in our lives. I was trying to convince Liz that we should do this together. She went back and forth and agonized over it, but she finally decided that this was not the direction she wanted her life to go in. So this led finally to our marriage breaking up.

But I was still in love with her. I have to say, and maybe it's obvious if you've read things I've written, that I've always been kind of a romantic. Even when I became a revolutionary, I remained a romantic—so it was heart-breaking to me. It was a very difficult thing. It was a life-changing decision in many ways, but I felt this is what needed to be done. I wanted for us to do it together. And, as I said, she did agonize over it, but when she decided that this wasn't the direction she wanted to go in, that was the final blow to our marriage.

When I moved to Richmond, I also to a large degree broke off relations with my parents, because they were still trying to influence my life in ways that I needed to break with, and I felt the terms of our relationship had to be radically changed. It had to be on the terms of what I was doing, there had to be a radical break and rupture there. So that was another big change in moving to Richmond. In fact, I didn't see my parents very much over the next several years, and when I did see them it was when I would take initiative to get in touch with them, because they didn't even know how to reach me—I basically cut off any kind of direct contact with them for that period of time. I still loved them, but this was something I had to do. It was very painful, but it was another break that I needed to make in order to carry through with the way my life was going and the way it needed to go.

I think there's an important lesson to this whole trajectory which ended up rupturing the relationship between me and Liz. It isn't that she was becoming a reactionary or something like that. She was still a progressive person, still someone sympathetic to and supportive of many of the things that I was active in, but our lives were just going in different ways, and the way she saw changing things was taking a different direction. Throughout her life she remained, as far as I know, a progressive person. Unfortunately, within the last few years she died of cancer. Things can develop, your paths can diverge, in such a way that you can't maintain an intimate relationship and you don't even see politically and ideologically eye to eye, in one sense. Yet, in the larger sense, you're still on the same side.

As I said, the break-up with Liz was tremendously heart-breaking. Of course, this was not the last romantic relationship I've had. Any other romantic relationships I've had since that time have had their own personal dimensions, of course—it is not the cardboard "commie" stereotype, or caricature, where supposedly there is no personal side to things, and people are stiff and unfeeling on a personal level. The relations I've had of an intimate character have always had that personal side to them, but in a larger sense, the direction those relationships have taken and whether or not they've continued has been largely influenced by the political and ideological direction and content of my life and of the other person's life.

And fortunately, at this time in my life, and for quite some time now, I have found someone who deeply shares the commitments and the goals that define my life, and though we have had to be apart at times, even for long periods, our relationship has grown deeper and closer as soulmates united in romantic love but also in our common goal of radically changing the world and achieving communism.

## *"The Baddest Motherfucker on the Planet Earth"*

Looking back on the period from 1964 to 1967, this was a time when the world was going through dramatic and rapid changes. Week to week, month to month, and certainly year to year, things were radically changing, and people in general of my generation—not just in the white middle class, but people in general—were going through radical changes in a very compressed and telescoped way. Beginning in the fall of 1964, I was in a real sense able to move beyond this whole battle with disease as the defining thing in my life—I had overcome that—although for a number of years after that I still had to be in touch with my doctor and to have tests to make sure that I wasn't having a relapse.

So everything for me was changing very rapidly, and by 1967 "everything" included my views toward revolution and communism. One of the main things that turned me in a communist direction, as I was becoming more and more radical and starting to have a revolutionary edge, even while it was still mixed in with some reformism, was something that happened one day when I went over to Eldridge Cleaver's house. Now Eldridge had some definite weaknesses, things that ended up pulling him back away from the revolutionary road actually, including some of his views toward women, but nonetheless he also had a lot of positive qualities and strengths.

And I remember I went to his house one day, and there was this big poster of Mao up on the wall. I was shocked, and I kind of gulped, but I didn't say anything. I didn't know how to ask about that right then, but a couple of days later I was talking to him on the phone and I said, "Eldridge, why do you have that poster of Mao Tsetung up there on your wall?" And he replied: "We have that poster of Mao Tsetung on our wall because Mao Tsetung is the baddest motherfucker on the planet earth." So I thought, "Wow, that's heavy," because I knew that these Panthers were pretty bad, pretty heavy, politically and in every other way—standing up against the police and all that brutality and murder and the whole system, really. What Eldridge said about Mao didn't convert me into a communist right away, but it was another thing that made me think to myself: "I've got to check this out. I've got to get one of these Red Books that more and more people seem to be reading." The Panthers carried around the Red Book a lot—they read it, and they promoted it. In fact, I remember going to a May Day rally in 1969 in San Francisco with about 5,000 people, led by the Panthers, all holding up Red Books. That was the character of the times, this was the direction in which a lot of people were being moved, and I was being moved that way too.

Since that time there has been a kind of "revisionist history" that has grown over the years, which presents things as if the Panthers were never really that much into the Red Book, that it was only a way to raise money from Berkeley radicals, etc. But the truth is that, not just in the Bay Area but in other areas as well, as the Panthers spread around the country, there were many Panthers who seriously read the Red Book, as well as other writings by Mao, and used the Red Book to carry out criticism and self-criticism. For a time, this was very integral to their whole internal cohesion.

All this had a big influence on me. In this period of three years, more or less, from the fall of 1964 to the fall of '67, I had gone through many changes in my personal life, but above all in the whole way that I saw society and the world and the struggle to change it and where that all had to go.

# Chapter Eight

# Getting Down with Revolution

O ne day in early 1967 I just happened to come into *Ramparts* about an hour after a very dramatic thing had happened, and when I heard what went down I was really upset that I missed it. Betty Shabazz, the widow of Malcolm X, came into town, and one of the things she was going to do was an interview with people at *Ramparts*. Huey and some other Panthers met her at the airport and escorted her into San Francisco, to the *Ramparts* office. They had their guns with them that they carried for self-defense, and as they got out of their cars, some cops drove by and saw them and screeched over to a halt, and they jumped out and pulled out *their* guns. One cop in particular kept trying to get Huey to put away his gun. Huey had his shotgun pointed down, so it wasn't aimed at the cop, but he was clearly not going to back down. This whole tense showdown occurred, and finally the cops had to back down. The Panthers had protected Betty Shabazz, and they had taken a clear-cut stand. This was electrifying, and people were still buzzing about when I got to *Ramparts*.

## The Panthers in Action

Although I was extremely frustrated about having just barely missed this, I got a very vivid account of what happened, especially from Eldridge. And I'd heard other accounts of other very intense encounters and confrontations the Panthers had with the police. I remember Bobby

Seale told me one time that, after going out on a number of their self-defense patrols, Huey said: "I need a break. I need to rest." And he went to bed and slept for something like two days before he could get up, because this was so intense.

Shortly after that, and this was not long before I moved to Richmond, there was a police murder in North Richmond, which was this unincorporated area just adjacent to the city of Richmond itself, and right near San Pablo. This young Black guy named Denzel Dowell was shot and killed by the police out there—they claimed he was burglarizing a liquor store and that he tried to run away, so they shot him and killed him. Of course, it was deemed justifiable homicide, and the Panthers had gone out there to the Sheriff's office (the cops who had jurisdiction in North Richmond) to register their outrage, and they'd taken their guns with them.

I still vividly remember this story where one of the Panthers was quoted in the paper. He had his shotgun with him when they were going up to the Sheriff's office to protest that the police killing of Denzel Dowell was really a murder, and one of the reporters who was there asked him, "Are you going to take that shotgun with you into the Sheriff's office?" And this Panther replied: "Righteous on that." I knew this guy and I could just picture him saying that. This was close to the time when the Panthers went to Sacramento with their weapons to make a political statement, to protest a law that was being passed that would make it impossible for them to do their armed self-defense patrols in the way they'd done them.

I knew North Richmond by reputation. Even the people I knew who were generally considered to be really "bad" regarded North Richmond as a place you didn't go. It was legendary. In fact, right around this same time, I went with some friends of mine to a basketball game between Contra Costa College, which was in Richmond, and Merritt College in Oakland. At one point, a fight almost broke out between players from each team, and one of my friends leaned over to me and said, "That guy there from the Merritt team is not going to fuck with so-and-so, because his dad is one of the biggest gangsters in North Richmond." That was the kind of reputation that North Richmond had.

Well, at one point Eldridge said to me: "Why don't you go out there to North Richmond and do some investigative reporting—try to find out more about this?" Naturally, I was kind of uptight about doing this, but I went and I asked around. People didn't know me and they were kind of reluctant to talk to me, so I asked my friend Billy to go out and talk to people—I got him paid by *Ramparts* as an investigative reporter. He came back and told me that most people said that Denzel Dowell might or might not have been involved in a burglary there, but the cops just shot him down, just murdered him. I did some other investigating in addition to that and we ran the story in *Ramparts*.

Then, a little bit later, the Panthers had this big rally there. They had a couple of rallies in North Richmond, one of which I spoke at along with Eldridge and some others, but even before that, there was this really dramatic rally at the house of Denzel Dowell's family. This was another time when Eldridge said to me, "Why don't you go check this out?" So I got in my car and I drove out to North Richmond, still having this whole image of North Richmond in my mind from people I had grown up with and these stories I had heard—but it was important, so I went. I got there and I parked my car, and they had this rally going on at the home of Denzel Dowell's mother. Up and down the street were these armed Panthers in a very disciplined formation, and Bobby Seale was on top of the garage roof giving a speech. The cops didn't dare come right into the area, but they had a helicopter circling above, and Bobby Seale was giving this speech, pointing at the helicopter, saying, "This is what the pigs do" and comparing it to what the U.S. military was doing in Vietnam.

I went up to one person I knew from another context who was part of the formation of Panthers and I said, "I sure hope you all know what you're doing." He said, "We know. We know what we're doing. We got it together." It was a very clear statement: we're not just messing around here—this is a serious thing we're doing, and we're doing it in a serious way. So that whole scene and Bobby Seale's speech and then what that guy said to me made a dramatic impression on me. This was just as I was getting ready to move to Richmond, so in a sense this was another introduction to that whole move.

### Moving to Richmond

Toward the end of 1967, it was time to make the move. It was time, as Mao had put it, to "integrate with the masses." We were trying to take radical and revolutionary politics, as best as we understood them, particularly to poor white people, which was what the Panthers, SNCC and other Black nationalist forces were urging. So, in a basic sense, that was our mission, but we didn't really have any idea how to go about it. We just knew we had to move there. That was the first thing, just literally move there. We had an orientation that we were still going to relate politically to things happening at Berkeley and other parts of the Bay Area and other important political struggles, but we were going to try to orient ourselves toward really, deeply immersing ourselves there in Richmond, and not just always go back to those places that we were more familiar and more comfortable with every time we wanted to do anything culturally or socially. So it was a big move and a big change for us.

Ideologically, we were into a real mixed bag. We thought of ourselves as revolutionaries and we were for socialism—sort of—but with a little bit of Mao, a little bit of Che, the influences of the Panthers and revolutionary nationalism all part of this mixed bag. That's where we were at and it was typical of a lot of radical people at that time. And it wasn't just the radicals in the Bay Area who were into this kind of mixed bag, but people more generally throughout the country and even in other parts of the world. Things are very different now, but at that time, even a lot of bourgeois heads of government in the Third World—say in Algeria or India—would talk about socialism of one kind or another in some sort of favorable way. So there was a lot of mixed bag ideology around and we were just a part of that.

Then we tried to figure out, "Okay, what are we going to do practically to begin trying to integrate with people here socially and culturally, and what are we going to do to start doing some political work with them?" So we started hanging out in bars to get to know people and going to local events. I always hated beer, but I started drinking beer so I could hang out and socialize with people. Politically, we decided, "Well, let's go investigate things they're doing with poor people here." So one of us went to this meeting of the local group that was set up under the whole Johnson "Great Society" anti-poverty program. It was a government-run group there in Richmond, but we decided, "Well, maybe we'll meet some interesting people there anyway." And we did meet a few interesting people that way, but I remember the person who went to the meeting coming back and describing how it was just this whole bureaucratic thing. It was captured in this diagram that they had with the President of the United States at the top, then all of these other government agencies, and then down at the bottom is "us," said the person who was running the meeting—this was actually a poor person from the neighborhood, but they were being turned into a hack by this whole program. Our comrade who went to the meeting finally couldn't take it anymore, and he got up and said, "The first thing we need to do is turn that chart upside down!" And that was our first political foray.

At the beginning, it was just a couple of us guys there. We were radicals, revolutionary-minded. We even had this sort of macho image of ourselves as revolutionaries. Now, as it turned out, as we did more work there, we started working among all different kinds of people, women as well as men, Black people, Latinos, Native Americans—but our goal initially was that we were going to hook up with poor white people. And so the first people we started drawing around us a little bit were a number of these young white working class guys, poor whites who lived in the area where we were.

## The First Political Steps

After getting to know them a little bit socially, we decided: we've got to do something to break the ice here politically. What could we do? Well, we lived in this house where the bedrooms we were staying in were upstairs and the living room was downstairs and we used some other rooms downstairs for a mimeo machine—back in those days, that's how you did things, you ran off flyers on mimeograph machines—and we had typewriters and things like that down there. So we took all the newspapers we could find—movement newspapers, regular newspapers—and we clipped out everything we could find where people had gotten into it with the police, like a police attack on strikers in Newport News, Virginia, cases of police murder, cases where the Panthers were defending themselves and Black people against the police, cases where Latinos were getting into it with the cops. All the way around the living room walls we pasted up these pictures and then we put captions below all of them. So one day, okay, here it goes—some of these guys we were hanging out with came over to our house. We opened the door and welcomed them in, and their eyes went really wide and they started walking around the living room almost as if they were in a museum, quietly looking at these pictures from beginning to end. And it was very interesting. Their response was very good. It was very favorable. They identified with the people who were being brutalized by the police and the people who were fighting back, and so this broke the ice politically.

During this time we were pretty sure our phone was being tapped, because you'd hear these clicking sounds and things. So, more to make a statement that we were aware of this than to actually get it fixed, we called the phone company and said we wanted someone to come out and see if our phone was being tapped. So this fairly backward guy came out. He walked into our place and he did the same thing—he looked all around our living room at these pictures—and he knows he's there to check to see if the phone is tapped, and he says, "What are you guys, spies?" "Man," we said, "just check the phone." Then he checked it and said he couldn't tell if it was tapped or not.

So this is how we began our political work. We started increasingly to involve the people we were meeting in various political activities— both things we did locally but also having them go with us to demonstrations in other places, and political meetings, and things like that. And then pretty soon through these first contacts and in other ways we started meeting other people; and again, while our initial mission was to go work among especially the poor white youth but more generally among poor white people, our contacts had friends who weren't all white and many different kinds of people were attracted to what we were doing— mainly younger people but some who were older, women as well as men, Blacks, Latinos, Native Americans, and these white proletarian youth. We started developing a kind of a political center there and of course it became known after a little while to the police in San Pablo and Richmond and the Sheriff's office, partly because we were also doing support work for the Panthers there. This was after the Huey Newton shootout incident, and his case had become a major political battle. So we started doing work around that in Richmond and that created quite a bit of controversy, but also brought forward some more advanced people.

## The Working Class: Practice and Theory

As I mentioned before, moving to Richmond was a big step we knew we had to take, and it had to be a situation where we were standing on our own in every way, so we had to work to support ourselves. We got jobs at local steel mills or other small plants, or we worked in gas stations or similar jobs, and for two reasons: to support ourselves financially but also, again, as part of integrating with the masses, to get to know people who had these different kinds of jobs.

I worked at a small steel mill for a short time, until I got laid off.

There was what we call a multinational workforce—Black, Latino, and white—and there were a lot of interesting experiences I had in the relatively short time I was there. Things came down in small ways as well as big ways, like during what became known as "the May '68 events" in France, when France was basically shut down by the combination of a youth revolt and younger proletarians getting into it, and this led to a general strike for a short period of time. This was a major event in the world at that time, and I brought a big article about it from one of the local mainstream papers in to work with me during the course of this. There was this young Black guy named Leon who worked in the same part of the steel mill that I did, and I was becoming friendly with him. During lunchtime he came over and looked at this article about France —he studied it for a while, and then said, "We need something like that here."

We started talking about this, and there was this other guy, a young white guy I knew who was sitting with a different group of people eating lunch—you still had this phenomenon of social segregation, where white people would eat lunch with other white people, and so on—so he says to me, "Hey, why don't you come over and have lunch with us?" This put me in a difficult position. I wanted to involve him in talking about what was going on in France, but under the circumstances I wasn't going to go eat lunch with the group he was hanging out with. So I said, "Well, why don't you all come over and eat lunch with *us*?" And that's actually what happened, and we all talked about the May '68 events in France. So on the job, as well as in the neighborhoods, we were trying to do a lot of political work as we got to know people.

These jobs didn't pay anything to speak of. You could get by, but that's about it. We'd buy these old cars and fix them up a little bit, just so they could run (and this is how I learned to work on cars, because I'd never done that before). Then you'd drive them for a few months and junk them, buy another one for a couple of hundred bucks and do the same thing all over again. So we were kind of living hand to mouth like that. Some of the places we lived in, you'd go to bed and turn off the lights, and then if you'd get up and go in the kitchen and put the lights on—roaches everywhere. Some places, the roaches were crawling up the walls even before you turned out the lights. These were the conditions that the people we wanted to work among had been living in and suffering under their whole lives.

We were reading a lot of different things at that point—a mixed bag again. We were reading *The Wretched of the Earth*, by Frantz Fanon, reading a lot of stuff from revolutionaries of various kinds—nationalists, Marxists, and so on—and reading the Black Panther paper. And we started to read some of the "classics" of Marxism. Of course, we read the Red Book. But we started doing some deeper study, too, from a lot of different sources at that time. Not only did we understand that it was important to go to the proletariat in the way we were doing, but we also recognized that you had to get a deeper theoretical understanding to give a framework for everything you were doing. So even though we were still in somewhat of a mixed bag ideologically at these beginning stages in Richmond, we did appreciate from the beginning the importance of theory. At the same time as we were very active in a lot of different things, we were reading everything that we thought had anything to do with radical politics and revolution and socialism and communism.

## Peace and Freedom

We still felt it was important to relate to all these movements—the students and the youth, the Panthers, and other radical movements in society. We still considered ourselves part of that whole broad general uprising, if you want to put it that way. In particular, and this is actually portrayed briefly in the movie *Panther*, the Panthers and especially Eldridge were interested in forming some kind of an alliance with the Peace and Freedom Party, another one of these radical reform movements focussed on electoral politics, which was developing in California and working to get on the ballot.

On the one hand, it was an electoral thing. But, on the other hand, its politics were directly in opposition to the Vietnam War and part of the general radical politics of the time, even though it had mainly a middle class base and its politics reflected that. Now you have, for example, the Green Party. At that time, you had this Peace and Freedom Party (which I think still exists in various places), and it was a more radical phenomenon because the times had generally become quite radical. In fact, the Peace and Freedom Party spread beyond California, and it eventually ran Eldridge Cleaver for president in 1968, although that was a process of a lot of struggle. And that gives you an idea of what the politics were in those times.

Eldridge in particular, and the Panthers more generally, saw this as an important phenomenon and thought it was important to develop certain alliances with it. So while we were out in Richmond, Eldridge came to me and said, "Why don't you work with this Peace and Freedom thing, try to get this off the ground more and also make it more radical?" I agreed to do this, so I was sort of splitting my time, in a certain way, between being in Richmond doing all the things we were doing there and, at the same time, being involved in these other efforts, like around the Peace and Freedom Party as well as relating to other broader movements.

In order to get the Peace and Freedom Party on the ballot, they had to have a certain number of signatures of actual registered voters, representing a certain percentage of people who'd voted in the last election. Time was running out to get on the ballot and they still were short of the signatures. Someone came to me and asked me if I wanted to be part of this tour that they were putting together to help make a final concerted push to get over the top and get the necessary signatures. We were going to go all around the state, from north to south, to rally people and get registered voters to sign these petitions to get the Peace and Freedom Party on the ballot.

A small core of people from the San Francisco Mime Troupe volunteered to do agit-prop skits as part of this crew, and then I was the speaker. One guy had bought an old farmworkers' bus and converted it for his own use, and he volunteered to drive us around. And we got a musical group to come with us too. We'd pull into an area and the musical group would get on top of the bus and they'd play music and gather a crowd. Then the Mime Troupe people would do a skit about the CIA and Vietnam and things like that. And then I'd get up and give a rap, doing exposure around the Vietnam War and exposing the system, then calling on people to sign up for the Peace and Freedom Party to oppose all this. And so we'd go from town to town doing this.

One of the interesting sidelights to this story is that the musical group who did this was actually Santana. This was just when they were starting out, and they volunteered to be part of this and they stayed with it for a few weeks under very difficult conditions. A lot of times we slept on the floor, or we slept in the bus, and they had to get up on top of a moving bus and play music. So I have to give them credit. They even felt a little badly that they finally had to leave, so then they did a benefit for Peace and Freedom later, which also contributed to getting it on the ballot. Of course, at the time, they were just starting out—so Santana, if you want to put it that way, wasn't Santana yet. Carlos Santana and the band were literally there, but it wasn't the Santana that it became. It was just starting out. So that was kind of interesting, too, and it's another one of these things that you look back on later and recognize: "Oh, that was very significant."

We started out in northern California and we went down to L.A. and then we were going to head up to Bakersfield to try to rally people to the Peace and Freedom Party—and we actually did get some people there to sign up, I will say. And if you know California and Bakersfield, that's an achievement. Bakersfield is a very proletarian town but it's not what you think of as a center of radical political activity.

But, before getting to Bakersfield, we experienced what turned out to be a major "detour." As we were heading out of L.A. for Bakersfield, we were going through Hollywood and we recognized that we had a few hours extra, so that we could relax a little bit. We had been going, going, going, and sleeping on the bus, sleeping on the floor, and often doing two or three rallies a day. So we said, "Let's take a little time out, have a little fun before we go at it again," and we decided to catch a movie.

We found a parking space for the bus right next to a high school, about a block away from the movie. We parked and we were going to walk to the movie. But the guy who drove the bus remembered that while he could lock the front door in the bus, there was a little door, almost like a trap door, at the back that he needed a padlock for. So he said, "OK, I'm going to get the padlock. You guys hang out here until I get back, then I'll lock it up and we'll go into the movie."

We were hanging out there, just waiting for him to get back, and all of a sudden we notice we're right next to the athletic field in this high school, and here's the high school ROTC marching around, being put through its paces by this guy acting very much like a drill sergeant. He was actually a football coach, I think, or an athletic director at the school, but he was also doubling in this role as a drill instructor for the ROTC. And of course, as we sat and watched this a little while, it was too much of a provocation—we started chanting anti-war and anti-military slogans. And we started singing these songs that these guys had made up in Berkeley about Mao and the Chinese Revolution, like:

"The thoughts of Chairman Mao are the best we've seen,
They make the fields grow fertile and green.

From the U.S. workers to the Viet Minh,
The thoughts of Chairman Mao will always win.
The thoughts of Chairman Mao will always win."

So we're singing these and other similar songs like this, quite loudly, while the ROTC is being put through its paces. This created a big uproar, and the drill sergeant guy comes over and starts yelling at us and telling us to get the hell out of there. And some of the ROTC guys are yelling at us. We hadn't planned a demonstration, we were just frankly goofing a bit, but there was a serious side to it, too, because this ROTC marching around in our faces *was* a provocation. So finally, the drill sergeant guy told us, "If you don't get out of here, I'm going to call the cops." Well, we weren't really looking to get arrested that day, so we decided to get out of there and go see the movie. But there was a complicating factor.

### The Flavor of the Times

Now you have to understand the times. These were wild, crazy times. And we had all this band equipment, people had all their belongings, and we often had to leave them on the bus overnight and one or more of us would have to sleep on the bus to protect all this stuff. So a couple of us actually had guns with us. Now, we didn't bring them along to shoot anybody. But we did feel we needed to be able to defend ourselves in case we were attacked at night or something like that. And in California at that time, even though they changed the laws to try to prevent the Panthers from doing their armed patrols, there still were ways you could legally carry guns in the state, and we were very conscious of staying within those rules.

But now we're in a difficult situation. What are we going to do with these guns that are on the bus? We realized that if we leave, they might just bust the bus driver when he comes back and impound the bus and then what are they going to make out of it if they find these guns on the bus? They were just pistols, they weren't howitzers or anything, but they might make something out of it. So we made a difficult but in the end a foolish decision, which was that I and this other guy would take the guns with us, and just get out of there with them so they wouldn't be an issue.

Well, of course, that didn't work. Now, I was very careful. I took the bullets out of the gun, because, as I said, we weren't looking for a shootout. I gave the bullets to one of the other people who was with us and said to the others with me: "I want you guys to be witnesses. This gun is not loaded, and I don't even have the bullets on me so I can't load it."

So we headed off, but I didn't want to put the gun I was carrying in my pocket, or under my shirt, or anything like that, because then it would be a concealed weapon, which was illegal. I was holding it out where everybody could see it, which made it in conformity with the law, but also much more of a big deal. And all of a sudden, I hear someone yell: "They've got guns! They've got guns!" So I'm saying, "Oh, shit!" and we're trying to get out of there as fast as we can. We're trying to just get away from the whole scene and somehow regroup and still go to our movie! We're still naively thinking we're going to go to this movie which, ironically enough, was *Bonnie and Clyde.*

We get a couple of blocks away and this police car comes tearing around the corner and screeches to a halt. The cop jumps out, and he doesn't pull out his gun yet, but yells, "Stop! Halt!" I'm holding this gun at my side. I turn around, and for the first time he actually sees the gun. But, of course, the report had already gone out on the police radio: "Dangerous people in the vicinity of the high school with guns." So he sees this and I'm standing about 20 feet from him. And as soon as he sees my gun, of course, he goes for his gun. He's trying to pull it out, but he's got this snap on his holster, and he's having trouble undoing it, so he can't get his gun out right away—fortunately. Like I said, I wasn't looking for a shootout, so I just walked up, put my gun on the top of his police car, and showed him, "Look—it's not loaded." But, of course, he doesn't give a shit if it's loaded or not, let's put it that way. So he pulls out his gun and points it at me and his hand is shaking, and I'm saying, "Oh fuck! His gun can go off even if he doesn't deliberately shoot me. It could go off by mistake!" Then a bunch of other police cars come up and the cops take us and slam our heads down on the hood of the police car and handcuff us.

Of course, these are the times: I'm getting into it with these cops even while they have us handcuffed and are holding guns on us. One of them says, "I thought you people were for peace." And I say, "No. We're not pacifists. We're against oppression and oppressors." He asks: "What does that mean—'oppression and oppressors'?" I say: "You know

—like you!"

So they tightened the handcuffs more and took us down to the local precinct, and a detective comes in and he starts giving us a bunch of shit —and I'm giving it back to him. And then finally he says to me, "If I hear one more word out of you, I'm going to charge you with armed robbery." "What armed robbery?" "The next one that comes on the ticker." So I decided tactically I'd be quiet for a while.

Eventually we got bailed out. When we went to trial we were charged with loitering around a school and disturbing the peace. So then we had to decide, how are we going to fight this case? We were discussing our legal tactics and I said, "Look, I know all about relying on the people and everything. But our defense is going to be very technical because we got busted in the area of a school; we had guns, even though we weren't intending to shoot anybody, and we didn't do anything illegal with the guns. A middle-class jury we're likely to get is not going to be very sympathetic to us in this situation. Even if they might be able to be won over to some of our political views, they're not going to be sympathetic to us in this situation and also they're not going to care very much about the 'technical nuances' of a first amendment defense." That was our defense—that we were exercising our first amendment rights, when we were chanting slogans and marching around doing a spontaneous protest of the ROTC.

So, at my suggestion, we decided to just go with what they call a "bench trial"—in other words, to be tried by the judge, without a jury. This, again, came out of the legal training I got year after year as a kid. "Let's go with a bench trial. Just have a trial by the judge and let's remind the judge every time we can that if he doesn't uphold our first amendment defense, we're going to appeal." So, during the trial, every time he got a chance, our lawyer would get up and remind the judge that we would appeal if we lost. For example, they had a blackboard in the courtroom and they would draw a diagram of who was where at a given time, and our lawyer would get up and say: "Your Honor, could we have that drawing on something more permanent, like a piece of paper, in case we need to preserve it for our appeal, if we have to appeal a conviction here." And finally the judge said: "Mr. so-and-so, I am very well aware of your reminders that you are going to appeal if this verdict goes against you. It is no longer necessary to continue reminding the Court of that fact." As it turned out, the judge *did* acquit us of all the charges on the basis of our first amendment defense. So we ended up getting out of that whole mess, but it was a pretty hairy thing.

### "Rocking" Dow Chemical

One more story from this Peace and Freedom tour—again, to give the flavor of the times. We went to San Jose State to do one of our Peace and Freedom rallies, but it turned out that there was a demonstration that day against Dow Chemical. Dow Chemical made the napalm that the U.S. military used to terrorize the people of Vietnam—napalm is this burning jellied gasoline, just a horrific thing. There was that famous picture, which was printed in *Ramparts* and many other places, of this small Vietnamese girl running naked down a roadway after a napalm attack. When we got to the San Jose State campus, we didn't even know about the demonstration; we were there to do our Peace and Freedom thing, but there was this rally, so we joined in. I think that there were Dow Chemical recruiters on campus or something like that, so there were hundreds of students there protesting. It was a really tense situation. During the course of the rally, people came around with big handfuls of rocks, passing them out to people and saying, "Put 'em in your pockets in case we get attacked by the police."

So we all took them and put them in our pockets. And, sure enough, after a little while, the police attacked the demonstration. Well, I never used the rocks. Very early in this whole fracas that broke out, this one cop started going after me. He threw a punch at me, and I blocked his punch, and I managed to land a punch to defend myself. Then, instead of continuing to fight with me, all of sudden I see this coward cop pointing over my shoulder to somebody and he yells, "Get him!" And before I have a chance to do anything, two other cops come from behind me and jump me, and then one of them put his nightstick across my throat. This happened to other people as well, and a number of us, including myself, were very close to passing out from this, or worse, and the only thing that saved us was the presence of the media there—whenever someone from the media would be around, the cops would loosen the chokehold just enough for us to breathe. Then they put us on a bus and we were taken down to jail. I ended up doing five days in jail for that.

Just like in L.A., when they busted me, I started mouthing off to them. It was interesting—there were some Hell's Angels there who had gotten busted for something else, and we were all in the same holding cell. The cops were trying to instigate these Hell's Angels to attack us, but that did not happen. So then they took me into this holding room to take my fingerprints and they were taking down my "facts," like name, birthdate, and all that kind of stuff. And at one point, they asked, "Where were you born?" And I said, "Washington, D.C., the capital of this foul place." And of course, they got very pissed off at that. And one of them said to the other, "Why don't we put Rudy in there with him?" Rudy was some other cop, I figured. And I said, "Yeah. I want Rudy. Put Rudy in the cell with me." So I'm going into my cell—and like I said, we were at this time sort of full of ourselves, kind of like macho revolutionaries, so I'm in my cell doing push-ups yelling, "Put Rudy in the cell with me, put Rudy in the cell with me!" But they never did put Rudy in the cell with me, for whatever reason.

When we were having our court hearings, we had these plea bargains—that's how I got five days. We'd get up before the judge and plead guilty, but unless they had something really big on somebody, the judge agreed to give light sentences, because it was a political demonstration and they kind of wanted the whole thing to go away. I still remember very vividly that there was one guy who got up before the judge—a guy I later found out was in the CP—and he started telling this story about how he was just there to protest and he didn't believe in violence and he didn't get into any violent activity. And so the judge said to him, "Well, then, how do you explain the fact that when you were arrested, your pockets were full of rocks?" And the guy replied: "Well, your Honor, you see, everybody was coming around passing out rocks. And when they came to me, I knew if I refused to take them, I'd be accused of being a petty bourgeois Left Hegelian, so I just took 'em and put 'em in my pocket." And the whole courtroom, even the judge, just cracked up. But that gives you a flavor of the times, not only the activism of people but also the intellectual, theoretical, and ideological ferment and debates that were going on.

### Free Huey!

The Peace and Freedom Party, as I said, was sort of a radical reform electoral movement which had its positive side, but also reflected the politics and the character of the people who were the basis for it—mainly middle class white people. It was a good thing they were becoming radicalized, but they also had their limitations. And so it wasn't by any means automatic that the Peace and Freedom Party would take up defending and supporting Huey Newton. I and a number of other people waged and won that battle, and the Peace and Freedom Party's stand in support of Huey was important as a political statement and also in bringing forward a number of people in and around the Peace and Freedom Party to become active in the struggle to free Huey.

During this same time period, early in 1968, the Panthers had a big rally for Huey in the Oakland Auditorium, to build political support on the occasion of his birthday.[15] They had that famous chair that the Panthers had taken the picture of Huey sitting in—they had made a poster out of that, and it was a very popular poster—and it was sitting there empty to symbolize the fact that they wanted Huey back among them. Many people who had been part of SNCC were there—James Foreman, Stokely Carmichael, Rap Brown. And I remember even Curtis Mayfield and the Impressions came there to lend their support. They couldn't come there in their "official capacity" with a band because of contractual complications, but they came and sang "We're A Winner" a capella—and that was a really nice moment. And, of course, Eldridge spoke and Bobby Seale spoke. I also spoke at that rally representing the Peace and Freedom Party. So that was an expression of the struggle that we'd waged and a further development of the struggle we were waging to win forces like those who were grouped around the Peace and Freedom Party, as well as others more broadly, to take up the case of Huey Newton in particular, but also more broadly to support the Panthers.

I went to a number of Huey's court appearances—in fact I happened to be there for some of the dramatic moments in the Huey court case—and I went to the rallies that were held outside. On one of these occasions, somebody (even to this day I don't know who) pulled down a flag from a flagpole around the courthouse, and different people were passing it around; some people were trying to tear it, and others were trying to burn it, but it turned out that it was very difficult to tear or to burn. And, after a few minutes of this, the cops were starting to gather to attack, and I said, "Let's just get rid of this fucking thing."

---

15. Film of this rally, containing portions of the main speeches, is currently available in the videotape *Black Panthers*, by the French filmmaker Agnes Varda.

Now, the courthouse was across the street from Lake Merritt, this small lake in Oakland. And there was this underground passage that went underneath the street, so you could go from the courthouse over to Lake Merritt. My idea was, I'll take this flag, run through that passageway, get over to Lake Merritt, and just throw the flag in the lake, and that'll be the end of it. It will show the "appropriate respect" for the flag, but we'll be done with it.

So I get about halfway through this tunnel—I'm running—and all of a sudden I hear footsteps behind me. I look over my shoulder and someone who is obviously a plainclothes cop is chasing me. At the other end of this tunnel, there are two stairways that go up, one to the right and one to the left, and they go out to the grounds of Lake Merritt. This cop is running behind me, when all of a sudden two other plainclothes cops come down the stairways in front of me—one from my left and one from my right. What am I going to do here? I think back to my football days. I'm running with the flag, and I'm not going down, I'm not going to get tackled. So, when the cops in front of me get to within a few feet of me, I lower my shoulder into them and, one after the other, they go down. At that point the guy behind me jumps me. I managed to shake him off—but, unfortunately, as happens sometimes in football, too, I lost my balance and fell just at the crucial moment, and then they all three piled on me and busted me. I ended up doing thirty days for desecrating the flag.

As it turned out, the courts were forced by the struggle that was waged to hand down sort of a mixed verdict in the Huey Newton case —they found Huey guilty of manslaughter, not murder, and he was sentenced to something like fifteen years. Two years after that he was freed altogether on appeal. Beyond that, though, taking up this legal defense in a very politically aggressive way played an important part in spreading the politics and program of the BPP and helping them to expand— though, ironically enough, this very expansion brought with it contradictions that they were ultimately not able to surmount, especially in the context of the vicious, literally murderous, repression that was brought down on them.

In April 1968, Eldridge Cleaver and Bobby Hutton and some other Panthers were involved in a shootout with the police in Oakland. Bobby Hutton was shot down and murdered by the Oakland police as he was coming out of a house where he had taken refuge. They ordered him to run, and when he ran they shot him and killed him.[16] And there was, of course, great outrage in the Black community and among people who were supporting the Panthers and progressive people generally. The Panthers held a rally at one point in the aftermath of this, and Marlon Brando came and spoke. He also went on "Johnny Carson" at this time, I remember, and created a tremendous uproar by telling the truth about what had happened, how the Oakland pigs had murdered Bobby Hutton — it was such an uproar that Johnny Carson invited the Oakland police chief on his show to give his version of what happened, to try to white-wash the whole thing.

Anyway, Marlon Brando came and spoke at this rally and then after-ward a few of us went back to the rather small Panther community office. Just a few people could fit into the office and eventually the others there left to go off and do things, and Marlon Brando and I were sitting there. It was like the incident when I was sitting in the room with Muhammad Ali. I said to myself, "I've got to say something to Marlon Brando." So I finally worked up my courage and I said, "Mr. Brando, you see, I'm a communist." Actually, I was just becoming a communist at that time, but anyway, that's what I said. He looked at me and he launched into a long story which, as I recall, was a story of one of the Native American peoples, and I believe the point of the story was to pro-mote the collective and cooperative way of life. That was his answer to my saying that I was a communist. And then there was a long silence after that, before people came back to take Marlon Brando to the airport.

---

16. Bobby Hutton was the first member of the Black Panther Party, after Huey Newton and Bobby Seale; he was 15 when he joined, 17 when he was gunned down.

# Chapter Nine

# *Becoming a Communist*

$\mathbb{A}$t that time, there were just a few of us in our core group in Richmond who considered ourselves conscious revolutionary activists. But we were meeting a lot of people, and people were starting to hear about some of our work and to call us from different parts of the Bay Area, and even other parts of the country, asking about what we were doing. Also, we started hooking up with other people who had similar politics to ours. We were moving more in the direction of recognizing that we had to get much more clear ideologically and in particular that we had to become more firmly grounded in communism and communist theory. So, we were moving in that direction, and we were meeting with, talking and struggling with other people who had similar politics.

At a certain point, we decided that we needed to form some kind of an organized group, not just in Richmond but more broadly in the Bay Area. So I wrote up a position paper, which we took around to other people, and it became the basis of discussion and the basis of unity, more or less, for drawing people together—originally just a handful—to form some kind of a group. We didn't exactly know what kind of a group. It was still sort of a mixed bag ideologically, but clearly we were for revolution, as we understood it, and moving in a direction of being for socialism and communism, as we were beginning to understand *that* more fully.

## Leibel Bergman

About this time I came in contact with someone who would play a very important role in developing me fully into a communist and in lending more ideological clarity to our efforts in forming the organization that we did form in the Bay Area late in 1968, which we called the Revolutionary Union. That person was Leibel Bergman, who had himself been in the Communist Party in the 1930s, '40s and early '50s. (He had also been in PL for a brief period after that, before deciding that it was not really going in the right direction and could not provide the needed alternative to the revisionism of the CP.) Leibel was a veteran communist, but he broke with the Communist Party in 1956 when they took up the Khrushchev program of in effect denouncing and slandering the whole experience of socialism in the Soviet Union up to that time. Khrushchev did this largely in the form of denouncing Stalin, but this was part of his renouncing the basic principles of socialism and communism. Leibel had criticisms of Stalin, and as we developed our theoretical understanding in the Revolutionary Union we began to deepen those criticisms of Stalin, but we saw that just negating and trashing the whole history of the Soviet Union under Stalin's leadership was going to lead you back into the swamp of embracing capitalism.[17]

That's one of the things that I came to understand through a lot of discussions with Leibel. He had written a paper criticizing this move on the part of the CP in the U.S., to take up this Khrushchev program. And it wasn't just denunciation of Stalin; along with that, and with that denunciation of Stalin as kind of the battering ram, Khrushchev started promoting his "Three Peacefuls": "Peaceful Coexistence" between capitalist and socialist countries; "Peaceful Competition" between socialism and capitalism; and "Peaceful Transition" to socialism from capitalism. In other words, Khrushchev started promoting the idea that revolution was no longer necessary, that somehow through electoral parliamentary

---

17. Joseph Stalin led the Communist Party of the Soviet Union from the mid-1920s up to his death in 1953. Shortly after his death, Nikita Khrushchev took the reins of power and instituted a form of capitalist rule under a fairly threadbare socialist cover. For more on Bob Avakian's evaluation of Stalin—his overall positive historical role and accomplishments, along with his serious shortcomings and grievous mistakes—see, among other works, *Conquer the World—The International Proletariat Must and Will.*

means and peaceful means in general you could achieve socialism—somehow the imperialists were going to allow you to bring into being a socialist society, and ultimately a communist world, without using violent means to try to suppress that and drown it in blood. Leibel rejected that, and he wrote a paper criticizing it which got circulated in the communist movement not only in the U.S. but internationally.

As a result of that, Leibel had been invited to China. So he'd gone to China around 1965, and he was there when the Cultural Revolution broke out. He was there for several years during some of the high points of the upsurge of the Cultural Revolution, and then he came back to the U.S. At a certain point, he approached me and said, "Well, you seem to be very radical-minded and very active, and you seem to be strongly against white chauvinism" (that's the term he used). He thought I had the potential to be a communist, and he decided to work to develop me into one.

I began spending a lot of time with him, and he had a big influence on me in getting me to read more communist theory. I read things like *The History of the Communist Party of the Soviet Union*. I started reading more than just the Red Book, going further into Mao's *Selected Works* and other writings by Mao about the Chinese revolution and about communism. I started reading Lenin's writings on imperialism, and his famous work *What Is To Be Done?*, as well as various works by Marx and Engels (although it would be a few years before I managed to launch into the study of Marx's *Capital* and—after some initial frustration and difficulty in understanding Marx's method of analysis—I was able to work my way through it and learn a great deal in the process). I was also discussing and struggling over big political and theoretical questions with Leibel.

Leibel would struggle with me—sometimes subtly, and sometimes quite sharply. For example, there was a meeting in Berkeley which had something to do with supporting the struggle of the Angolan people—Angola was still a colony of Portugal at that time, and Angolan revolutionaries were waging an armed struggle for independence. People at this meeting were debating back and forth about Angola and the freedom fight there, and I got up at one point and made this speech supporting the Angolan people's struggle and said: "It doesn't matter if the Portuguese think the Angolans are a nation. It doesn't matter if everybody here thinks the Angolans are a nation. It doesn't matter if I think the Angolans are a nation. What matters is that they believe they're a nation. So they should be able to be free."

Leibel was there at the meeting, and afterward he talked to me about this. He said: "Well, you know, you made a lot of good points, but the way you put it is not right. It's not a matter of what anybody, even the Angolan people, just thinks. It's a matter of what's objectively true, what's the reality. And since it *is* true that they are an oppressed nation, a colony, then they *should* be supported in fighting for liberation. But it is not a matter of what anybody thinks. It's a matter of what the reality is." That was a big lesson for me that I've remembered to this day.

Around this time a book came out that had a lot of influence in the radical movement. It was written by Regis Debray, who is now a bourgeois functionary in France, and it was called *Revolution in the Revolution*. It basically put forward the Castro-Che Guevara line on how you make revolution, particularly in Latin America, and argued that you didn't need a party to lead it, you just needed a military "foco," as they called it—that is, a military force that would be both a political leadership and a military leadership and would go from place to place fighting and supposedly spreading the seeds of revolution.

I was very influenced by this book, and so were many other people I knew. But the thrust of the book, the essential position it was putting forward, was not correct and influenced people in the wrong direction. I recall arguing vigorously with Leibel about this for hours, because I was being swayed by Debray's arguments. And at one point he got very frustrated with me—in the course of this argument, he slapped me on the thigh and said, "You know, you're an asshole" because I was being stubbornly resistant to his arguments, which were actually more correct than mine, and he got frustrated. But finally, I remember the thing that really stuck with me. He said: "This whole line about how you don't need a party is really wrong, because without a party there is no way you can really base this among the people"—he was talking about an armed struggle for revolution in countries of the Third World. I asked why.

"Because," he said, "in order to base it among the people, you have to do political work among the people. You have to organize the people to actually take up economic tasks, to carry out transformations in the economy and meet their economic needs, to make changes in their conditions and their social relations, as well changing the politics, the culture and ideology; and in order to do that, you have to have a political force that isn't just moving around with the army from place to place but is rooted among the people and actually mobilizing and leading them politically and ideologically. The military is a separate force, which may do political work, but it can't substitute for sinking deep roots and leading the people to carry out these transformations. That has to be done with the leadership of a party, and its cadres—it can't be done by an armed force which is made up of full-time fighters, and which has to move from place to place in fighting a war." That was a very profound point; it struck me very penetratingly at the time, and it has stayed with me since.

## Red Papers 1 and the
## Formation of the Revolutionary Union

During this period, I wrote some articles for various movement newspapers, especially about Huey and the Panthers. Then the next year, 1969, there was this major oil workers strike in Richmond, which became a big deal in the whole Bay Area and even had a big impact around the country. We were actively involved in that strike, and in building support for it, and I wrote a number of articles about this for a movement newspaper, appropriately called *The Movement*.

I was also doing more theoretical writing because we were starting to form these collectives of revolutionaries which we then united into the Revolutionary Union, and we were writing position papers to develop the basis of unity for that organization. We actually formed the RU in late 1968 but announced its formation publicly when we published our manifesto in what we called the "Red Papers" (the State Department would publish "White Papers," so we decided to call our publication "Red Papers"). We put out *Red Papers 1*, which had our statement of principles, some summation of the history of the communist movement and polemics answering attacks on communism, and descriptions of some of the work we were doing in Richmond. So I was writing a lot at that time, as well as being involved in internal discussion and debate with others who founded the Revolutionary Union, including Leibel.

In forming the Revolutionary Union, one of the things we recognized as crucial was the question of what kind of leadership is needed once you start confronting the fact that a revolution is necessary and you understand it has to be socialist and that the ultimate goal is communism. The Panther Party was already out there, and there was a point when Eldridge came to me and said, "Why don't you just join the Black Panther Party and be a secret member of the Central Committee of the Black Panther Party?" And I thought about this and discussed it with people I knew, and I think he discussed it with some others in the Panthers. But I decided that this was not a good thing to do, and that rather than being a secret member of the Black Panther Party, the thing to do—and this was our general view in the Revolutionary Union—was to develop organizations which would all contribute to the eventual formation of one unified, multinational communist vanguard. By "multinational" we meant that people of all races, or nationalities—Black, Latino, Native American, white, Asian—would all be united in this one vanguard party. And that was our objective in forming the Revolutionary Union—to contribute to the development of such a multinational communist vanguard.

There were a lot of other significant forces out there at that time, like the Panthers, which had come out of a revolutionary nationalist current; other groups which had developed among Latinos and other oppressed peoples, and others who had come out of radical "New Left" politics; and there was a question of whether and how we were all going to make a leap to unite on a communist basis—which, when we formed the Revolutionary Union, is what we understood to be necessary. But that was going to be a process of development and of ideological struggle, frankly, and we saw *Red Papers* making a contribution to that.

We tried to present what we were doing in forming the Revolutionary Union modestly—not in the bourgeois sense of being self-effacing or something, but corresponding to what we actually represented. We were just a fledgling organization that was putting forward these principles. We wanted to discuss and debate this with people, and we wanted to move to an eventual vanguard party. We didn't at that time see ourselves as that party. But we were trying to move toward that and make as much of a contribution as we could to it, through practical work and also through theoretical work and ideological struggle with other forces. So when we published *Red Papers 1*, we put out the goal of forming such a party at a future time—as soon as it could be done on the correct basis. And we put forward our views of a communist understanding of U.S. society and of the world and of revolution.

That's what *Red Papers* was about—and it made a big impact, for a lot of reasons, including the fact that on the front cover of the first *Red*

*Papers* (*Red Papers 1*), we boldly put forward the pictures of not only Marx, Engels, Lenin, and Mao but also Stalin. Of course, this was highly controversial. In *Red Papers 1* we raised certain criticisms of Stalin, but we put them in the framework that "these are *our* mistakes, these are mistakes of our movement and our struggle and not something we're going to stand outside of and attack like petty bourgeois or bourgeois critics and slanderers." And, of course, this created tremendous controversy. I remember I spoke at Columbia University sometime shortly after *Red Papers 1* came out. I went there knowing that this was going to be controversial. I jumped right into it and talked about why we'd put Stalin on the cover. There were several hundred students and others there, and there was a lot of back-and-forth about this. It was very controversial, but it also had a very significant impact.

### The Struggle in SDS

I've talked about why we were opposed to the Communist Party and their whole revisionist position that took revolution entirely out of the picture and somehow tried to present a socialism that had revolution ripped out of it, which is of course ridiculous and reactionary in fact. But we were also opposed to groups like PL (Progressive Labor Party) and these Trotskyite groups who had a very narrow—what we call today "workerist" and "economist"—position of "it's just the workers against the bosses," who saw everything in very narrow terms like that. PL (and most of the Trotskyites) actually saw revolutionary nationalism as a negative phenomenon. They did not recognize that, although contradictory, it was mainly positive—even overwhelmingly positive, and in some ways representative of the most advanced revolutionary expressions of masses of people at that time. They just saw it as a negative phenomenon, period. PL denounced nationalism in general, even revolutionary nationalism. In essence, they reduced national oppression to a matter of ideas —just racism—without recognizing that Black people are actually an oppressed people and indeed an oppressed nation within the U.S., and there are other minority nationalities in the U.S. which have a whole history of being oppressed, which isn't only a matter of some racist ideas or simply discrimination, but has a whole historical development, an economic basis, and political and social and cultural manifestations. PL and the Trotskyites—or at least the more "pure" Trotskyites—failed to recognize all that and denounced and opposed struggles against national oppression that were expressive of nationalist ideology.[18]

Earlier I mentioned the book by Regis Debray, *Revolution in the Revolution*, and how Leibel Bergman sharply struggled to get me to recognize what was wrong with the basic position Debray was seeking to popularize. But there was one sentence in that book which still makes me laugh, though I became convinced that the basic line Debray was putting forward was fundamentally and seriously wrong. Debray wrote, "Has anybody ever seen a concrete analysis of concrete conditions from the pen of a Trotskyite?" Although that may have been a slight exaggeration, Debray was getting at something very real there—hitting at the completely idealist tendencies of the Trotskyites (followers of Leon Trotsky), who instead of proceeding from reality in the struggle to transform society, seek to impose their fanciful notions *on* reality. Although they are always talking about "socialism"—and often seeking to make support for "socialism" the dividing line in all kinds of mass movements—the only kind of "socialism" that people like that will ever have anything to do with creating is a "socialism" that they imagine in their own minds. And their outlook, and actions flowing from it, actually works against the living struggle to bring socialism, and ultimately communism, into being, in the real world. Concrete analysis of concrete conditions has never been the strong point of the Trotskyites—I remember laughing uproariously in agreement when reading that line from Debray.

So, as we were forming our principles of unity in the RU, we recognized the importance of combatting these various trends—revisionist and opportunist lines which were posing as "socialist" and "communist" while objectively opposing revolutionary struggles, and thereby doing a great deal of harm. We were putting forward a position sharply opposed to that and carrying out polemics and ideological struggle against these various trends.

By 1969, SDS (Students for a Democratic Society, formed in the early

---

18. Some of the less "pure" Trotskyite groups, most notably the Socialist Workers Party (SWP), took the mirror-opposite tack, and uncritically pushed nationalism of the most petty variety. In neither case were the Trotskyite groups able to see the ways in which nationalism could take on an "against-the-system" character, even as it fell short in being able to provide a way for people to rupture with and overthrow capitalism. With many Trotskyite groups it is a matter of fixating on one aspect—the shortcomings of nationalism—while Trotskyite groups like the SWP uncritically tailed various expressions of nationalism and failed to acknowledge its shortcomings.

1960s with a basic stand and program of striving to realize the promise of American democracy and make it live up to its proclaimed principles) was becoming more and more radicalized and various revolutionary currents were developing within it—and this wasn't just a handful of people. Thousands of people who were in and around SDS were debating questions of revolution and socialism and communism. All these different trends were contending within SDS, struggling over what direction this very broad revolutionary current among youth, in particular white youth, should take. And so we felt it was important to get into these debates and try to influence them in the direction of communism, as we understood it, and we got involved, in a big way.

SDS had these quarterly national conventions in different parts of the country, and the first one that I went to was in Austin, Texas in the spring of 1969. Three of us who were part of the RU got in a little VW bug and drove from the Bay Area to Austin, Texas, in a couple of days, without stopping. Some students at the University of Texas put us up, but we spent almost the whole time deeply immersed in debates and struggles at the SDS meeting. At that time, the focus of the struggle was against PL, which was opposing struggles for ethnic studies on campuses, denouncing this as nationalist and bourgeois. There was a lot of struggle against PL's attempts to take SDS in this narrow "bosses vs. workers...all-nationalism-is-reactionary" kind of direction.

We were working to expose and defeat that. But not only were we trying to win people away from that, we were also very importantly working to expose that what PL was putting forward was *not* communism, was *not* Maoism. I talked earlier about how someone I knew in PL wouldn't even defend the Cultural Revolution when I raised questions about it. But PL was still identified in a lot of people's minds with China and with Maoism until 1971, when they denounced China and actually jettisoned the whole idea of supporting socialism and instead started coming out with the notion that you should leap immediately from capitalism to communism, without going through the transition phase of socialism, because socialism had too many problems.[19] Of course, this was a leap—directly from capitalism to communism—that could only

---

19. For further discussion of the problems in PL's approach on this, see Bob Avakian's "MLM vs. Anarchism, Part 5: Making Revolution for Real in the Real World," *Revolutionary Worker* #923, at rwor.org.

take place in their minds. Nevertheless, they were still identified in 1969 with China and Maoism even though, as exemplified by the conversation I had with that PL guy, they were not really defenders of the Cultural Revolution and of Mao, even at *that* time.

A lot of people who were revolutionary nationalists but influenced by communism were completely turned off by PL. Some people might be drawn to it initially because it was always raising the slogan "fight racism," but when you got closer, you'd see that PL would denounce any kind of national liberation movement that didn't declare socialism as its goal. They posed the fight for socialism *against* national liberation movements and struggles. So this turned a lot of people off, but in being turned off, they thought this PL line was communism, that this was even a radical communism, that this was Maoism, or what was represented by China. So it was important to expose that this was *not* the case.

The next big SDS convention was set for Chicago, and everyone knew that this was going to be a major political event and that there would be a big showdown there. Right before that, we had published *Red Papers 2*, which put forward our understanding at the time of the united front as the strategy for making revolution in the U.S.; and a couple of us in the RU took a box of these *Red Papers* with us and drove from California to the Chicago SDS convention.[20] At that time it was already legal to make a right turn on a red light in California, though in a lot of other states, including Illinois, it was not yet legal. So we're driving along in Chicago and we come to a stoplight. We stop and there's no traffic, and so we make a right turn while the light is red. Someone else was driving, and I was sitting in the front seat next to this box of *Red Papers*. We go a couple of blocks down the road, and we get pulled over by these Chicago cops—one was a Black cop and one was Puerto Rican. They say, "You ran a red light." And the driver says, "When? I didn't run any red light." I'm trying to think fast, to get out of this, because I don't want this to turn into a whole thing where they end up busting us on some pretext, and then discovering these *Red Papers*. So I turned to one of the cops and say, "Look, are you talking about when we pulled up to a red

---

20. *The United Front Under the Leadership of the Proletariat* is now the Revolutionary Communist Party's strategy for making revolution and transforming society. At that time, the Revolutionary Union had a less developed understanding of this but held the same basic position, and that was put forward in *Red Papers 2*.

light, stopped, and then made a right turn?" And he says, "Yes, exactly."
I say, "You see, we're from California, and in California it's legal to blah,
blah, blah, blah, blah..." and they finally let us off with a warning.

We sold our box of *Red Papers 2* at the convention, and it came in
the middle of this huge ideological debate. SDS split basically in two
directions at this convention, with one led by PL and the other a kind of
coalition of people opposed to PL. But even then you could see that further splitting was going to go on, and it did—and SDS as an organization soon ceased to exist. The bourgeoisie, and others who want to paint
radical and revolutionary politics in a bad light, present this now as if
this were just a case of people becoming dogmatic fanatics and eating
each other up in these sectarian squabbles. But mass movements like
SDS, which had started off as a sort of radical bourgeois-democratic
organization of students whose objective was to make American democracy live up to its professed principles and ideals, had developed together with the times into a much more radical and revolutionary organization that had thousands of active members around the country and
tens of thousands or more who supported it, who had come to a general revolutionary position.

And as happens when things develop, things also divide out. As we
Maoists say, things divide into two. There were new questions posing
themselves: If you are going to be for revolution, *what kind* of revolution? How can you make that revolution? What kind of leadership do
you need? What kind of program do you need? What kind of forces do
you need to mobilize and unite? These were questions that were bound
to come on the agenda as the times were developing; the struggles in
society were intensifying, and thousands and thousands of people were
coming up against these questions.

Naturally, there is going to be debate and struggle, and not everybody is going to agree. And this wasn't because everybody overnight
became sectarian or "the revolution was eating its own children" and all
that kind of bullshit. People were running up against these big questions
*because they had made advances.* They were moving beyond the position
of seeking to reform an unreformable system. They were at the point—
or they were on the threshold, at least—of making a leap to something
beyond the limitations of this system, a leap to taking up communism,
or at minimum debating about whether it should be communism or
some other revolutionary theory and program that would bring about a

transformation in the whole society, and not just some bourgeois-democratic reforms.

## Weatherman

So naturally, there were these struggles. PL represented one trend that had a lot of influence within SDS. What became the Weathermen, or the Weatherpeople, represented another trend and then what was, broadly speaking, represented by the RU was a third trend. These were the struggles of the day, and I would still say today that our position was, among the three, the most correct or the most in line with the actual way in which the struggle had to be developed and what the objectives of that struggle should be, how it should be led and what forces should be mobilized as the main forces, who were the key allies, and so on—even though our understanding was very undeveloped and was obviously not fully correct in many particulars. Our basic position was that we needed a socialist revolution, as part of the worldwide revolutionary struggle whose ultimate goal was communism; that the proletariat would be the backbone force of this revolution, but that at the same time it was necessary to build a broad united front, unifying many diverse forces fighting against the injustices and outrages of this system, and that a key force for revolution was the struggle of the various oppressed nationalities; and that, to lead all this to revolution, there was a need for a single, multinational revolutionary communist party.

The Weatherpeople took their name from the line in Bob Dylan's "Subterranean Homesick Blues": "You don't need a weatherman to know which way the wind blows." Now, if you think about it, it's one thing for Bob Dylan to write that, but it's another thing to take that up as an ideological stand. It's very pragmatic. It rules out theory and analysis. It's correct to have a stand that we should not be armchair revolutionaries, that you actually have to change the world in practice and through leading masses in struggle; but if you throw out the need for theory and adopt that kind of pragmatic orientation, you're going to be whipped around by many different events and currents, and end up in a bad place and a dead end eventually—which in fact is what ultimately happened with the Weatherpeople, even though many of them were very sincere and dedicated people and very revolutionary-minded.

Anyway, at one point sometime in 1969—I think it might have been after the Chicago SDS convention, after this "don't need a weatherman" position paper had been written—Leibel Bergman said to me, "Why don't you go back there" (talking about New York and the area around Columbia in particular where a lot of the leaders of the Weatherpeople were centered) "and make Marxist-Leninists out of those people?" (Leibel had a way of putting things somewhat provocatively.) I said okay, and we got together the money and got me an airline ticket. I went back there and showed up and, since I knew some of them from SDS, I found out where they were staying and went and knocked on their door. They invited me to stay with them and I did. The place was full of people, so I slept on the floor, but there wasn't too much time for sleeping anyway —we had lots of discussion and debate and struggle, but they were set on a certain course and nothing that I said was going to convince them or did convince them to turn to a different course and, as Leibel put it, become "Marxist-Leninists." But it was an interesting experience. And even after that, when they split off and formed their own grouping within SDS, we continued to struggle with them because it was the view of people like Leibel and myself that there were many dedicated revolutionary-minded people among them who were going off in the wrong direction, and that it was important to try to win them to a more correct revolutionary orientation and program, as best as we understood that.

### People's Park

During this period we still maintained our connections to the Berkeley movement, and in fact the RU had collectives in Berkeley. When the oil workers strike broke out in Richmond in 1969, we went and talked about that to people in the student movement and others in Berkeley and mobilized people from the campus and among other forces in Berkeley and around the Bay Area to come out to Richmond in solidarity with the strikers. Simultaneously, there was a Third World student strike at San Francisco State, which was a very crucial struggle, and there was a similar strike at UC Berkeley. We developed ties with people in these strikes and also helped mobilize people from these struggles to link up with the strike of oil workers. And people in the RU were continuing to build the anti-war movement in Berkeley and other parts of the Bay Area. Those of us based in Richmond at that time took part in that in various ways, both building opposition to the war in Richmond itself but also being involved in other protests and demonstrations around the Bay Area more generally.

And then People's Park broke out. I was actually out of the Bay Area when it initially jumped off. As I recall, people associated with Jerry Rubin,[21] Stew and Judy Albert and some others, discovered this property that the university owned but was not using at that time, just a little bit off campus in the Telegraph Avenue area, which extends out from the south end of the campus. The university was planning to turn this into a parking lot, and these activists took the initiative to turn it into a park instead.

This developed into a major battle because the university was completely unyielding and was determined to "pave paradise and make it a parking lot," as the Joni Mitchell song says. The university administration threw down the gauntlet, and the people who were building People's Park refused to back off and carried forward what they were doing—and it became a gigantic struggle. That might sound a little improbable, but if you think about the context of things at that time and that the people involved were part of a broader movement, you can see why other people—even if they weren't actively involved at first or didn't think that was the main kind of activity that people should be directed toward—would still see this, in a broad sense, as part of the whole movement that they were part of. *Thousands* of people saw it that way.

And when the university moved against People's Park and brought the police down on it, people responded accordingly. This developed into a major struggle in which eventually the National Guard was called out. As a result of and through the course of this whole struggle, there was actually a form of martial law implemented in Berkeley during this period. People were forbidden to gather in crowds of more than a few. If you gathered on the street corner, the police would come and break it up. People would come by on motorcycles with stacks of literature and throw them on the corner and then drive off, and then other people would scramble, pick them up, and distribute them, because you weren't even allowed to do that. I remember driving somewhere in Berkeley and

---

21. Jerry Rubin, along with Abbie Hoffman, had founded the Yippies, a group that tried to infuse radical and confrontational politics into the hippie communities that had grown up around the U.S. Rubin and Hoffman played a major role in the Democratic Convention of 1968 and were subsequently tried for conspiracy, along with Bobby Seale and others, in a very wild trial. They were convicted, but the convictions were eventually overturned.

getting caught in a traffic jam, and I saw this cop standing out in the street—he had a gun pointed at somebody. So I got out of my car, and the cop wheeled and pointed the gun at my head. This kind of thing was going on throughout the city.

So things became very intense, and we in the RU decided that even though this wasn't the form of activity that we would have put our main energies into or focussed our attention on, and we weren't the initiators of this by any means, once it became a much bigger issue it was important to relate to it. So we put out leaflets and tried to mobilize as many forces as we could to support this struggle. I remember we put out one leaflet to the National Guard itself, because a lot of the people in the National Guard were not really "gung-ho" types—quite a few of them were sympathetic to the struggle and some of them were even people who had been involved in the movement. This leaflet had a drawing showing a normal person going through changes as they got into their National Guard uniform and were mobilized against the people, with this National Guardsman ending up as a pig—and the message was: don't let this happen to you. We passed out thousands of copies of that leaflet, to people in the National Guard as well as others. And we put out a number of other leaflets as well, calling on people to support the battle for People's Park.

Even though I was living in Richmond at that time, I myself got actively involved as the People's Park struggle crescendoed. At the high point of the struggle there were tens of thousands of people mobilized, with many of them demonstrating at the fence that the university had put up around People's Park to keep people out. I remember being right at the fence, and the National Guard was on the other side, inside the park, with their weapons loaded. We were shaking the fence, and it was swaying, almost coming down. And it was very clear that had we brought the fence down, they were going to open fire. This was even before Kent State and Jackson State. It was also clear that people were not prepared to take that next step, that it would have been a massacre that people weren't prepared for. So that didn't happen. People shook the fence, but they didn't knock it down.

## Confronting the Implications

During that upsurge around People's Park, a guy named James Rector was killed in one of the demonstrations. I was in that demonstration, but a few blocks away from where he was killed. That was a very heavy thing, obviously. That same day, the police not only shot live ammunition at people but also fired a lot of tear gas. And they had started using these tear gas grenades instead of just tear gas canisters. These were more dangerous because they not only had the tear gas and all the effects of that, but they would explode, on a delay. I remember the same day that James Rector got killed, I picked up one of these tear gas grenades to throw it back at the cops, and it exploded in my hand—and it took me about two or three seconds to work up the nerve to look and see if I still had a hand. Then I discovered that it was just a tear gas grenade, and my hand was still there.

As a footnote to that story, my father was a judge then and the deputy in his courtroom was a member of the county sheriffs who'd been mobilized as part of the police force attacking the demonstration that day. He came into court and in a nasty way said to my father, "How's your son?" And my father didn't know anything about this, so he said, "What do you mean?" And the deputy came back, "Oh, we were watching a film of the People's Park demonstrations the other day, and we saw that your son picked up a tear gas grenade and it went off in his hand." And my father told me later that he was very upset by this.

The tear gassing affected thousands of people, and many people had this experience of these tear gas grenades going off near them, if not literally in their hands. But the James Rector murder by the police was yet another step, another outrage, beyond that.

People had to confront the implications of this, but generally they were not freaked out by it. From the time I started working with the Black Panther Party, and as the struggle intensified and the repression became much harsher and more intense, I think *many* people sensed the high personal stakes, even the risk of death. And, in fact, during that time I knew that there were attempts to set me up to be killed. But I don't remember, to be honest, a lot of talk among activists about dying or the fear of dying.

To tell the truth, I felt, and most of the people I knew felt—and this might sound like a funny word in this context—very *joyous* about being involved in the struggle. We weren't in it because it made us feel good, but the fact is that you felt as if your life mattered and counted for something. I remember demonstrations where we chanted, "The whole world is watching." And, with the May Events in '68 in France, the Vietnamese people (who were obviously waging struggle on a whole other level), the struggles in Latin America, the things going on in the U.S. and, for people like me, the Cultural Revolution in China—with all that going on, you felt you were part of a whole wave of people who were trying to change the world, were *determined* to make a much better world. So that's what motivated you, and sure, I think there was a feeling that you could die, but I don't think that preoccupied people. And I don't remember talking about that a lot. The thought would go through your mind, but we were motivated in a different way and weren't thinking that much about whether we might die.

## Richmond Oil Strike – And Taking Revolution to the Working Class

When we started taking up what we then called Marxism-Leninism, Mao Tsetung Thought (and we now call Marxism-Leninism-Maoism), we recognized that in order for there to be a revolution, it had to involve and activate people beyond the students and youth, even though there were millions of them who were actively involved in radical struggles and politics in one way or another. It had to spread beyond the Black people and Latinos and Native Americans and Asians, beyond only the oppressed peoples. The revolutionary movement had to reach more broadly in the society—that was really what the call from SNCC to take radical politics to poor whites was about.

Originally, we'd gone to Richmond to work among the poor whites —and we continued to work among them as well as people of other nationalities—but, as we became more Marxist, it was contradictory. We understood we had to be more scientific about all this, but as we took up a more scientific, Marxist approach, we also took up some ideas from the international communist movement that had actually gone away from the revolutionary core of Marxism and had taken things more in the direction of trade unionism and economism—that is, the idea that the key thing is to center everything around the immediate economic struggles of the workers—and toward a "lowest common denominator" kind of politics. We picked up some ideas from the history of the international communist movement which, since the 1930s, had been influenced by a lot of economism and reformism, and which more and more identified socialism with trade unionism and gradualism. The CP, and some others who claimed to be socialists, were deeply into and deeply bogged down in that, but we were also influenced by that. We began to see the more stable workers in larger factories and other workplaces as being the key force for socialism and communism and revolution, and put less emphasis on those proletarians whose life conditions were more unstable and volatile.

Now the one thing that characterized us in the Revolutionary Union —and this is something that has sustained us all the way through—is that we knew you needed revolution. We knew you needed a socialist transformation of society and that the proletariat had to rule and lead society in doing that. We knew the goal had to be communism through-out the world. We never let go of those things, and we kept reading theory and carrying on ideological struggle and debates and polemics about what that meant and how to do that. Even when we made a lot of mistakes, which of course we did, and even when we were pulled in the direction of wrong lines, and in particular these "workerist" or trade unionist tendencies, we never let go of that fundamental revolutionary and communist orientation. Actually, in the U.S. at that time, the work-ers in the larger plants and the unionized workforces were relatively bet-ter paid and relatively well off, and were not the most readily radicalized sections of the proletariat. But that's something we had to learn through practice and also through continuing to study.

As I've mentioned in other contexts, people used to say to me in those times, "You're very ideological." Sometimes they meant that as a criticism, as if I were too ideological or spent too much time studying theory and things like that. But it's *because* we were very ideological and recognized the importance of theory, that even when we got off the track, we could eventually correct our errors by summing up both our own practice and historical experience much more broadly and by grap-pling with theory and ideological struggle. So we were still working our way through all this, and that was kind of the good and the bad, or the positive and negative aspects, of how we got into the Richmond oil strike.

This was a strike by a group of workers who were in a union. Their jobs were actually for the times relatively "high tech," as we'd say now, even though it was manual labor. And they were relatively well paid. But this struggle got very intense, and there would be company goons who'd come out and attack the strikers; and the police, of course, would back Standard Oil and the company goons, so you'd get into it with police, too. I remember at one point one of the workers who was actively involved in this oil strike, and with whom we were working, said something which captured the contradictoriness that I've been speaking about. He was talking to a group of students who'd come out to join the picket line. There was a battle with the company goons, and then we went back to the union hall. And this worker told these students: "I used to think that I was part of the Establishment, but now I know that I'm not." This was a section of workers that thought of themselves in that way, but through this whole experience, not just of their own strike but also having these Third World students, as they were called—Black and Latino and Asian and Native American students, coming from Berkeley, coming from San Francisco State and bringing a radical alienation and radical politics to them—through that mix these workers were becoming more radicalized.

So this was all part of what we were doing. We were trying to integrate, as Mao said, with these workers, at the same time as we were discovering, and discovered over a number of years in the course of doing this, that while it's important to win over this section of the working class, this was not the force that was going to be the most radical backbone force for revolution and that actually we were closer in our original orientation of going to the poor whites and going to lower sections of the proletariat overall, not just whites, obviously, but all nationalities. These are things that you learn through the back-and-forth of theory and practice and the turmoil of all of that. And it takes a while to sort all this out.

But, as I said, we understood the importance of theory; we understood it was *good* to be very ideological; we understood the importance of *summing up* practice. We'd carried out a lot of practice, but we also saw the need to sum it up as scientifically as we could at any given time; and we understood that this all had to be in the service of making a revolution and getting rid of this system and bringing into being a socialist system in which the proletariat would take the lead in ruling and transforming society; that you needed a party to lead this, you needed a vanguard force; and that fundamentally this had to be an international struggle, that the final goal was communism throughout the world. That's what kept us going through all the mistakes that we made.

As Lenin once said about the Bolsheviks, when they first went out to make revolution they were like peasants going off to war, picking up whatever weapons were at hand. He meant that metaphorically, he was referring to political and ideological "weapons"; and that applied to us in the RU, too, because you had this whole thing with the Soviet Union having gone down the tubes and becoming capitalist in the name of socialism, and the Communist Party in the U.S. having followed in the wake of that. So, in a certain sense, we were "starting over." Of course, the CP had a *long* history of being pulled more and more to reformism. I mean, after all, it supported Roosevelt and the New Deal as far back as the 1930s. So this was a long-standing tendency in the CP, but then it had gone completely into the sewer when Khrushchev came to power in the Soviet Union and put forward his "peaceful transition" and all that. So we had to kind of rediscover Marxism, and that's what a lot of people —not just those of us in the RU at that time, but a lot of people—were struggling over: rediscovering Marxism; rediscovering revolution; rediscovering what is the problem, what is the solution, what program and what ideology do you need, and how should this be led—or *should* it even be led, which was a big question then, too, as it is now.

## The Revolution Comes to Richmond

Because of the whole general upheaval that I've been describing, and all the back and forth over different ideas and programs, people were following closely what was happening all over the country. People in other parts of the country were very intensely following what was happening with things like People's Park, and people who didn't go to the Democratic Convention in 1968 were very intensely following that, and there were a lot of people who felt themselves a part of a whole movement, wherever things were happening. As one important dimension of this, there were over a hundred newspapers that eventually developed that were either written by or directed to GIs in the U.S. military—radical and revolutionary newspapers. And in different locales around the U.S., a lot of people were putting out their own newspapers. There were many different ways in which people were circulating their ideas and their experience, and many, many people were wrestling with all this. Of course, there were differences, but people were struggling out their differences, and even where you had differences, you would still unite in a lot of ways.

So, through this whole kind of process many people came to know about what we were doing in Richmond and the whole banner that we were trying to raise in practice as well as in theory of "going to the pro-letariat." A number of people were attracted to that, and people would get in contact with us. Some couples moved to Richmond and there were also individuals who'd come. A number of women came on their own to become part of this, and that was significant. As I said, we sort of started out, a few of us, with this view of ourselves as "macho revolutionaries," but we were changing—and being changed—in that, too. The women's movement was beginning to develop, and expressing itself in different ways throughout society. The RU initiated a major International Women's Day rally in San Francisco in 1970, but well before that all these different influences were all part of the ferment and upheaval that we were part of, and that were influencing us in important ways.

So we had sort of an inner core of RU people there in Richmond, but then there were broader groupings of people there who were working collectively and struggling collectively, and there were a lot of things going on in Richmond. At the same time, the RU was developing as more of an organization throughout the Bay Area—in San Jose and Stanford, in San Francisco and Berkeley, and in Oakland as well. And one of the most lasting and important things is that there are some peo-ple who got involved, who came to Richmond at that time, and who have stayed with things, in one way or another, all the way since then. People I can think back to, from the days in Richmond 35 years ago. At the same time, everything that this experience taught us became part of the development of a whole revolutionary line and program and strate-gy, and in that way it contributed to the founding of the Revolutionary Communist Party in 1975 and to its further development. So all of that was important at the time, but also made a lot of lasting contributions.

Through all this work in Richmond, we started meeting more peo-ple. We would meet adults who had kids, or we would just meet kids who were in junior high or high school. I remember one great walkout where the kids in one of the junior highs in Richmond busted out and climbed over the fence. This was in support of the farmworkers, so they went down to the Safeway, which was being boycotted by the farm-workers, and trashed it. It became a big thing. Dozens of them were busted and the action was written up and denounced in the local paper. But we mobilized support for this, and they all got off without having to go to juvenile prison. We would write and pass out leaflets and pam-phlets about local issues as well as national and international events, and a number of kids just loved to pass these out in the junior high and high schools, partly because they agreed with it and were part of the whole movement, and also partly because they knew it really pissed off backward teachers and principals and school authorities, and they loved that part of it, too. In fact, some of the kids we knew hardly ever went to school, and one of the rare times they'd go is when they could take our pamphlets or leaflets in and pass them out and stir shit up.

So we were doing a lot of that, and then in 1969 there was this anti-Vietnam "moratorium" declared, with big demonstrations against the war back east and in San Francisco. As part of that, we got together with the Panthers, who were also in Richmond, and decided to call for a walkout and rally on the same day in Richmond. This had some really key elements that were missing from a lot of the other anti-war demonstrations. We focussed it in a park right across from Richmond High. And Richmond High was like—well, I think I mentioned before that when I was at Berkeley High people would say, "Richmond High! Even the white guys are tough over there!" It had this whole proletarian character to it.

We knew a teacher who taught at Richmond High. I went to his class one time, not long after we moved to Richmond, and I gave this whole rap about Vietnam—the history of it, what the U.S. was doing and why it was wrong, and so on. And I could tell that the students in the classroom had never heard this kind of stuff. Their teacher was progressive, but they'd never heard this whole thing laid out like this, and maybe part of the reason he invited me to talk to them was that he figured I could do this more easily than he could—he could just say he was having visiting speakers or whatever. So, while I'm laying out this rap on Vietnam, I can see in their faces and their body language that this is new to them. Finally a guy raises his hand and I was preparing myself for an argument, because I knew kids like this were bombarded with the standard pro-war propaganda—and this was a new experience for me, too. But he said: "What took you so long? How come you haven't come and talked to us about this kind of stuff before?" So I said, "Well, you know, that's a good point, but now we *are* here."

So we were building on that kind of thing when we went to Richmond High and put out a leaflet and called for a walkout and a rally. And about 500 people came to the rally, which was very significant for Richmond—there had never been an anti-war rally on that scale before in a place like Richmond, and it was overwhelmingly these proletarian youth, Black, Latino, and white, who walked out from the high school. Then, at the end of the rally about two to three hundred of us went over and surrounded the draft board in Richmond, which was drafting people out of Richmond but was also a good symbol of the whole war and the military. And it was a very militant demonstration. We found out later that the draft board was packed with pigs, just waiting for any excuse to attack, though things didn't come to a major confrontation that day. But we made our point, and it was very important to those who took part, and the youth in particular, that they were part of this whole bigger anti-war movement but had also made their statement right there, in Richmond. This was one of the high points of our work in Richmond.

A little while later, when students were shot and killed at Kent State and Jackson State,[21] we were already doing work at the junior college in Richmond, Contra Costa College, as well as other places. We had waged a struggle together with students at Contra Costa to get the college to fund a day care center, because there were a lot of proletarian students there who couldn't afford childcare in order to go to school. That was an important battle, but we were also doing a lot of other kinds of political organizing and educational work—passing out leaflets, having rallies, giving speeches, and holding protests.

So when Kent State happened, I remember speaking at a rally at Contra Costa College. Basically the whole college, or a large part of it, had come to a standstill, and the level of unity there was very high. There were some students there, including some veterans of the military and the Vietnam War, who had some differences with us, but on that day we were all very tight in our outrage and our support of the students at Kent State. And then we learned about the murders of Black students at Jackson State, and that became a question that we took to the students and others in Richmond as well. It was a very powerful day—basically the campus at Contra Costa College came to a standstill. Because of all the weight that proletarian people have on them, Contra Costa College,

---

21. On May 4, 1970, National Guardsmen killed four unarmed students demonstrating at Kent State University in Ohio. Shortly after that, on May 15, state troopers killed three Black students demonstrating at Jackson State, in Jackson, Mississippi. The killings sparked a nationwide student strike, massive demonstrations and, in many cases, further battles with police and National Guardsmen.

like Richmond in general, had not historically been a place where it was easy for people to mobilize themselves politically. And, as that high school student had spoken to, people weren't coming to them to bring them an understanding of these things and to enable them to learn about the world. But this was changing through our work and through the general upheaval that was going on.

### Learning From The Proletariat – Deep Bonds

Mao wrote about revolutionary youth going to the masses of working people and how, in his own experience, he learned a great deal more from them than he brought to them, even though obviously what he brought to them was very important. And this was also our experience in Richmond and my personal experience. We made not only many political ties but deep personal ties and friendships and relationships of various kinds with people that I still look back on very fondly. I think of the people often and feel strong bonds with them, even today.

There were many people who taught me many deep lessons. I remember this one white proletarian youth who was really just a beautiful guy. He was open to learning a lot of things, but he also *taught* me a tremendous amount, coming from his whole life experience and what the practical realities were, the difficulties of becoming politically active with the weight that was on him and on his mother, who was working a low-paying job trying to support the family. I still think about him a lot, and I remember very sadly, in fact, the last time I saw him. He came forward and became very revolutionary-minded and, as I said, he taught me a lot, but he was also pulled down by drugs at the time, and the last time I saw him we had a very deep-going, honest talk for several hours sitting in a car in Richmond, and he confided in me that he was hung up on heroin, and therefore he couldn't stay active in the revolution. This was a heartbreaking thing to me.

There were also some individuals in particular with whom I developed very deep bonds, people who mean a lot to me personally, and from whom I learned a great deal. For example, William Hinton wrote this book *Fanshen* about the experience of the Chinese Revolution. I used to read that book to some people in Richmond who didn't have a lot of formal education. And it was amazing to me—it really struck me—how readily and deeply they identified with the people who were the main characters, the poor peasants who were rising up to change the world in

China, as described in *Fanshen*.

But also, early on, when I was reading to them, they would often stop me and say, "I don't know what that word means." So, after a while, when I was reading to them, I would be looking out for this and I would change some of the wording as I was reading, breaking words down into other words, while keeping the meaning so that they would get the essence of it. I wasn't watering down what was being said, but I was changing the language as I read, because the people I'm talking about had been denied almost literally any kind of formal education because of the poverty and difficulty of their circumstances. So I had to break this down into language that would convey the same meaning, but that they would be able to get. I would always do my best to read in a way that wasn't leaving them behind. And there would be struggle and criticism because sometimes I would forget or wouldn't do it very well—or I'd go too far and they'd say, "You know, I'm not an idiot."

I still remember this very vividly and fondly to this time, and I also learned a great deal from it. Sometimes people would ask me, "How is it that you give these speeches that break things down so people can understand them?" And I would cite this experience as one of the main ways that I learned the importance of doing that. This is mainly a question of your political and ideological understanding, or political and ideological line, as we say, and how to actually understand things well enough to be able to break them down and popularize them; but there was this dimension as well that was crucial for me. Along with the deep personal ties I made, this was also a great learning experience for me. I was very fortunate to have this experience where I had these kind of ties and personal relations with people where they would speak honestly with me, let me know when what I was saying, or reading to them, was getting across to them, and when it was missing the mark.

This is something that has remained very valuable to me up to today. And, on a personal level, I still have very fond remembrances and strong deep feelings of affection for the people I was so close to then.

# Chapter Ten

# *Taking Responsibility*

It was the Panthers who turned me in the direction of revolution and turned me on to Mao and who were the main impetus initially propelling me in the direction which led to communism; and this is true even though they themselves were a mixed bag ideologically, with revolutionary nationalism mixed in with some communist inclinations and communist tendencies and influences. Then, in 1968 and '69, Leibel Bergman was the person who in a more systematic way steeped me in Marxism and actually helped me make the leap to taking up the ideology and the theory of communism. Overwhelmingly, his role was a very positive one, even with some of the views and tendencies that he still carried from the old CP, which would later grow and come to eat up his better side in the context of new challenges.

## The Panthers – Differences Develop

As I developed more as a communist, I also began to develop some differences with people like Eldridge, Bobby Seale, and other Panther leaders. I still respected them greatly as revolutionaries, and had tremendous appreciation for the kind of vanguard role they had played in putting revolution on the map when the CP and others who were supposed to be radically changing society had basically ruled revolution out of order. But there were a lot of pulls on the Panthers and a lot of ways in which their ideology was a mixture, as I've said, of revolutionary nation-

212

alism and some communism, and they never made the complete leap to becoming really fully communists. And, as I was making that leap, I developed differences and struggled with them, even while I was still actively working with and supporting them.

They were encountering severe repression and they were being influenced by groups like the CP, which was sending members into the Panthers at the same time as they were viciously attacking them in their official capacity as the CP. The CP would work to influence things in many different ways; for instance, it would help with legal assistance, but then use that to try to exert ideological and political influence. I'm not saying the problem was all the CP or mainly the CP. More, the fundamental thing is that you have to make a leap and a rupture to become a thoroughgoing communist and take up Marxism-Leninism-Maoism, as we say today. And if you don't make that leap and rupture, then you get pulled by a thousand different influences and forces—especially when you are facing the kind of brutal and vicious repression that the Panthers were facing, when they were at the leading edge of the revolutionary current and force that was developing. And, in turn, when you face that kind of repression, that can make it even more difficult for you to make crucial ideological leaps and ruptures. As I was moving more fully in the direction of communism and they, frankly, were not, naturally our differences became more pronounced.

By 1969, partly at the suggestion of the CP and partly from the Panthers' feeling a need generally to deal with the repression they were facing, they came up with this idea of building a united front against fascism. They were basically saying that U.S. society was already fascist. I remember having a discussion with Bobby Seale where he put that forward, and I didn't agree with that. I didn't think it was scientific analysis. I knew there was tremendous repression the Panthers in particular were facing, being in a real sense at the leading point of the struggle against this system. But it was not scientific and correct to say that the society as a whole was fascist. Taking that position, and calling for a united front against fascism, was a way of trying to build a broader united front but doing it, frankly, by watering down the political stance somewhat and appealing to people more on the basis of bourgeois democracy. Now, it's not wrong to appeal to people whose viewpoint is still in the framework of bourgeois democracy to unite with you against repression. You have to do that. But essentially to make upholding bourgeois democracy the basis of unity, in the name of fighting fascism, represented a backing off of some of the more revolutionary positions the Panthers had taken, although they still upheld some of these revolutionary positions—I don't mean to oversimplify it.[23]

I remember in the midst of this, there was a meeting in Oakland that the Panthers had called to organize for this conference to build a united front against fascism. We in the RU had decided to take part in this and to fight to bring a more revolutionary and anti-imperialist line into this conference, as opposed to the more bourgeois-democratic line that people like the CP were pushing and that the Panthers, frankly, were being drawn to. So I came into this meeting in Oakland, and Bobby Seale was leading the meeting. As I walked in, I recognized a number of Black people that I knew were members of the CP, and my heart just sank because I knew what that represented. As I said, many people regarded me as "very ideological," and sometimes they used that as a point of attack, as if being very ideological were somehow bad. So, as I walked in and sat down in the meeting, Bobby Seale turned to me—well, he turned to everybody really—and said: "Oh, here's Bob Avakian. Have you come here to talk about ideology or have you come here to do work?" And I answered: "Well, I've come here to do both. But let me ask *you* a question. In the world today, there are basically two ideologies, bourgeois ideology and proletarian ideology"—then I looked at all the CPers in the room and I continued—"which ideology is in command in *this* meeting?" And then it seemed that the temperature in the room dropped twenty degrees, and there was a tense pause before we went on with the meeting.

Later in 1969, around the same time that Fred Hampton was killed by the pigs in Chicago while he slept, and about the same time as the L.A. police launched a massive assault on the Panther office in that city and sparked a shoot-out lasting several hours when the Panthers inside defended themselves, it became clear that there very well could be a plan by the government, coordinated nationally, to attack all the Panther offices and to murder as many Panthers as they could. So the leadership of the Panthers in the Bay Area, where the national headquarters of the

---

23. For more discussion on the complexities of the strategy of the united front under the leadership of the proletariat, see the series of articles "Revolutionary Strategy: Uniting All Who Can Be United," by Bob Avakian, at rwor.org.

Panthers was, put out a call to their supporters, and other people more broadly, to come sit in the offices and defend them against attack—to be sort of a shield against attack. And so a number of us in the RU mobilized a squad of people to go to the national Black Panther Party office, prepared to defend the Panther office and the Panthers in the face of attack.

At that particular time no attack came on the Panther national office in Berkeley, but while we were there some of the Panther members decided to do some political education. This was after Eldridge Cleaver, who had gone into exile, had gone to North Korea and sent back word about how great it was. And I didn't agree with this at all, because I'd done some reading about Kim Il Sung and North Korea, and I viewed Kim Il Sung frankly as more like a feudal monarch than anything having to do with socialism and communism. So when this Panther guy stood up in front of a packed room of people in the Panther national office and started saying, "Well, Eldridge has told us that Kim Il Sung is the real revolutionary—he's much more revolutionary than Mao Tsetung," I just couldn't let that go. Even though I was there to do whatever it took to defend the Panther office if it were attacked, I had to speak up. So I said, "Well, I just don't agree with that, Kim Il Sung is not more revolutionary than Mao. Kim Il Sung is not really revolutionary, and North Korea is not really socialist; Kim Il Sung is not an outstanding communist leader at all, let alone a great leader like Mao." So, of course, a lot of tension resulted from this, and it carried over beyond this particular situation.

This gives you an idea, once again, of the complexity of things. We were developing some differences with the Panthers, but when it was a question of defending them, particularly against vicious attack from the state, there was no question that we were going to rally to their defense and put ourselves on the line for that—even while we carried out struggle with them over major ideological questions of great importance.

Now, the ideological struggle I was engaged in with the Panthers was complicated because some of the Panthers' thinking about what section of people are the revolutionary force, what they called the "lumpen proletariat," was a matter of their partly talking about the lumpen proletariat but largely talking about lower sections of the proletariat that I have since come to more fully recognize are a driving force and a key force in revolution, especially the youth among them. And, as I said earlier, we in the RU at that time had this view of going more to the organized, unionized workers in some of the larger factories and plants. So, it was contradictory because in one sense their idea of who was the revolutionary force might have been closer to reality than ours at that time, but the *ideology* that they were mobilizing or seeking to mobilize people around was not a scientific revolutionary ideology and couldn't lead all the way to revolution, and definitely not to socialism and communism. So that was kind of the contradictoriness of it.

But, despite our ideological differences, we did participate in the united front against fascism conference that the Panthers held, and I spoke there, struggling for an anti-imperialist and revolutionary line in opposition to particularly the influence of the CP and the way in which the CP was once again seeking to drag things down to the "lowest common denominator," raising the banner of fighting fascism in order to uphold bourgeois democracy and make that the basis of unity of the movement.

### The RU Goes National

By 1970, it had been a couple of years since the RU had been formed. The RU had developed into a fairly significant disciplined, organized force of revolutionaries in the Bay Area. Overall, we were still hoping that the Panther Party, or at least key forces that were part of or around the Panther Party, as well as some other revolutionary forces, would be part of the formation of a single multinational communist vanguard. Forming such a party was still our objective, but we realized that we would have to play more of a role in this than we'd recognized before or were capable of playing before. We saw that, all around the country, there were people who had formed revolutionary collectives and generally associated themselves with communism. And the movement was at a high peak. Perhaps, if you weren't part of that whole experience, it's difficult to really grasp this, but literally millions of people were, on one level or another, sympathetic to and supportive of the idea of revolution at that time. Hundreds of thousands who were actively involved in the struggle had revolutionary sentiments and aspirations, and there were literally not just hundreds but thousands of people who were trying to organize themselves in some kind of revolutionary way, although often with a mixed bag of ideologies.

We recognized that if we didn't do our best not just to remain a force in the Bay Area and hope to link up with others eventually, but to draw together right then as many forces as we could around the country who could be won to a communist line and program, and to do that on a multinational basis—if we didn't do that, then this whole upsurge and in particular the most advanced forces within this upsurge were in effect going to be lost and dissipated, and no vanguard communist party would emerge from this high tide. If we didn't make a leap then to being organized on a higher level, if we didn't take more responsibility for this struggle to form a new, genuinely communist and revolutionary party, however long that took; and in particular if we didn't go throughout the country and try to pull together, into a single organization, people of all different nationalities who could be united on the basis of a communist line, then the prospects for bringing such a new party into being would be greatly set back.

Looking back on those times, it's possible to say, "Well, maybe a revolutionary situation could have fully emerged at that time." There was the political upsurge and crisis around Kent State and Jackson State, which came in response to the Nixon administration's expanding the war much more fully into Cambodia, bombing and invading Cambodia. This was in the face of years and years of protests and rebellions and militant demonstrations and fighting in the streets against this war—Johnson had even been forced to not run for reelection—and yet here's the government escalating the war again. This radicalized millions more people and helped—or propelled—them to make another leap. And this was on top of all the protests and rebellions that had gone on, and reached a high peak, for several years, throughout different parts of society. So the situation was very ripe, but partly because of our own primitiveness, ideologically and politically, we in the RU didn't fully recognize the potential right then.

But, what was of great importance, and what we *did* recognize, was that in order for there to be a revolution, there needed to be a vanguard force, a united revolutionary communist party, and people of all different nationalities and groupings, who had come forward in different parts of the country, had to be pulled together. We recognized that it wasn't yet time to form the party, but that a crucial next step had to be made. And that was to make a leap in developing the Revolutionary Union as a pre-party formation, to develop it further as a leading force within this whole revolutionary upsurge, to develop it further as a multinational organization, drawing together revolutionaries of all nationalities, and drawing together people from all these different streams across the country who'd come to a revolutionary position. That would be a key step in laying more of the groundwork for the formation of a vanguard party that could lead the revolution.

For that reason, as the summer of 1970 approached, Leibel Bergman came to me and some others in the RU and proposed that we go on a nationwide tour—get in a car, a few of us, and drive around the country and try to link up with and win over all these different revolutionary forces throughout the country. And that's what we set out to do, in the summer of 1970.

### On the Road

This tour actually had a false start. We'd borrowed a car from one of these newer comrades in the RU, but it wasn't a very big car and it was so loaded down that when we got a few miles out on the highway it started rocking from side to side, and when we put the brakes on, it would start shaking. That wasn't going to work, so we went to another comrade and borrowed his car. But he said, "the only problem is that sometimes it won't start." So fairly frequently during this trip I had to get underneath the car and get a screwdriver and put it to *just* the right spot on the starter motor to get the thing to spark and start up. Nevertheless, we took off.

All over the country, off the '60s, collectives were forming which were communist, or "halfway communist," and we were seeking to link up with these people and have discussion with them and try to win them to become part of the RU. We mainly traveled in the midwest and the east. We went to Baltimore, where we stayed in an apartment in the city that was too small for all of us, so a bunch of us slept on the floor, including Leibel, who wasn't that—I was going to say, "wasn't that young then," but he was actually younger then than I am now, so I have to be careful. But we slept on the floor and stayed with these people who had a collective in Baltimore. And we went to Philadelphia and New York and New Jersey, and up into New England, and then into Ohio, and sometimes a couple of us would make a side trip to go talk to students in places like Penn State. We went through Michigan and Illinois, and other places in the Midwest—everywhere we went we were searching out people who were either part of, or knew of people who were part of, these collectives that were forming.

There were four of us—Jane Franklin (who would later split from the RU), Leibel, another comrade, and myself. We'd stay at people's places, we'd get into a lot of discussion and struggle, and sometimes it went better than others. When we went to places like Jersey City, I remember being struck at the time by the devastation of large parts of the city. Even at that time, three decades ago, there were just huge numbers of burnt-out buildings that looked like they'd been through a war or just allowed to rot. And there were a lot of junkies around—it was very stark conditions. One of the people we were meeting with in New Jersey would talk about how you would be walking down the street there and people would pop out of nowhere to try to sell you drugs, asking "are you looking...are you looking...?" That became kind of a joke when we were talking with these people—we turned it into a thing of "are you looking...for communism?" (Since that time, from what I have learned, Jersey City has become one of those "re-invented cities" where sections have been rehabilitated and essentially gentrified for people with more money, while other sections have been left to rot even further.)

In Ohio, we met with a group of people based at Antioch College who had formed a more or less communist collective. But it was a newly formed collective and they were still going through a lot of changes themselves. And the work we did with this collective shows you the other side of Leibel Bergman, because while he had a very positive side that he brought to the RU and brought to my own development, he also had this pragmatic, whatever-works kind of streak that he'd picked up from the old CP.

The old CP had at least two big faults: they tailed after American patriotism and "American democracy"; and they were extremely pragmatic, especially from the mid-1930s on. They just put themselves under the umbrella of Roosevelt and the New Deal and became the "best Americans." When the CP sent people to the Abraham Lincoln Brigades to fight in the Spanish Civil War, the joke went around—which had a definite reality to it—"How can you tell who's in the CP?" And the answer was, "It's those people who know not just the first verse but every verse to the Star Spangled Banner."

So there was a history of tailing after American patriotism. Leibel used to tell us this story about a big unemployed demonstration in the

'30s, where this crowd milled around, not knowing what to do, and then he said the big dramatic moment came when a veteran from World War 1 picked up the American flag and said, "Let's go, boys." We used to always tease Leibel about this—"What's so fucking great about picking up the American flag?!" But that was the CP and that was the tradition that he came out of, even though he broke with it when they followed Khrushchev all the way into the swamp of just totally betraying revolution, socialism and communism.

The other thing that was very strong in the CP, a big tendency in American society that they had taken up—and which was also a big weakness of Leibel—was pragmatism: whatever works, in the short run, whatever gets you over, is true and good.

And this came out when we were meeting with this collective of people at Antioch. The question came up: what does it take to be a part of the RU, what principles do you have to agree to? We started getting into this discussion, and the question of Stalin in particular was very controversial. I mentioned earlier how I'd gone to Columbia University with *Red Papers 1*, with the pictures of Marx, Engels, Lenin, Mao, and Stalin on the cover, and this was a very controversial issue. Now, again, we didn't uphold Stalin uncritically, we had many criticisms and we've since developed them further and deepened them in the RCP. But still, from an historical perspective, we were upholding Stalin as the leader of the first historical experience in building socialism, in the Soviet Union. We were, and are, firmly of the view that in evaluating and, yes, in criticizing, what was done in the Soviet Union it is necessary to keep in mind—and is completely ahistorical and nonmaterialist to ignore—the extremely difficult circumstances in which this took place. This was an unprecedented struggle, there was no prior experience in building a socialist society, and it had to be carried out in a situation where the Soviet Union was, from the beginning, surrounded, threatened, and outright invaded and attacked, by imperialist powers, with tremendous losses, including more than 20 million Soviet citizens killed during World War 2. All this was a big issue in general in the movement that developed during and out of the '60s, and it was an important question for the people in this collective at Antioch. So they started raising questions about that, and Leibel said, "Oh never mind about that, you can just come in and we'll work all that out later." And I was saying, "No, no, no, wait a minute, these are important issues, there's no point in having people come in on just any old basis—we'd end up splitting because the basis of unity wouldn't be deep and it would just be a kind of opportunist alliance." Well, we finally resolved that, on the correct basis, through further discussion and struggle, over the question of Stalin and other important questions.

## Cuba, Vietnam...and the Soviet Union

It was important, as a matter of principle, that the basis of unity on which we built the RU really be founded on something real, that it be deeply founded and not just superficial. But the importance of this was further underscored, as I was becoming increasingly aware then, by the fact that differences were beginning to develop inside the RU itself. These differences centered around a range of ideological and political and even organizational questions, and a different line on these questions was being formulated and fought for by Bruce and Jane Franklin, who had been part of the RU since shortly after its formation. The Franklins had been organizing people at Stanford University and in the Palo Alto area. The Franklins claimed at the time to be upholding Mao and to be organizing people on the basis of the RU's principles, but increasingly they were doing something different.

At that time in the communist movement there was a very strong current of people who identified with China and took up the Red Book and followed Mao, but who were also influenced by trends like that represented by the Vietnamese Party. The Vietnamese seemingly maintained an independent stance, siding with neither China nor the Soviet Union in the great struggle and split that had developed in the international communist movement, once Khrushchev had come to power and began pushing his revisionist theses and in fact moving to restore capitalism in the Soviet Union. But in fact, despite their seeming "neutral stance," the Vietnamese were largely and increasingly in the Soviet camp. And the same was true of Cuba.

Now a number of people in the U.S. had gone to Cuba and were bringing back the "Cuban variety" of pro-Soviet politics and ideology, and the Franklins were trying to recruit people like that into the RU. So there was a lot of turmoil about that kind of thing, because those of us who wanted to be consistently Maoist, as we say now, didn't want people coming into the RU who would be bringing in these seemingly centrist but in reality pro-Soviet revisionist positions. We didn't want to bring in people who were supporting Cuba and refused to draw clear and firm distinctions between what was represented by Cuba, especially now that it was clearly in the Soviet camp, and on the other hand the revolutionary line which was represented by Mao and China.

I remember that, just about this time, Venceremos Brigades were organized to go to Cuba: people would go and cut sugar cane and they would basically be propagandized by the Cubans; it was a way of getting people into the pro-Soviet camp. It is important to realize that at that time most people who were coming forward as radicals and revolutionaries and beginning to consider themselves communists were very turned off by the Soviet Union, because they could see that there was nothing revolutionary about the Soviet Union. However they understood it, and whether they had a really deep scientific understanding of this or not, they saw the Soviet Union as just another world power contending for its interests—and they recognized that its interests and what it was doing in the world had very little, or really nothing, to do with revolution. Revolutionary-minded people were turned off by that, but then these other countries like Vietnam, which was standing up to the U.S., or Cuba, which in its own way was defying the U.S., were more attractive to people who were radical but hadn't really gotten deeply into communist philosophy and its scientific viewpoint and method for understanding the world. So a lot of ways in which the Soviets tried to influence people like that would be through the Vietnamese or through the Cubans. And, with regard to people in the U.S. in particular, Cuba was a very important vehicle for this—hundreds, probably thousands of people, mainly youth, went down to Cuba on these Venceremos Brigades.

Around the same time as we were doing this tour around the country, the RU sent a few comrades to be part of one of these Venceremos Brigades and to struggle with people during the course of this. Since we recognized that a lot of radical and revolutionary-minded people were being drawn to these Brigades, we wanted to influence them toward Maoism, as we would now say. So we sent these comrades down there, but when you are among other people, in certain circumstances you may influence them but they influence you as well. And that is what happened with the comrades we sent on this Venceremos Brigade. This came out when we had a meeting with these comrades after they had come back from Cuba. Some of us in leadership of the RU, including myself and Bruce and Jane Franklin, were talking with these comrades about their experiences in Cuba and what they had learned, and at one point one of our people who'd been on this trip to Cuba started referring to "the Sino-Soviet split." So I stopped him and I said, "Wait a minute, we don't talk about the Sino-Soviet split—you mean the struggle against Soviet revisionism that China is leading?" And immediately Bruce Franklin jumped in and said to me: "I don't think you have the right attitude here, this is a bad method you're using. We sent these comrades down to Cuba and, now that they've come back, we should be trying to learn from them." I responded: "Well, I'm very anxious to learn as much as I possibly can from them, but one thing I don't want to learn from them is revisionism."

So this was the situation and the struggle that was developing inside the RU itself at the same time as we were setting out to spread the RU around the country. As a matter of general principle I was concerned that we not bring people into the RU on the kind of pragmatic, "whatever works," basis that Leibel Bergman was pushing. But also more particularly I was concerned about this because of this situation where the Franklins, who were an influential and leading force within the RU, were trying to bring in people who would bring about a weakening of the communist position in the RU—who would represent a revisionist influence, to put it baldly, right inside the RU. Especially in those circumstances, I was very concerned to ensure that, when we went on this tour to spread the RU around the country, we would be spreading communism and not some centrist, eclectic mish-mash of communism and revisionism, which wouldn't have any solid foundation and would fall apart or degenerate into an opportunist organization.

You see, one of the characteristics of the movement at that time was a lot of eclectics—a little bit of this, a little bit of that, without clear lines of demarcation over some fundamental matters of principle. People were newly coming forward and hadn't sorted out a lot of these things. You'd see people who would have a Red Book and then a t-shirt with a picture of Che Guevara on it—they weren't drawing distinctions between these different lines, they hadn't gone deeply into what *really* is communist philosophy, what *really* is the communist viewpoint and method, what *really* is a communist program. Anything and everything that was more or less opposed to U.S. imperialism was often thrown together by people, or seen as all part of the same thing.

A process was going on, among some people, of sorting all this out, but then there was a much broader movement where a lot of this eclectics characterized things. And it was very important to draw the distinction between what characterized the broader movement, on the one hand, and what characterized those who were uniting on the basis of communism, and seeking to build a new, genuinely revolutionary and communist party that could act as the vanguard for the whole struggle. Within the broader movement, to have many different ideologies and programs contending, and even mixed up with each other, was natural and, in a basic sense, fine. But to have that within a *communist* organization was the kiss of death.

In the RU, as a communist organization, we had already drawn certain clear lines of demarcation. We already were very clear on the role of Cuba—that Cuba was in the camp of the Soviet Union fundamentally, and in fact its apparent centrism actually served the Soviet Union as a revisionist power which was itself "social-imperialist," socialist in name but capitalist and imperialist in deed and in essence. We'd drawn those distinctions and understood the role of Cuba in that way. And while we continued to support the Vietnamese people's struggle against U.S. imperialism, and regarded this struggle as heroic—and recognized that in some ways, in a practical sense, at least, it was on the front lines of the fight against U.S. imperialism—we'd also seen that the Soviet Union was increasingly exerting its influence within that struggle, utilizing the fact that the Vietnamese were up against this great world power and offering weaponry—even though they didn't offer them their most advanced weaponry—to fight the U.S., and then using that as political and ideological leverage. Yet, even though the RU as an organization had made these analyses and drawn these lines of demarcation, people like the Franklins and others were trying to blur those lines and to bring people into the RU who were, at best, unclear about these crucial questions and at worse represented a kind of centrist, pro-revisionist position.

## Striking Out Boldly

Looking at the situation overall at the time, I saw all the more reason to get out there very boldly to spread the RU, even with these conflicts within the RU. There was a lot of ferment going on and a lot of people were engaging the process of trying, at least, to sort out these different lines, tendencies and political trends. They were trying to come to an understanding of the "correct line," as we say. Today, when I hear all these attacks on "political correctness," I shake my head, because smuggled into this seems to be the notion that somehow being "politically correct" is a bad thing, as if being politically *incorrect* were somehow a good thing. Of course, dogmatism is not a good thing, being unable to distinguish between what is really a major matter of principle and what is a minor matter is not good and can lead to bad consequences. But, really, much of the attack on "political correctness" is an attempt to undermine the very necessary opposition to and struggle against profound injustices and outrages which are in fact built into the system in the U.S. and its role in the world. Fundamentally, I have to agree with Mao: not having a correct political, and ideological, line is like having no soul. By "line" I mean your analysis of reality and of how to change it—what kind of change you see as necessary and how you see going about the realization of that change.

So there was all that ferment at that time, as a result of the whole upsurge through the '60s and into the early '70s. I and other leaders within the RU felt that if we didn't dive into this ferment and struggle to win people to a communist line, then we would lose a lot of these people, a lot of them wouldn't get clarity on these questions. And, if we didn't bring people together in one organization, then even if some people got more clarity on these questions, they would remain sort of isolated from each other—and it's very difficult to maintain yourself as a communist organization with just a small number of people isolated from others in pockets around the country. It was necessary for people to become part of an organization nationally that could all pull together and struggle out some of these questions together, and on a certain foundation. So we really felt we'd be dissipating a lot of this development if we didn't expand. There were these "new communist forces" coming forward, who in a general sense were rejecting the Soviet Union and recognized that it had nothing to do with communism or socialism or revolution, but were still trying to thrash out questions like: what is the road to socialism, and what should socialism be like, and what about communism—is that the ultimate goal and how you do you get there? And what does this mean in a country like the U.S.?

People recognized that the U.S. is very different than Russia was in 1917, or China in the 1930s and '40s; so, while a lot could and should be learned from those revolutions, making revolution in the U.S. was a very different, and of course very daunting, challenge.

All these big questions were getting thrown up by the development of things, and lots of people around the country were forming groups and collectives of various kinds to try to grapple with them. So we felt that, in a real sense, there was opportunity but also a necessity to go out and link up with and struggle with these groups and try to pull them together on the basis of the line that the RU had in fundamental terms united around.

Even while I was aware that there were these different lines, or different tendencies, developing within the RU, we did have a set of principles that we'd put forth in *Red Papers 1* and these principles of unity were supposed to be the basis on which we were united and on which we brought new people into the RU. And these principles didn't include things like support for Cuba or other "centrist" and revisionist positions! But just because you have principles that you united around at one time doesn't mean that that's the way things stay. Struggle develops, different things happening in the world influence people, different trends develop and take shape within any organization, and especially if you're engaged in practical struggle and engaging with other trends and other forces in the movement, it is once again a matter where you influence them and they influence you. You're not existing in some sort of rarified, "pure" situation, sealed off from the larger society; these trends penetrate into your organization and exert their influence. And that's what was happening in the RU.

But at this time, in the summer of 1970, this hadn't fully developed yet, it hadn't yet come to a head. If, as happened a few months later, we had been right in the midst of an all-out, full-blown struggle between two different lines, two fundamentally different positions and analyses, then we wouldn't have been able to go on this tour to spread the RU, or it would have been a big mistake to do so. But things hadn't yet ripened to that level, and it was actually a good thing we did embark on this tour, because we were mainly able to win people to the correct position, in accordance with our principles of unity, and to build the RU as a national organization, which was the outcome of this tour.

But then the struggle did erupt in a full-blown way inside the RU a few months after that, and the people who had newly come into the organization were confronted with this struggle within the organization that they'd just joined, although that struggle mainly took its most acute expressions in the Bay Area, where the RU had developed over a couple of years and where these opposing lines had become more full-blown.

## Nationalism...and Marxism

The tour itself was full of interesting and challenging experiences, which shed more light on key questions of line. From back before Leibel left the Communist Party in the late '50s, he had known this guy, DH. Within the CP some sort of a caucus, or a sort of a semi-secret group, had formed that was supposed to be more radical than the CP itself. And this guy DH had been part of this grouping in a loose sense, even while he had also been part of the Chicago area Panthers for a while. DH's father had been in the CP, and Leibel had known his father, and so, when we went to Chicago, DH was one of the people we met with.

We got into a discussion about the RU principles and how we were based on Marxism-Leninism and Mao Tsetung Thought, as it was then called. So we started discussing and debating a bit about how this ideology applied to different questions in the world and in the U.S. itself. And, at one point, we were talking about the national question—that is, the oppression of Black people and other oppressed nationalities, what the socialist revolution represented in terms of ending that oppression —and how the RU approached that. We were having some back and forth about how to analyze and understand this question and in particular how would the emancipation of Black people fit into the larger socialist revolution in the U.S. And I remember DH saying, "Well, no white person can tell me that they know more than I do about the Black experience and what it means to be Black in the U.S.—or even that they know as much about that as I do." This was directed at me, because he and I were getting into some struggle about certain aspects of this. So I said: "Well, if you're talking about *perceptual* knowledge, I agree; if you're talking about *conceptual* knowledge, I don't agree." And the temperature in the room went down about twenty-five degrees.

What I was saying was, "Look, if you want to talk about the direct aspects of this experience—what it feels like, what it means in that sense, to be Black in America, of course what you're saying is true. Somebody who is not Black is not going to be able to know that in the same way and experience that directly in the same way. But if you're talking about how to analyze that experience and put it in the context of the

larger society and the world as a whole—and how that fits into the overall revolutionary struggle, the crucial role it plays in relation to that
overall revolutionary struggle and the transformation of society and the
development of socialism and ultimately communism throughout the
world—if you're talking about analyzing all *that*, then it's not a matter
that if you're Black you automatically understand that more correctly or
more fully than someone who's not Black."

Otherwise you would get into "identity politics," as it's called now,
where only people who have a direct experience of a particular kind of
oppression are said to be able to really analyze or have anything substantial to say about that, and fundamentally you can't have a unified
understanding of reality and you can't unite people around a larger program to transform the society as a whole and uproot all oppression. That
is what we were battling out—and the same question, of course, is being
battled out now. But through the course of this, for whatever reasons,
DH did decide to become a part of the RU, and in fact after a certain
while he became a leader within the RU, and then later a struggle sharpened up with him and others over some of these same questions, when
these questions posed themselves more acutely a few years down the
road.

## Anarchism...and Marxism

That was one important experience of this tour, but it was one of
many. With different groups and different collectives there were different experiences and different questions that came up as key things to dig
into and struggle over deeply. Among some collectives, especially those
that had formed among students, questions arose about the dictatorship
of the proletariat: why do you need a state through which the proletariat
rules society and suppresses the overthrown bourgeoisie and other
counterrevolutionary forces? There were certain tendencies toward
anarchism: "Okay, we need to overthrow this system, but once we do
that, why do we need to suppress anybody then, why do we need a state
at all? Since the new society will be in the interests of the great majority, we won't need a state."

Questions of this kind had to be battled out in order to unite people
on the basis of a communist line. And, while we didn't understand it as
fully as we have come to understand it over 30 and more years since
then, even then we had a fundamental understanding that at this stage

of history, societies are divided into classes and that this system is ruled by a capitalist class; and that when you overthrow their rule, the capitalists are not just going to give up, they're going to try every way they can to undermine and destroy the new society you're building and to regain power so they can restore capitalism. And we had a basic understanding that, besides the overthrown capitalists, new elements will emerge within socialist society who don't want to see the socialist transformation of society carried out, or don't want it carried beyond a certain point, because they still enjoy certain privileges—these forces will jump out to oppose the advance of the socialist revolution, and you have to have a state that prevents them from seizing power, or else the old society will in fact be restored, with all the suffering that means for the masses of people.

### Dogmatism...and Marxism

Many of these questions got battled out on this tour, and it was a very lively and exciting process. There were just the four of us out there on the road, and besides all the ideological struggle, we had some hairy experiences driving late at night, or early in the morning, when we were all exhausted. One time Leibel took a wrong turn and was going the wrong way on an interstate highway in Ohio. For a little while, we didn't even realize that we were going the wrong way, because it was dawn and there wasn't a lot of traffic yet, but then we saw some cars up ahead of us—coming toward us, on the same side of the highway! Somehow, we managed to turn the car around quickly and avoid a disaster. As the saying goes, that was all part of the experience. And somehow, having escaped with our lives, it added to the whole feeling of adventure—it became one of those stories you tell with a certain odd kind of fondness, even though you would never want to repeat the experience!

In Maryland we heard about this guy named Robere who had committed to memory a large body of the "scripture" of Marxism, as he treated it—in other words, he'd memorize it and then recite it and try to intimidate people. These people in Maryland told us how he'd come in and destroyed their collective with his dogmatism. Most of these people in this particular collective were white and Robere was Black, so they were reluctant to struggle with him, and that kind of merged with the way in which they were awed by the fact that he could regurgitate long sections of what Mao or Lenin had written. This experience, too, held some important lessons—about the destructive force of dogmatism and the danger of blindly tailing things like nationalism.

People, of course, did need to grapple with theory at that point, and many were. They were reading Lenin, many people had the Red Book and some were getting into other writings by Mao. People were also studying things by Marx—at least the *Communist Manifesto* and perhaps some other writings by Marx—and maybe a very few people had read *Capital*. That's why this guy Robere was able to influence and awe people—they had some appreciation of the importance of theory, but some of them had a hard time distinguishing the living study and application of theory from an approach that reduced theory to dogma, and even went to ridiculous lengths of memorizing and regurgitating it.

Marxism is not a scripture, it's not a religious dogma, it's a scientific approach to reality. But it can be *turned into* religious dogma. At that time, many people were new to this theory, and there is a tendency, whenever you're new to anything, to be somewhat mechanical about it. If you recognize at a certain point that you need to take up theory, there can be a tendency to take it up somewhat mechanically, to not really have a correct approach to theory itself or a correct understanding of the relationship between theory and practice. So, especially when you are new to this, you can get into a kind of dogmatic tendency yourself, and then if somebody comes along who is even more dogmatic than you are, or has committed to memory and can regurgitate a lot of theory, it might seem as if they are really deeply steeped in it. This is a wrong and harmful approach to theory in general, and it is an especially wrong and harmful approach to Marxism. Marxism is, and must be, a living, critical, creative, scientific approach to reality—Marxism is not a dogma. And if it gets turned into a dogma then it becomes something very bad instead of something very liberating.

This Robere was a peculiar case, but among other people, including some students and intellectuals who take up Marxism, there can be a tendency toward a "scholastic" approach to Marxism. For example, I knew someone who was reading all forty-plus volumes of Lenin's *Collected Works*. I saw him one day and I said, "Hey, Mike, what are you up to?" and he replied, "Volume 40." He was reading all of Lenin's works, but he was doing it in a way that was divorced from practice, and so it was turning into its opposite. Instead of a living, scientific approach to understanding and changing reality, he was in effect treating it as a dogma.

Many people, on the other hand, were more influenced by pragmatism—"we just gotta go out and do it, we just gotta go out among the people and talk about revolution." They didn't recognize or appreciate the need for revolutionary theory to *guide* what they were doing. These different tendencies existed within the various collectives we met with, and we were struggling through all this as best we understood it at the time.

I think that we in the RU were able to handle the relationship between theory and practice in a basically correct way because, from early on, there were a few veterans of the communist movement—Leibel Bergman in particular, but a few others as well—who helped us develop an understanding of the importance of theory, and of linking it with practice. Despite certain pragmatic tendencies and certain tendencies toward reformism, which became more and more pronounced in Leibel as things developed and we faced new and difficult challenges, he nevertheless did bring a basic grounding in Marxism to us and fought for that to be taken up by the embryonic group that became the RU. We had an important, and not very common, combination—or, as we say, synthesis—of people like myself and others who were very definitely activists and very much involved in all different streams of the struggle of the time, people who had become very radical-minded and were influenced in a very radical way by the Panthers and other forces, both in the U.S. and internationally, on the one hand; and, combined with that, we had the body of Marxism that had been brought to us and which we'd begun to take up and to grasp in a beginning way, and which as time went on, we were able to more deeply immerse ourselves in and grapple with.

So we were able, through the *Red Papers* and through our work overall, to present that sort of a synthesis, and people could sense that. That had a fairly significant impact. When we went around on this tour people knew about the RU from *Red Papers* and from "the talk in the movement," if you will—they knew that we had these two elements together, theory and practice, including the practice of actually working, in a beginning way, to take revolutionary politics and ideology to the proletariat.

A couple of years later, we in the RU had an encounter and confrontation ourselves with Robere. In the spring of 1972, there was a major anti-war demonstration in the east, and in San Francisco tens of thousands of people mobilized once again against the Vietnam War. We had decided in the RU that, while it was good to have these broad-based demonstrations, there was a real problem in that the leadership of these things was generally pretty mainstream, with a lot of mainstream politicians and other similar types featured as the spokespeople of these demonstrations, and this set the tone for the whole thing. We knew that there were a lot of people who opposed the war with more advanced sentiments, and that it was important to organize a more advanced or more radical expression within this larger demonstration.

So we set out to organize what we called an anti-imperialist contingent, and when it finally all came together on the day of the demonstration it was really beautiful—there were something like five thousand people in this contingent, and it was bordered by red flags. This contingent put out very advanced slogans in support of the Vietnamese people and calling for their victory in the struggle against U.S. imperialism. There were thousands of people chanting these slogans, people in the contingent and others among whom these slogans resonated and caught on, and as we marched into the stadium where the rally was being held, the sounds of these slogans were reverberating and the red flags were flying, and it was very powerful.

But in building this contingent we got into a lot of struggle with people who wanted to turn this into a very sectarian kind of thing, in the guise of being super-revolutionary. Had they prevailed, it would have turned off a lot of people. They were running this dogmatic kind of nonsense that would have been laughable if it weren't so potentially damaging—like insisting that there be something against feudalism in the name of this contingent, even though that did not make any sense in the context of this demonstration.

So we had to fight to defeat this kind of dogmatism, and in the course of this we encountered this character Robere, whom we had heard about from people in that collective that he wrecked in Maryland. He had come into the Bay Area and was part of this whole dogmatic, sectarian effort to in effect wreck the anti-imperialist contingent we were building for this anti-war demonstration. At one point, there had been a meeting to build the contingent, and I talked to someone the next day who'd been at the meeting, and she said: "This really strange thing happened, this guy came into the meeting when we were trying to discuss how to build things, and he started spouting all these long quotes from Mao and Lenin." I listened to her account of this, and it struck me that this sounded very much like this guy Robere, and it turned out that it was indeed him.

Well, we were able to successfully defeat these efforts to turn this contingent into a sectarian fiasco that would have turned off many people, and we did have this beautiful contingent—but these are the kinds of things you have to deal with, some of the craziness that would grow up sometimes among people who were trying to take the revolutionary upsurge of the time and turn it inward and distort it into something very sectarian and dogmatic.

So that was the struggle we had to wage, and it became clear that not only was this guy Robere trying to take over this coalition, but he was trying to wreck the RU. From what we'd heard from people in Maryland, and then through further investigation we'd done, we had learned that he had a whole history of leaving groups in shambles around the country, playing on people's egos or intimidating them and setting different people off against each other. But as soon as we recognized what this was, we were able to repulse and defeat it, because even though we were still primitive in a lot of our understanding of things, we had certain fundamental principles that we were united around, including that when there were differences you had to struggle things out in a principled way, and we were about trying to mobilize people as broadly as possible to take on this system, and not just attempting to grow a little sect in a hothouse.

It's one thing to challenge people with revolutionary politics in a lively way; but it's another thing to come to them like a religious sect and turn them off in the name of revolution and turn them off to communism. Also, we'd fought through the question of what kind of organizational principles a communist organization or party has to base itself on, so that it can pull together in a united way and can struggle in the correct way over differences, or just over questions that are unresolved. And because we'd fought some of this through, this kind of assault on our organization didn't have the effect of disrupting it and reducing it to a shambles, as it had with some groups. Despite the negative character of all this, it did provide another valuable experience in recognizing the real destructive effect of sectarianism and dogmatism, and how that really has nothing to do with making revolution and nothing to do with communism.

## Women's Liberation and Proletarian Revolution

For myself personally, I began going through a further transformation in terms of understanding women's oppression, as a result of coming into contact with and taking up communist theory. There were also other influences—the women revolutionaries that I knew, the beginning upsurge of a women's movement. But it was particularly the whole tradition and theory of communism that had a big influence on me in that way. There were certain influences from the history of the international communist movement that were in the direction of trade unionism and reformism, but there were also some very important positive traditions and influences—including International Women's Day, that had been institutionalized in a positive sense and made a significant part of the history and tradition and ongoing practice of the communist movement internationally. And there was the whole analysis, from Marx and Engels, down through Lenin and Mao, about the emancipation of women and how that was an integral part of the whole socialist revolution and the struggle to reach communism.

Becoming a communist and taking all that up was the central way in which I began to undergo radical transformation myself on this question. As I said, when we first went to Richmond we saw ourselves as sort of "macho revolutionaries." There were women who came to Richmond, sometimes as part of couples who moved there and sometimes on their own, and that had an important influence. Some of them were very strong and independent, both in terms of their thinking, but also just in the whole way they dealt with everything. And there was the radical development inside the movement, as well as more broadly in society, of what became the feminist movement, or the women's movement, and some of it wasn't just more narrowly feminist, some of it had a communist perspective, at least in a general sense.

All these different influences had an important effect, but I think what was most essential within all this was a communist understanding of the oppression of women and the pivotal role this played in the development of class divisions and oppressive society overall, on the one hand; and, on the other hand, the pivotal role that abolishing all that and completely emancipating women played in the overall struggle to end all oppression and establish a society, a world, without class divisions and without oppressive relations.

And you can't separate that from the impact of revolutionary China at that time. When you start studying and learning more about the Chinese revolution and the experience building socialism in China, you very quickly come to see what it meant that this was a society that was steeped in feudal oppression before the revolution triumphed in 1949. They were not just taking on and uprooting capitalist forms of oppression, including of women, but also these deeply rooted feudal relations, customs, traditions and ideas. 1970 was only twenty years, more or less, from the triumph of that revolution, and you'd see that there were women like Chiang Ching in the leadership of the Chinese Communist Party, but more to the point you'd read things like the *Peking Review* and *China Reconstructs* and other publications that came out of socialist China, and you'd see women active and playing crucial roles in all different spheres of Chinese society, even though—as the Chinese comrades themselves acknowledged—they still had a long way to go. I was struck recently by watching that movie, *Crouching Tiger, Hidden Dragon*, because that is set, obviously, in pre-revolutionary China, and you see how deep the feudal stuff was. If you look at that movie and you are aware of what happened in China after the revolution, you can't help thinking "my god,"—if you'll pardon the expression—"within 20 years or so after the revolution triumphed, they'd made these tremendous transformations." And not only in an overall sense, but specifically with regard to the role and status of women in the society.

I still remember, for example, seeing Barbara Walters on a morning talk show in the early '70s, doing this little segment on shoes from all different parts of the world. And when she got to China, she had these shoes that were worn by women who had bound feet in the old feudal Chinese society, where the feet of women would be bent under and their bones broken to make their feet petite and "dainty," and supposedly sexually appealing in that way. She was showing these little shoes that women had to wear after their feet were mutilated in this way, and she commented, "Well, they need an equal rights amendment in China—which in fact they have." And it was striking: here's Barbara Walters having to acknowledge that women, as she put it, had "an equal rights amendment," that in fact they had gone a long way toward achieving not just equal rights but an emancipated position and playing crucial roles in China, even though as I said, and as the Chinese openly talked about, there was still a long way to go with that.

They were only a few decades out of feudalism, and there was also still a lot of bourgeois stuff with regard to women to uproot. Still, the transformations they had carried out—and the contrast not only with feudal society but with a "modern" bourgeois society like the U.S.—was very striking. I saw this very clearly when I visited revolutionary China. This was true on every level—the relations among people, and in particular between women and men, were so radically different from anything I'd seen before. For example, the kitchen workers and waiters in the hotel where we were staying would engage you in friendly casual conversation but would also talk with you about world affairs and what was happening in the U.S., as well as what was going on in China. Some young women who were university students from another part of China were spending a certain amount of time working as staff in the hotel, and there was no subservience in their relationship, nor was there any standoffishness. They came up and were very interested in who we were and what we thought about all kinds of things. I remember that when I came back from China and put on the TV in the U.S., how starkly it stood out—everything is this fucking commodification of sex and in particular of women's bodies. And that was three decades ago—all this is even more overt and grotesque now! All that had been strikingly absent from China and the culture there.

## Going Forward

The summer 1970 tour to expand the RU had been very successful. We did unite with a good number—if not all, or even a majority—of people and collectives we met with around the country, and we came off this tour with an organization that had a presence in many significant parts of the country, including New York and the East Coast and Chicago and other parts of the Midwest. We had engaged in many important discussions and struggles, influenced many people and deepened our own understanding in the process. And yet, at the same time, a struggle was ripening right within the RU and came to a head only a few months after this tour was completed, in the fall of 1970.

# Chapter Eleven

# *Revolution or Adventurism?*

$\mathbf{A}$s we developed the RU as a national organization, we were still looking beyond that to how we were going to get to a single unified party that could be the leadership of the whole revolutionary movement that had emerged, and could go out and do revolutionary work among people in society who hadn't yet been brought forward into the revolutionary movement. This was part of our basic understanding, we'd spoken to the need to do this in *Red Papers*, and we were wrestling with this goal in an ongoing way.

## The Questions Are Posed

The RU had now spread throughout the country and had an organized, structured way of relating to the people and collectives in other parts of the country who had joined it. But the leadership of the RU was still centered mainly in the Bay Area. And as we started having discussions in the Bay Area about how the party was going be formed, it turned out that people grouped around the Franklins had a vision that we needed to go over to the armed struggle against the system more or less immediately and that the party had to be built in accordance with that.

Others of us felt strongly that this would be suicidal and disastrous. We were up against a very powerful ruling class, a very powerful state, and, in order to launch a revolution, it is necessary to have a revolutionary situation—a profound crisis in society in which tens of millions of people could potentially, at least, be rallied to the side of revolution. Now, there were millions who were sort of generally favorable to a revolution at that time, but there were still millions and tens of millions more who were not—not necessarily that they were opposed to it, but they hadn't been brought into the stream of struggle and the upheaval of the time. You needed to go "take the revolution to them," so to speak—not in the sense of actively "getting it on" right then, but by spreading the message of revolution and going out and uniting with them and leading them in struggles that they were prepared to, or could be won to, take up, while at the same time moving and leading them to take this in a more radical direction, toward the goal of a revolution. And when *all that* came together with a revolutionary crisis, *then* we could "get it on."

Another dimension to all this—and this also developed into a sharp struggle with the group headed by the Franklins—was their view that the revolution was basically, as it was said in the terms of those times, "a third world thing." In this view, the revolution was going to be led by—and its essential forces were going to be overwhelmingly, if not entirely, drawn from—people of the oppressed nationalities: Black people, Latinos, Native Americans, Asians, and so on. They argued that the "third world peoples in the U.S." were already ready to get it on with the system right away, and that was an essential reason why the armed struggle had to be launched right then. Furthermore, those "third world" forces had to be declared and institutionalized as the leadership of the revolution. That's what revolution in the U.S. was about, as they presented it.

Our argument was that, yes, there *was* a revolutionary mood broadly among Black people, Latinos, Native Americans, Asians and so on, but first of all, that wasn't uniformly true. There were definitely revolutionary elements and revolution had a lot of initiative among these sections of the people, but even there, in their broad masses, people were not yet won to revolution, especially as something to be immediately fought for. And more than that, they existed within, and were aware of existing within, the larger society where people were not so much in a revolutionary mood. Yes, there were sections of the youth, including youth and students among white people, who were radicalized and in a revolutionary mood. But that just wasn't true for the broad sections of the population.

You know, if you're Black or Latino in this society, you are aware of the larger picture of society, and when you think about whether you want to rise up against the system, you think about what you will have to go up against. And even if you haven't studied all kinds of theory and thought it through in that way, you still have a certain sense of this, and you have a sense that unless more people are brought to the revolutionary side, you will be crushed. So even that tends to temper your revolutionary mood—not that you don't have certain radical sentiments, and not that you wouldn't love to see a revolution, or a radical change in society, not that you don't burn to get this oppression and the whole long history of that off your back. But you still look around and ask: what's out there, and could it succeed? And we felt that even that revolutionary inclination, if you will, among large sections of the oppressed couldn't be given full expression unless we won broader sections of the people to revolution by taking revolution to them, linking up with them in struggles that they were more prepared to wage and then developing and, as we say, *diverting* that onto the revolutionary course.

So, in basic terms, that was the struggle that shaped up within the RU. We felt that revolutionary preparatory work, of a political nature, needed to be done and that this needed to come together at some point in the future with the development of a profound, radicalizing crisis in society overall; the Franklins, by contrast, were saying that "third world people in the U.S." were ready for revolution, they were going to lead the revolution, and the vanguard had to be built and structured in accordance with that.

Of course, there was a lot of manipulation and opportunism, because people like Bruce Franklin were still maneuvering to actually lead and direct things, even while talking as though they should step to the side and let "third world people lead." But more than that, it was fundamentally not a correct view of how you would make revolution in a country like the U.S.

In some ways the key philosophical and methodological questions at issue were also involved in that struggle I had with DH when he became part of the RU. When you're talking about how to make revolution, how to understand the society and how to change it, that's something that has to be put on the table, studied, wrestled with and struggled over by everyone who is willing and anxious to take up that challenge. And the answers don't come to anybody automatically. Certain people may have an impulse toward revolution if their life experience is full of oppression, but that doesn't translate automatically into understanding the whole context for that oppression and how to get rid of it and how to build a whole new society and bring into being a whole new world. Coming to that understanding is a matter of taking this up scientifically and getting into the theory of it, studying society and the world in a deep and comprehensive way, and grasping the essence of things and the way in which they are moving and changing. Everybody who wants to bring about this kind of change should be brought forward and unleashed to take up this challenge, and everybody has to pitch in and do that. There are no people who, merely by virtue of being part of an oppressed group or nationality, are "automatically" able to do that, or inherently able to do it better; nor, on the other hand, are there people who, merely by virtue of being from the dominant, oppressor nationality (white people in the U.S.), have less ability, or somehow less right or responsibility, to contribute to that. So that was another key part of the struggle we had with the Franklins.

It wasn't *just* the RU that was going through this, nor is it just some sort of inevitable feature of communist formations that they turn inward and fight among themselves. Big questions were up, which I'm speaking to here, about how to actually take up the challenge of making revolution and transforming society. Making a radical change in a society like the U.S., completely overturning the system and bringing into being a socialist society, doing that together with people throughout the world who are fighting the same battle, and getting to a communist world— that is a big, big, big challenge. People who had become radicalized and revolutionary-minded through the whole '60s experience were coming up against these problems. Let's say you start out among Black people and you're building the struggle there. And you come to realize that you can't solve these problems within the confines of this system. Once you get to that point, then you have to take it the next step and say, "okay, what *does* it take, and how do we do that?"

## The Split in the Panthers

Lots of different forces were confronting the same objective problems of making revolution, especially in a country like the U.S., that the RU was running up against. There were struggles within different groups, including the Black Panther Party, over essentially the same questions. Now the Panthers weren't founded on thoroughgoing communist principles—their ideology was a mix of communism and other ideologies, in particular revolutionary nationalism—but nonetheless they were coming up against the same contradictions. Although they were not proceeding systematically and thoroughly as communists, they were trying as revolutionaries to figure out what to do. And, in some significant ways, the split within the Black Panther Party parallelled, or was very similar to, what was going on inside the RU.

On the one hand, you had Eldridge Cleaver—who was out of the country, in exile, at that time—and the forces who looked to him for leadership within and around the Black Panther Party. They were saying, "We have to go underground, we have to develop armed formations and we have to get it on right now." And then there was Huey Newton, who'd come out of prison during this period, who said, "No, if we do that we're going to become isolated from the masses of Black people, we're going to bring down the state on us, we're going to be crushed and the masses are not gonna support us."

But, unfortunately, Huey's response to that Eldridge line was to more or less openly go into reformism—"we just have to do things to meet the needs of the people"—and he formulated it as "survival pending revolution." With that orientation, it wasn't just a matter, on his part, of recognizing that revolution was not immediately on the agenda, but it basically got put off the agenda into never-never land. The politics of Huey and those who followed him became essentially reformist and based on meeting the needs of the people within the system, which (a) you can't do on a mass level—if you could, you wouldn't need a revolution; and (b) if you approach it in that way, you don't actually build toward a revolution.

The important point here is that these struggles were not a matter of a bunch of communists and other revolutionaries fighting among themselves simply for petty and sectarian reasons. We were running into big questions, big contradictions as we say, in terms of how to make revolution in a powerful, imperialist country like the U.S. The whole movement was running up against them and struggling out these questions, in one form or another.

## Settling the Questions

Inside the RU, as this struggle was going on, there were some people who were firmly in the camp that myself and some other leaders of the RU were in, and there were other people who were firmly in the camp of the Franklin group; and then there were a number of people in the RU who were unclear about this, especially at the beginning—this is often how things are at the beginning of a major struggle. But waging this struggle was complicated by the fact that while the RU was a communist organization, founded on communist principles, within the RU there were also some of the influences of what was called the "New Left" at that time. The New Left had some very positive aspects to it, in particular rejecting the conservatism, as it was seen, of the Communist Party. But it also had some influences from the mainly middle class forces among which it had emerged and in which it was mainly based. One major expression of this was an anti-leadership tendency.

So the political unclarity and differences merged with a certain anti-leadership tendency that existed more broadly in the movement, but was reflected inside the RU, and as the struggle unfolded within the RU, there was a widespread feeling among RU members that they didn't want "the big leadership honchos" battling it out. So we wrote up papers. I wrote many of the papers that refuted and polemicized against the Franklin position; and they, in turn, wrote up their position papers, and then we circulated all these papers in the organization. And since we "big honchos" were not supposed to go around and get involved in this, on our side we had what we called "flying squads." Our forces were mainly centered in the East Bay, in Oakland, Berkeley and Richmond, as well as in San Jose, and we would meet with the people on the next levels or the basic levels of the organization, have sessions with them to go deeply into the questions, and then they would go to the areas where the Franklin people were stronger, or to other places like San Francisco, where people were more confused and unclear, and they would battle it out with the forces who represented the other line. Through the course of this, we won over the majority of people in the Bay Area and ultimately we won over the great majority of people in other parts of the country who had just joined the RU. So we consolidated the majority of the RU around our position.

As for the Franklin trend, they went off, joined with a few others and formed a group called Venceremos and tried to put some version of their line into practice. This didn't last very long and, while it lasted, it had a negative effect in a number of ways. And then Venceremos split apart,

# Photos

The author and his family: Dad Spurgeon, older sister Marjorie, Bob, his mother Ruth, and younger sister Mary-Lou.

Traffic boys "being put through their paces"; the author in inset photo.

Singing
doo-wop,
with ninth
grade best
friend.

The author as high school quarterback: "a little guy, brimming with confidence."

Graduating high school.

The author in revolutionary China, 1971, with two new comrades.

The old and the new generations, in revolutionary China.

On the docks, Shanghai, 1971; the author in the center, and Leibel Bergman, second from left.

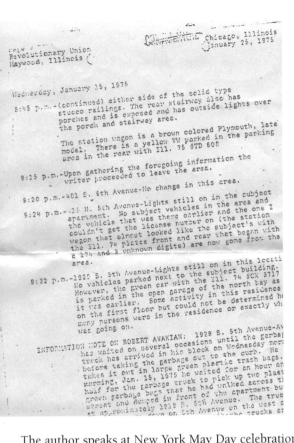

Chicago, Illinois
January 25, 1975

Re: [illegible]
Revolutionary Union
Haywood, Illinois [illegible]

Wednesday, January 15, 1975

8:45 p.m.—(continued) either side of the solid type
stucco railings. The rear stairway also has
porches and is exposed and has outside lights over
the porch and stairway area.

The station wagon is a brown colored Plymouth, late
model. There is a yellow VW parked in the parking
area in the rear with Ill. 75 #TD 608

9:15 p.m.—Upon gathering the foregoing information the
writer proceeded to leave the area.

9:20 p.m.—401 S. 6th Avenue—No change in this area.

9:24 p.m.—416 N. 5th Avenue—Lights still on in the subject
apartment. No subject vehicles in the area and
the vehicle that was there earlier and the one I
couldn't get the license number on (the station
wagon that almost looked like the subject's with
the Ill. 74 plates front and rear that began with
a 194 and 3 unknown digits) are now gone from the
area.

9:32 p.m.—1929 S. 5th Avenue—Lights still on in this locati
No vehicles parked next to the subject building.
However, the green car with the Ill. 74 #CX 3717
is parked in the open garage of the north bay as
it was earlier. Some activity in this residence
on the first floor but could not be determined ho
many persons were in the residence or exactly wh
was going on.

INFORMATION NOTE ON ROBERT AVAKIAN: 1929 S. 5th Avenue—A
has waited on several occasions until the garba
truck has arrived in his block on Wednesday morn
before taking the garbage out to the curb. He
takes it out in large green plastic trash bags.
morning, Jan. 15, 1975 he waited for an hour an
half for the garbage truck to pick up two plast
green garbage bags that he had walked across th
street and dumped in front of the apartment bu
at approximately 1918 S. 5th Avenue. The truc
[illegible] down on 5th Avenue on the west e
[illegible] the trucks a

FBI surveillance files detail
minute-by-minute movement of
the author and associates, 1975
(left); FBI photo of author's
house, mid-1970s (above). In
June 1971, FBI director L. Patrick
Gray noted to subordinates that
"This is the kind of extremist I
want to go after HARD and with
innovation."

The author speaks at New York May Day celebration, 1975.

Mao Tsetung Memorial, New York,
September 1978: Bob Avakian outlines
his analysis of the massive changes in
China following Mao's death.

Posters building support for
Bob Avakian's defense against
felony charges as a result of
the demonstration against
Deng Xiaoping.

Police attack on demonstration against Deng Xiaoping's visit in Washington, D.C.;
author, second from right, was charged with felonies carrying total penalties of
over 200 years.

The author on a nationwide speaking tour as part of the effort to politically defeat the charges and develop a revolutionary movement, 1979.

One-on-one with Bob Avakian.

The author speaking in D.C., late 1979, after the charges were initially dropped; they were later reinstated, then finally settled for good in 1982.

The author in exile, in front of the Wall of Communards in Paris, 1981.

Photos in this section on pages 1 through 4 courtesy of the author, except inset on page 1 from website of Jim Dean, www.english.udel.edu/dean; page 5 (bottom) and page 6 (top 2 photos) courtesy of RCP Publications; page 6 (bottom) ©1979, The Washington Post, printed with permission, photo by John McDonnell; page 7 (both) and page 8 (top) courtesy of the Revolutionary Worker/Obrero Revolucionario; page 8 (bottom) courtesy of the author.

and basically nothing positive came out of that.

One of the important things that came out of this struggle within the RU was *Red Papers 4*, in which we published the position papers and polemics from both sides. As I said earlier, these questions were not confined to the RU. But so long as the Franklins were in the RU and there was a chance to win them to a correct line, we did not want to publicly air the debate; doing so would have made it more difficult to carry out the struggle within the RU on a correct and principled basis, and then to settle the question within our organization. And, if the Franklin group could have been won away from their position, that would have made it possible to unite virtually the whole organization around the correct line.

But once the struggle within the RU had been resolved, and led to a split, we thought it was very important to put out these documents, as a way to enable people very broadly in the revolutionary movement to grapple with the issues more deeply. This publication of both sides of the debate in a major two-line struggle like this would become something of a tradition and hallmark, so to speak, of the RU and later the Party.

## Taking on Baggage from the International Communist Movement

Even though we were essentially correct, and the Franklin group fundamentally wrong, our position was contradictory. On the one hand, even looking back on it now, more than 30 years later, with everything we've learned since, I would say we were overwhelmingly correct and positive. In other words, we were correct about what was necessary to make a revolution *in basic terms*. And we were correct in rejecting a path that would lead people to getting isolated and crushed, no matter how good or even heroic their intentions and desires might be.

At the same time, in carrying out this struggle we had gone more deeply into the history of the international communist movement to draw lessons to apply to our situation. While we were essentially and even overwhelmingly correct in this, we also got from the international communist movement certain tendencies which had developed over a number of years, especially under Stalin's leadership, toward reformism and toward economism—that is, a basically trade unionist approach of centering the struggle of the workers around their economic demands and basically reducing the workers' movement to a battle around day-today needs. Along with that, we saw the workers who were in more stabilized employment situations and in larger factories as being the most important force for revolution and socialism, and in this there was a significant aspect of a mechanical approach that we'd taken from the international communist movement.

One of the distinguishing and most controversial features of the RU, which I've spoken to, is that we upheld Stalin. Of course, we did not uphold Stalin uncritically—we recognized and spoke to serious errors that Stalin made, and since then we have continued to deepen our understanding of that—but we have upheld Stalin with historical perspective. Stalin led the first attempt to build socialism, under very difficult circumstances, and led important advances in building socialism in the Soviet Union over several decades. While there were many mistakes made in the Soviet Union under Stalin's leadership, some of them quite grievous, there were also many great achievements. But, at that time, we hadn't fully recognized and taken account of the fact that, to put it somewhat provocatively, while Stalin had led in the building of socialism in the Soviet Union and had made contributions to the international movement, at the same time over the period of several decades and up through World War 2, Stalin had basically undone a great deal of Leninism in the international communist movement.

For example, Lenin had said that the model for a communist should not be a trade union secretary but a "tribune of the people," someone who exposes the system in all its manifestations (and not just the struggle of the workers against the employing class) and on that basis shows people the need for socialist revolution and leads people in that direction. But, to a significant degree, Stalin made the model of a communist a good militant trade union leader, who talks about socialism. Not instantly and immediately, but over a period of decades, that had been a significant aspect of Stalin's influence. And while we never took this up in its crudest form, or simply reduced our work to the trade union struggle—while we never abandoned the goal of revolution, nor failed to do agitation and propaganda about the need for revolution, socialism and ultimately communism—these economist tendencies exerted a significant pull on us.

Also, Lenin and the Bolsheviks stood out for saying that the workers in the imperialist countries—and Lenin included his own country, Russia, in that—have no interest in "defending the fatherland" and that when the fatherland goes off to wage war, as an imperialist power, the workers should oppose that war and unite with the workers and oppressed people throughout the world; they should *not* line up with their own ruling class but should take a position which Lenin characterized as "revolutionary defeatism," that is, welcoming the setbacks and defeats of their own ruling class in war and utilizing that to advance toward revolution to overthrow that ruling class. And, in fact, in World War 1, the Bolsheviks were literally the only socialist party of a major power who held to and applied that internationalist and "revolutionary defeatist" position. This was a hallmark of Leninism. But Stalin had to a significant degree undone that, too. He came out with this whole theory about how, in the several decades after World War 1, the workers in the imperialist countries had actually gotten a stake in the fatherland—they'd won certain concessions, they'd formed trade unions, they'd won more democratic rights—and so they actually had something to defend in the fatherland. That's the line that Stalin and the Communist International put forward in the period leading into World War 2 and then during World War 2 itself, once the Soviet Union was invaded by Nazi Germany and the Soviet Union became a major battleground of the whole war.[24]

In other words, what we were getting from the international communist movement was contradictory, very sharply so in some important respects. We got the basic principles of communism, which we have kept and which have kept us going in a revolutionary direction, but we also got a lot of things that were corrosive of those correct communist principles, and they influenced us in the direction of trade unionism and even reformism.

As Maoists we say, "things divide into two"—that is, into their contradictory parts, or aspects—and you have to determine what is the principal and defining aspect. Was the main thing about the RU at that time these reformist, trade unionist and economist influences, or was the main thing that we were correctly assessing how to go about making revolution? The main thing was the latter. We were correctly assessing this, in the main and in essence, even though our understanding was primitive, and even though it was significantly influenced by these negative tendencies.

---

24. For further analysis by Bob Avakian of Stalin's position in relation to World War 2, see "Conquer the World: The International Proletariat Must and Will."

## Reviving Revolutionary Traditions

But as a result of going back to the history of the international communist movement, which the RU had done from its beginning, we also took up some very important positive things, including the celebration of May First as a revolutionary workers' holiday and of International Women's Day as a day to mark the struggle for the emancipation of women. Both of these holidays had been popularized and given expression throughout the world by the international communist movement, and we revived these as communist traditions in the U.S. And, again, though there was some influence of reformism and economism, essentially we took these as *revolutionary holidays of* the working class *to* the working class.

In 1970 the RU sponsored and organized the first International Women's Day rally in San Francisco in many years. It was a real revival of this as a revolutionary holiday, which was taken to working women, as well as men in the working class, and to other sections of the people as well. As I recall, it was in Delores Park in San Francisco, and it was a powerful and moving, revolutionary International Women's Day of several hundred people. Along with reviving International Women's Day as a revolutionary holiday, the RU published *Red Papers 3*, which was devoted entirely to the woman question. It consisted of theoretical and strategic analysis of the oppression of women and how it can only be ended through revolution and advancing to socialism and communism, as well as reports about the work that comrades in the RU were doing in various parts of the country, working for example in the phone company and among other sections of women workers.

In 1971, we had a May Day rally, and it was the first time that May Day had been taken to the working class, especially as a revolutionary holiday, in quite some time. I had moved to San Francisco at that time, in order to help provide leadership for the RU as a whole in the Bay Area, and I was mainly organizing in San Francisco for May Day, but the actual celebration was set for a park in Oakland. We took a busload of people from San Francisco, and as we crossed the Bay Bridge into the East Bay, and then got into Oakland and then turned onto the street that went up a little hill toward the park, all of us were very nervous, sitting on tenterhooks as they say, biting our nails—"is there gonna be anybody in the park?"—because we'd really gone all out to build for this revolutionary holiday. We came up the hill, and the road leveled off, and there was the park—and we could see there were already a couple of hundred people gathering in the park. So we got all excited and overjoyed: there was May Day as a revolutionary, socialist, communist holiday in that park, in the middle of a proletarian district in Oakland. So that was one of the fruits of our generally coming to a communist position, but also of the struggle with the Franklins and the deepened determination that we had to take revolution and socialism and communism broadly to the working class and win people to this. That's how we were approaching things at that point.

# Chapter Twelve

# *Going to China*

U nder the influence of first Eldridge Cleaver and then, much more deeply, Leibel Bergman, I had really gotten into studying Mao and the whole experience of the Chinese Revolution, especially the Cultural Revolution. When I get into something, I like to get into it *deeply*, and this was no exception. But even more, what was compelling to me was that the more I got into this, the more I began to get a sense of how you could make a revolution and prevent it from being sold out and betrayed—how you could keep it going until you really did uproot, as Marx had said, *all* the oppressive social and class relations, and all the oppressive ideas that they generate.

I was far from unique in this. Tens of thousands of people in the U.S., and millions worldwide, looked to China as a beacon and, on one level or another, had some sense of the importance of the Cultural Revolution. But if you were living in the U.S. back then, the possibility that you could actually go there and see it for yourself didn't seem in the offing, so to speak.

## Seizing an Opening

Then, in 1971, China was beginning to carry out an "opening to the west." Henry Kissinger had made his secret trip to China, and Nixon would make his first trip to China the next year, in '72. If you were a U.S. citizen you couldn't go to China up to that time without the possibility

248

of facing consequences, perhaps of a very serious nature, from the U.S. government. But because of the changes in U.S.-China relations, a greater possibility of going to China was opening up. Leibel Bergman, who had lived in China for several years during the Cultural Revolution and still had ties and contacts there, took some initiative to organize a delegation from the RU. Someone from the Young Lords Party, Pablo Guzman—who at that time called himself Yoruba, and that's what we called him, Yoruba—was also a part of this delegation of people that went to China in the fall of 1971.

I, of course, was extremely excited about this. A lot of big things were going on at that time—this was the same time as the uprising at Attica prison in New York state. In fact, I think we actually left for this trip just before the Attica uprising came to a head with the bloodbath that occurred, unfortunately, when Governor Rockefeller called out the state troopers to put down the uprising, and the state troopers murdered dozens of prisoners in cold blood and even killed a number of guards whom the prisoners were holding as hostages. There was still a lot of revolutionary upheaval going on at the same time as we were embarking on, and extremely excited about, this trip to China. I remember we had to wait and wait and wait to go, and up to the last minute there was the question of whether the whole thing was going to fall through—and then we finally were able to go. We took the long way around on an Air France plane that stopped in places like Athens, Cairo, and Karachi, which I believe was then the capital of Pakistan. The anticipation and excitement was building up as we flew from one place to another, just touching down for a few short hours, then taking off again, and it reached a high peak as the plane came down over China and we flew over miles and miles of cultivated farmland. Then an airport came into view, I think it was in the city of Canton where we first landed, I can't remember that for sure, but I will never forget the large portrait of Mao that greeted us at the airport. I was unbelievably excited—here we were, finally, in the People's Republic of China.

## Struggle in the Chinese Leadership

But big historical things were going on in China at the time that hadn't yet come to the surface. A struggle with Lin Biao, who was a leading figure in the Chinese Communist Party and was even being hailed as the closest comrade and successor of Mao, had just come to a head.

Apparently Lin Biao had taken the position that, in the face of mounting threats from the Soviet Union to attack China, the Chinese should conciliate with the Soviet Union. Mao's position was that China should stand up to the Soviet Union, but at the same time, and as part of that, it should try to deal with the Soviet threat partly by opening to the West and using that as a way of lining up forces against the Soviet Union.

So we were coming in all excited, full of wide-eyed enthusiasm about going to China, in the midst of all this struggle going on, which we weren't, by any means, fully aware of. We flew from Shanghai to Peking (Beijing) and arrived shortly before October 1st, which is the anniversary of the victory of the Chinese Revolution in 1949, when Mao stood in Tienanmen Square in the capital and proclaimed: "The Chinese people have stood up." We were very much looking forward to the celebration in Tienanmen Square because, every year through the Cultural Revolution, a million or more Red Guards and others would throng into Tienanmen Square with their Red Books, and Mao would come out on the balcony with other leaders and they'd wave Red Books.

Then, a few days before October 1st, some of the people from the Chinese government who were relating to our delegation came to us and said, "Well, this year we're going to do things a little differently. We're not going to have one big celebration in the central square, Tienanmen, we're going to spread out the celebration in parks all over the city, so more people can be involved." We were all disappointed, because we weren't going to be able to see Mao and masses of people in Tienanmen Square. But when I went back to my room, Leibel came over to talk to me, and I was shocked to find out what the real deal was.

I was heading the delegation, but Leibel was the one who had a lot of the contacts in China from having lived there, and he took me aside and said: "You know, this is a bunch of bullshit about how they want to have it in the parks so more people can take part." He went on: "What's really going on is that there's been a whole struggle between Mao and Lin Biao, and Lin Biao has gone down, so they can't have this big celebration in Tienanmen Square because Lin Biao won't be there, and everybody in the country will learn that he wasn't there, and it will create a big stir. They're not prepared to talk about all this, yet, so that's why they're not having a big celebration in Tienanmen Square."

And then he started telling me all the different stories he was hearing from people he knew in China, what he used to call "back-alley rumors." You know, I laugh when I hear people talk about how everything is so tightly controlled in "totalitarian" societies, that the only source of information people have is the official government source. There was all this talk, rumors flying all around, among the Chinese people—much of which proved to be rather accurate.

So then I knew—oh shit, something big is going on. I'd gone there full of almost naive enthusiasm, and then I was hit with this. And I also got a glimpse into what would later become a fuller degeneration in Leibel's outlook: the way he was talking to me about what was happening in China struck me even at the time as being mired in bourgeois conceptions. We got into these big arguments, because he was saying, "Oh that Mao—anybody gets close to him and down they go. First there was Liu Shao-chi..." Liu Shao-chi had been the president of the People's Republic of China and second in the party to Mao—and then he was exposed and denounced as a "capitalist roader." Leibel had supported that. He could see that Liu Shao-chi's policies would weaken socialism and were not about supporting revolution in the world—and that, in fact, they would lead back to capitalism—so fine, criticize him and knock him down from his leadership position, which they did through the Cultural Revolution. But now Leibel started looking at things the way the bourgeoisie does, as if struggles among communist leaders are all just a matter of personal power trips and ego.

I was familiar with this outlook, even from my own limited experience, because within the RU, as the struggle with the Franklins had come to a head, we had a meeting with a broader grouping of people in the RU from different parts of the country. Most of them hadn't really been deeply involved in this struggle, and a number of them tended to adopt the same kind of attitude—"Oh, this is just a big ego trip, and you should criticize yourself for splitting the organization." It took a while to win people to see that, no, there were important, fundamental issues that were being fought out, different lines that led in very different directions, and the outcome had real consequences. We'd won these new people in the RU to that understanding, but it took a while; and here was Leibel, taking the same kind of stance toward what was happening in China, even though he had a wealth of experience to enable him to know better.

So we got into a very sharp argument. I was responding to him by saying, "That can't be the issue—just that somebody gets close to Mao, gets too powerful, and so Mao has to knock him down. There have to be questions of program and line, some substantial issues here, that are being battled out." We went back and forth on that, and I was shocked not only to hear about this struggle in China but also to see indications that Leibel was abandoning a Marxist approach and falling into bourgeois theories and bourgeois "psychological analysis" in confronting what was happening in China.

### Transformations – Seeing a New Society

Of course, those of us on this delegation had all gone to China with great enthusiasm. We wanted to see first-hand this vibrant revolutionary socialist society where the Cultural Revolution was going on and the Red Guards were going out to the countryside and linking up with the peasants and taking revolution to them, and the people were bringing about all these changes in all the different spheres of society. And within the limits of what you can do on a trip of this kind, which only lasted six weeks, we did get to witness many of these great transformations. Even though I had been hit with this whole Lin Biao thing, I nevertheless continued to have tremendous enthusiasm for what I was seeing and learning there.

We had a lot of discussions with people, and we visited a number of different places in the country. We went, for example, to one of the rural areas, where they had built the Red Flag Canal. They were diverting a river through a mountain so that a whole, larger commune of people would have irrigation for their farmland, rather than just one or a few villages closest to where the river ran. We talked to the Iron Women's Team that had drilled through this mountain—they told us how they had lowered themselves, on cables, down a sharp rock face, so they could plant dynamite to blast through the mountain, in order to divert the river through it. This was in a society where, only a couple of decades before that, it would have been impossible to imagine people doing something like that—and impossible in particular to conceive of women doing anything like that.

There were all these really exciting and uplifting things. We felt the whole spirit of "serve the people" that was popularized throughout the society, and we saw living examples of revolutionary transformations. We'd come upon situations where the men and women would be engaging in friendly competition to do things like sweeping up in the house. Again, you think about China coming from a feudal society less than twenty-five years before that, and here you had these big changes in the relations between men and women. Even though this was a small example, in a sense—and even though, of course, many backward ideas and practices still persisted and were still contending with these more advanced things—this friendly competition captured both the "serve the people" spirit and the pervasiveness of the changes that were going on between men and women.

We would have discussions in factories with workers who were reading Engels' *Anti-Duhring*, which is a major theoretical work of Marxism, and who were reading other works of Marxist philosophy and debating all these big questions. In a number of factories we talked to members of what they called "three-in-one leadership committees," or revolutionary committees, in which party members and administrative personnel from the factory, together with workers selected from the shop floor, made up the committee that led the whole factory. This was a very exciting development and a whole new thing even in the history of socialism, let alone in contrast with what goes on in capitalist society.

We visited a hospital and saw how, as a result of the Cultural Revolution, they had actually instituted the practice of doing anesthesia with acupuncture. Our delegation went to three or four operations—for things like stomach cancer—and it was very advanced medical practice, but they were also integrating traditional practices from Chinese culture into an overall system of medicine which for the first time was geared toward serving the ordinary people, and as a result of the Cultural Revolution was being spread throughout the countryside, where the vast majority of Chinese people lived.

We talked to people on cultural teams. China was still a backward country, it was only a few decades from feudalism and domination by imperialism—a society where, for generations and centuries, the masses of people in the countryside were barely hanging on and millions were regularly starving, even in the "better" years. Things like movies and other cultural productions were known in the cities, although even those were overwhelmingly for the elite, well-to-do Chinese and foreigners, and virtually none of this existed in the countryside, before the revolution. We saw people who, on bicycles, were taking movie projectors to spread revolutionary culture, the culture of the new socialist society, in the countryside.

We saw truly wondrous things.

## Lin Biao and the Complexities of the Struggle

Yet, at the same time, I was aware that there was this whole struggle going on inside the Chinese Communist Party over monumental questions like how to deal with the threat of attack from the Soviet Union. This threat, we've since learned more fully, was very real. Beginning in the late 1960s, the Soviet Union was actually developing plans, it seems, for a major attack on China, including perhaps the use of tactical nuclear weapons. I remember that our Chinese hosts took us through these air raid shelters that they had in Peking and other cities, vast networks of air raid shelters under the city. They told us a story about how some other, more bourgeois-type American visitors had come to China and, upon seeing these shelters, had asked: "What are these air raid shelters for, what are you protecting against?" And the Chinese replied: "Against attack from you or the Soviets." This threat was very real—and increasingly it was coming from the Soviet Union.

So this set the context for what became a big struggle within the Chinese party, with Lin Biao arguing against an opening to the West and insisting that they should more or less conciliate with the Soviet Union —that this was the way to deal with the Soviet threat. And Mao rejected that.

This was very complex. Lin Biao was the Defense Minister, and he was formally the head of the army, although Mao was still acknowledged as the ultimate leader of not only the party but the army as well. Essentially, the army was led by the party, so really the party—and Mao, as the head of the party—were the leaders of the army. But, *institutionally*, Lin Biao was the head of the armed forces. And, while the army played largely a political role through the Cultural Revolution, it was after all the army, and after a certain point there was a tendency for the country to be turned into something like an army camp. Not that they had guns pointed at everybody's head, but from what a number of people have said, the whole society had the feel too much of an army camp.

Now, the Chinese army was vastly different than an imperialist army. In the revolutionary days, when China was a socialist country, they didn't have all those stripes and fruit salad all over the officers, and they didn't have saluting and yes-sirring and all that absolute authority of officers. The relation of the army to the masses of people was vastly different than it is today—the Chinese People's Liberation Army had a whole tradition of being closely linked with the masses of people, and this tradition had been carried forward after the revolution triumphed and power was seized in 1949. Still, you don't want the whole society to be run even like a revolutionary army. At a certain point in the Cultural Revolution, Mao said that it was time to move away from that, and to reduce the role of the army in everyday life and in the political affairs of society. But Lin Biao resisted that.

All these different issues were being fought out, and they'd just come to a head when we got there. So, for me, this visit to China represented a sharp contradiction. On the one hand, I was tremendously inspired by these real-life transformations that we were seeing all over the country. But, at the same time, I was learning about all this struggle that was coming to a head, and they were canceling the massive October 1st celebration in Tienanmen Square.

## A Lesson

I also got a lesson in what we communists call democratic centralism—the way in which issues, including differences within the party, are discussed and struggled out through the channels of the party, and then are decided by the leadership of the party, drawing on the discussion and struggle throughout the ranks of the party, and how decisions of this kind are not broadcast to the world until these issues are resolved and the party is unified around them.

I got a living illustration of that because we had a group of translators accompanying us as we went around visiting all these different parts of China and—as I learned when I went back to China a few years later and talked to some of the same translators—by the time we were traveling around the country, they already knew about the struggle with Lin Biao and the fact that Lin Biao had died in an apparent attempt to flee the country. (It was reported that he had been attempting to fly a plane toward the Soviet Union and had crashed. I don't know all the ins and outs of this, I'm not privy to that, but that was the story we heard.) This had happened by the time we arrived in China just before October 1st, 1971. And later, when I returned to China, these translators told me: "Yes, we knew this by the time of your first visit, but when we went out to some of the outlying areas, because things were being communicated from the center out, and this was being taken down, rung by rung, through different levels within the party and the government, there were places out in the outlying areas where this news, and the presentation of the beginning summation of this, had not yet reached."

So we would go to a museum, for example, in a remote rural area, and here was a picture of Mao and right next to that a picture of Lin Biao, and they were still being presented as close comrades. I remember this woman in one such museum giving us a rundown—this was a museum on the history of the Chinese Revolution—and she was telling us all about the history of the Chinese Revolution, and at one point she said: "During the Long March, Lin Biao, Chairman Mao's closest comrade and successor, did thus and so." Of course, at that point, Lin Biao was no longer considered to be Chairman Mao's closest comrade-in-arms and successor. But that hadn't gotten out to this remote rural area, so the translators were dutifully translating all this talk about Lin Biao in very glowing and positive terms.

Later, when I went back to China, I said to them, "Well, you must have known at that time that this was no longer what was being said and being summed up." And they replied: "Yes, we knew, but if we hadn't done our duty and translated things as they were being presented, we would have just caused tremendous chaos, because then the people in that area who hadn't yet been informed about what had happened with Lin Biao, would have all of a sudden known from us that something was going on of a monumental nature—and that's not the way they should have found that out." So I learned a great lesson from that about the correct way and the correct channels and means through which you do things, and the systematic way in which you do them, so you don't have a party degenerate into factions, and become a bunch of bourgeois cliques. It is not a matter of keeping things from the people, but of finding the way that they can take them up systematically and dig into them deeply.

But it was quite a jolt to learn this about Lin Biao, to be there less than a week and be confronted with this reality. I didn't agree with the approach that Leibel was falling into. It didn't make sense to me that something of this magnitude could be reduced to just a matter of ego and personal power struggles—I wanted to know what the fundamental issues were. I wanted to know what was in contention, what were the different programs that different forces were fighting for. We had been through this kind of experience within the RU, in our struggle with the Franklins, and so I had at least a beginning sense of how these things go, and that they're not just ego contests. I won't say that ego never plays any part in it, but essentially and fundamentally when you have a split of that proportion, it's because there are fundamental differences about the direction that people think things need to take, and what policies are needed to deal with what people are confronting. I was trying to figure this out, in terms of what had happened in China. It wasn't discouraging to me, but it *was* a jolt and it immediately caused me to come to grips with the fact that all this is more complex than I'd understood up to that point.

### Running Into Huey

So all these exciting and inspiring things were going on at the same time as I was learning about the complexity of it. And then there was this very poignant experience.

As it turned out, Huey Newton was on a trip to China at the same time as our delegation. I was developing a friendship with Yoruba at that time—we were hanging out together and talking about a lot of things, we had a lot of the same musical interests, and so on, and there were a lot of things we could talk about that we had in common, as well as some experiences that were very different. And then at one point we saw Huey Newton walking around in a park while we were in Peking. Leibel said to me, "Look, given your history with him, you have to go talk to Huey Newton, you can't avoid it." As I have discussed earlier, we had developed our differences with the Panther Party, and things were even a bit strained, but I knew Leibel was right. Yoruba wanted to go meet with Huey, too, because he'd always looked to Huey as a revolutionary leader and admired him. So the two of us, along with another person from our delegation, went and approached Huey and we arranged to go over to the room where he was staying.

But as we were sitting in Huey's room talking, it didn't feel like the same Huey Newton. He didn't seem to have the same revolutionary enthusiasm. This was a very painful experience for me, because it just reminded me that this was not the Huey Newton that I had known and learned so much from a few years before. And Huey seemed very pained and anguished himself—it seemed to me that, while he was doing his best to maintain a friendly and cool exterior, just beneath the surface was a very troubled person, who did not seem comfortable in his own skin.

## Learning an Important Lesson

This trip was right around the time of a war between India and Pakistan, and the Chinese summarized their position on this to our delegation. And that was a learning experience, as we say. You can learn positively, and sometimes you learn by negative example. This was a learning experience of the latter kind.

The Chinese gave us their explanation for why they opposed the creation of a separate state of Bangladesh in what had been East Pakistan. In essence, they were supporting the ruling class in Pakistan in forcibly and brutally attempting to suppress the breakaway of Bangladesh, which, partly because of the intervention of India, Pakistan was ultimately unable to prevent.

The Chinese party cadre who ran this down to us, said "Look, don't repeat this publicly, but of course we know the government of Pakistan is a government of landlords and capitalists—but this is an attempt by India, with the Soviet Union behind it, to dismember Pakistan, so we have to oppose it." Now this was a big, controversial issue in the movement around the world, including in the U.S. We listened to this explanation and then, when we got back to the U.S., a number of us actually worked on a pamphlet that put forward the Chinese explanation, and we tried to defend it as best we could. And there were also other issues, like Chinese support for this oppressive government in the Sudan, which had brutally repressed the opposition—we tried to explain that too, on the basis of what the Chinese had told us.

But basically the Chinese position came down to opposing whatever the Soviet Union was supporting. Especially around the Pakistan issue, there was also the fact that India was a long-standing enemy of the Chinese revolution and there had been border clashes where India made incursions into Chinese territory, and more recently the Soviet Union had aligned itself to a significant degree with the Indian ruling class as part of an encirclement of China by the Soviet Union. (As I've discussed, the Soviet Union had degenerated into an imperialist power in its own right, while still having the pretense and disguise of socialism, even though that was becoming more and more threadbare.)   Basically, China's actions were dictated by a certain kind of *realpolitik*, to be honest, which was based on seeking to prevent their own country from being attacked, and dismembered, by the Soviet Union. That was a very real concern but, frankly, the way they were going about it, and in particular the way they were seeking to rationalize it, was not correct.

But, at that time, we became convinced by their rationalizations—we actually got drawn into the logic of what they were putting forward—and so we publicly, and even somewhat aggressively, defended this. We put out this pamphlet and distributed it within the broader movement, and we boldly argued for it, and I guess it had some influence. But these arguments were really not defensible, and we later summed up these were errors that China was making in the face of very real threats and dangers.

It was not a minor matter that you had the U.S., which was still fundamentally antagonistic toward China as a socialist country, despite the Nixon visits—that was just a tactical maneuver by U.S. imperialism—and you had the Soviet Union, right on the border with China, which was very hostile to China and regarded it as a thorn in its side and a threat to its role as the head of the "socialist camp" and which was anxious to weaken and cripple China, if not outright subjugate it and dismember it. So these were very real threats and dangers that China had to deal with. Nevertheless, the positions they took, and still more the rationalizations they developed—for example in the case of Pakistan, where they ignored, or didn't base themselves on, the fact that besides the maneuvering of certain bourgeois forces in what became Bangladesh, and besides Indian expansionism and the Soviet Union behind it, *there was a genuine mass upsurge of people against the highly oppressive and brutally repressive rule of Pakistan* —these rationalizations were wrong. So we learned through that, we summed up fairly soon after that this was wrong, that the Chinese were making errors and that we should not join in seeking to rationalize those errors.

We learned a great deal from that mistake. We learned the importance of thinking critically, and not blindly accepting or following anything, even in relation to China, which remained, despite some errors it was making, a genuine source of inspiration and strength for the whole revolutionary movement around the world. And overall, we returned to the U.S. with an even greater determination to carry forward the revolutionary struggle and even deeper confidence in our cause.

# Chapter Thirteen

# *Consolidating the Revolutionary Union*

I went back to the U.S. and the Bay Area. But since we'd developed the RU into a national organization, it became increasingly clear that we needed to establish a national leadership that wouldn't be just what had grown up sort of "organically" in the Bay Area, but would be more able to act as a leadership for the whole country. So we made a decision to take another step in more fully consolidating the RU as a national organization, by establishing its headquarters and its leadership in Chicago. The RU already had organization in Chicago, but we decided that it was necessary for me, and a few others, to make this move to Chicago in order to strengthen the RU as a national organization and in its ability to contribute to the formation of a new vanguard communist party.

We didn't see ourselves as immediately moving to build the new party, however. We thought there still needed to be a period where those who were basing themselves on communist principles accumulated more experience in applying that in practice, in taking it to the working class in particular, and lines and approaches could be clarified on that basis. So we saw ourselves doing three main things, at that point: we were continuing to build the revolutionary movement among the masses, with a particular focus on the working class; we were doing important theoretical work; and we were trying to develop the unity of the communist movement itself, clarifying differences as part of struggling for a higher level of unity. And we thought this move to Chicago would further all that.

## Moving to Chicago

I moved to Chicago in the spring of 1972, and this was a big move for me. Since the time I was three, I had lived in the Bay Area. I had been to Chicago for a New Politics Convention in the '60s, and one of the first things that struck me was how dirty it was. It was a gritty, industrial city, and you could smell it from twenty miles away.

When I first moved to Chicago, I drove across country with another comrade in the RU. We got one of these deals where you get somebody's car that they'd left in one part of the country and basically you could drive it back for them for free. Actually, the owner of this car lived near Detroit, in Grosse Point, Michigan, but he'd left his Lincoln Continental in the Bay Area, so we drove it to Chicago, and then I drove it to Grosse Pointe, Michigan, after dropping off the other person who was with me. I delivered this car to this exclusive residence in Grosse Point, where I couldn't even get inside the guard gate. Finally, the guy came down and I turned his car over to him, and then I got on the bus to downtown Detroit, and from Detroit took a bus back to Chicago.

I hadn't yet gotten an apartment in Chicago, so I didn't have a place to stay. Although there were RU members in the Chicago area, I didn't know too many of them yet, and I didn't have their phone numbers or their addresses for the most part. The person I knew best and knew how to contact was DH.

I arrived in Chicago about midnight. I knew the general area of the city that DH lived in, so I took the "el" train up to that area and when I got close I called, to let him know my situation and ask if I could stay with him. But he didn't answer his phone. So here I was—stuck out in the street at midnight, nowhere to go and no one else I could contact very easily. I walked over to his house, carrying a suitcase. I knocked on his door, and I could see that there were some lights on. I knocked and I knocked and I knocked; then I rang the bell. No answer. So I wandered around, feeling increasingly uneasy, because I was caught between whoever is out in the street at that time of night, doing whatever they are doing, on the one hand, and the pigs on the other hand. And I was carrying a suitcase. I kept calling and going back and knocking on his door, calling back and knocking, but still I was not getting any answer; I could tell somebody was there and he's refusing to answer. So finally, I had just enough money to get a cab—there was no more public transportation running at that hour—and I went out to Maywood, west of the city, and after wandering around for a while longer, I finally found the house of somebody I knew, and they let me sleep on their floor.

I later found out that the reason DH let me wander around in the streets in this kind of frankly desperate situation for hours is that he had a woman with him and he didn't want to be bothered letting me in. As a little postscript to this story, on a more positive note, the cab driver was this young white guy who'd been a college student at Northwestern; we got into talking about music, and he asked me if I liked jazz, and I said I had listened to some jazz but I wasn't really into it that much, and we started talking about John Coltrane and other jazz artists, and at one point—this really struck me—this guy says, "You have to understand *this* about jazz: What's coming out of those horns is all the frustration and anger of Black people for all their oppression for decades and centuries."

### Maywood

After a short time, I got an apartment in Maywood, a suburb a few miles west of Chicago. Maywood was a very interesting suburb—at the time I moved there, I think it was about half Black and half white, and a very proletarian town. Maywood also had this high school, Proviso East, about a mile from where I lived, that usually had a good basketball team, so I liked that, too. For three years while I was there Glen Rivers, who later played and then coached in the NBA, was on their team. I went to a lot of their games. I also found out where the playgrounds were that had good basketball, and I started hanging out there and I would play ball with some of the guys who were on the high school team or who had just graduated. So, those were the positive aspects of the move.

The negative side was that, in this midwestern setting, the town would like roll up the sidewalks at 9 o'clock. The lights would all go out and I was like, "What the hell's going on here?" I was used to a little more night life than that, a little more vitality. But the fact that Maywood had playgrounds with good basketball where I could hang out made it easier for me to get to know a number of people, and that kind of eased the transition for me.

In thinking of Maywood, I remember a story which is a little funny, which has something of the flavor of Maywood, and which is more than a little illustrative of DH and what he was all about. There were mainly Black people living in the apartment building I first moved into, but the discrimination was very blatant. I didn't have a job at the time, I had no references or anything, and still I got the apartment. But I later found out that if you were Black and wanted to live in that apartment building, you had to have employment, you had to have references, and so on. Anyway, I moved into this apartment and the unfortunate people living underneath me were this working class Black couple—they both had jobs and they both had to leave early for work. And when I first moved into the apartment above them, I didn't have much money, I couldn't afford much furniture, and I certainly couldn't afford rugs in the apartment. I would have people over, and sometimes we would talk loudly, the way you do when you have a bunch of people all together. We would walk on the bare floors right above these people who were trying to sleep, because they had to get up early to go to work. Finally one day, one of them came up and knocked on my door—I think I had been vacuuming the floor, and obviously it was making a big racket. I opened the door and there was this guy standing there, my downstairs neighbor, and he says: "Would you please think about buying some rugs?" He went on to say that I was making a terrible racket and they couldn't rest, and a lot of times I kept them awake at night, and it was disrupting their whole rhythm. But I couldn't afford rugs right then.

And then things got worse because one night DH came over with these friends of his, including this guy, Jerry, who'd been in the Panthers and this other guy whose nickname was "Home Before Dark" (he'd had this nickname since he was a kid: "Home Before Dark"). So "Home Before Dark" and Jerry and DH were there, and DH said he was going to make up this drink that I believe was called a "black pearl," which consisted of, not regular rum, but 151-proof rum, which is 75 percent alcohol, and a bunch of fruit juices. When you drank this it just tasted like a real sweet fruit drink—and then all of a sudden it would sneak up and lower the boom on you. I think DH wanted to get me drunk to see what would come out of me when I was in that state, because he always liked to probe for people's weaknesses—he was that kind of an opportunist, with a real hustler streak. But the more I drank these "black pearls," and the more they affected me, the more I started talking, with unrestrained enthusiasm, about how great socialism was going to be. And I could tell that DH was getting more and more frustrated with this. This is not what he wanted to hear coming out of me.

Then, about two in the morning, after we had been drinking these "black pearls" for quite a while, things started getting really loud and raucous. And these two guys, "Home Before Dark" and Jerry, who were both very big, started wrestling in my apartment, in a mainly friendly way—and then, all of a sudden, my apartment door was open and they were out in the hallway wrestling. And then, worse yet, they tumbled down the stairs—I was on the second floor, and there was this railing at the edge of the stairs and then a little space behind the railing where the wall was. And one of them, "Home Before Dark," went crashing through the railing and fell a whole floor down on his back, while Jerry was teetering there, about ready to fall. I ran over and helped him get back away from the edge, and then we went running downstairs to see if "Home Before Dark" was okay. Ironically, because he was so drunk, it turned out that he actually wasn't badly hurt, just a little bit bruised. But then, just as we were picking him up and figuring out how to get him to the hospital or whatever, the door of these downstairs neighbors opens, and they stick their head out, and Jerry turns to them and says, "What are you doing? Get back in your apartment!" I felt badly about that, and it didn't exactly improve my relations with my neighbors, but stepping back from this a bit, the whole thing was sort of funny.

### Fred Hampton's Legacy

Fred Hampton was from Maywood, and he had led the Panthers in the Chicago area. I had followed very closely the whole outrage when he, along with Mark Clark, was murdered by the pigs in Chicago in December 1969. The newspapers and the authorities had put out this story that the Panthers were the aggressors, that they'd fired on the police and the police were only firing back in self-defense. But then the Panthers led tours of people through the apartment where Fred Hampton and Mark Clark were shot, showing that all the bullet holes were made by bullets coming from the *outside in*, and that what the police and media claimed were bullet holes from inside out were actually *nail* holes, and things like that.

I was very aware of and I had tremendous respect for Fred Hampton, though I knew him, so to speak, more from a distance, as compared to the relationship that I had with leaders of the Panthers like Bobby Seale,

Huey Newton, and Eldridge Cleaver. When I got to Chicago, I discovered, not surprisingly, that all the comrades in the RU had been tremendously influenced and inspired by Fred Hampton and, of course, tremendously devastated by the way in which he was murdered. This was one of the strengths of the RU comrades in that area. Even though we had developed differences with the Panthers, the influence of Fred Hampton was a very positive one overall. He would openly proclaim that he was an all-the-way proletarian revolutionary—he would popularize that stance. By the time I moved to the Chicago area, it was several years after he had been murdered, and the Panther organization wasn't at the high point that it had been while he was alive, although there were still Panthers in that area, and there were some people who had been in the Panthers who either joined the RU or worked very closely with it.

Of course, it wasn't just the RU comrades in that area, but many, many people throughout the country had been moved by Fred Hampton and had made a leap in their revolutionary commitment because of his influence—the whole way in which, before he was killed, he boldly put forward: "You can kill a revolutionary, but you can't kill the revolution." When people saw how he was just shot down in cold blood by the police, this caused even more people to make the leap to becoming revolutionaries.

## The RU's Early Practice

As I referred to earlier, from the international communist movement the RU had taken up the orientation that you have to go to the working class. But, again, this was contradictory—or, as we say, it divided into two. There was the positive side, and the main aspect of things, which was that we were taking *revolution*, and socialism and communism, to the working class—to Black workers, Latino workers, white workers, and so on. On the other hand, our understanding of that and how to do that was colored by a lot of the influences that I described earlier from the international communist movement as it had developed under Stalin's leadership, with a lot of what we refer to as "economist" tendencies, tendencies toward narrowing the struggle of the working class to its own more immediate and narrow interests.

As part of "going to the working class," the RU comrades in all these different areas were putting out newspapers that had a sort of general socialist character, but weren't explicitly communist. There *were* things of an explicitly communist character in them—articles about China, for example, as well as articles supporting revolutionary struggles around the world, including the Vietnamese people's struggle against U.S. imperialism—but that wasn't their level of unity.

We were mainly directing these newspapers to the workers in the factories, although we did sell them more broadly—we would sell them at demonstrations as well as in different neighborhoods. This reflected the fact that, on the one hand, we had a national organization, but we hadn't yet developed it to the point where it could put out a single newspaper that would be a unified voice and instrument, if you want to put it that way, of the organization as a whole, on a national level. These local newspapers had generally the same perspective, but they wouldn't always have exactly the same take on different issues that arose, or they wouldn't all emphasize the same things at the same time.

There was a strength to this, but there was also a weakness. The strength is that we were able to speak to local issues more, and there was a certain diversity that was good. But these monthly papers could not make an analysis of key issues in a timely way, because they were monthly papers, and they didn't have a unified analysis coming out from a single center that the whole organization could pull together around, and then take initiative around in accordance with the particular conditions that comrades were working in, in the various local areas.

We were also continuing to work in the anti-war movement and among the students, although this was after the big upsurge of the '60s, and after Kent State and Jackson State, and the student movement was not on the same mass scale as before, and didn't have the same powerful revolutionary current. But there were still fairly broad sections of students and youth who in various ways were in rebellion against the system, and we were trying to relate to that, while our focus was on going to the workers in the factories and taking revolution, socialism and communism to them, as best as we understood that.

## Red Papers 5

I was sort of unofficially the leader of the RU by this time, but that wasn't an entirely settled question; and, while we had an elected collective leadership that was centered in Chicago, within that collective core of leadership we didn't have an official "leader of leaders," as we say now.

I was sort of unofficially assuming that position, and things were evolving in that way, but it wasn't yet clear at that point how the whole question of leadership was going to be approached. Part of the reason we didn't make a big point about having a leader, especially one that we would publicize, is that we regarded ourselves as still a formation that was building and contributing toward the development of a party. We didn't regard ourselves as that party. So we didn't want to be, in effect, pre-empting some things by declaring a leader, in a public way at least.

Developing theory—actually applying Marxism to the questions we faced and learning in the process—was essential at this point. And one of the ways in which I was providing leadership within the RU, besides playing an important part in developing policies and tactics for different struggles, was through doing a lot of theoretical work. I especially focused on one of the most important questions in relation to revolution in the U.S., which is what we call the national question—that is, the situation of Black people and other oppressed nationalities in the U.S., what is the means for ending their oppression, and how does this relate to the radical transformation of society as a whole?

In the movement of that time, no one had yet made a thorough and thoroughly correct analysis of this question. The Black Panther Party had in their better days put forward an almost classical colonial model, at times comparing the situation of Black people in the U.S. to that of Algeria under French rule. Other forces had gone with a view that focused almost exclusively on the privileges that had been granted to white workers as the heart of the matter—this was the "white-skin privilege" line. A few groups tried to claim the situation of Black people still fit into the 1928 resolution of the Comintern (Communist International), which characterized Black people as primarily peasants and said that the heart of their struggle revolved around their right to self-determination, the right to form a separate Afro-American Republic in the south; while this reflected at least some of the reality of the period in which this Comintern resolution was written, by 1972 it was badly out of date and something of a theoretical Procrustean bed. (Procrustes was an innkeeper in classical Greek mythology who forced everyone who slept in his inn to either cut off part of their legs or to be stretched out so they would fit into the bed he provided. "Procrustean" has become a metaphor for a method that attempts to torture reality to make it fit into pre-conceived notions.) PL, as well as many Trotskyite groups, utterly negated the national question, and the CP maintained that this oppression could all be reformed away under capitalism. So clearly a great need existed to arrive at a correct analysis of this decisive question.

We devoted an entire issue of *Red Papers*—*Red Papers 5*—to an analysis of the Black national question, and I did much of the research and analysis and the main part of the writing for that issue of *Red Papers*.[25] It had a big impact within the RU but also in the movement more broadly—a lot of people and groups united with it, and there was also a lot of criticism and debate—so this was one of the most important ways in which I was providing leadership at that time.

## The Guardian Forums

The "Guardian forums," which took place during this general period, were also part of the "pre-party ferment" that was going on. They were sponsored by the *Guardian* newspaper and billed as party-building forums. We saw this too as an important arena to address and a way to sharpen up the big questions in the movement. The *Guardian* actually represented a form of "revisionism-lite," I guess you could say. It was basically in the camp of the Communist Party and the pro-Soviet revisionist viewpoint, but it represented a kind of "left pole" within that. They were trying to appeal to and draw in people who were disgusted by the open reformism and revisionism of the CP. I talked earlier about how the CP openly and viciously attacked the Panthers, for example, and many people were obviously disgusted by that. But the *Guardian* represented a slightly more left version of fundamentally the same politics.

These forums were aimed especially at what was the called "the new

---

25. *Red Papers 5* covered the history of the development of African-Americans in the U.S., from colonial times to 1970; it analyzed the class makeup of Black people in the U.S. and how they fit into the overall social structure; it critiqued a range of other views on this question; and it also included "work reports" from RU comrades on their practice in working to unite the working class as a whole against this oppression, as well as in building caucuses of Black or Chicano workers in the workplace. Most essentially, this *Red Papers* showed that the movement against the oppression of Black people as a people and the proletariat's struggle for socialism were at one and the same time distinct but inextricably interconnected social currents, bound together by a thousand links. The RCP has held to this essential position ever since, even as it has modified and deepened its analysis as it has learned more and things have further changed and developed.

communist movement" at that time—people who rejected the Communist Party and were grappling with the question of forming a new party that would be a real revolutionary vanguard. So the *Guardian* had a series of forums on a number of different issues: the national question, how to work in the working class, how to build the party, the woman question, the united front—I don't remember all the specific issues, but around a number of issues like that they had forums where representatives of different trends and groups would speak and debate. So we took part in these—I spoke at one of them and other RU comrades spoke at others. These forums were a part of the sorting out, if you will, of different lines; and from our point of view, it was part of drawing a clear line of demarcation between real communism and phony communism, or "revisionism," which means revising the revolutionary heart out of Marxism and communism and reducing it to just drab reformism—sometimes reformist dogma, but reformist nonetheless.

Although we didn't have a weekly newspaper at that time, the RU did begin a monthly newspaper, *Revolution*, shortly after we set up our national headquarters in Chicago. *Revolution* both wrote about the struggles going on and tried to put them in a revolutionary context, and also did exposure of the imperialist system and carried out polemics with other trends and organized forces in the movement, and addressed important theoretical issues. So this too became a critical element in our all-round efforts of the time.

### Agonizing Over McGovern

Shortly after we set up in Chicago, George McGovern came on the scene as a presidential candidate running on a promise to get the U.S. out of Vietnam. This became a big question. Many people who had been drawn into supporting the "peace candidate" Eugene McCarthy or then Bobby Kennedy in the '68 election had since become totally alienated from the bourgeois electoral process and become much more radicalized. But, in 1972, the McGovern campaign was drawing a lot of people in the movement—many who hadn't moved to a full revolutionary position, but even some who had been inclined in that way—back into the bourgeois electoral framework. Whether to support McGovern or not was widely debated in the movement. This was true even within the RU itself. And, here again, the reformist side of Leibel Bergman asserted itself.

Leibel was arguing very vigorously and vehemently that, as he put it, "it's our internationalist duty to the Vietnamese people to support McGovern, because McGovern will put an end to the Vietnam War and Nixon will escalate it." This was not something that I, or the RU as a whole, simply dismissed. We didn't just say, "oh, McGovern, he's a bourgeois candidate, end of discussion." I personally agonized over this a lot; I did a lot of reading, a lot of study, trying to understand in a general sense what is represented by conflicts within an imperialist ruling class, and then more specifically what was represented by *this* conflict—not just the electoral contest in itself, but what larger conflicts within the ruling class and the imperialist system did this represent, or not represent. To what degree were there really serious differences?

I wrestled deeply with this question: Could it actually be true that this was an exceptional case, where which bourgeois candidate got elected might make a profound difference? Was it really true that whether or not McGovern got elected would determine whether the U.S. would pull out of Vietnam or, on the other hand, escalate the war? I and others in the RU agonized over all these kind of questions, trying to understand the realities of the conflicts within the ruling class and what was going on in the world more broadly and how did this election fit into that; and trying to understand more deeply the principles of Marxism and how they applied concretely to this situation. I came to the conclusion, and the RU as a whole was won to the position, that we should *not* support McGovern, and that in fact whether or not the Vietnamese people would prevail in this war and whether the U.S. would be forced to withdraw from Vietnam would not be determined on the basis of whether McGovern or Nixon got elected.

In fact, Nixon was re-elected in a landslide, and a lot of people who were drawn into the McGovern campaign got very demoralized by that. And yet, within a few months after Nixon's re-election, even though Nixon ordered a Christmas-time escalation of the bombing in Vietnam, in January of 1973, the agreement was signed which began the withdrawal of the U.S. from Vietnam. By 1975 the puppet government of South Vietnam, which had been installed and kept in power by the U.S. since 1955, was toppled and Vietnam was reunified under the leadership of the Vietnamese Workers Party, the party founded by Ho Chi Minh. So this whole idea that only by electing McGovern could the Vietnamese people prevail and could the U.S. be forced out of Vietnam—this was proven in practice to be completely wrong.

But, of course, we didn't know exactly how all this would work out as the election was approaching. We had to study and wrangle deeply with this to come to a basic understanding of what was correct and would really represent the upholding of our internationalist responsibilities. Through that process, we united the RU around the position of "Victory through our struggle not through the elections," and fought for that line within the broader movement. That was actually a very wrenching process. As I said, this wasn't a matter of just adopting a facile approach of "this is an imperialist election—bourgeois candidates, who cares, they're all the same." We actually wrestled very deeply with the concrete situation, as well as the larger questions that this was bound up with, to figure out what stand to take.

So we "stood aside" from the elections in the sense of not supporting one candidate or another. But we mobilized people to oppose the war right at the time that the election was taking place, and that was an implementation of our slogan, "Victory through our struggle not through the elections."

## Nixon and Watergate: "Throw the Bum Out!"

But life is always changing, and you have to examine things in real life and not have a dogmatic approach. So when the whole Watergate thing broke out, and Nixon started getting in trouble and there was a real question of whether he'd be impeached, or forced to resign, Leibel came forward with something that I *did* think was correct. He said, they're in a lot of turmoil, and we should join in and make more trouble for them—"kick em while they're down." He came up with the idea that we should put forward the slogan "Throw the Bum Out, Organize to Fight," which is what we did.

We viewed this as being different than the election, and here's why. In the '72 election (and to some degree in the '68 election, through which Nixon first became President) some people insisted on the orientation of "anybody but Nixon." But if you take that kind of stand in the context of an election, you're saying hold your nose and vote for a Democrat, whether you say it openly and explicitly or not. And when you do that, you essentially put people in a passive, politically disarmed position. But in a context where there wasn't an election—and this whole Watergate thing was an internal, fratricidal struggle within the ruling class that was causing all kinds of shit to come to the surface and causing them all kinds of problems—we thought it was good to add fuel to that fire by popularizing the slogan, "Throw the Bum Out, Organize to Fight" and actually mobilizing people in that spirit and with that orientation. This was taking advantage of a conflict that was becoming very acute within the ruling class, in order to advance our struggle. Even though there may have been some reformist notions mixed in with this, fundamentally it wasn't a slogan or an approach which sided with one section of the ruling class, it wasn't a matter of being a tail on the Democrats, the way you would if you'd urged people to vote for McGovern in the election (or if you did this "indirectly," by taking a stand of "anybody but Nixon"). The unity between these two positions —refusing to support McGovern in the '72 election, and raising the slogan "Throw the Bum Out, Organize to Fight" during Watergate—was the criterion: would our position reflect reality and would it enable people to take conscious action, independent of the bourgeoisie, and develop their class consciousness and revolutionary understanding?

By the end of 1972 we had made important progress in consolidating the RU as a national organization and in laying the basis to form a genuine communist party. An important aspect of this was a developing unity with other revolutionary groups. This unity would pose new opportunities and new challenges—though not precisely the ones we anticipated.

# Chapter Fourteen

# *Unity, Struggle...and Principle*

During the early 1970s, we in the RU continued to work toward the development of a single multinational revolutionary communist party, and a key part of that was focused in our efforts to link up with and unite, and struggle, with other forces that had come out of the different streams of the movement and the radicalization that had gone on in the '60s. And, of course, among the most important of these streams were the different struggles of the oppressed nationalities—Black people, Puerto Ricans, Chicanos, Native Americans, Asians and others—in the U.S.

I mentioned earlier that Yoruba from the Young Lords Party had gone with our delegation to China. During this same general period, the Young Lords Party had begun to turn more and more toward Maoism, and they changed their name from the Young Lords Party to the Puerto Rican Revolutionary Workers Organization, which reflected this turn. And there was the Black Workers Congress, which grew out of the development of revolutionary organization among Black workers in the auto plants in Detroit, and then organized Black revolutionaries in other parts of the country. At this time, the Black Workers Congress too was moving more fully in the direction of taking up Marxism and Maoism.

## The National Liaison Committee

So we sought out these other organizations which we'd begun to work with in various ways and laid on the table that we needed to con-

273

sciously work toward the development of a single multinational communist party, a new revolutionary communist party. And through the course of discussion we united around this as a common objective. This took organizational form in what was called the National Liaison Committee, which had representatives of the Black Workers Congress (BWC), the Puerto Rican Revolutionary Workers Organization (PRRWO) and the Revolutionary Union (RU). The objectives of this National Liaison Committee were to develop closer unity on two fronts: common *practice* in the various mass struggles, and a common *line and program* for a unified party, through joint summation, study and debate. And in fact a lot of good work was done, much of which was centered in New York, where the PRRWO was mainly based, but also in various places in the Midwest. This Liaison Committee actually had a significant effect in mobilizing masses of people, including around revolutionary May Day, but also in other struggles that were going on, on various fronts, and in developing closer ideological unity and more of a common approach toward a party.

But within this there were a lot of contradictions that were yet to be fully confronted, and would have to be struggled through in order to make the leap to unify all these forces into a single party. And, as is not surprising given the nature of U.S. society, one of the main questions on the table was the national question. How do the struggles and movements of Puerto Rican people, of Black people, of Chicanos and Native Americans and Asians — how do these struggles relate to the overall revolutionary struggle? How does the emancipation of these peoples from their oppression as peoples relate to the general, broader struggle for socialist revolution? How, on the one hand, do you avoid these struggles being subordinated to a more narrow reformist kind of movement or liquidated in the name of "working class unity"; and, on the other hand, how do you develop them, not in a narrow, nationalist way which ends up accepting the framework of capitalist society, but in a way that is part of a socialist revolutionary struggle to transform all of society? These were questions that the whole movement was confronting, and contradictions and conflicting views on these crucial questions remained within the broader framework of unity that was being forged in practice and in theory within the National Liaison Committee.

## *Who Should Represent?*

Here I have to say that an important question arose when we were deciding who should represent the RU in this National Liaison Committee. DH, who joined the RU during our national tour in 1970, was more and more asserting that he should be playing a leadership role in relation to the Black members within the RU in particular, and he was pushing that he should be the RU representative on the Liaison Committee. Leibel, interestingly enough, was opposed to this, on what I later came to see was a correct and important basis. Revolutionaries of different nationalities were confronting the question of how to develop closer working relations and, more fundamentally, ideological and political unity. People who had come out of a more nationalist framework and had then taken up Marxism were confronting what it means to be working in a common way with white people who had become communists. Leibel was arguing that we should confront this straight up, and that I should be the representative to the Liaison Committee. Rather than having this issue be sort of "an elephant in the room" that nobody is talking about directly, let's get it right out there by having me there as the RU representative, and in that context let's work together and work through this issue as part of the broader struggle that needed to be waged to develop the unity to a higher level.

But at that time I took the mistaken position: "Look, there are enough contradictions, the key thing is to develop the Liaison Committee and to get good struggle going over these questions, to put forward our understanding of them, and to push the struggle forward in that way. And let's not make it more complicated by adding the factor of myself, as a white communist, being the RU representative. Let's let DH represent the RU and put forward our line."

Well, there were two problems with that. As it turned out, DH didn't put forward our line, he put forward a rank reactionary nationalist line, not even a revolutionary nationalist line. He was sort of a combination of a pseudo-communist revisionist from the CP and a very narrow, reactionary nationalist, which actually included a lot of racism and chauvinism toward other nationalities. As things sharpened up, he came out more fully with a lot of this really disgusting stuff: he actually referred to Hawaiians as "pineapples," and he insisted that Chicanos were really white people. So that was one problem—he wasn't going to put forward our line, as it turned out.

But the other, and more fundamental, problem was that, even though everybody had moved to a position of considering themselves communists, there was tension because people who are not white have a lot of negative experience with white people, even white people who seem on a certain level to be friendly or comradely. And Leibel was right, the best way to deal with that was to put me in the Liaison Committee as the RU representative, to directly confront this problem and struggle it through in that context, rather than seeking to avoid or "soften" this contradiction by having DH be the RU representative. But, partly because I was confused about this and didn't join with Leibel's more correct approach, we ended up with DH as the RU representative.

As it turned out, there was a lot of forward motion through the Liaison Committee. PRRWO and BWC both united with the position of *Red Papers 5*, as well as the need for a multinational communist party. But there were certain unresolved contradictions that came to a head. Should we institutionalize the notion that Black workers had a special role in the revolution and raise the slogan "Black workers take the lead"? That was one expression of the differences.

But even more central in the way this came out was the whole question of whether in the communist movement, and within the party that was to be formed, there needed to be some formal "guarantees" or built-in structures to make sure that the Black people and people of other oppressed nationalities wouldn't be sold out by the white people. Instead of selecting leadership on the basis of demonstrated ability to grasp and apply a communist line, and to lead party members to grasp and carry out a communist line, should we instead have a structure in which so many people would have to be of one nationality, so many of another nationality, and a majority would have to be non-white in the leadership in order to guarantee that this party would stay on the revolutionary path, and in particular wouldn't stab the struggles of the oppressed nationalities in the back?

## No Guarantees Against Selling Out

Well, as bitter experience has shown, the fact is that just having people of a particular nationality in leadership, or having a majority of leadership drawn from the oppressed nationalities, doesn't provide a guarantee that you will stay on the revolutionary road. These formalistic, so-called "guarantees" are not real guarantees at all. There are, and can be, no such guarantees. Staying on the revolutionary road is a matter of struggle—struggle to grasp, and win people to, a revolutionary line and to forge ahead on that basis, resolving the very real contradictions that have to be confronted in seeking to make revolution. And the problem is that seeking illusory "guarantees" of that kind, based on percentages of different nationalities in leadership and so on, undercuts the actual and essential struggle to grasp and apply the correct line.

The "correct line" isn't some abstract dogmatic notion; it involves developing your understanding in a living sense of the actual problems that you're up against in making revolution and how you solve those problems. What concrete strategy, tactics, and policies do you need to develop, how do you mobilize people and what overall vision and goal is this all guided by, and what overall framework does it fit into? How do you correctly handle the relationship between the revolutionary struggle you're seeking to build in a particular country and the whole worldwide struggle, and how do you resist the pulls to undercut or to stand back from support for revolutionary struggles in other parts of the world in order not to incur more repression against your own party? Questions and challenges of this kind are very acutely posed, particularly in a country like the U.S. All these are big questions that don't get resolved on the basis of having so many people of one nationality or another in leadership, but can only be resolved on the basis of struggling to gain a correct understanding of these contradictions and fighting through all the complexities that are involved and which continually arise, often in new forms, at each new stage of the struggle.

Grasping and uniting around the correct understanding and orientation toward all this was the leap and rupture that needed to be made in order to bring into being a party that really could *be* a communist vanguard, out of this whole revolutionary upsurge that had occurred through the period of the 1960s into the early '70s. And this was the stumbling block that the leaders of the BWC and the PRRWO could not get over or did not leap beyond—this was the rupture they would not or could not make.

Now, some members of the BWC and of the PRRWO did end up becoming part of the Revolutionary Communist Party (RCP) when it was formed, in 1975, including Carl Dix, who later became the RCP National Spokesperson; but the leadership of these organizations—and, under their leadership, most of the people in these organizations—did not make this leap. They insisted instead that not only in the broader movement, but also institutionalized within the party itself, you had to have structures in which a certain number of people, and even a majority, would be of the oppressed nationalities to supposedly guarantee that they wouldn't be sold out. Ideologically, this represented not rupturing with nationalism, it represented the expression of nationalism within a communist organization, and an undermining of the principles on which a communist organization has to be based.

In the U.S. you have many different nationalities of people, and one of the key factors in making a revolution in this country is going to be developing the struggle, including among white people, to take on and uproot the whole history of oppression of Black people, Puerto Ricans, Chicanos, Native Americans, Asians, and so on. You are never going to make a revolution in this country without that being central and pivotal. But you're also never going to make a revolution without a vanguard that bases itself on a scientific approach to these questions—and to every other decisive question—a vanguard in which everybody contributes and struggles with each other on the basis of striving to grasp that scientific approach, and *on that basis* battles out what is required to make revolution and to transform society and the world, to put an end to all oppression.

This is what we were confronting at the time of the National Liaison Committee. This is what we, in the RU, were fighting for as the basis on which the party and its leadership had to be unified, whatever particular individuals made up that leadership. And this is what the leaders of the BWC and the PRRWO, whose ideology was still a mixture of communism and nationalism, balked at. (For a short period in this Liaison Committee there was an Asian group, I Wor Kuen, which partly out of nationalism—they were mainly based among Chinese—and partly out of an attraction toward communism, had sort of taken up Mao. Then they dropped out of the Liaison Committee, largely for the same reasons —they could not or would not make a leap to being fully communist and systematically taking up the communist outlook and method.)

## The Struggle Sharpens Up

These questions were posing themselves with BWC and PRRWO, they were posing themselves in our leadership with DH, and they were also coming up in the practice and thinking of our own ranks. So to deal with them, I wrote a paper on the relationship between what we called the national and class struggles, which we put out in our ranks as an internal bulletin ("National Bulletin 13").

We criticized some tendencies in our own work to limit our work with white workers to trade-union issues, and among Black workers to tail—in other words, to just go along with and not challenge—a certain nationalist understanding and to confuse that with communist consciousness. Both of these tendencies expressed a lack of faith in the ability of workers, whether oppressed nationality or white, to grasp their interests *as a class*—not in a narrow sense, but as the class whose mission it is to do away with capitalism and, eventually, abolish class divisions altogether. We also criticized a tendency that we had fallen into, to in effect put off the question of actually building the party, and we said that now the different approaches had pretty much sorted themselves out and it was time to move more seriously towards an actual plan to build that party. Of course, these problems weren't limited to us, and we gave this internal bulletin to the other organizations in the Liaison Committee as well, with the hopes of generating struggle with them on a good basis.

Well, it did generate struggle, but of a rather antagonistic character. One of the leaders of BWC at the time, who later criticized his position and joined the Party, wrote in retrospect that part of BWC's and PRRWO's turn to Marxism had come off their difficulties in building their organizations, after a certain point.[26] They thought that Marxism would lead to relatively quick and easy solutions to these problems and, in particular after uniting with *Red Papers 5*, that they would immediately turn things around. When this didn't happen right away—and it didn't happen mainly because of larger factors, having to do with the general ebb in the revolutionary struggle in society—they began casting about for something else "that would work," and began pushing for a more nationalist approach. They argued that they needed to build up their base before a party could be formed—again, as part of that "guarantee" thinking I spoke to earlier—and that combining more nationalism into their communism was the way to do that.

---

26. See "Marxism, Nationalism and the Task of Party Building," by D.B., *The Communist*, Vol. II, Number 1.

So these two directions were clearly coming into conflict, and then BWC chose to respond with an open polemic criticizing our "National Bulletin 13" as being racist and national chauvinist.

## Bundism or Marxism?

We characterized this nationalist entrenchment as *Bundism*. In this we were drawing from the history of the Russian revolutionary movement. Russia, before the revolution, was called "the prisonhouse of nations," because there were so many nations and different national minorities that were oppressed under the regime of the Czar. Within the socialist movement in Czarist Russia there was a group based among Jewish workers that called itself the Bund, which wanted to be part of the overall socialist movement but said that it had a special role in upholding and protecting the interests of Jewish workers, who were bitterly oppressed in Russia.

Lenin waged a very sharp struggle with these Bundists. He pointed out that communists have to base themselves on the interests of the proletariat as a whole. The goal of socialism and communism, and the radical restructuring and transformation of society and the world on that basis, is what all communists, of whatever nationality, have to base themselves on; and trying to have different communist organizations that see themselves as upholding the particular interests of a particular oppressed group within the proletariat would lead back to nationalism and to the reinforcing of national divisions and not to a revolutionary transformation of society.

Now this same basic line was finding expression within our movement and specifically within the Liaison Committee. This struggle also erupted very sharply within the RU because DH, who was supposed to be representing our line and our organization within the Liaison Committee, was actually pushing this nationalist line within the RU as well as promoting it on the Liaison Committee. So we formulated this as a struggle of Marxism vs. Bundism. Or to put it another way, the fundamental question was: Are we going to be communists and base ourselves on that common ideology and struggle, and on *that* basis unite around the correct way forward to make revolution, with all the difficult problems and complexities that this involves, particularly in a country like the U.S.; or are we each going to retreat into a position of "my nationality first," raising that above the overall revolutionary struggle? If we do the latter, we're not going to have a unified party, we're not going to have a unified line, and most fundamentally, we're not going to have a way in which we can all struggle on a common basis, and a scientific basis, to grasp the correct approach to all these different contradictions, including how to uproot national oppression.

We insisted on the need to unify on the basis of analyzing reality as it actually is, in all its complexity, and in all its changingness, as the common scientific method and approach. BWC and PRRWO saw this kind of method and approach as a fetter and, after the painful break-up of the Liaison Committee, they thought they would roar ahead on the basis of what was objectively a combination of dogmatic pseudo-Marxism and revolutionary nationalism.

In fact, they didn't. They turned more inward and they weren't able to move ahead. To a significant degree, that was because we were *all* confronting the fact that the movement of the '60s had ebbed, and it wasn't going to be continuing forward on a high tide in the way it had; and we didn't know when there would be another high tide—nobody could predict that with certainty. But, at the same time, out of all this the question was very acutely posed: What do you do to bring forward a unified revolutionary vanguard force, so that everything that came forward in that upsurge is *not* lost, and you have something to build on for when the next upsurge comes, something that would carry forward in a consistent revolutionary and communist direction even before there was another upsurge?

These were the questions everybody was confronting, but because BWC and PRRWO came up with wrong answers to them, and clung to and refused to rupture with their attempt to eclectically combine nationalism with a Marxism that was becoming more and more dogmatic, they didn't go forward, and in fact they turned more and more inward and began to get more and more sectarian and even split apart among themselves.

That was a very painful thing to see. These were people with whom we'd worked closely, people with whom we had developed a real comradeship; we had hopes and expectations of uniting to form a party together with them—which would have been a tremendous thing, if we could have done it **on a correct basis**. But they were now heading for the cliff. The party, when it was formed, as the Revolutionary Communist Party, USA, in 1975, was a tremendous leap and did mean that something lasting and invaluable for the communist revolution came out of that whole '60s upsurge; but the fact that these other forces came right to the brink and wouldn't go forward was really heartbreaking and wrenching.

## The Night of the Lepus

I took part in the last Liaison Committee meeting, as one of the representatives of the RU (this was an expanded meeting, in which each organization had a number of representatives). In a real sense, this whole thing had a tragic aspect to it, yet there was a sort of ironic humorous moment when we were in New York for the final National Liaison Committee meeting, and the people from the BWC and the PRRWO were setting up the meeting. They were supposed to get in touch with us to let us know about the arrangements for the meeting. We waited and we waited, and waited and waited, and they were having trouble getting a place for the meeting. Finally they told us they would call us back in a number of hours, and we were getting so tense, in anticipation of what we knew would be a very heavy meeting, that we decided that we needed some relief. So we decided to go to a movie.

We picked out the stupidest movie we could find, one of these schlock horror movies called *The Night of the Lepus*, about these mutating gigantic rabbits that were going around rampaging and ravaging the people in the surrounding towns, eating people and generally creating havoc. And I remember sitting in this movie theater, watching this ridiculous movie, knowing we would soon get the call to go to the Liaison meeting and thinking: as stupid as this movie is, it is not as excruciating as what's coming in this Liaison meeting.

And sure enough, the meeting was excruciating. The whole thing just unraveled and blew apart on the basis of the differences that were becoming extremely sharp in the context of needing to make the leap that was before everybody, in order to form the party—the leap and rupture to being communists, in a consistent and thoroughgoing way, to being internationalists, to being Maoists in the fullest and most fundamental sense.

There were a lot of people, particularly within the oppressed nations and nationalities around the world, who admired and respected Mao because he was a leader of an oppressed Third World country and had led the people there to stand up. That kind of sentiment, respecting Mao on that basis, can be a positive thing in certain contexts, but that's not the same thing as *really* being a Maoist, actually being a *communist*. That was the question before people, and that was the stumbling block the leaders of PRRWO and the BWC could not or would not get over. This was heartbreaking, and the meeting was wrenching, because that was the question on the table and it lay at the root of a number of bitter disputes.

It would have been easy, on a certain level, for us to just accede to their demands, but that would have been forming an organization on an opportunist basis, not on a basis of everybody striving to be communists and to grasp the communist outlook and methodology and apply it to all the extremely difficult and complex problems that lie on the road to making revolution. Instead, we would just have had different "interest groups" ("identity groups") and factions within the party, and that would either have ripped the party apart or turned it into a bourgeois mishmash masquerading as a communist party, like the CPUSA, a party with no unified line or orientation towards making revolution and radically transforming the world. We refused to do that. We hadn't gone through everything we'd gone through just to bring into being yet another opportunist, revisionist group—another, perhaps even more pitiful, version of the CP.

It was tempting to give in, because it would have smoothed some things over in the short run, and we could have all gone off together to form a party. But it would have been a serious setback to form a party on that basis.

## Deepening the Struggle Against Narrow Nationalism

Instead, we carried forward and deepened the struggle of Marxism vs. Bundism (or communism vs. nationalism). We were firm that, if we are going to form a genuine communist vanguard, then we have to unite on the basis of communism, not on the basis of nationalism of even the most revolutionary kind. We can unite with all kinds of people in the practical struggle who are nationalists of various kinds, including obviously revolutionary nationalists. But *as communists, in forming a communist party*, we have to unite on the basis of communism—*that* has to be the common basis of unity and the common principles that everyone strives to apply.

On one level that might seem obvious, but it wasn't so obvious at that time, because much of the revolutionary upsurge had come out of the struggle against national oppression, and spontaneously the distinction between communism and various kinds of revolutionary sentiments, including revolutionary nationalism, was not so clear. Many people were arguing that you could combine nationalism and communism, or that revolutionary nationalism was "applied communism" if you were part of an oppressed nation or an oppressed national minority. So we had to carry out an ideological struggle to clarify these questions and draw crucial lines of demarcation; within our own ranks there were some people who had followed DH, or on their own had gravitated toward the line of confounding and eclectically combining communism and nationalism. But more broadly, this was a big question in the movement.

We published *Red Papers 6* with documents from both sides of this struggle, and we went deeply into this question and its many ramifications. For example, what does it mean if you say Black people are a nation—do they have the right to self-determination? Yes, we said, but how does that fit into the larger objectives of socialist revolution and transforming all of society on the road toward communism? We carried out study and theoretical work and ideological struggle around these questions, and in *Red Papers 6* we published a lot of the work we'd done and conclusions we'd drawn, because these were crucial questions that needed to be take up by the broader movement.

I remember, for example, a big controversy at that time was around whether the struggle to establish a separate state in the Black Belt South was the heart of the Black people's struggle. The BWC was arguing that it was, while our position was that there is a right for Black people to do that, and this right must be firmly upheld, but that was not the heart of the struggle, and to make it the heart of the struggle was to take up a nationalist position that led away from the objective of socialist revolution to transform all of society and uproot all oppression. We emphasized that the *right* to do something, including the right to set up a separate state, is not the same thing as the advisability of doing so under all conditions.

This was a big struggle, and it required a lot of work to come to a correct understanding of this. I went to libraries in the Chicago area, doing research day after day, in order to analyze what had actually happened to the Black people who lived in this historic area of the Black Belt in the South (which was called that because of the color of the soil), a crescent of land that ran through much of the deep south and other areas where Black people, in their overwhelming majority, had been exploited and oppressed, from the time of slavery up until World War 2. Beginning around the time of World War 1, and then really accelerating during and after World War 2, Black people in large numbers were dispersed from that area, both through being pushed off the land because the white owners were mechanizing and didn't need as many Black laborers on the land, and through the "pull" of better jobs and better social conditions in the north. The conclusion to be drawn from this extensive research and study was that, on the one hand, large numbers of Black people still lived in the Black Belt South, but even there they were now living mainly in the urban areas, not in the rural farmlands, because of profound changes that were occurring in southern agriculture; and, at the same time, millions of Black people had left the south altogether and were now living in urban areas in the north. And under these conditions, the setting up of a separate state in the Black Belt South, while still a right of Black people, was not at the heart of Black people's struggle—it didn't correspond to breaking the most decisive chains of oppression that were shackling them, in the conditions in which they were actually living, with the changes that had gone on in the several decades since World War 2 especially. Our understanding of this was greatly deepened as a result of extensive concrete investigation and analysis, and theoretical work and a lot of ideological struggle to get further clarity on this question.[27]

## On the Real

During this time, I had some interesting personal experiences which served as sort of a commentary on, or perhaps a counterpoint to, this whole ideological struggle we had been engaged in. When I moved to Maywood and I sought out and found the good basketball courts to go to, there were a number of occasions where people were testing me out. For example, there was this ice cream and hamburger joint in Maywood called the "Cock Robin," and one of my favorite things to do, after a day of playing basketball, was to go to the Cock Robin. One day I was at the Cock Robin having a hamburger and a milkshake—it was early evening, and one of the guys I knew from playing basketball was sitting in his car.

---

27. See "Living Socialism and Dead Dogmatism," *The Communist*, Volume I, Number 2.

He called me over, and he said: "Hey, how's it going? Get in the car, let's talk." I did, and we talked for a while, and I realized that this was partly a friendly gesture on his part, and partly he was testing me out—like, "okay, it's one thing when you come to our courts, you hang out and play ball with us, but what about when you're away from the courts—are you gonna hang with us now, or are you gonna act like you don't know us?"

There was another guy I knew from playing ball, and one day I walked into McDonald's and he was working there. I'm standing in line, the line is moving and I'm getting close to the cash register where he's working. I know he's seeing me, but he's not saying anything to me or making any gesture to acknowledge me. So finally, I get up to the front of the line, and he comes out with, "May I help you, sir?" And I say, "C'mon man, what is this, you don't talk to nobody when you're not on the basketball court?" So then he cracked up and started joking around with me. And obviously this was another situation where he was wondering if I was going to act all different and not even acknowledge him.

This guy who worked in McDonald's, I think his name was Raymond, and he had an older brother named James. James was a very good basketball player, he could really leap, and for whatever reason he liked to play on the same squad with me. And we used to hang out and talk. At about the time the struggle with the Bundists was coming to a head, James and I were talking about different things going on, and in particular what was happening with Black people. And thinking of what people like DH were always arguing, I said, "Well, you know, some people say that really, deep down, Black people just hate white people." And James replied, "Well, not really"—and then we went into a whole discussion of the complexities of this. "Yeah," he said, "there is a lot of racism, in a lot of different ways, and some white people do a lot of nasty shit, and you gotta really test people out to see if they are for real or not; but no, I don't go around hating all white people, and most Black people I know don't either."

I thought this was a very interesting conversation in its own right, but it was also something to reflect on in relation to the struggle with the Bundists, because DH was always pushing that really deep down all Black people just hate white people. And it struck me that, while James had a sophisticated understanding of a lot of things, and was pretty militant in his sentiments about racism and the oppression of Black people, he was not a revolutionary and by no means a communist, and yet his outlook was lofty, and not narrow and petty in the way that, ironically, the outlook of DH, the so-called communist, was.

Another time in the same period, for some reason there wasn't much going on at the basketball courts where I usually hung out, so I asked somebody where was another place to play ball, and they directed me to this park on the west side of Chicago. I drove down there and I got into some games, and the team I was on won a few games, but then we lost so we had to sit down and wait until our turn came around again. It was a Saturday afternoon and a lot of people were playing, so we had to wait quite a while to get back on the court, and I got into this conversation with this guy who'd been on my team about what was going on with the government and politicians, and in particular how did you look at Kennedy. This guy was talking about how when Kennedy came in, it made a lot of difference for Black people, Kennedy did a lot for Black people, and so on. And I was arguing, it's not really that Kennedy did things for Black people, Kennedy wasn't really *for* Black people, it's just that there were changes he had to go along with. We're going back and forth, and finally he says to me, "Well, you know, maybe you just have to be Black to see it, but there was a world of difference after Kennedy came in." So I said, "Well, look, I'm not saying that there were no changes made from the time Kennedy came in. What I'm saying is that it wasn't Kennedy who did this out of the goodness of his heart. I'm saying there was a tremendous struggle waged by Black people which a lot of people supported, things were really shaking the country up, and Kennedy had to make some changes to try to keep this from getting completely out of hand."

There was a fairly long silent pause, and then he asked me, seemingly out of nowhere, "Do you play baseball?" And I answered, "No, not really." He went on: "You know, we're looking for another pitcher for our semi-pro baseball team." I reflected on this for a second, and it seemed obvious to me: this is not really about baseball at all, this is this guy's way of saying, "I get it now, you're not arguing that these changes weren't important for Black people, you're just saying they came about a different way, through the struggle of Black people. Now I understand where you're coming from."

## Chapter Fifteen

# *Building the Party*

The destruction of the Liaison Committee confronted us with a difficult situation. We had tried to go down the road together with these other forces to forge the unity to build a party and then that was blown apart, for the reasons that I've discussed. So now what do we do? And here again, I have to give credit to Leibel Bergman. He insisted that "We have to go ahead to form the party anyway, because if we don't seize the moment to unite as many people as we can to form the party now, everything that came forward in this upsurge of the '60s is ultimately going to be lost." So that is what we set out to do.

Once we'd come to the understanding that we had to carry forward with the building of the party, even in the face of this setback with the National Liaison Committee, then we recognized that this had to become the main and central task for the period of time until the party was formed—and this had to be a relatively short and telescoped process. We couldn't drag it out or we'd lose the momentum and we would lose and dissipate the people who'd come forward out of this whole upsurge of the '60s and into the early '70s—we would lose the chance to bring them together as an organized vanguard force, and therefore nothing permanent, in terms of revolutionary leadership, would come out of that whole upsurge—which would obviously be a major setback and defeat. And we recognized that in order to carry forward and culminate the party-building struggle, we had to continue and

288

deepen the process of distinguishing different lines and programs.

These are not just abstract, academic questions. They concern the basis on which people are going to be and need to be united in order to form the party. Around what kind of program are they going to unite? What is your understanding of who are the forces for revolution—or even what kind of revolution is needed—and how do you go about working to bring forward these forces for revolution? Obviously these are gigantic questions in any revolution. But they are especially important to be battled out, and to get the most clarity and unity around, in a country like the U.S., given everything that you're up against. It is a major, even a *monumental* challenge to make revolution in a country like this while at the same time doing this in a way that contributes to and is part of the whole world revolutionary process to abolish imperialism and thoroughly transform *all* societies and relations based on exploitation, oppression and inequality. Especially given this momentous challenge, you have to struggle to get clarity and to determine what really is the road that will lead toward that, even while you will continually have a great deal more to learn as you carry this forward. So, in order to have a solid foundation, you have to recognize and draw basic dividing lines, and sharply distinguish what will really lead to revolution from what will lead away from it.

### Going on Tour

We were carrying out discussions and struggle with different forces around the country, but as one leading edge of this party-building process in 1974 I went on a speaking tour around the country, representing the RU and putting forward our views on the building of the party. In connection with this speaking tour, we organized private meetings and discussions with different people and groups in many cities across the country, from the northwest to the Bay Area to the midwest, the east, and the south.

The speeches I gave were very polemical: As I said, we had to draw lines of demarcation clearly and sharply in order to unite people on a solid and correct basis to actually take up the challenge of leading a revolution in a country like this. So the speeches would lay out the need for a party and why that was a crucial thing to bring forward out of this whole upsurge, but then they would criticize different lines that had currency in the movement. I argued against the line that we didn't need a party, or that vanguards were a bad thing, but I also hit at different lines and programs that were put forward concerning the basis of unity of the future party that were different from what *we* recognized to be the necessary basis and program.

I also polemicized against the dogmatic tendencies that had arisen within the newly developing communist forces. I talked earlier about how the PRRWO and the BWC had retreated not only into nationalism but also into dogmatism. They put forward that basically the only task was to build the party, and they made theoretical work essentially the be-all and end-all in relation to building the party. They took the stance that to even get involved in the mass struggles that were going on was—and here they borrowed a phrase from Lenin and mis-used it—"bowing to spontaneity."

Lenin meant that when you're working among the masses, you shouldn't just tail after their understanding and where they're at, at a given time; instead you have to, as he put it, *divert* them and their struggles onto the revolutionary path, and through the course of all your work show them the necessity and the possibility of revolution and organize and lead them for revolution, and not for something else, something less. But the BWC and PRRWO and other similar groups and tendencies distorted this into saying that being involved in the mass movements and mass struggles at all was "bowing to spontaneity." This was just a dogmatic distortion that was combined with their retreat into nationalism.

There were also forces who were falling into the opposite error, putting forward the position that Lenin actually *was* polemicizing against—that is, a reformist position that would put revolution off the map, or into an indefinite future that really had nothing to do with the work you were doing today. In their view, you *did* have to completely immerse yourself in the day-to-day struggles, whatever they were, and leave the goal of revolution out of the picture, or talk about it only as a vague abstract thing. Along with this went a lot of what Lenin characterized as *economism*—which I have spoken to earlier, in terms of influences on the RU itself—a view that when you go to the working class, you reduce your politics down to the level of trade-unionism, you make everything revolve just around the day-to-day struggles of the workers for wages and working conditions, and you leave the broader political struggle and beyond that the strategic political and revolutionary goals out of the picture. So I also polemicized against that as part of this tour.

These speeches and public meetings were, as you can imagine, very lively. There would usually be hundreds and hundreds of people at the public meetings, because the question of the party was a big question among a whole section of people who'd come forward out of the upsurges of the '60s and early '70s. I'd give a speech, and it was very polemical, and then we had question-and-answer sessions, which were generally very heated, because many, many groups and tendencies would mobilize people to come and raise their questions and disagreements.

Some of this would be on a high plane politically and ideologically, and some of it would frankly be down on the ground, narrow, petty and even personal attacks—like someone would get up from a group like the October League, which was a group that called itself Maoist but was moving toward forming a party on an essentially reformist basis, and they'd attack me for being "the son of a judge." That was the level of "ideological struggle" they often dragged things down to. There had been a big strike in the Bay Area, and my father had issued an injunction against the strikers, limiting the picketing. So then people who were on this level would say things like, "How can you be a communist? Look at what your father did." And I would make the point: "First of all that's my father—this is me, I'm a grown adult, I have my own views and actions. Second, let's put this into context and draw the most important lessons from it. I happen to know this judge you're talking about, and on a personal level he's a good guy, and on some issues like discrimination, and the rights of defendants, he's made some good rulings. But the point is, this is all within the framework of an oppressive system and a set of laws that serves this system. So in the final analysis, it doesn't matter whether he's a good guy or not, he's following the law and the law represents the interests not of the proletariat, the working class, but the interests of the capitalist class. And when he follows the law, naturally it's going to result in these kinds of rulings, against the interests of the working class." So I tried to use even these personal attacks to make some important political points and bring out the nature of the system, and how even a good-hearted person, which my father was, when acting as a judge was operating within the confines, and had to follow the logic and mechanisms, of a system that is oppressive and exploitative.

But in the main, the things raised were on a higher level and dealing with more substantial questions—not personal attacks but ideological and political disagreements—and we would battle these out, back and forth, in the question-and-answer part of these meetings, following the speeches I gave. A couple of other comrades accompanied me on this tour, and they would also take part in the private meetings with different people and groups. So it was a very lively process and a very invigorating experience. We certainly clarified the differences much more sharply for a lot of people, and we did bring forward some people to join in the process of bringing the party into being, including some people who hadn't previously been part of the RU.

## The RU and the Mass Struggle

Even as we recognized that party-building had become the main task and we had to put our main emphasis into that for a certain telescoped period of time—and this party-building tour was one major reflection of that—we also were continuing to carry out mass work of various kinds. As I said, we rejected the dogmatist position that the BWC and the PRRWO were retreating into, which insisted that you should withdraw from the mass movements. So there was much mass work that we continued to carry out. There was the whole initiative I talked about earlier in terms of the crisis developing around Nixon in 1973 and '74—our position of "Throw the Bum Out..." There were still mass demonstrations in the early '70s against the Vietnam War, until the U.S. actually began withdrawing. And we continued the work we'd been doing in the working class.

Very importantly, the struggle we waged against narrow nationalism had actually unleashed the comrades in the RU to more aggressively and dynamically take up the struggle against national oppression, in many different forms. In the Bay Area, the RU took on a dragnet against Black men in San Francisco ("Operation Zebra," I think it was called) and the police murder of a Black youth in Oakland named Tyrone Guyton. We were able to both unite with the outrage within the community and help give that organized expression and, very notably, comrades were able to mobilize workers in the factories, other workplaces and the unemployment lines to take on these struggles, both at work and in the streets.

The RU also built nationwide support for the Chicano workers, overwhelmingly women, who went on strike at the Farah plants in the southwest, a struggle where three different forms of oppression—

national, class, and women's oppression—were very intertwined, and where comrades drew links between these different struggles and movements.

## In the Mines

One of the main struggles that we were involved in, in the period of '74-'75, even as we were moving toward the formation of the party, involved the miners in West Virginia. In the early '70s, some comrades I had worked with in Richmond, who had previously spent time in West Virginia as volunteers in government anti-poverty programs, raised that, "We really should do work among the miners in places like West Virginia, they are part of a really impoverished, exploited section of people in Appalachia and an important section of the working class."

So we decided that we would, in fact, send some of these people who'd been in West Virginia before, as well as some other comrades, to the mines. It was really a tremendous thing that people volunteered to go to the mines. Working in the mines is a very difficult and dangerous job, and life in those areas of Appalachia is not an easy life by any means. And a number of comrades, including the ones who made the suggestion to do work there, and others who volunteered, plunged right into this.

We set out to take socialism and communism to what we saw as an important section of the working class. And we did play a leading role in the formation of what became known as the Miners Right to Strike Committee, which led a number of major strikes in the area of West Virginia, in which tens of thousands of miners were involved. At the same time, as we learned more fully through our work there, there was a big "disconnect" between the trade union militancy of a lot of the miners, which was very developed, and their political consciousness and ideological outlook, which was not on a very high level.

This was a rural area, steeped in a lot of religious, even fundamentalist religious, tradition. The comrades who worked in the mines would talk about the raging debates they'd have with the other miners, some of whom were also part-time preachers, who would always be going around Bible-thumping. Working in the mines leaves people covered with coal dust, so at the end of the shift everybody heads for the showers and then people would hang around in the shower rooms afterward and there would be these arguments and debates. Our comrades would get into arguing with these miner-preachers about evolution and things like Noah's flood and how that flood didn't really take place.

I remember a funny story that one comrade told later—this was a person who'd done a lot of theoretical study and understood a lot of different scientific questions very well. So he was able to argue very strongly about why evolution was a fact and take on all this fundamentalist religious nonsense. One time, everybody had cleared out of the shower room except this comrade and then, just as he was getting ready to leave, one of the miners came back, looked around to make sure nobody was there, then said to the comrade: "I'm only gonna say this once. I think this religion stuff's a bunch of bullshit too." And then he walked out. So this gives you a sense of both the atmosphere and some of the ideological work and struggle that our comrades were carrying out within it.

I also know from talking to some of the women comrades who were down there that this was a very difficult area for them to try to live and work in. On the one hand, there were just beginning to be a few women coming into the mines as workers during the time our comrades were there. Overwhelmingly, and almost entirely, this was a preserve of men —the men worked in the mines and the women mainly didn't work or sometimes had jobs, or part-time jobs, in various places but, with very few exceptions, not in the mines. In general, it was a very suffocating atmosphere for the women who had grown up there, and in certain ways it was even more suffocating for the women comrades who had come out of a whole different scene, where culturally and politically and in other ways they were actively involved in a lot things. They would tell stories of how they would meet women in West Virginia who had this hunger to know about the broader world, but who then at a certain point would often retreat and pull back, because it was very difficult for them to break out of the narrowing and suffocating confines of the situation there, and many of them didn't see any realistic alternative.

So this was a very contradictory experience. We did lead a lot of mass struggle and we were trying to do revolutionary work and bring forward socialism and communism. But, while the miners would unite militantly with us in trade union struggles, it was very difficult to win them to a *revolutionary, communist class consciousness.*

This work we did in the mines had its own particularities but it was also representative of the kind of work we were doing in many different parts of the working class. We were leading strikes, including wildcat strikes that weren't authorized by the union, in auto and in other industries where we were working. And we were continuing to take part in the broader political movements, although these were undergoing something of an ebb. The Vietnam War, or at least the massive involvement of U.S. forces in that war, had come to an end, and other struggles that had come out of the '60s were also ebbing to a certain degree.

We were doing a lot of work among the unemployed as well. There was a significant amount of unemployment in the early and mid '70s. We were not only trying to organize people to fight for jobs and benefits but also, once again, seeking to bring broader political consciousness and the goal of socialism and communism to the unemployed workers. And we would mobilize people who were unemployed not only to fight around that issue but to take part in broader political events and struggles, including bringing them to May Day and International Women's Day rallies and demonstrations, as well as involving them in other political struggles of the time. This was all part of our understanding of how to develop an all-around struggle in which the working class comes to the fore as the leading force and allies with and leads other strata and movements in society toward the goal of a socialist revolution and ultimately communism.

### *"Are You Still Not Drinking Coke?"*

Several times I've mentioned my friend Billy, whom I'd known since high school. He had been in my younger sister's class, a couple of years behind me, but we overlapped for a brief time in high school, although we only casually knew each other at that time. Then, when I'd gotten sick and I'd gone back to do tutoring and working with some of the athletes in other ways at the high school, I'd gotten to know him in a deeper way. I remember very fondly that, when I first started going out of the house, after I got sick and was engaged in a long struggle to get over the kidney disease, and I was very self-conscious about how I looked because of all the side effects of the cortisone I was taking, Billy came right up to me and acted as if everything were just perfectly normal and there were no reason to be reluctant about talking to me. Something like that meant a lot to me at the time, and it stayed with me—that's the way I am—and after that I always had a very fond place in my heart for him.

After Billy got out of high school, he got married right away and he needed to get a job. At that time my father had certain contacts with people in the longshoremen's union, so I went to my father and asked him if he could help. And we actually helped Billy get a job as a long-shoreman, or at least got him into the longshoremen's union. But there were two levels of longshoremen in the union, and he was in the lower level, so he didn't get very much work. I remember asking him one time, "How's it going with the longshore job?" He said, "Aw man, I quit going to the union hall. I hardly ever get work, and besides, all the people who hang out in the union hall are the same people I hang out with in the pool hall and in the street anyway, so why the fuck should I go to the union hall?" This, again, was a reflection of the fact that he had one foot in the proletariat and one foot in "the life," as they say — different hustles and schemes that were "on the other side of the law."

But when I saw him, we would often get into talking about what was going on in the world. One time, I was running down to him what was happening in South Africa and in particular the role that Coca-Cola played in supporting the apartheid government in South Africa and oppressing the African people there, and how therefore I was boycotting Coke. He was very interested in this, and every time I'd see him after that he would ask me, "Are you still not drinking Coke?" After a certain point, I'd given up this particular form of protest, and I explained to him, "Well that gesture in and of itself didn't really do much, so I've given that up, but I still feel the same way about what Coca-Cola is doing in South Africa and about South Africa as a whole." Yet, every time I'd see him after that, he'd ask me, "Are you still not drinking Coke?" — and both of us knew that this was a metaphor for bigger things than just Coke, or even just Coke's role in South Africa. So Billy had these conflicting, contradictory sides, but he was always interested in what was going on in the world and supportive of the political things I was into, and he was the one who introduced me to people who in turn introduced me to Huey Newton and Bobby Seale. He was someone I enjoyed talking with, someone I learned a great deal from, and someone who meant a lot to me.

In 1974, when I was living in Chicago, one day I came home and there was a message that Wilma, the woman he'd married right out of high school, was trying to reach me. So I called her back and she gave me the sad news that Billy had been killed. And the way he died was really excruciating.

He was killed in a confrontation in this area of Berkeley, Sacramento

Street, that was more or less bounded by Walker's Pool Hall at one end and Stubby's Pool Hall at the other. I used to go down and look for him there, that's where he hung out a lot. I remember being down there looking for him one day when the news broke that Martin Luther King had been assassinated. There were these two guys parked in their car in front of Walker's Pool Hall. I'd seen them before when I'd go in the pool hall looking for Billy. But this particular day they clearly had just gotten the news about Martin Luther King, and one of them came up to me and, sort of half as a warning and half as a threat, said, "Today, you better get out of here." And so I did.

But I was somewhat familiar with this scene in the area, in this stretch of Sacramento Street, where Billy was killed. As I later heard the story, he was in some kind of after hours joint, sitting at a table talking with somebody who'd gotten into some shit with some other people, and both he and the other guy were shot. But what made it especially excruciating was that it was something like an hour before the police and an ambulance came, and during that time Billy bled to death in this place.

Even though, since moving to Chicago, I hadn't been able to keep up with him the way I did when I was living in the Bay Area, and I hadn't seen him for more than a year, this was a deep personal blow to me.

Since I had moved to Chicago, my relationship with my parents had also gone through further changes. As I explained earlier, in order to make the kind of leaps that we had to make in moving to Richmond and going to the proletariat, and given the political and ideological differences that existed with my parents at that time, our relations became pretty estranged, and I largely cut off contact with them for a number of years. Not that I completely broke off things with them, or that our relationship was fundamentally antagonistic, but for quite a while I didn't see that much of them. We saw a lot of things differently and I was living a very different life than they were—and a different life than they wanted me to be living, to be honest.

By the mid-'70s, there was still tension between us, but two things had happened. One, while my parents initially supported the Vietnam War, they had later come around to opposing it, and they were principled enough to admit they had been wrong. And, more generally, while my father was then a judge, he was the kind of judge who, for example, made rulings against discrimination in the selection of juries. He was that kind of a liberal judge, and I've heard from many lawyers, including progressive lawyers, who say that in my father's courtroom you would get a fair deal, that things wouldn't be as stacked against the defendant as they were in many other courtrooms. He was still a judge, and that was an objective fact, which I've spoken about earlier, but our political and ideological differences were not as great as they had been before. So I was getting to be a little closer with my parents at this time, but our lives still didn't intersect very much and there was still some tension there.

### *"Time Has Come Today"*

By 1974, after the party-building tour, the RU recognized that the time had come to move more immediately to the formation of the party. We developed a journal called *Forward to the Party, Struggle for the Party*, which was not just an internal RU journal but was a vehicle for everybody who became part of this party-building process. The RU also developed Programme Discussion Committees, where people could struggle over the actual application of Marxism to making revolution in this country and through that develop a Programme for the new party. This journal was addressed to the people who were in these Programme Discussion Committees and in general were part of the process of going to the party.

There were a few people from the BWC who joined the party at the time it was formed, or soon after it was formed, and there were some people from the PRRWO who did the same—this was not a matter of huge numbers, but it was still significant. And there were some people who were in some other organized formations in various parts of the country who joined in this party-building process, a number of whom became part of the party when it was formed. There were also others who weren't part of any organized group or formation, but were just revolutionary-minded individuals who came forward in this party-building process.

The journal *Forward to the Party, Struggle for the Party* provided a means through which people involved in the party-building process could express their opinions and carry on struggle over questions relating to this process. We had written a draft Programme and draft Constitution, and people made criticisms and suggestions for changes in those documents, or just put forward their general views on the party and the goals of the revolution. So this journal and these discussion committees provided an organized form through which people could thrash out these issues and also come to a decision about whether they wanted to go forward to be part of forming the party. This went on all over the country. Some people who took part in this process ended up deciding they didn't want to join the party, but many of them remained supportive. And a number of people who were outside the RU were brought forward through this process and became part of the formation of the party.

It was through this process that we identified and focused on the key questions and the key controversies that needed to be put on the table, and on the floor of the founding congress of the party, to be thrashed out. You can't discuss literally every line of a draft programme or constitution—you have to focus on issues that become concentration points of key questions and matters of principle, and/or the issues over which there is the most controversy and struggle. The Programme Discussion Committees and the journal *Forward to the Party, Struggle for the Party* also helped to identify those key questions so that in organizing the founding congress we could focus on those questions.

Within the RU itself, of course, there was very concentrated focus on these questions, and a lot of struggle—it was a period where people were doing their political work in the day and then at night studying Marxism, summing up their practice, debating questions and writing for the journal. There was a lot of vibrancy to this process, but there were also some negative elements—both in terms of ideological and political line and also in terms of method, or how people were approaching this process—that were finding expression and gaining some momentum.

# Chapter Sixteen

# Exposing the Soviets, Struggling with the Chinese

$B$efore talking directly about the founding of the Party, and to give a fuller sense of the context in which this occurred, it is worthwhile to discuss important changes that were going on internationally, and how we were responding to that. I mentioned earlier that the struggle with the BWC and PRRWO—and, really, the whole process of building the Party—occurred in a situation where the revolutionary upsurge in the U.S. had been ebbing, and this was one important objective factor setting the context for things. But this ebb occurred in a still larger international context. The U.S. had begun to pull out of Vietnam and was somewhat in the position of regrouping and shoring up its empire, while the Soviet Union was beginning to push out and much more fully challenge the division of the world in which the U.S. reigned as supreme imperialist. And, as I touched on earlier, China was facing a threat of Soviet invasion and the direct massing of thousands of Soviet troops on its northern border, and was making adjustments in its international posture.

So it wasn't just that within the U.S. struggles had run up against certain limitations and begun to ebb; the situation had begun to change on a world scale as certain dynamics and trends played themselves out, or at least went through important shifts.

All this presented new challenges to revolutionaries. The model of the world, if you will, that the people who had gravitated to revolution had operated on in the 1960s no longer described the world as it was in 1973 or '74; and this posed a very acute need for the revolutionary movement to deepen its theoretical understanding in order to maintain its bearings and rise to the new situation.

## The Soviet Union: Flawed Socialism or State Capitalism?

One of the very sharp questions posing itself by the early '70s was the essential nature and role of the Soviet Union. Was the Soviet Union still a socialist country, as it once had been? Or, as we argued, had it since the time of Khrushchev been taken back down the road to capitalism, in the form of revisionism and state capitalism? Was it a force for revolution, or at least for opposing imperialism in the world; or was it, as we said, a "social-imperialist superpower," socialist in name but imperialist in essence and in deed?

This was a big bone of contention. Many people criticized the Soviet Union but said that while *it* wasn't very revolutionary, Vietnam and Cuba after all were revolutionary, and they would pull and force the Soviet Union to be more revolutionary. We would argue, no, the Soviet Union is using, for its own imperialist ends, various struggles against colonial domination in the world. For example, in places like Angola, we would maintain that the goals and objectives and the content of what the Soviet Union is doing does not constitute supporting revolution but misusing people's struggles in order to divert them into serving the Soviet strategy of contending with the U.S. in various parts of the world and exerting its own interests as an imperialist power, a social-imperialist power. This was a big debate within the movement.

Even some people who had one foot in Maoism often had the other foot in an eclectic, centrist position which ultimately covered over the nature of the Soviet Union and apologized for it. They would argue that the Soviet Union is supporting the struggle against the U.S. in the world, so that proves the Soviet Union actually is socialist or at least can be made to support revolution, and anyway it's better than the U.S. And we would insist that, no, these are both imperialist powers, the Soviet Union has a socialist guise but it is now in essence and in its deeds an imperialist power, and even when it appears to be supporting struggles against U.S. imperialism, it is acting out of its own imperialist needs and interests.

You could go round and round on this, but in order to sort this out, you had to get down to the fundamental issues. You couldn't just look at the different phenomena that occurred in the world, like the Soviet invasion of Czechoslovakia in 1968, on the one hand, or the Soviet military aid for rebel forces in Angola, on the other hand, taken by themselves. You had to get to the essence of the question—the essential nature of the Soviet Union. So we did a lot of theoretical work and research to dig into the nature of the economic foundation of the Soviet Union. What was the economic system in the Soviet Union at that point? Was it a socialist system or was it a capitalist system? And, proceeding from that, what could we understand about the essence of the relations, economically, politically, and militarily, that the Soviet Union had with different states and groups and forces throughout the world?

### Revisionism in Power Equals Capitalist Restoration

We made an analysis, based on our research and theoretical study, that the Soviet Union was, in fact, a country where capitalism had been restored, not (at that point) in the classical form of "free market" capitalism, but in the form of state capitalism. We published a new issue of *Red Papers*, *Red Papers 7*, which was devoted to this question and went into it in great detail. Now, at that point, our analysis and our understanding of this question was still only in the developing stages, but we did make a leap in putting together both theoretical and concrete analysis of the workings of the Soviet system, beginning with its economics, which is the foundation of the politics and ideology and culture and the military and international policies of any society. All that flows from the fundamental nature of the economic system. So we analyzed, both from a theoretical standpoint but also in terms of the concrete workings of the Soviet economy, that this was a system where capitalism had been restored, where the pursuit of capitalist profit had become the guiding principle and ruling dynamic within the Soviet economy (and in its relations with the economies of other countries) and that *this* ultimately governed what the Soviet Union did in the world.

This was around 1974, in the period just before the party was formed, and one of the main tasks that I took up was working with a team of comrades in the RU, and some people not in the RU, to undertake this very extensive research and theoretical study and then to systematize that into an analysis of the Soviet Union that later became *Red*

*Papers* 7. I wasn't doing most of the direct research or writing of the initial drafts; but I was discussing with the team the conceptual and methodological framework for this project. In other words, how do we conceive of going about doing this investigation and this analysis and how should we approach it? And then, as the team was writing drafts, I was reading the drafts and making comments and suggestions for rewrites, as well as for further areas of investigation and analysis.

This was very invigorating, as well as extremely important. People in groups like the Communist League[28] were insisting not only that capitalism had *not* been restored in the Soviet Union, but that theoretically it was *impossible* for capitalism to be restored in a country once it had become socialist. I remember in a polemic of theirs, they used this metaphor: "once a baby has come out of the womb, you can't stuff it back into the womb," which was not at all an appropriate analogy or a correct understanding of what had actually happened in the Soviet Union.

In opposition to this, drawing from pathbreaking analysis by Mao, we argued that socialism itself, where it does exist, is a society in transition from capitalism to communism, and is full of and driven forward by contradictions between, on the one hand, the old capitalist relations and elements which are being eliminated but are not yet fully abolished and uprooted and, on the other hand, the elements and forces in society leading to the ultimate achievement of communism, where these remaining capitalist relations will be fully overcome and eliminated. To take one example, socialism still contains a division of labor between mental and manual workers—a division of labor which is characteristic of capitalism and, actually, all class society. Communism is a society where such divisions will no longer exist—where everyone will partake fully in both mental and manual labor—but you can't just declare that this has been accomplished, overnight; there has to be a transition. Throughout the course of this transition, this division contains the *seeds* of exploitative and oppressive relations, and if policies are not pursued to step by step eliminate this, then capitalist relations will grow within the socialist society, and forces favoring capitalist restoration will feed on that and gain strength.

---

28. The Communist League was another group which was declaring that it was going to form a new party, and in fact did form the Communist Labor Party in 1974, though it didn't last for very long after that.

So it is completely contrary to reality to argue that capitalism cannot be restored in a society after it has advanced to socialism. To fail to recognize, or to blindly ignore, this danger of capitalist restoration in socialist society will only disorient and ideologically disarm the masses of people and those who are seeking to lead them out of the hell of capitalism and to a radically different and better world.

We addressed these issues in *Red Papers 7*, as well as other polemics that we wrote around this question. This was all part of a very lively, vigorous, vibrant process of struggling things out to form a party that would really be a communist vanguard—a revolutionary communist party, as we eventually called it.

In some important ways *Red Papers 7* broke new ground for the movement and put the criticism of the Soviet Union on a much more materialist footing. And as things would develop in the world—with the death of Mao and then the coup by revisionists in China in 1976, and the further pushing out of the Soviet Union in (imperialist) contention with the U.S. at the end of the '70s and into the '80s—this understanding of the nature of the Soviet Union would prove to be very important. In the late '60s the Soviet Union was not contending with the U.S. in the same way it did in the 1970s—the Soviet revisionists were more concerned with consolidating their home base at that time, and they were, in a real sense, letting the U.S. slowly bleed in Vietnam. So many forces that were turning to revolution in the '60s could see, on a perceptual level, that the Soviet Union was not about revolution or really challenging U.S domination in the world. But the people who had, in the late '60s, united on a basic level with the idea that the Soviet Union was no longer socialist, and certainly was not revolutionary, could not deal with the huge changes which were germinating by the early '70s and which would soon blossom—in rather ugly ways. Some people, in part because they lacked a real understanding of the distinction between revisionism and Marxism, ended up supporting the coup in China; others drew opposite conclusions and recanted their former criticisms of the USSR. But none of these trends could maintain their revolutionary bearings, to a significant degree because they had not made a thorough, materialist analysis of things in the first place. And this emphasizes the importance of things like *Red Papers 7* and the importance of devoting the time and resources to making that kind of analysis of decisive questions.

## Return to China: Raising Questions...

In the midst of all this, in the fall of 1974, I went back to China on a trip with Leibel Bergman. This time I went with a little different view and with different objectives.

I mentioned earlier how, after our first trip to China, we'd come back and put out a pamphlet defending and seeking to explain the Chinese position on controversial international issues, in particular what was going on in Bangladesh—China's support for Pakistan in seeking to suppress the breakaway of Bangladesh from Pakistan. Well, as I said, we learned some lessons about uncritically accepting and rationalizing everything a country does just because it is socialist and just because, in an overall sense, it plays the role of a bastion of socialism and of the communist movement in the world and is in a real sense a beacon light and source of inspiration. That *was* the role that China was playing then, but that didn't mean that everything China did should be uncritically supported. Marxism is, and has to be taken up as, a critical revolutionary approach to reality, and as Marx insisted it has to constantly interrogate reality and interrogate itself. So this is something we learned, partly through the overall process of developing and engaging the struggle in all the different realms, including the theoretical and ideological realm, and more particularly as a result of the mistake that we'd made earlier in uncritically supporting what China was doing.

So Leibel and I went on this trip with a lot of questions that we wanted to raise about what was going on, especially with Chinese foreign policy and international relations at that time. That was a big purpose of this trip. We wanted to talk about why, for example, did China appear to be supporting Marcos, the reactionary dictator in the Philippines and the stooge of imperialism, when not only was he a great oppressor of the Philippine people, but there was actually a communist movement and a people's war led by the Communist Party there against the Marcos regime and against imperialism? Why were the Chinese saying positive things about Marcos and portraying him in a positive light? Why did they have the Shah of Iran—who was a brutal despotic ruler over the people of Iran and had a vicious torture squad, the Savak, which terrorized the people of Iran—why were the Chinese upholding him as a positive figure? Why were people like Haile Selassie—who, Rastafarianism aside, was a brutal oppressor of the Ethiopian people—

being upheld and put forward in a positive light by the Chinese government? And why did it appear that China was either not supporting, or seemingly cutting back support, for revolutionary struggles in different parts of the world that China had supported previously?

We also raised the question of Pinochet in Chile, who in 1973 had carried out a vicious coup against the reformist, social-democratic government of Salvador Allende. Pinochet, with the backing and support of the CIA, had overthrown the Allende government and then murdered and tortured thousands of people. Later, when I myself went into exile in France, I met a number of Maoists from Chile who'd been forced into exile, along with thousands and thousands of other Chileans. The Chinese did not denounce this coup, and in fact did not aid people who were victimized in this coup and seeking refuge; China in effect supported the Pinochet government. This is another thing we were very upset about and raised when we went to China in 1974. One of the great ironies and, in a real sense, a further tragedy of the events in Chile was that the revisionists—including not only the influential pro-Soviet Communist Party of Chile but also Castro in Cuba—had put forward the Allende government as a model for change, openly promoting the dangerously illusory notion that this showed that the peaceful road to socialism was possible. The coup that put an end to the Allende government, and in which Allende himself died, drowned this illusion in the blood of the Chilean people. But, because of the policies and actions of the Chinese government (along with the work of the revisionist propaganda machinery), it was not the revisionists who were discredited so much as China and even Maoism.

We knew that raising questions about these policies of the Chinese government was going to make things pretty hot, but we felt it was important to put these things on the table. We went prepared to do that —that was our orientation and that was one of the main purposes of this trip to China.

Now, I in particular was still very excited about going to China, where great things were going on in terms of the transformation of the institutions of society and the relations between people, and of the culture. China was still carrying forward the Cultural Revolution, and this was very exciting and inspiring. So I didn't go there with an overall negative view, by any means. But even with my excitement and enthusiasm for the tremendous revolutionary process going on in China, I was also going with some questions that troubled me.

One thing about this trip that I've laughed about afterwards, because it's sort of ironic, is that Leibel knew other people who had lived in China, and before we left on this trip, he had gone and talked to some of them. And when Leibel explained that we wanted to raise certain questions and get into discussions with the Chinese Party representatives about these matters, one of these people said, "Well, if you're having trouble getting people to really discuss these things you want to talk about, and you really want to get to somebody who will talk to you straightforwardly, ask to speak to Chang Chun-chiao."

Chang Chun-chiao was someone who was later attacked and arrested as part of the so-called "Gang of Four." He was actually a leader of the people who continued to uphold and fight for Mao's line against Deng Xiaoping and the other revisionists who seized power in China and then took it back down the capitalist road after Mao died. At the time of our visit in 1974, however, although we knew generally that Chang Chun-chiao was a leader who'd come forward in the course of the Cultural Revolution in Shanghai, and had become a major leader in the whole country, we didn't have a full sense of the internal struggles going on within the Chinese party. We understood there was struggle, and we knew some things about the role of different people, such as Chang Chun-chiao, but that was only in broad terms, and we weren't privy to all the ins and outs of this. While we were in China, we thought about this advice to ask to speak to Chang Chun-chiao, but we decided not to pursue that, because we knew enough to know that it would be a bad idea to inject ourselves into whatever internal struggles might be going on inside the Chinese party. But I always wondered what would have happened if we had asked to speak to Chang Chun-chiao. That is kind of an aside but, especially since the coup in which Chang Chun-chiao was arrested, and which led to the restoration of capitalism in China, it is something I have often thought about.

## ...And Getting No Answers

We did raise the tough questions we felt we had to raise, and we pretty much got no answers. What we got instead, not once but twice, was a representative of the Central Committee of the Chinese Communist Party giving us this whole presentation about what at the time was called the "Three Worlds Theory." This theory argued that there were basically three different forces in the world: there were the superpowers, the U.S. and the Soviet Union, and they constituted the first world; then there were lesser capitalist and imperialist states, which were not really treated as if they were imperialist in this conception, and they constituted the second world; and then there was the third world, the countries of Latin America, Africa, Asia and the Middle East, which were oppressed by imperialism. But, in reality, as part of this three worlds theory, the Chinese were distinguishing and identifying the Soviet Union as the main danger and main enemy among the two superpowers.

In fact, the Soviet Union *was,* in immediate terms, the main danger to China—if an attack were to be made on China at that time, it would most likely come from the Soviet Union, and the Soviets were actually making preparations for such an attack, as I've discussed earlier. But we rejected the idea that, on a world scale, you should just identify the Soviet Union as an enemy and essentially put the U.S. and all of its allies and puppets, like the Shah of Iran and Marcos and Haile Selassie, in the camp of friends, or potential allies. And, in fact, that was the effect of this "Soviet Union main danger, main enemy" line—in this conception, the Soviet Union was really the *only* enemy.

As part of this three worlds theory, the position was being put forward openly that even imperialist states in Europe, and Japan, should be united with against the Soviet Union. And I recall a funny moment, after a Central Committee member gave us this whole rap, where he put forward the formulation: unite with the third world, win over the second world, and oppose the first world—which actually meant oppose only the Soviet Union. When this presentation was completed, we took a break, and Leibel and I went back to my room. We were sitting in my room talking about this presentation and Leibel says, "All this talk about winning over the second world—win them over to do *what?*" I remember breaking out laughing, because that was precisely to the point: What kind of unity, for what purpose, could be built with the capitalist and imperialist states of Europe and Japan?

An irony in all this, however, is that Leibel ended up a couple of years later supporting the revisionist leadership in China, headed by Deng Xiaoping, which not only allied with certain imperialists, but just completely brought China under the domination and exploitation of imperialism once again, even as Deng & Co. were striving to push forward their own bourgeois interests, to "modernize" China along capitalist lines and make China a powerful country within the framework of imperialist domination. But at that time Leibel very strongly, and with great sarcasm, rejected this notion of uniting with the capitalist and imperialist countries. "Win over the second world to do what?!" he said very emphatically and sardonically. So that gives a sense, and a flavor, of the struggle that went on during that trip to China, even while we continued, as I said, to be very enthusiastic about the overall character of China as a socialist country, the revolutionary transformations that were being carried forward through the continuation of the Cultural Revolution, and the inspiration and lessons that provided for revolutionaries and communists all over the world. Sometimes things can be acutely contradictory, and I was struck with how this was so during that visit to China in 1974.

## Shooting Hoops...and Hold the Sea Slugs

Just a personal note to inject here: Basketball was becoming a big thing in China at that time. Wherever you'd go, in work places or residential neighborhoods, you'd see basketball hoops and basketball courts. And especially during my first trip to China, but also somewhat during the second, I kept insisting to our Chinese hosts, somewhat jokingly but also with real conviction: "I really have to play basketball, we have to take time out to play basketball." And I remember that during the first trip they organized a game that some of us played with the staff of one of the guest houses where we were staying. And that was a lot of fun. We had important things to do, important places to visit and discussions to have, but playing basketball was also important!

On these trips to China, in each city after you had visited different places and held meetings, they would host a banquet and there was a lot of great food—and then some food which some of the members of the delegation had a harder time with. A number of people had a hard time with sea slugs. This was considered a real delicacy in China. But it wasn't something people on the delegation were familiar with, and not only the taste but the texture of it was somewhat difficult for a number of people on the delegation, including myself to be honest. But just as our hosts were seeking to be polite with us, we were trying to reciprocate. So the first time they served us sea slugs, they came around and asked me, as the head of the delegation, "How do you like them?" And I replied, "Oh, yes, they're nice." Well, after that, every place we went they kept giving us sea slugs. And finally, I had to go and very apologetically say, "You know, I don't want to be ungrateful, but a number of people on the delegation just really don't like sea slugs, so we'd appreciate it if you don't keep giving them to us." That was a clash of cultures, so to speak, but it was all handled among comrades. I tried very hard not to make it like a typical "ugly American" thing or an affront to Chinese culture, and they tried very hard not to be insulted and to take it in the right spirit.

## Comrade Chin

During one of the trips to China, we were in Shanghai and we met with one of the leading people there whose name, as I recall, was Chin Tsu Min, and he enthusiastically upheld the line of supporting the Cultural Revolution and Mao. During this visit he gave us a very interesting and thorough presentation about what was happening in Shanghai. In particular he talked about what they were doing with the economy in Shanghai and the advances they'd made in production. It was clear, especially in retrospect, that he was doing this because Shanghai was a revolutionary center in China, and the line of attack of the revisionists was that all this revolution was hurting production. Shanghai was the place where, after the revisionist coup in 1976, the people's militias actually fought the army, the regular army, for a couple of days, even though their attempt to resist the coup was finally drowned in blood. So Shanghai was known to be a revolutionary center and the attack on it and on people like Chang Chun-chiao, who came out of Shanghai and was one of the leaders of the so-called Gang of Four, was that they weren't concerned with production.

In any case, comrade Chin gave us a long presentation about what they were doing with the economy and the advances they were making in production on all different fronts in Shanghai. I remember being struck by that at the time and, reflecting on it later, I realized that this was in part to inform us and in part to answer these attacks that were being made.

So anyway, after this long and very interesting discussion we had with this guy and other people there representing the leadership in Shanghai, we had a banquet, at the end of our visit. Often at these banquets they would have Chinese wine, and there would be toasts—you might have as many as six or seven toasts, or even more, during the course of a banquet. And, of course, some people hold their liquor better than others. Well, I noticed that whenever we'd have a toast, comrade Chin would take his little wine glass and dump out the wine. So after three or four times, I called him on it. I said, "Hey, you're not drinking your wine, what's going on here?" And he came back: "I can't drink wine, I get red in the face when I drink wine." So, I said, "C'mon, c'mon, that's no excuse." All this was in good fun, and so he started drinking a little bit, and sure enough, he did get red in the face. But he also loosened up a bit. We were eating this dinner of Shanghai fresh water crab, and it was really great—unlike sea slugs, everybody loved this—and then at one point comrade Chin just waxed eloquent, enthusing about the crab, and he concluded with: "The person who invented crab is a genius!" And we all roared with laughter.

I remembered that very affectionately—and then I thought about it very bitterly when I learned that he'd been executed as part of the revisionist coup.

# Chapter Seventeen

# *Founding the Party –*
# *A High Point...and a Low One*

T he whole party-building process culminated in 1975, when we held the Founding Congress of the Revolutionary Communist Party, USA. On the one hand, the Congress represented an important leap, in that a vanguard party did in fact get brought into being through this whole process and as a result of this whole upsurge of the 1960s and early '70s. So, in the main—in the principal aspect as we say—this was a tremendous achievement and a tremendous step forward.

On the other hand, to be somewhat deliberately provocative, the time of the founding of the Party and right afterward was, looking back on it now with perspective, also the *low point* of the Party—it was when we were most deeply influenced by the economist and reformist lines and tendencies that I've discussed.

There were people within the Party itself, people who had been part of the RU, and even leaders within the RU, who had a more worked-out economist and reformist position. These people, as things developed more fully, actually became an organized faction. There were already strong tendencies in that direction within the Party as a whole, and this came to a head in 1976—just a year after the Founding Party Congress —when the revisionist coup in China happened and our Party was confronted with the question and the challenge of how to understand that and what stand to take toward it. There were already, broadly in our Party, influences toward economism and reformism, toward just sort of burrowing into the working class and in some ways tailing after not even the most revolutionary-minded sections of the working class.

But then there was this group that we later dubbed Mensheviks, because they were ideologically and politically akin to the Menshevik trend in the Russian revolution, which opposed Lenin and the Bolsheviks from an economist and reformist position. The struggle with this Menshevik faction within our own Party came to a head and took a big leap when the coup in China happened. But it was already beginning to assert itself at the time of the founding of the Party, in 1975.

They really had a different view. They wanted to be like the old Communist Party, only "better"—or not like the Communist Party in its very worst days, when it was openly supporting Roosevelt and sections of the bourgeoisie, but the Communist Party when those kind of tendencies were strongly expressed but weren't fully developed. They wanted to adopt a mixture of Maoism, on the one hand, and revisionism and reformism, on the other hand—that's what it amounted to objectively—and they were already pushing for this at the time the RCP was founded. This was asserting itself both in terms of what they were arguing should be in the Programme of the Party, but also in their style and methods of work and of struggle, which was a combination of reformism and extreme sectarianism and factionalism.

It was very evident, even at the time of the Founding Party Congress: There were not only two different views that were co-existing, while struggling with each other, within the Party that was formed, but also two very different styles and methods of work. These people, who became the Menshevik faction within our party, had a style of work and of relating to people that I didn't recognize as having anything to do with communism. They were petty and nasty, and if they didn't agree with you they would use underhanded and unprincipled methods to try to undermine you, and they'd attack you in an opportunist, unprincipled way, and even on a personal level. Some of this was already rather strongly in evidence at the Founding Congress, and a number of people who weren't part of the faction were troubled by this, and asking, "What's going on here?"

## Two Opposed Views, Two Opposed Styles

I remember attending a meeting in New York City right before the Party Congress, where I was very struck by this. After the party-building tour, as part of the party-building process, I went around to different parts of the country to listen in on the different discussions that were going on, particularly within the RU, but also more broadly sometimes. People were wrangling with the things that were in the journal *Forward to the Party, Struggle for the Party*, and different position papers were being written up by people in different parts of the country, and then they were being discussed and debated. But you weren't supposed to be forming lines and opinions *as groups*. Individuals could form, and should form, different ideas and viewpoints about the different issues that were being discussed and debated. But different parts of the RU weren't supposed to be solidifying and forming groups, or factions, in essence, around different positions.

As a leader of the RU—and in fact by this time it had been announced internally within the RU that I had been elected the Chairman of the Central Committee of the RU—because of holding that position I did not intervene in these discussions. As the leader of the RU, if I had intervened, it obviously would have had an influence one way or the other, and that was not appropriate in this "bottom-up" process, so I went to learn and investigate but didn't take an active part in the discussion. I asked some questions sometimes about how people saw this or that, but I was very careful and scrupulous not to take sides, if you will, on the different positions that were being discussed and debated and not to act in a way that would undermine the process of discussion and debate.

But when I got to New York, where this developing Menshevik faction was headquartered, there was a meeting that I went to where they were discussing some position papers on what were called "intermediate workers organizations." These were mass organizations we were trying to build among workers who were more politically advanced; the idea was that these organizations would be more politically advanced than the trade unions but intermediate between the trade unions and the party—in other words, they weren't communist, but they weren't just trade unions either—they were more politically radical and had a broader political orientation than the trade unions, even while their basis of unity was not revolution, socialism, and communism.

In fact, there was a lot of dispute and struggle within the RU over what *should* be the basis of unity of these intermediate workers organizations, and the people who were part of this developing Menshevik fac-

tion wanted these organizations to be more trade-unionist and economist—more like a militant labor federation—and they attacked people
who were from the west coast and other places who were putting forward that these organizations should have a broader political perspective
and mobilize workers in broader political struggle. So, in a beginning
way, the tension and struggle was already asserting itself between a more
narrow, reformist, economist view and one that, yes, had some of those
influences but was also seeking to bring a broader political perspective
and ultimately a revolutionary perspective to the working class, including through our work as communists in these intermediate workers
organizations. In this RU meeting in New York, the discussion was going
back and forth, and at one point this young comrade, who had been on
the party-building tour with me, gave this impassioned, bitter denunciation of a position paper from the west coast that was arguing for a more
political character to these intermediate workers organizations. And she
ended her denunciation by saying: "This line is fucked up, it's wrong and
it's not the line of the New York district."

I was taken aback by this, because in this process different district
organizations of the RU were not supposed to take positions. Plus the
whole spirit and style of this was completely contrary to the spirit in
which people were supposed to be engaging and discussing these questions. There was no comradeship in it, it was just a bitter attack and
denunciation of other people who were part of the same organization
and part of the same party-building process. After the meeting, I went
up to one of the leading people from this New York district, and I said:
"What's this bullshit? What are you doing, forming a faction here? We
don't have 'district lines,' we're not supposed to be organizing people
around lines going into the Congress. It's supposed to be a 'bottom up'
process where individuals put forward their own views and we struggle
it out in that way and culminate the 'bottom-up' process at the Founding
Congress." And this leading person just tried to shine it on and make
some lame excuse: "Oh that's just her, she just got carried away." But
obviously it wasn't "just her." This was part of a whole organized effort,
infused with a factional spirit and a factional purpose.

So these things were already beginning to emerge and assert themselves, even at the time of the Founding Congress—these reformist and
economist influences were exerting a pretty generalized influence within the RU, and then at the founding of the Party, but they were also being

fought for in an organized way by what became this full-blown Menshevik faction.

## Taking a Wrong Turn

Still, even with all that, the fundamental thing about the Party that was formed—its "saving grace," if you'll pardon the expression—was that, at its core, it did continue to uphold and recognize the need to be based on a radical transformation of society: the overthrow of capitalism, the building of socialism and the advance to communism world-wide. That remained the bedrock of the Party. And then, at the same time and in contradiction to that, there were a number of erroneous ideas and outright wrong positions being fought for by different people, positions which would have ultimately undermined the revolutionary and communist nature of the Party. But there remained an essential and fundamental grounding in the principle that the reason we're going to the working class, the reason we're working among other strata, the reason we're trying to build a united front led by the working class, as we understood that then, is because we want to overthrow capitalism and get to socialism and ultimately a communist world.

Those two things were in contention: on the one hand the basic and bedrock communist foundation of the Party, and on the other hand those tendencies and influences which would have undermined and eventually completely undone that foundation. At the time the Party was founded, the main and fundamental thing was its bedrock communist grounding. But the economist and reformist tendencies were growing and were asserting themselves more and more strongly, and they *did* affect and color the Party and its character and its internal life, right from the time it was founded.

Right after the Founding Congress we had a meeting of the Central Committee elected by the Congress, and this represented, in a real sense, the height, or depth, of economism within the Party. In the early '70s, a lot of members of the RU who had gone to the working class had in fact ended up among the more exploited and poorer sections of the proletariat. But then there was this contradiction that I talked about earlier where, under the influence of Stalin in particular, the international communist movement had gone more in the direction of insisting that the communist movement must be based among the workers in the large-scale industries—and in the U.S. in particular these were the better-paid workers who, in the aftermath of World War 2 and the situation where U.S. imperialism was the dominant imperialist power in the world, had been given some of the spoils of imperialist plunder and, in significant numbers, were relatively well off and even somewhat conservative in their outlook.

As we've come to grasp more deeply since that time, one of the important features of imperialist countries is what Lenin called a "split in the working class." There are the more bourgeoisified sections of the working class that are paid more and experience all these conservatizing influences from having a more bourgeoisified existence. And then there are what Lenin referred to as the lower, deeper sections of the proletariat. Ironically, at the time of the founding of the Party, drawing from the international communist movement *after* the time of Lenin, we believed we were doing the right thing by moving to concentrate more systematically among what were objectively the more bourgeoisified sections of the working class. And, along with that, in the Programme adopted at the Founding Congress, it was actually said that the center of gravity of our work should be the economic struggle of the workers.

Now, especially those of us whose orientation had remained one of seeing the need for revolution, and who were inspired by the vision of a whole new, communist world, were not particularly interested in or inspired by the notion of becoming trade-union secretaries, literally or in our political and ideological orientation; we saw this concentration among the workers in the larger factories and workplaces as a necessary part of building a working class movement that would be developed into a class-conscious revolutionary movement. That was still our orientation. But in fact we were working in ways and adopting policies that were undermining that, and this was becoming pretty acutely contradictory.

This was very sharply expressed at this first Central Committee meeting, following the Founding Congress. Mickey Jarvis, who became one of the main leaders of the Menshevik faction, gave a presentation on concentrating our forces in the major industries, like auto and steel—in fact, we ranked these industries in order of importance, largely on the basis of how large-scale the factories in these industries were. Jarvis was out of the old CP—in fact, the first time I saw him was at an SDS meeting where he jumped up on a table holding a bunch of CP pamphlets and yelled at the people there, "Okay, all you petty bourgeois creeps, here's the real working class program." He had this whole background in the CP—his parents had been in the CP and, even though he was fairly young when he was a member of the CP and even though he'd left the CP, he hadn't by any means shed all the influences of that kind of outlook and line. So he gave this whole presentation at this Central Committee meeting—and I don't want to misrepresent this, this was with the approval of the Party leadership as a whole—about the major industries that had the highest concentration of workers, like auto and steel and electronics, and how we have to orient ourselves to go into these factories and we have to center our work around the economic struggle of the workers, especially in these industries.

And, to be honest, there was some enthusiasm for this within the Party: there was a feeling that by doing this we would win the working class to socialism—at least that was the objective of those of us who still strongly had the orientation of seeing the need for socialist revolution. But, in fact, this was a profoundly mistaken orientation and direction. It's not that we shouldn't have worked among those sections of the workers, especially when they did engage in strikes and other struggles, but that shouldn't have been where our work was rooted and—as we came to see more clearly in a little while—the center of gravity of our political work shouldn't have been in the economic struggle of the workers in general, and particularly not of the more bourgeoisified workers.

But in mapping out this approach of going systematically into the big industries and in making the center of gravity of our work the economic struggle of the workers, particularly in these large industries, our whole orientation became almost like that of a slightly left-wing trade union organization. In addition, when you do political work among people, it's not a one-way street—you influence them, but they influence you as well. You're "sharing weal and woe," as the Chinese used to say —you're getting to know people and their problems, you're learning from them, you're coming to understand better how they see things, and inevitably you're being influenced, to one degree or another, by their outlook on things. In one aspect, that is good and even essential, if you want to really unite with people and bring them forward to communism— but, on the other hand, especially if you're doing political work among people whose situation, while they may be generally held down by the system, is not *that* dire, or extreme, there can be certain conservatizing influences from them that creep into your own outlook, and that you're going to have to be aware of and struggle against. This was aggravated by the ways in which we were mistakenly concentrating our efforts among a section of workers who *were* better off—and on account of that more influenced by the reformism and the American chauvinism that saturated the official "labor movement." That was skewing and affecting even many of the better comrades who had a more revolutionary spirit.

And, frankly, this carried over into internal Party life. To be blunt, I found this a very depressing time. Party life was being reduced more and more to these narrow economist and reformist terms, and the whole vision of revolutionary politics, of ideological struggle, of building a broad political movement to take on the whole system, and the vision of how all that would be led—and diverted, as Lenin put it—toward a socialist revolution: that whole vision was getting lost. And that got reflected in internal Party life, which became very dreary for a while.

## Country Music

We had all been affected by this economism, even on the level of culture. For example, a number of people, including myself, started listening to a lot of country music, because while we knew we had to bring forward the workers from the oppressed nationalities, we also recognized that it was necessary to bring forward the white workers, to win them to the fight against discrimination—against national oppression, as we say, or against racism, as it is popularly put—and win them in general to a socialist and revolutionary perspective. And, as part of the overall economist influences within the Party, the idea got taken up that, in order to do that, you had to really immerse yourself among these workers, not only practically, but also culturally. So a number of us were listening to a lot of country music, and I have to say that I'm a sucker for a beautiful song. Some country music songs are very beautiful, in fact, so it wasn't just that I held my nose and listened to this music—some of the songs I actually liked, and some of them had a little bit more rebellious spirit too. There was Kris Kristofferson and Willie Nelson and Johnny Cash, and I also liked this Chicano country singer named Johnny Rodriguez. I remember he had this song "Riding My Thumb to Mexico," which I liked because, while it was a love song in one sense— or a song about a relationship that didn't work out—it also had an a kind of "outlaw" feel to it. So I actually liked some of this music.

But then, just to jump ahead a little bit, as the struggle with these

Mensheviks was developing and sharpening up, particularly after the revisionist coup in China, I went to a Jimmy Buffett concert. I had listened to some Jimmy Buffett songs, because Jimmy Buffett sort of had one foot in the youth culture and one foot in the country-western culture. He came to Chicago and he had his band called "The Coral Reefer Band"; and of course "reefer" was a play on words—on the one hand, it referred to the Caribbean influences in his music, but then it was also...reefer. And at this Jimmy Buffett concert there was a lot of reefer: there were a lot of jokes from the stage, from Jimmy Buffett and the band, about reefer, and a lot of people in the audience were smoking reefer. In this audience there were some youth from the middle class, but there were also a lot of young white proletarians who were there, who were into all of this. And this might seem odd, but even in the form of all this talk about reefer, and the people joking about it, there was a certain rebellious edge, and it made me think: we've gotten into tailing after the intermediate sections of the workers, or even the more backward among the white workers. There are workers, including among the white youth, who are more alienated and rebellious than many of the more stable and more conservative-tending workers among whom we had been focusing much of our work. It is right to have a strategic orientation of winning as many as possible of the more intermediate workers, and even more backward workers, to socialism, but this should not be our main focus. In that way, this Jimmy Buffett concert, while in and of itself a small thing, was a part of provoking questions in my mind politically and ideologically.

At the same time, throughout this period I had never stopped being drawn to the culture that I'd developed a love for as a youth, namely Black culture and R&B music at that time. While I was listening to country music, I was also listening to the main Black radio station in Chicago. I remember in particular that there was a disk jockey on that station who used to do these little routines, especially late at night, and he had this one character he portrayed, Rudolph "Hat-Tipped-to-the-Side" Browner. It was a comical routine. There was a lot of nonsense mixed in with it, but it was really funny, and I used to especially look forward to when that routine would come on the radio.

## The "Saving Grace"

Returning to the situation in the Party, those of us who weren't part of this developing Menshevik faction still had a basic revolutionary and communist orientation—and that's the reason why we found internal Party life so depressing right then. But we continued to seek ways to assert a revolutionary orientation. I remember that, not long after the Party was founded, I wrote a couple of articles for *Revolution*, which was the monthly paper of the Party at that time. Among other things, these articles spoke to how the Party branches should take up ideological and political tasks and not just the trade union struggle. I thought I was merely calling attention to some basic principles, but even this became very controversial and, as I learned later, was bitterly attacked in a factional way by this developing Menshevik clique within the Party, which essentially regarded any diversion from the narrow trade union struggle and any talk about broader political issues as an abomination.

The basic thing, the thing that sustained me, was that I didn't join the revolutionary movement—and I didn't join the movement before I was a revolutionary or a communist—to wallow in narrow petty reforms. Even before I became a communist, I was motivated by the recognition that radical changes were needed in society and the world. When I became convinced that we had to go to the working class in order to make revolution, however we understood that at the early stages, then that is what I joined with others to do. But we didn't do that —at least I and others who shared the same viewpoint didn't do that— and we didn't form the RU or lead in forming the Party, in order to just become a slightly left trade union. We still held to the orientation that the purpose of all this is to get rid of this rotten, foul, oppressive, horrendous society and everything this system does to people all over the world, and bring into being a radically different and better world—a communist world. That's what this is about. Otherwise, what's the point?

That orientation led us into struggle against the growing economist and reformist tendencies within the Party. It wasn't that we set out to defeat this developing Menshevik faction—we didn't even realize at that time how developed this faction was, or how firmly committed they were to this sort of economist, reformist path. It was just that we were still in this for revolution and communism, so we kept trying to find the ways to get it back to that. That's why I wrote these articles shortly after the Party was founded, because we had to keep that orientation alive, we had to keep bringing that to the forefront. The more things were being carried off in this economist and reformist direction, the more pronounced became the need to assert the opposite of that, the need to bring forward a revolutionary orientation. And, as a result, I and others found ourselves increasingly locked in struggle with these other people within the Party, as we realized that they were actually committed, as a matter of orientation and outlook, to this more reformist and economist position, whereas we had been influenced by this but increasingly found these influences in contradiction to our fundamental revolutionary and communist orientation.

### Eldridge Finds Jesus

Just around this time, Eldridge Cleaver suddenly popped up in the news again. After the 1968 shootout in Oakland in which Bobby Hutton was killed, Eldridge had gone into exile in Algeria, and then France, and I had lost touch with him. I hadn't seen him, or even heard much about him in years—and then, all of a sudden, here comes this news story about how Eldridge has discovered Jesus! I think he told this story about how he was looking out at the moon in Paris one night and he saw Jesus in the moon. This was a revelation to him, and he'd become a Christian, even a Christian fundamentalist. And I have to say that, when I read this, I thought: Yep, that's Eldridge. Because, while I had a lot of respect for him when he was playing a revolutionary role and he made many positive contributions—and I've said many times, and will say again, that he had an important positive influence in terms of my development, turning me on to Mao and radicalizing me and helping me rupture with some reformism and go in a revolutionary direction—at the same time there was always a bit of the hustler in Eldridge. And when I heard that he claimed to have seen Jesus in the moon, I said: "Yeah, right, he wants to come back to the U.S. He's tired of being in exile, and this is the way he is trying to get back into the U.S. without having to go to jail."

In fact, I heard a funny story that sheds further light on this. Years later someone who used to be in the Black Panther Party just happened to bump into Eldridge somewhere. And this former Panther said to Eldridge, "Hey, Eldridge, what's all this shit, now you're a big conservative and you're into all this religion and everything. What the hell is that all about?" Well, Eldridge invited him over to his place, and Eldridge took out a joint, lit it up, and then said: "Look, brother, we've *seen* all the revolution we're gonna see." And that was Eldridge's explanation for why he'd done what he'd done, which made perfect sense to me—obviously I don't agree with him that we've seen all the revolution we're gonna see, but it made sense that this is what Eldridge would do if he thought that.

# Chapter Eighteen

# Revolutionary Work in a Non-Revolutionary Situation

## A Target of Surveillance

Ever since the time that I'd become known as a radical and then as a revolutionary activist back in the Bay Area, and even more so once the RU had been formed, I was constantly under surveillance. I told the story earlier about how, from the early days in Richmond, we were pretty sure our phone was being tapped. I also remember, for example, that in Berkeley in the late '60s, there was a demonstration that ended up marching to the police station. I was standing there talking to a couple of other people I knew in the movement while the rally was being held in front of the police station, and I was commenting on the fact that the guy who was notorious to all of us as the head of the Red Squad in the Berkeley Police Department had just retired from that post. And I said to these other people in the demonstration: "Who's gonna come around and surveil us and harass us, now that so-and-so has retired?" And, all of a sudden, there's this tap on my shoulder, and I turn around and this guy sticks out his hand, and says, "I will, Bob, I'm the new head of the Red Squad."

But once the RU was formed, it was increasingly targeted by the political police—the FBI on a national level and the different Red Squads that existed in different parts of the country. In fact a few years after the RU was formed, just after the split with the Franklins, a committee of the U.S. House of Representatives did a whole investigation and report on the RU, which of course wholly distorted what we were about.

So surveillance and attempts at infiltration by the political police were a fact of life—not that we accepted it, but you had to recognize it as part of the conditions you were dealing with. And after the Party was formed and I was publicly identified as the leader of the Party, this became much more overt. In Maywood, for example, there would constantly be cars which didn't belong to any of my neighbors parked near my house; in particular there was one guy who would park down the street a little bit from where I lived, and he would sit there, sometimes for hours, taking note of any cars that came to my house, writing down their license plates, and watching my comings and goings. Later we did a Freedom of Information Act (FOIA) inquiry and we found out that not only had he done that, but he'd gone through our garbage. We were aware that the political police did this, so there was a continual struggle: we would never put our garbage out at night; we would always get up early and try to put it out just before it was collected, but these political police agents would still try to scramble and steal our garbage after we put it out and then go through it.

This one guy in particular wrote up a whole diagram of our house, indicating through which windows someone could see different things going on in the house; and, of course, you have to think—the implications are pretty heavy—what is the purpose of drawing up diagrams like that? To my understanding, that kind of diagram was used by the police in the murder of Fred Hampton in Chicago. So while this surveillance was, in one sense, "all part of what was going on," making diagrams of your house, and indicating where someone could get good vantage points to see into various parts of the house, was very heavy.

We had realized much of this, but not quite the full extent of it until we got this FOIA material. But I can remember many times leaving my house and, as I was driving, a car would follow me for three or four blocks, and then eventually either I'd lose it or it would take off going somewhere else. So this was a constant presence, day in day out for years when I lived in Maywood, and especially after the time that the Party was formed and I was publicly put forward as its leader.

## *Struggling for a Revolutionary Orientation*

Getting back to what was going on with the Party at that point, some of us, as I said, had begun to question at least elements of the Party's work and, to a certain extent, its orientation. And in 1976, we had a Central Committee meeting in which I gave a talk which was then published as a pamphlet, "Revolutionary Work in a Non-Revolutionary Situation." We recognized, those of us who were still thinking about and oriented toward revolution, that the revolutionary upsurge of the '60s had passed. Even the '60s upsurge had never fully ripened all the way to a revolutionary situation, although in my view it had come pretty close and there were significant elements of that. But now we were in a very different situation than that '60s upsurge, and no one could say for how long, but for a certain period we were going to be in a situation that was non-revolutionary and which, in fact, might not be characterized by the same kind of upsurge that took place in the '60s. So, if you're a revolutionary, and you continue to be oriented and inspired by the goal of socialism and communism, what do you do in that kind of a situation? This talk I gave addressed that and spoke to how we had to develop a broad political movement and raise the sights of the working class to broader political questions and be guided by a revolutionary and a communist orientation and not sink down into tailing after the terms of the more intermediate or even backward workers, and not just accommodate ourselves to the ebb in this situation and to the non-revolutionary character of it.

As it turned out, and as is perhaps clear from things I have said already, this was highly contentious and the developing Menshevik faction within our Party bitterly hated this. But, at the time, I didn't conceive of it as a polemic against them. I saw it as something of a struggle against certain tendencies that were taking the Party in the wrong direction, but I didn't see it then as a matter of fully developed struggle against another group or faction within the Party that was fighting for a whole other orientation. I just thought I was trying to help correct and struggle against certain tendencies that were pulling us away from where we needed to go, along with the objective pull of being in this kind of a non-revolutionary situation that wasn't marked by a massive upsurge in the same way as, say, a decade earlier, or even five years earlier. This talk had a significant impact on the Party, but also it became highly contentious, as I learned later, even at that Central Committee meeting. And in its aftermath, the Mensheviks within the Party bitterly attacked and began to factionalize against this position—even though as the Chair of the Central Committee I'd presented the outline of what I was planning to say to other leading people, and none of them had objected or disagreed.

These were the kinds of unprincipled methods these people would use. At leadership meetings heading into this Central Committee meeting, I laid out: "This is what I think the situation is, this is what I think we need to say, this is what I think we need to discuss, this is what I'm planning to put forward at the Central Committee meeting"—and none of them said, "No, no, that's wrong." But then, when I presented this to the Central Committee meeting, they attacked it in a factional way, behind my back and in a way that avoided and undermined the channels of the Party through which disagreement and struggle is supposed to be carried out.

### Gutter Tactics

And they used very underhanded methods against my wife at that time, in order to make her life miserable and to get at me. She and I got married when we were in the Bay Area; we were married for a number of years and had moved together to Chicago (although we later split up and she ended up leaving the Party). But in this period of time, while we were in Chicago, and especially after the Party was formed, these people were deliberately targeting her as a way to go after me, and just making her life absolutely miserable—tormenting her, attacking her at every turn that they could, undermining her in whatever role she was playing within the Party and in her work, and just making her life miserable. I can remember a lot of times when she couldn't sleep at night. They were just making life impossible for her.

And, to show you the depths to which these people sank, the depths to which someone can sink when they adopt a position and an orientation and outlook that is totally opportunist and unprincipled: After the struggle with this Menshevik faction came to a head over the question of China and what stand to take toward the revisionist coup—with this faction insisting that we should support the coup and those of us who prevailed in that struggle insisting that we had to denounce it for what it was—after that came to a head, and this faction split from the Party after being defeated in this struggle, my wife and I had to change our phone number. We had an unpublished number, but it was known to many in this Menshevik faction. And we started getting these obscene phone calls, where people would call up and ask for my wife by name and then start all this heavy breathing into the phone and saying all this obscene stuff. And when we looked into this, we discovered that some of these Mensheviks had written, in men's bathrooms, things like: "If you want a blow job, call so-and-so"—the name of my wife—"at this number." This is how low these people went, this is how thoroughly disgusting they were, and just to call it "unprincipled" doesn't even really capture how despicable it was.

It is a disgrace to think that people who call themselves communists would descend to that level. But even before they sunk to that level, they were in many different ways making life completely miserable for her—these are the unprincipled methods that people can sink to when they are in the position of attempting to defend an indefensible, opportunist line.

## Taking On the Bicentennial

Nonetheless, I and others were trying to keep alive the communist and revolutionary character of our Party and have that guide the nature of our work, and we were insisting that we had to take up broader issues than just the trade union struggle among these better situated, better paid, more bourgeoisified workers.

At that time, in 1976, the bourgeoisie was making a major political and ideological offensive around the 200th anniversary of the American revolution in 1776. They were calling for big celebrations in the major cities on July 4, and they were putting an awful lot of effort into this. It may be hard to remember—or if you weren't alive then, it may be hard to imagine—but through the course of the 1960s millions of people in this country became very alienated not just from specific government policies, but from the foundations and values of American society altogether; they became very skeptical and even bitter about all the talk about how great America was and all that—they had seen and experienced too much of the truth, and there was a lot of anger against what people called "the system" and what many had begun to understand to be imperialism. Many people had become very alienated from patriotism and very scornful of all this "my country right or wrong" type talk. And while there were a lot of people who were reacting against this very positive development—with their "love it or leave it" bumper stickers and mindsets—the people who were alienated and radicalized had a lot of initiative and a lot of conviction.

But, as I explained earlier, there was some regrouping by the ruling class in the early '70s and some ebbing of the struggle. So the bourgeoisie was very anxious to, and saw an opening to, use this Bicentennial to "put that behind us"—to bring those who had become disaffected back into the fold and to seize initiative to "rehabilitate" the notion of America as the greatest country in the world and the "leader of the free world." They had an ideological objective—promoting this patriotism—and they had a political agenda too, which was tied in many respects to what they understood to be the growing prospect of war with the Soviet Union. So the question before us was whether we were going to find the ways to take this on, or keep ourselves buried in the trade union struggle. And we were able to win the Party to take this on.

There were different demonstrations at the time of the Bicentennial, but we in the leadership of the Party formulated the policy and put out a call for a demonstration that would mobilize the proletariat, and also other sections of the people, around the theme of opposing the system in a broad way. And we came up with a slogan to popularize that: "We've Carried the Rich for 200 Years, Let's Get Them Off Our Backs." Those of us who were adhering more to a revolutionary and communist line were trying to infuse that slogan with a basic "against the system" thrust. And in line with what I've been discussing about the divisions within the Party and different views and visions of what we should be all about, there was struggle within the Party over what should be the character of this demonstration. But we eventually united that it should have this basic anti-system thrust and that we should mobilize proletarians and people from other sections of society to come to Philadelphia and make this statement at the time of the Bicentennial.

And that's what we did. We had a march and rally there, and it was very highly contested because Rizzo was the mayor of Philadelphia at that time, and he ran it like a feudal fiefdom. He had viciously attacked the Panthers in Philadelphia when he was police chief, and now that he was mayor, he was saying, in effect, "They're not gonna have this demonstration in *my* city."[29] So there were a lot of tactical questions that had to be fought out in how we responded to this. They were trying to trap us into saying that we were going to have this demonstration anyway, whether or not they gave us a permit, but we refused to get drawn into those terms. We just said, "We're gonna fight this through and win, and we're gonna have our demonstration"; but we refused to get drawn tactically into making statements that we were going to break the law—which was what Rizzo and some of the media were trying to trap the people organizing this demonstration into saying. And we were able to carry through with it.

We had a march and rally which was very powerful, especially in the face of the attempts to suppress it, and it was very significant because it did raise a banner of radical opposition to this system, and it did have a significant contingent, if you will, of people from the proletariat who came from around the country to make this statement in this way. So it was a very significant demonstration and rally. I remember I spoke at the rally on behalf of the Party, and it had a very radical feel to it.

But, even though Rizzo, et al., had to back down and were unable to block the march, right up to and during the march and rally, they were continually making threatening noises as if they might attack it—they even posted sharpshooters on the rooftops during the march itself—and this set the whole context in which we had to carry through this demonstration.

### Vietnam Vets...and VVAW

As part of the same demonstration, vets were mobilized around the slogan "We Won't Fight Another Rich Man's War." Vietnam Veterans Against the War endorsed this demonstration and played an important and major role in it. Their contingent was quite powerful; it brought together several hundred vets from around the country in an important political statement at a time when, as we had analyzed, the dangers of world war were beginning to grow.

---

29. Rizzo went on to persecute the MOVE organization in Philadelphia and to launch a vendetta against the radical Black journalist—and now death-row inmate—Mumia Abu-Jamal.

Now a lot of things have been said about Vietnam Veterans Against the War, or VVAW, and what happened with it, by some people who don't know anything about it actually, and by some other people who do know but are not telling the truth about what happened.

As I've spoken to several times, one of the things that everybody was running up against was that the upsurge of the '60s and early '70s had ebbed. This was having an impact on the Party too—that's why we had to raise and struggle for the orientation of revolutionary work in a non-revolutionary situation. Part of that upsurge had been a tremendous alienation and radicalization among GI's, especially those who'd fought in Vietnam, but also more broadly, right within the imperialist military. Eventually, I think there were more than a hundred radical newspapers that were either put out by GI's or addressed to GI's. There was rebellion, sometimes very sharp rebellion, within the military in Vietnam, against officers and sometimes against being ordered into battle. Even in the military jails in Vietnam, where they imprisoned the troops who rebelled, there was further rebellion.

There was this great demonstration, Dewey Canyon III, where thousands of veterans mobilized in D.C. and threw their medals back, and declared that they didn't want medals for what they'd been made to do as part of the imperialist military, and denounced the Vietnam War. It was very broad, and it was a very tremendous thing. And out of this came this organization, VVAW, Vietnam Veterans Against the War. But by the mid-'70s, the Vietnam War had ended, the puppet government of South Vietnam had been defeated militarily and overthrown, and the country had been united under the leadership of the Vietnam Workers Party (even though that Party was marred by a lot of revisionist influences and lines). So by this time, in the mid-'70s, there wasn't the same upsurge overall, and it wasn't the same situation in the military. There were many vets who had been radicalized, but they too were being affected by the fact that this ebb had set in, that you were in a non-revolutionary situation, and there wasn't the same upheaval. This was the objective context for what was going on among all sections of the people, and also the situation that everybody who was seeking to build a movement of opposition and struggle against the system was facing.

In VVAW the question came up as well: What do you do in this kind of a situation, how do you maintain and carry forward VVAW in these circumstances, even though there is not going to be the same phenomenon of a mass radical movement of vets that there had been at its high point? And different lines developed—within the Party as a whole and among people who'd come out of this veterans movement and were part of the Party—about what to do among the veterans. And, as is not surprising, the people in the Party who were increasingly into the Menshevik faction wanted to narrow the vets movement down to something that was centered overwhelmingly on the question of vets' benefits and things like that. And others of us who opposed that orientation said, those issues are important to take up, but it has to be in a broader, more radical context of opposing imperialism. These were differences that emerged within the Party, and among leading people in VVAW who were members of the Party.

Sometimes people mischaracterize this as if somehow the Party came in and "wrecked everything" from the outside. But in fact we were very integrally involved in VVAW by this time, including in the leadership of it; and the truth of it is—even if some people don't want to acknowledge it at this point—that a number of people, on *both sides* of this developing struggle over the direction of VVAW, were all in the RCP —they just had different lines: one a more economist line, as applied to VVAW, and one a more broadly political anti-imperialist line. And so this was another way in which the struggle with this Menshevik faction was developing inside of the Party, including among people who were on different sides of this developing dispute and struggle over what direction for VVAW, as well as more generally what direction for the movement and for the Party itself.

## Debating the Question of War and Revolution

At the 1976 Central Committee meeting of our Party, we had decided that we needed to give more attention to broader political issues. In my report to the Central Committee in 1976, I gave increased emphasis, and collectively the party leadership started giving increased emphasis, to the growing danger of world war. This is something that Mao had pointed to even in the early 1970s, but we recognized this danger was growing and coming more to the fore. We started calling attention to this, as well as putting forward the general line that we had to oppose all imperialism and to build the struggle internationally against all imperialism—including not only the U.S. and its imperialist bloc but also

Soviet social-imperialism and its bloc.

In line with this, we needed to raise the banner of anti-imperialism broadly, and at the same time to struggle out some questions that were sharply posing themselves among radical and progressive people, over how to understand the role of different forces and different struggles in the world. In particular, how should we understand what role was played in the world not only by U.S. imperialism but also by the Soviet Union. Was the Soviet Union a progressive, positive force, was it a friend and ally of people fighting for liberation? Or was it misusing struggles for national liberation and against colonialism in Africa and other places for its own imperialist aims and distorting and diverting those struggles off of a revolutionary path? These were the questions addressed in part in *Red Papers* 7, but the situation had intensified since then and besides, there were more people who needed to be reached with this analysis.

So we organized a conference on international questions, which was held in New York. Now, of course, we didn't know this when we were planning the conference, but it ended up being held just after the coup in China, in the fall of 1976, so there were a lot of issues very sharply swirling around that conference, most of all: how did we understand that coup? Our party—in large part because by this time we had a fully developed Menshevik faction within it—had not yet come to a unified position around this, but we were beginning to take up this question just as this conference was held. So this obviously made this conference more complex.

The conference had workshops and discussions about the struggle against imperialism in many different parts of the world, and then in the evening we had a three-sided debate between myself, representing the RCP; William Hinton, who had written the book *Fanshen* and done a lot to popularize the Chinese revolution but who was at that point sort of uncritically following the Chinese leadership, particularly with regard to the international arena; and Dave Dellinger, a long-time anti-war activist. We had tried to get someone openly supportive of the Soviet Union and that whole revisionist camp to be part of this debate, but we couldn't find anyone who would do that. Dave Dellinger took part as someone who put forward the position that the Soviet Union is no good, but that U.S. imperialism is the real evil in the world and we have to support any struggle against U.S. imperialism—and we have to look at the role of the Soviet Union more or less entirely in relation to that. And particularly in places like Angola[30] and other countries in Africa, for example, where the involvement of Cuba would be the means through which Soviet influence would be extended into these struggles, then Cuba—as opposed to the Soviet Union—was put forward by people like Dellinger in a more positive light; and by extension, therefore, even the Soviet role was seen in that positive light. So this was the debate: How do we understand what's going on in the world with these struggles and the role of these different world powers and other forces?

Our position was to oppose both superpowers and to uphold revolution against U.S. imperialism and Soviet social-imperialism all over the world. Hinton was putting forward the line coming out of the Chinese leadership—which, as I've discussed earlier, identified the Soviet Union as the main enemy, or in reality the only enemy. The Chinese position, as articulated by Hinton in that debate, was to unite all who could be united against the Soviet Union, including even the U.S. and other imperialist and reactionary states in the U.S. camp. The Dellinger position was sort of the mirror opposite of that: Unite everybody against the U.S., including forces in the Soviet camp, and in particular support those within the Soviet camp who were seemingly taking a more radical anti-(U.S.)-imperialist stance, like Cuba.

A lot of people were (and are) confused about Cuba, but the fact was that because Cuba had become totally dependent on the Soviet Union, economically, politically and otherwise, it went right down the line in

---

30. In 1974, the fascist regime in Portugal was overthrown by a military coup made up in part of officers who wanted to pull the Portuguese army out of its African colonies of Angola, Mozambique and Guinea-Bissau. Anti-colonial insurgencies had developed particularly in the latter two colonies. But in Angola the armed struggle had not made much progress. There were three main factions among the Angolans which were contending for power: MPLA, which was backed by the Soviet Union; UNITA, backed by South Africa and, later, the U.S.; and FNLA, widely acknowledged to be a wholly owned subsidiary of the CIA. But MPLA and UNITA each had something of a mass base in different tribal groupings and regions of the country, and neither represented a force that aimed to fundamentally break with imperialism. Shortly after the Portuguese pullout in 1975, the South African army (backed by the U.S.) stormed into southern Angola in a move to wipe out MPLA and install UNITA as the ruling party; the Cuban army came to the aid of MPLA; and the result was a bitter proxy civil war, the main content of which had to do not with the liberation of the Angolans, but the relative geopolitical positions of the U.S. and USSR.

supporting the Soviet Union when it came to any really important matters, including the Soviet invasion of Czechoslovakia. But many people still tried to keep inventing ways in which Cuba was somehow an independent force, even though it could not be denied that it consistently allied with the Soviet Union. We argued strenuously against that and maintained that the international struggle had to be directed against both imperialist camps.

There were about fifteen hundred to two thousand people at this conference and debate on the international situation. The debate was a significant clash of different positions on crucial things having to do with the international situation and the struggle against imperialism, and as such, was very lively. It also had repercussions inside our own Party, sharpening up the question of whether we were really going to be internationalists and support revolution throughout the world, or whether we were going to take a position which, in one form or another, would end up accommodating to imperialism. This became interwoven and closely bound up with the struggle that was coming to a head in our party with the Menshevik faction, particularly focused now over what stand to take toward what was in fact a revisionist coup in China, which had taken place just before this conference.

This struggle would determine the fate of the Party.

# Chapter Nineteen

# "Bitter Sacrifice Strengthens Bold Resolve"–Mao

## The Death of Mao Tsetung

Mao Tsetung died on September 9, 1976.

When Mao died we all knew it was a momentous thing. We knew that it was going to have monumental implications. But right at the time he died, we didn't and couldn't fully understand what that would mean.

We did know that the struggle inside the Chinese party had been sharpening up before Mao died. I used to get the *Peking Review* mailed to my house every week, and one day in the spring of 1975 I opened it up and there, featured on the front page, was this article by Yao Wen-yuan, who was later arrested as one of the "Gang of Four." This article analyzed the basis for revisionism and capitalist restoration in China, and in particular its expression right inside the Chinese Communist Party. The article was called "On the Social Basis of the Lin Biao Anti-Party Clique," but it was one of those Aesopian things that was ostensibly talking about Lin Biao yet was really referring obliquely, or perhaps not so obliquely, to the people who were currently fighting for a revisionist line inside the party. And, as soon as you saw an article like that, you said, "Wow, something heavy is up."

That was followed the next month by another article, this one by Chang Chun-chiao, called "On Exercising All-Round Dictatorship Over

336

the Bourgeoisie." This article also analyzed, in more depth, the contradictions within Chinese society—and socialist society in general—and their concentrated expression within the Party, which made it possible for socialism to be overthrown and capitalism to be restored. This made the fact of sharp struggle inside the Chinese Communist Party even more clear, and these articles were followed by a round of open, society-wide struggle in China against capitalist-roaders and criticism of revisionist lines in various spheres. So, by the fall of 1976, a year and more later, there was a lot of struggle—and then Mao died. We had a definite sense that big things were up and the struggle was likely to intensify, but we didn't quite understand how everything was coming to a head right then.

We put out a statement on Mao's death, and we had memorial meetings around the country. I spoke at the one in Chicago and posed the question: Who will be Mao's successors? I answered that *we* will—the communists and the revolutionary proletarians throughout the world, including in the U.S., would step forward and take up Mao's banner. And that was our orientation.

But then, about a month after Mao died, I woke up to hear on the radio that leaders of the Chinese Communist Party had been arrested: Chiang Ching, Mao's widow; Chang Chun-chiao; Yao Wen-yuan; and Wang Hung-wen (who had also come forward in Shanghai during the Cultural Revolution). They were being denounced as a "Gang of Four" that supposedly had opposed Mao—but I had a strong feeling that that was just a shabby device to cover over what was nothing less than a coup against the whole direction in which Mao had been leading the Chinese people, and a blow against Mao's line of continuing on the socialist road and keeping the goal of communism as the guiding star.

This coup sharpened everything up, and it put the death of Mao into this whole new context. Right away it was clear to myself and some others in the leadership of our Party that the only thing that had held back this coup for some time had been Mao himself. As long as Mao was alive, the revisionists within the leadership of the Chinese Communist Party couldn't carry out these arrests and pull off this coup; but no sooner had Mao died than these revisionists moved against those who had been fighting to keep China on the socialist road, denouncing them as an anti-socialist "Gang of Four." So the basic terms of what was *really* going on were clear to me, more or less from the beginning.

I remember listening to the radio, right after the coup, and they were reporting how in Shanghai, which had been a stronghold of the revolutionary forces, the people's militias were fighting the PLA, the regular army in China. And I was going, "Come on, militias, overturn and reverse this coup, and save socialism in China." But they were brutally defeated within a couple of days. And then you had to confront the reality not only that Mao was gone (which was itself a tremendous loss), but that *China* was lost as a socialist country, as a bastion of revolution and socialism and a guiding light and a source of inspiration for oppressed people all over the world.

This was a terrible and stunning setback, an almost incalculable loss.

## A Division in the Leadership

At the beginning, when the coup happened, there wasn't anybody in the leadership of the RCP who would openly come out and support it. The initial reaction of myself and some other leaders of the Party was that this was a revisionist coup, a terrible thing. I think the reality of it was that, for a little while, the dust was still settling, so to speak, and perhaps for some people it had not really sunk in that revisionist forces had definitively seized power and won out. So during that brief period nobody within the Party leadership came out openly in support of the coup. But, as soon as the dust did settle and it became clear that the so-called "Gang of Four," and all the revolutionary forces they represented in the Communist Party and in Chinese society more broadly, were being crushed and decimated, with some of them being executed and others imprisoned—as soon as it became clear that this was the situation, *then* some of these people in the Menshevik faction within our Party, such as Mickey Jarvis, *did* start to act differently. At first this seemed to be mainly in the form of raising questions: "Well, wait a minute, maybe it's not so clear that these people like Chiang Ching are actually the revolutionaries, maybe they really are a counter-revolutionary 'Gang of Four.'"

And this is where Leibel Bergman went off the deep end. Some of his better qualities were already being seriously undermined by bourgeois influences and ways of thinking that were increasingly marking his outlook, particularly in the form of pragmatic and reformist tendencies from the old Communist Party which he'd never completely shed and which, in a sense, co-existed with the better and more revolutionary and communist side of him. But these revisionist tendencies didn't really come to *characterize* his outlook and approach until this coup happened. At that crucial turning point, these negative tendencies just ate up everything else, and Leibel went completely over to the side of supporting the coup. He started upholding and praising Deng Xiaoping— whom everybody in our Party had understood to be a revisionist who was taking the same road Liu Shao-chi[31] had taken before, the road of restoring capitalism while claiming to be building socialism. But, all of a sudden, Leibel Bergman started saying, "That Deng Xiaoping, he's not so bad—he's a 'tough cookie,' he doesn't buckle under to anybody."

This led to intense arguments and struggles. I replied: "Yeah, but what is the *content* of this 'tough cookie-ness?' What's he fighting for, what's his program, where will it lead? When Mao was alive, it was clearly understood, and we all agreed, that this would lead back to capitalism. Now, what are you saying?" "Well," Leibel would insist, "it isn't so clear now that this is the case." It seemed that, among other things, Leibel just couldn't confront the fact that socialism had been overturned in yet another country—that, as had happened in the Soviet Union, a revisionist clique had seized power in China. His pragmatic tendencies, which were always there—and which sometimes strongly asserted themselves—started really coming to the fore and dominating his outlook.

Leibel might just as well have said, and in effect he did say: "Well, these people won out, so what can we do? That's the way it is, and we might as well 'make a virtue of necessity.' It's much better if we can still say that China is socialist. So let's not get into all this stuff about analyzing what's really going on. Let's just accept what the people now in power in China say—that these other people who were arrested weren't *really* the revolutionary forces inside the Chinese Communist Party, but were actually against Mao, and despite all appearances they were really the counter-revolutionaries who were trying to undermine Mao and take Mao's whole thing in an ultra-left direction, which would destroy it all."

---

31. Liu Shao-chi had been the head of those Party members—and in particular Party leaders—who were fighting to take China in a capitalist direction; he became the chief target of the Cultural Revolution. Deng Xiaoping had been Liu's second-in-command and had himself been targeted and sharply criticized in the Cultural Revolution, only to be brought back in the wake of the Lin Biao affair.

This kind of pragmatism began to assert itself very powerfully in Leibel. In addition, people like Leibel and the others who were heading this Menshevik faction looked to Chou En-lai as a model communist. He was the kind of practical administrator who got things done and, at the same time, to put it a certain way, Chou En-lai was also very "French." That is, he was urbane and cosmopolitan, and many intellectuals could feel very comfortable around him. That can be a good thing, if it's in the service of a revolutionary line. But it was clear that Chou En-lai himself had a very strong pragmatic streak, and that he had been attempting to reconcile all these different contradictions within the Chinese Communist Party and ultimately was protecting all these revisionists like Deng Xiaoping, which had the effect of enabling them to regroup and eventually seize power. Deng and his cronies were greatly aided by the way Chou En-lai was trying to put stability and the development of the economy above everything else in China—and, in particular, above the struggle to combat revisionism and prevent capitalist restoration.

Writing in the context of the outbreak of World War 1 and the "collapse of the Second International"—with most of the parties that were part of that international socialist organization degenerating into a position of supporting "their own" ruling class in that imperialist war—Lenin talked about how sharp turns in society and in world events will temper and strengthen some but break and shatter others. And the latter is what happened with Leibel. The revisionist coup in China led him to abandon the communist outlook and method and communist principles.

I remember that at one point I was insisting that we couldn't just go along with what had happened in China, that it was our responsibility to analyze this and if, as I believed, such an analysis led to the conclusion that in fact a revisionist coup had taken place, it was our responsibility to oppose it, openly and vigorously. And he shot back: "There you go again, you gotta tell everybody in the world what to do. Let the Chinese people figure out what's right and wrong in their country, it's not up to us to tell them about what's happening in China."

And I replied: "Yeah, but *you're* taking a position. It's not a question of taking a position or not taking a position. We will be taking a position one way or another, whatever we do. You're supporting these people who've come to power and who, as I see it, have pulled off a coup. That's a position—not opposing this coup is supporting it. So that's a position. Saying China is still socialist is a position of supporting what's happened in China. So don't tell me it's none of our business to take a position. You're taking a position, you just don't want to take a position against this coup because you don't want to admit or face up to what's really happened—or maybe you *like* the direction in which these people are taking China, where it's gonna be a more 'business-like' society where they put developing the economy and 'modernizing' the country above everything else, regardless of the character of the economy and of the modernization and who is served by all this. Maybe you don't care that this is gonna be done along capitalist lines and with capitalist principles and will subject the Chinese people to horrendous oppression and exploitation once again under the rule of these bourgeois forces and the domination of imperialism. But don't tell me that I'm being arrogant to take a position. You're taking a position too, you're just taking the opposite one, so let's not pretend that's the issue."

## Unfolding the Struggle

The coup in China and the struggle that erupted within our Party over this brought everything to a head. But a party is a precious thing— a vanguard party is absolutely essential and indispensable for people to make revolution, for the proletariat to seize power and transform society, for the oppressed people to rise up and put an end to all oppression. So you don't just willfully or mindlessly split apart a party like that. You try to win over and unite as many people as you can, on a revolutionary basis, within the party. You don't seek unity at any cost, you don't do it on the basis of throwing out principles—but you don't just lightly fracture apart a party.

Some of us were getting more and more clear that a revisionist coup had in fact taken place in China and that this would have horrendous consequences for the masses of Chinese people, which of course has proven to be true—but which is rarely, if ever, talked about these days in the mainstream bourgeois media. The imperialist media, when it "covers" China, focuses on the elite minority, on the bourgeois forces in China; the masses of people are rarely mentioned. All the terrible suffering that they've been subjected to since Mao died and the revisionists seized power—that, of course, is not a focus of the imperialist media. But that was what those of us who opposed this coup were focusing on —what this will mean for the *masses* of people in China, and throughout the world, what it will mean for the world revolutionary struggle.

The record is very clear on Deng Xiao-ping: he not only brought about capitalist restoration in China, and opened up China and its people once again to imperialist domination and exploitation, but he completely abandoned any pretense of supporting revolution, or even any *talk* of revolution in the world.

So these were the stakes we were facing. And the question was sharply posed: How do we unite the Party around a correct understanding of this on a principled basis? I myself, and other comrades who recognized what was up, also recognized that we faced the tremendous challenge of trying to correctly unfold things in the Party in order to preserve the revolutionary character of our Party and at the same time win over the greatest number of people to the correct position. There was another comrade in the very top leadership of the Party who had the same understanding of this that I did. This was very important for me, both personally as well as in my ability to lead the Party as a whole, because in the top leadership core things were sharply divided: in addition to this comrade who was solidly with me on this, there were Leibel Bergman and Mickey Jarvis, who were supporting the revisionist coup with increasing vehemence. This other leading comrade and I, who were firm in our opposition to the coup, had to go to meetings with Bergman and Jarvis and discuss Party work and various political and ideological questions, at the same time as we were sharply divided over this life-and-death question of what was happening in China.

I recognized that if we were going to correctly unfold this struggle inside the Party and win as many people as possible to a correct position on this and unite the greatest number of people, we had to do it in a principled way, and in particular with means and methods that would enable the greatest number of Party members to grasp the essence of what was involved and to determine where they stood on that basis. You can't apply unprincipled methods and have a principled outcome.

So what did this mean? One thing it meant was that you couldn't factionalize. A faction is a group inside a party with its own views, its own network and its own discipline. You can see how that would undercut the unity and discipline that a serious party needs, but it also actually subverts the search for truth. In a situation like this one, where we were split on the highest level of leadership over what was right, we at least needed to formulate the questions that people should be studying and the principles that people should be using that could help them arrive at the truth, or else people would just get bombarded with the one-sided stuff coming out of China and the slant coming from the U.S. media, the whole thing would be very disorienting and the membership as a whole would not be in a position to contribute to arriving at the truth. So you couldn't just go around to anybody in the Party and try to influence them, in whatever way you could, toward the view that you held. You could, and should, debate it out on the highest body you sat on, but when you "took things down," so to speak, you couldn't be putting out your own take on things or you'd have the Party as a whole going in different directions and *not* in a position where we were applying some unified standards, and the same basic framework, to carry out investigation and debate and get at the truth.

In short, it was necessary to unfold this through the appropriate channels of the Party and the correct procedures of Party functioning, so that all Party members would be fully involved and able to wrestle with the decisive questions in the deepest way. But this was difficult to adhere to when the people within the Party who were upholding the coup had no such compunction. They had an unprincipled position and they had unprincipled methods that went along with it. They were opportunists all the way around, so they didn't hesitate to factionalize. In fact, I didn't really realize the full extent of this until the struggle came to a head, and then people started telling stories about how, even before the coup in China, but in a much greater way after that, these people were factionalizing. They were factionalizing for their line everywhere they could, on every possible occasion.

For example, I spoke earlier about intermediate workers organizations and different views within the Party about how to build them. Well, the RCP made efforts to build an organization of that kind, drawing together workers from many different parts of the country, and in 1977 a convention was held of the National United Workers Organization (NUWO). More than a thousand people, from many different industries, representative of more advanced politically aware workers, came to Chicago for this convention. But it was shot through with both the economist influence of these Mensheviks, and their constant factionalizing with others inside the Party, and even some people who were not in the Party. The Mensheviks saw this as an opportunity for them to go around and get into it with everybody about what was happening in China and the struggle within the RCP. But, as a matter of basic orientation, if you wanted to win people to the correct line on the correct basis and have an outcome that would unite people on the basis of principle, then you had to be principled in how you went about it. So, even in the face of this factionalism, those of us who opposed the coup in China resisted pulls to retaliate in kind.

It was ironic. I remember one time we confronted one of these Mensheviks and pointed to concrete evidence of how they had been factionalizing all over the place. And their answer was: "So what, you've been doing the same thing." And we pointed out that, as a matter of fact, we had *not* been doing the same thing. This was also a matter of principle to us. We adhered to Party organizational principle while we were carrying out this struggle because we recognized that there was an important unity between the line you were fighting for and the principles you applied in fighting for that line.

Sometimes, as a result of adhering to this principle, it would get very lonely, because there was almost nobody for me to talk to. I couldn't even talk to my wife at that time about this, since she wasn't on the same level of top party leadership that I was. So while she was being subjected to all this horrendous shit by the Mensheviks, which I referred to earlier, and while she was witnessing all this factionalizing, I couldn't talk to her about how I viewed the issue at that time—because that would have been violating Party discipline and principle.

### "Everything Seems Very Stable"

But, as I said, there was one comrade in particular who was on the same level of leadership as I was, so we could talk about everything without that being factional. Everybody on that level of leadership knew what everybody's position was, and the two of us were open and aboveboard about all this in discussions with others on that level. At one point this other leading comrade headed a delegation of Party members to China. This was the last time we had a delegation go to China. It was several months after the coup, and part of our overall approach to resolving this question was to send a delegation to China to investigate. Some people on the delegation were part of this Menshevik faction, and then other people weren't part of any faction and had a range of views, but the delegation collectively was assigned the task to go and investigate without formulating definite opinions about what they saw, and then to report back to the Party leadership.

Well, this comrade leading the delegation was faced with one of the most difficult situations that you could possibly be in. At the end of the delegation's visit to China, they had one of these banquets. And a member of the Chinese Communist Party Central Committee came and officiated at this banquet. In the course of this, he tried to put this comrade leading our delegation on the spot. He said to him: "You have heard all this stuff in the foreign press about how much instability and upheaval there is in China. You have been around to all these different places and seen all these things, now what do *you* say about this?" Obviously, he was trying to get this comrade to say, "Oh, everything's fine." But this comrade said: "Well, everywhere you've taken us, everything seems very stable." He cut right down the middle of this and maintained principle without taking a side one way or the other. When I heard this story, I thought: what a brilliant way to avoid a trap and give an answer that was in accordance with the mission of this delegation!

Now the people on this delegation who had been organized by, or influenced by, this Menshevik faction were not only arguing for their position but were pressuring this comrade who headed the delegation to take a position in support of the coup. But that wasn't the assignment of this delegation. They were supposed to go and investigate, and report back to Party leadership—this was part of the overall process through which this crucial question would be resolved.

So the delegation didn't take a position. They came back and reported to the leadership, and I was *very* glad when the delegation returned —not only because the results of their investigation were important but also, on a personal level, because once again there was someone I could talk to about all this. After he returned from that trip to China, we used to sit up late at night talking and going over articles in the *Peking Review*. The *Peking Review* was now being put out under the direction of the revisionists who had seized power, so it was giving us their side of things; but we also pored over issues of the *Peking Review* that had come out before the coup, like the ones with the articles by Yao Wen-yuan and Chang Chun-chiao that I referred to earlier. We'd go through these issues and thrash all this out, comparing and analyzing the different lines, over and over again; and we would read and discuss things written by Mao, as well as other Marxist theory—things which shed light on the situation and provided important theoretical grounding. Then we had to go to meetings with these Mensheviks, who now included Leibel

Bergman, and fight for a principled way of unfolding this struggle in the Party.

## Focusing on the Cardinal Questions

I, together with this other leading comrade, adopted the tactics of focusing the attention of the whole Party on what we called the "cardinal questions" involved. That is, as best as we understand them, what are the questions of outlook, of program, of policy, that have been put forward by the two sides in this struggle in China—i.e., by those who are now in power, and by those whom they've arrested and denounced as the "Gang of Four." At the time, the people behind the coup were using their monopoly of the media to just gossip about, slander and really vilify the "Four," often on the level of personal attacks, and to obfuscate the real differences. But we insisted on analyzing *lines*, as we say, and where will these lines lead? What interests do they represent and what kind of direction do they represent for society?

Since there was sharp disagreement over all this within the Party leadership, those of us who opposed the coup and upheld the so-called "Gang of Four" insisted that at least the Party leadership should unite around focusing the attention of the Party as a whole on these cardinal questions. These Mensheviks couldn't find a basis to oppose that. They wanted us to just come out and support the coup, but since we refused to do that they had to go along with this method of identifying and focusing attention on key questions and certain key lines of demarcation. My orientation and aim was to unfold this so that people throughout the Party would be strengthened in their ability to grapple with and evaluate what was going on in China and what was represented by the two sides, and as part of this we were able to force these Mensheviks to agree to certain criteria for evaluating what was happening in China. These were criteria that it would have been extremely difficult for them to openly oppose at the time.

One of the clearest and most important examples of this was what stand to take toward Deng Xiaoping. Deng had been criticized as a "capitalist-roader"—and had been made the focus of a mass campaign of criticism—during the last year and a half of Mao's life. In fact, Deng had a whole history of advocating and trying to implement lines and policies that would set China on the capitalist road—and, of course, after Mao died and the revisionists seized power in China, Deng was not only "rehabilitated" but quickly assumed the leading position in China and then fully implemented these lines and policies, with the result that in fact capitalism *was* restored in China. And, as a matter of fact, after being defeated within our Party and then splitting from the Party, Mickey Jarvis, Leibel Bergman and the rest of the Mensheviks came out openly in support of Deng Xiaoping.

But, before that, given the fact that within our Party Deng Xiaoping was clearly identified as a representative and advocate of the capitalist road, these Mensheviks found themselves in a position where they were forced to agree to Mao's evaluation of Deng. Another factor in this was that, when the coup was pulled off, Hua Guo-feng was nominally the leader of the government of China, and nominally the author of this coup. And, for a short time, Hua made a pretense of continuing the movement to criticize Deng Xiaoping. The truth was that Deng Xiaoping was the real force behind the coup, but for a short time this was not so glaringly obvious.

For these reasons, we were able to force the Mensheviks to agree to the criterion that if Deng Xiaoping is rehabilitated politically, and once again resumes a leadership position in the Chinese Party and state, that will tell us that something is very wrong. We had people throughout the Party study and discuss Deng's actual program and the criticisms of it by Mao. We united people that Deng Xiaoping is a capitalist roader, and what happens with him now that these new forces are in power in China will tell us something very important about what road *they* are on. The Mensheviks within our Party couldn't oppose this guideline because that verdict on Deng Xiaoping had not yet been reversed in China. He hadn't yet been rehabilitated, and moreover everybody knew that this was Mao's verdict on Deng Xiaoping; and this new leadership, nominally headed by Hua Guo-feng, was still pretending to be upholding what Mao was all about. Under these circumstances, the Mensheviks had to go along with this criterion, and this was very important.

We insisted on other important criteria and guidelines which the Mensheviks were also in a difficult position to oppose: What are the new leaders in China going to say about the Cultural Revolution? Are they going to continue to carry forward the Cultural Revolution? If they claim to be upholding Mao's line, they should continue to carry forward the transformations that were brought forward through the Cultural Revolution. Or are they going to start undoing those things? Are they going to start abolishing the revolutionary committees? These revolutionary committees were a new form of administration in institutions throughout China, combining representatives of the masses with administrators and Party cadre, and also simplifying administrative functions and reducing bureaucratization. Is the new leadership going to start replacing this with bourgeois structures and methods, like one-man management? What are they going to do about the policies for production? Are they going to keep to Mao's line of "putting politics in command," motivating people in production on the basis of their having a grasp of what the production is for and how it serves the revolutionary transformation of society and aids the world revolution, and inspiring people with the ideal and the vision of continuing on the socialist road toward the goal of communism and building the economy to do that? Or will they try to motivate people on the basis of "bourgeois right"—working more to get more income—piecework, bonuses, and other "material incentives"?

Another key criterion and guideline concerned a crucial political formulation. Mao had developed the theory that the main danger of capitalist restoration under socialism comes from people in Party leadership who take the capitalist road—who uphold and fight for policies that would put capitalist principles in command and would lead back to capitalism—and that, consequently, the class struggle under socialism is *concentrated* in the struggle against people in authority taking the capitalist road (as opposed to dispossessed exploiters or petty proprietors who do not hold high party positions and are not in a position of exercising authority and key decision-making with regard to the economy and the society as a whole). This was integral to the line identified with Mao and a qualitative advance in the understanding of the nature of socialist society and of the continuing class struggle within that society. Would the new leaders uphold and actually apply this understanding, or would they simply pay lip service to it, distort it—or outright overturn it?

Once again, the Mensheviks couldn't oppose these criteria because a basic understanding of these things was generally grasped throughout our party, and because these principles hadn't yet been openly denounced and overturned in China itself. They were stuck. And by putting out these criteria within the Party, we established a good foundation for people to be able to evaluate what had happened in October of 1976, when the "Gang of Four" was arrested, as well as the subsequent course of events in China.

Then one by one the criteria were put to the test. Deng Xiaoping got rehabilitated. Then crucial transformations that had been brought forward through the Cultural Revolution were repudiated and abolished. And the new leadership came up with eclectic new "versions" of Mao's line—they focused class struggle *away from* the struggle between the two roads and the two lines, as concentrated in the leadership of the Party—and, before long, especially once Deng Xiaoping was fully rehabilitated and openly back in power, they began abandoning talk of class struggle and revolution altogether.

But because of the way we had proceeded, comrades throughout the Party had the best possible basis to evaluate what could otherwise have been very confusing and disorienting events and to correctly understand what was going on. The majority of Party members were able to recognize that those who had seized power in China were in fact reversing the whole course that Mao was leading the people in, and were just putting into practice that line of Deng Xiaoping, which comrades could understand to be a line of restoring capitalism.

Now eventually, the hard core of this Menshevik faction—and others who followed them without thinking that much, frankly, or who gravitated toward this sort of revisionist line anyway—went along with all these changes in China. But, despite all their factionalizing and other unprincipled methods, they were not able to carry the day in the Party, and the great majority supported the position of opposing and exposing the coup, upholding the revolutionary legacy of Mao, and upholding those who had gone down fighting in defense of that revolutionary line.

## Coming to Grips

While it was extremely important that this struggle was won within the Party—and won on the basis of principles and methods that enabled Party members and the Party as a whole to be strengthened in their grasp of the key questions involved and of the means for engaging those questions and arriving at a deeper understanding of them—the fact remained that what had taken place in China was a tremendous setback.

I, as well as others in the Party and in the international communist movement, had to come to grips with this. It was a very bitter pill. But it did not shake my belief in the practicability or desirability of socialism and the ultimate goal of communism. What it did do, as had previous negative developments that I'd been forced to confront, was to make me more aware of the complexity of the whole process of moving from capitalism to communism. Not just everything that is involved in getting to the point where it is possible to overthrow capitalism in the first place, but then the process, and struggle, of continuing on the socialist road, to carry forward the radical transformation of society toward the goal of communism and to do that together with people throughout the world struggling for the same goal. It brought more fully to life things that Mao had pointed out about the danger of capitalist restoration in socialist society. I came to understand this more acutely, and at the same time I recognized that we had to confront and engage this more deeply in order to understand how to not only make revolution and seize power but how then to continue to advance through all the twists and turns on the road of socialist revolution, in order to bring into being a world that the masses of people—the great majority of people throughout the world who are suffering horribly under this system—need, in order for their oppression to be uprooted and ended, a world in which these masses, and ultimately all of humanity, would want to live and in which they could really come alive.

# Chapter Twenty

# *Split!*

This internal process of focusing comrades' attention on the big questions that were being posed about the direction of China, and what that said about revolution and counter-revolution, lasted for about a year. As that process was unfolding, of course, the struggle was intensifying within the leadership of the RCP, and the Menshevik faction grew more and more overt and organized, and aggressive, reaching everywhere they could within the Party. So, both because the year-long process of providing guidelines and focusing the attention of the whole Party on the cardinal questions involved had laid a sufficient basis, *and* because the internal struggle and the Menshevik factionalism was intensifying, it was time to bring this to a head and decide the issue. A meeting of the Central Committee of the Party was called, to resolve the struggle.

## Revolutionaries Are Revolutionaries... And Must Be Supported

In preparation for that, I wrote a paper called "Revisionists Are Revisionists And Must Not Be Supported; Revolutionaries Are Revolutionaries And Must Be Supported," which was later published in the book *Revolution and Counter-Revolution*.[32] This paper was circulated

---

32. In addition to this paper by Bob Avakian, the book *Revolution and Counter-Revolution* also contained a long paper, in response to Avakian's paper, written some months later by the Jarvis-Bergman group, after they had split from the Party; it also contained a rejoinder to this from the RCP, as well as several papers debating questions of line related to making revolution within the U.S. This book delves in considerable depth into many issues of socialism which can only be alluded to here.

among members of the Party's Central Committee, in preparation for the upcoming meeting. It set forth my view (which was shared by the other leading comrade I have referred to) that what had taken place in China was a revisionist coup, and that those who had been arrested and denounced as the "Gang of Four" were in fact the genuine revolutionaries. The paper analyzed why this was the case, and it spoke to a number of contentious issues and answered attacks on the revolutionaries that were appearing in the *Peking Review*, which was now being put out by this revisionist ruling group in China. It also answered the main arguments that the Menshevik faction within our Party was raising—things they had taken up from the revisionists in China and to some degree had put their own particular "spin" on, as is said today. This was a clearly polemical paper, and it made very clear to everybody who read it that there was an intense struggle between two fundamentally and antagonistically opposed positions. And that's how we headed into the Central Committee meeting.

The people on the other side did *not* write up a comparable paper putting forward their position. They were free to do so, but they didn't —and this was characteristic of the way they chose to carry out the struggle. They didn't want to put forward a fully developed position that people could then answer and refute. They chose instead to repeat a lot of gossip and raise a lot of doubts and secondary issues in order to obfuscate the question and try to undermine the process by which people could focus on and come to a determination about the key issues. Their opportunist line had to be, and was, accompanied by opportunist methods.

But right up to the Central Committee meeting, I continued to meet with, and to have discussion and struggle with, the people who were heading up this faction. We were discussing Party policies and actions in general, but we were principally discussing and struggling over this whole question of China. And right before we left to go to the Central Committee meeting, Mickey Jarvis, who was one of the main leaders of this Menshevik faction, called me up on the phone. I guess the FBI must have gotten quite an earful, because here we were talking on the phone about all these issues that were in contention, about who were the revisionists and who were the revolutionaries on the two sides of this struggle in China. Jarvis seemed to be having second thoughts and to be more open to considering the position that I had been arguing for. He seemed to be asking questions from that vantage point: "Well, there are just a few things that I still am uncomfortable about or am not clear on, so could you explain those?" As it turned out, he really just wanted to hear my arguments one more time so he could try to sharpen his own opposing arguments in preparation for the Central Committee meeting, and to do that he was pretending that he was being won away from, or at least reconsidering, his position.

At one point I even told him, "You know, I feel like Charlie Brown with the football—one more time it's gonna get pulled out from underneath when I go to kick it. But, okay, I'll go through it with you one more time." So I tried to explain, as fully and patiently and as exhaustively as I could, the answers to the questions he was raising—knowing that it was very likely that this was all just dissembling and maneuvering on his part. Still, I felt it was right and necessary to try one more time to convince him; and if, even at that late date, I'd been able to convince him and we'd been able to win this Menshevik faction away from their opportunism, there would have been fewer obstacles to uniting the Party more fully around the correct position. So that's why, even though I had very serious doubts and suspicions about what he was up to, I went through this process with him.

### Showdown

As I said, the time had come to hold the meeting and decide the issue. And as I was getting ready to go to this meeting, my wife at that time, who by then had read the key documents and was clear on the terms of the struggle, said, as we headed off for the Central Committee meeting, "Do you think we can win?" And I replied: "I don't know, but we can't lose." My meaning was clear: either we were going to win at this Central Committee meeting, and from there win and consolidate the majority of the Party around the correct line; or if the opportunist line won out at this Central Committee meeting, we were going to split and take as much of the Party as we could with us, because this was a life-and-death issue over which there could not be compromise.

If you read the Constitution of our Party, you'll see that the Central Committee has standing committees, and there was a standing committee meeting immediately before the larger Central Committee meeting. And at this time, Mickey Jarvis presented a paper, a little two- or three-page paper, which didn't say anything except the Gang of Four are no good and we should uphold the people who are in power now in China —the people who, in fact, had pulled off a revisionist coup. In other words, he hadn't budged at all from his position. But neither did he come in with a paper that actually sought to substantiate this position and to answer with any substance all the things that were in the position paper that I had written. It was just really a paltry and disgusting maneuver on his part. So, recalling the whole dishonest way in which, only a few days earlier, he had pretended to be reconsidering his position, I started off this standing committee meeting by saying: "Comrades, friends, double-dealers, back-stabbers and snakes in the grass." Thus the tone was set going into the Central Committee meeting, because he had been opportunizing right down to the last minute, and now it was all out in the open.

In order to get to the Central Committee meeting, I had traveled by airplane with this other comrade I've referred to, who had led the delegation to China and who firmly united with me in opposing the coup. During the airplane ride, we were discussing what he should say about this at the Central Committee meeting. Our orientation and approach for the meeting was to keep going until everybody on both sides had their say, as thoroughly as they wanted to, and then we were going to bring it to a head and resolve the issue. So, he and I were talking about what he would lay out as part of his presentation on the issue. We went through a number of different arguments that we'd heard from the Mensheviks, and we were developing our refutation of that; and, as we were talking, he was taking extensive notes to prepare and organize what he wanted to say at the Central Committee meeting. Then we got off the airplane and were continuing on our way toward the meeting, and it turned out that his notes somehow got left on the airplane. We joked afterward that the people working on the airplane and some of the passengers perhaps got an education in these world-historic issues about China and socialism and communism. Nonetheless, we had to go through the whole thing again, and he once again made notes and prepared his remarks; and when the Central Committee meeting started, he was the first person to speak and went on for a number of hours refuting the arguments of the Mensheviks and laying out a very clear and cogent analysis of what had happened in China and its implications.

The Central Committee meeting proceeded from there, and people did speak as long as they wanted to. Some people spoke for a relatively short period of time, maybe 20 or 30 minutes, and others spoke for hours, but we had a thorough airing of both sides of the issue, and it went on for days. In fact, the last day before we brought things to a vote, we just went all night long—we started early one morning and we just went all the way until the next morning. I was the last person to speak. I started late at night and continued until early the next morning, summing up the key points and answering arguments that had been raised by the Mensheviks. Then I asked if anybody had anything else to say. No one did, so we brought it to a vote. And the Central Committee majority voted to adopt as the line of the Party the position that was set forth in the paper that I had written, "Revisionists Are Revisionists And Must Not Be Supported; Revolutionaries Are Revolutionaries And Must Be Supported."

## The Real Deal

Now I have to say: I really did, and do, like that title. It encapsulates, in a simple yet provocative way, the fundamental point: "Look, you can bring up all the rationalizations and bullshit and opportunist obfuscation that you want, but here's the deal—and you know it: These people are revisionists, they're taking China down the capitalist road, and we're not going with that; these other people they've arrested and suppressed are the revolutionaries—and you know it—and we're going to support what they stand for, even though they have been defeated."

One of the things about pragmatism—and it's been a very strong streak in the American "Left" and the Communist Party historically, as well as more generally in American society—is the idea that if you win you must be right, and if you lose you must be wrong; "everybody loves a winner" and nobody has any use for a loser. According to this view, whatever "works" is right, whatever wins out is true. Well, it was necessary to go straight up against that and say, no, objective reality is not determined by who's prevailing at a given time in a struggle, or what's more popular at a given time among a section of people or generally in society—that does not make something true. There is objective reality, and there is objective truth. Truth is an objectively correct reflection of reality as it actually is. It's not whatever is convenient, it's not whatever is winning out at the time.

Pragmatism was a big ideological and philosophical component of the outlook of these Mensheviks. This took two main expressions in the context of the struggle over what had happened in China. On the one hand, they actually liked the revisionism that was coming out of China —to them it was more "practical." Never mind that it represented the practical application of capitalist principles. At the same time, they gravitated to the pragmatic logic that "these people are now in power, so how can we go against that?—what they say must be true because they won out, they're in power." These two pragmatic tendencies reinforced each other in their thinking. So we had to take on that whole outlook, and the position paper I wrote—and in a concentrated way its title, "Revisionists Are Revisionists And Must Not Be Supported; Revolutionaries Are Revolutionaries And Must Be Supported"—very clearly called that out, and said, "No, if they are revisionists, which they are, we are not going with them just because they won out in the short run. And the people they have arrested and denounced as the 'Gang of Four' were Mao's close comrades; the line they were fighting for is Mao's line, it is the communist position and represents the socialist road, and even though it's been defeated in the short run, we have to continue to uphold that."

## Pretending Unity, Preparing to Split

After the vote was held at the Central Committee meeting, and the line put forward in the position paper I wrote had prevailed, then all the Mensheviks there, except for Leibel Bergman, pretended to make self-criticism and to unite with the majority position. We sang "The Internationale" together as the meeting ended. But, as became clear before long, no sooner did they leave the site of the meeting than they began factionalizing again.

Since they were based mainly, although not entirely, in New York and the east coast, we had recognized that while we had defeated them politically and ideologically, it was also necessary to take certain organizational steps to break up this whole faction they had developed over a period of time. By decision of the Central Committee, most of them remained in positions of leadership in the Party, though in many cases not quite the same prominent leadership positions they had held before. I regarded it as important for them to continue to be part of the leadership, because it was still necessary to try to win them over, even at this point, and to unite the Party as fully as possible. We wanted to continue struggling with them and get them to play a positive role in uniting the rest of the Party, in particular those who had been part of their faction or who had been influenced by it. But they abused this. As soon as they got back to their strongholds in New York and the east coast, they resumed factionalizing to oppose the Central Committee position.

We sent other comrades into these areas to assume the key leadership roles, but also to continue seeking unity on a principled basis with these Mensheviks, who were still nominally members of the RCP. Instead, the Mensheviks raised their factionalism to a whole new level, and formed what they called a Revolutionary Workers Headquarters within the Party, declaring that they were going to basically take over the Party and install their revisionist line as the line of the Party. Well, they didn't succeed in that. They did win over a section of the Party, particularly in their strongholds, but they didn't succeed in taking over the Party or winning over a majority of the Party.

I remember very clearly one of the decisive organizational steps we had to take. The Mensheviks were trying to make it appear that the line and the actual leadership of the Party was still an open question, and a matter up for struggle. They insisted this was not a settled issue and that, "there are two headquarters inside the Party, and people should go with us, the Revolutionary Workers Headquarters, because we're just as legitimate as that other headquarters"—even though that "other headquarters" represented the majority of the Party's Central Committee and the position it had adopted was the outcome of a whole process which lasted more than a year, and involved the whole Party, and which had culminated in a Central Committee meeting where the issue was thoroughly discussed and analyzed and the opposing lines exhaustively debated and then voted on. But they tried to obliterate all that and act as if the issue, and in fact the Party itself, were "up for grabs." So in addition to deepening our refutation of their political and ideological line, we insisted: "No. There is one Party. It has taken its position through its channels and procedures and through a whole process in which the entire Party has been involved, culminating in a meeting of its highest leadership body. *This* is the Party, and you're either in *this* Party, or you're not. You're either in or you're out." And in the areas where the Mensheviks were fomenting this reactionary factional rebellion, we called on comrades who wanted to remain in the Party to re-enroll in the Party and to re-establish their dedication to the Party, to its ideological and political line and to its organizational principles.

This completely infuriated these Mensheviks, because it just cut the ground out from underneath their attempt to say that the questions of what is the Party's line and who is the Party's leadership were not settled; and it also rallied the comrades who wanted to take the correct revolutionary position to come forward and rededicate themselves and declare their determination, not just to remain with the Party organizationally —although that was a key step—but also to grasp and to take up this crucial line that had been adopted by the Central Committee.

## What If...?

As I said to my wife right before this Central Committee meeting, I was not sure we would win this struggle. The Mensheviks knew whom they could count on going into the meeting, but I had *not* lobbied and politicked, so I didn't. I had a sense of where some people stood, but mostly I was waiting to see how people fell out at the meeting. As it turned out, no one outside the Menshevik faction sided with them, and even some of the Mensheviks began to waver and ended up abstaining when the issue finally came to a vote.

But had I lost, yes, I would have split the Party. I would have resigned first and then I would have talked to everyone I could about the issues involved and the stakes and why they were of such a magnitude as to compel me to take such a drastic step. I would have fought as I hard as I could, but in a *principled* way. I would *not* have lied. I would not have pretended to go along with the majority as a ruse to keep my leadership position and then go behind the Party's back, so to speak, to rally "my people." I would not have tried to confuse the issues when clarity was demanded.

The reason is that there actually *is* a unity between your ends and your means at any given time. And if you use means that are not in line with your communist principles, that don't serve getting to the world you're trying to get to, you will find yourself getting further from that world and actually undercutting your goals—and in the end, turning into the very thing you started out opposing.

## Deepening and Broadening

We had to defeat this factionalism and unite the Party as thoroughly as possible, internally—this was, of course, the key step that needed to be taken. But we also needed to *deepen* our analysis of the struggle that had gone on in China and what it represented. This was crucial for Party members and in terms of the internal life and cohesion of the Party. Even beyond that, we needed to put this analysis out more broadly in society and the movement. Many people in the U.S., and in other parts of the world, were trying to figure out what was going on in China: what the contending forces and programs and lines represented, in particular the people who were now in power in China, and what was this all leading to? So we undertook further study and analysis both to deepen the grasp of this within the Party, and also to put this out more broadly.

At that time, within the U.S., but also internationally, there was a great deal of confusion and disorientation about China. Even among the Maoist forces, more than a few got taken in by the revisionist coup, or in one way or another went along with it, and as a result lost their bearings further. Some of them even self-destructed, in effect, immediately or over a period of time, as a result of supporting what was objectively counter-revolution, even though some of them perhaps thought that they were supporting revolution. Regardless of people's subjective understanding and intent, objective reality has its effect; when you go down a certain road and you keep going on that road, one thing leads to another, and many parties around the world which had considered themselves Maoist were undermined and destroyed by taking the wrong turn and supporting the wrong side at this crucial divide. Some were unwilling or unable to face up to and analyze deeply what had happened; because what was objectively involved was a profound setback, they did not want to acknowledge what had happened and draw the bitter but necessary lessons.

At the same time, a number of Maoist parties and organizations refused to go along with the revisionist coup in China, but there remained the task of analyzing what had happened and why. The position paper I wrote, "Revisionists Are Revisionists...Revolutionaries Are Revolutionaries," was an important but beginning step in that direction, and it was necessary to deepen that. As part of that deepening, I began writing a series of articles in *Revolution*, which was the monthly newspaper of the RCP at that time, about Mao's contributions and development of communist theory and strategy on a whole series of questions: the political and military strategy for revolution in countries like China, i.e., countries that are under imperialist domination and internally are feudal or semi-feudal; how to develop the socialist economy and transform the economic relations so as to serve the fundamental interests and needs of the people and overcome the remaining elements of capitalism; the dictatorship of the proletariat, and how that can be a revolutionary state that moves society forward toward communism; Mao's development of Marxist philosophy; and the whole question of how to develop a culture that serves socialist society and the advance to communism, as opposed to a culture that encourages and fosters the ideas and orientation that lead back to capitalism. I began writing this series of articles to deepen and systematize this analysis and to provide more of an all-around framework for understanding these questions. And these articles eventually were put together and published as a book, *Mao Tsetung's Immortal Contributions*.

## The Mao Memorials

We also needed other means and vehicles for popularizing our understanding and trying to help people get clarity about these world-historic events. Because, again, there was a lot of confusion out there and a lot of contending analysis. Some of it came straight from the bourgeoisie, which of course was distorting the whole thing and obscuring the real issues. And then some of it came from other forces in the progressive and radical movements, who had, at best, a very eclectic understanding. And, more broadly, a lot of people were just sort of at a loss to understand what had happened in China.

As one of the main vehicles for bringing a more comprehensive and systematic analysis of this to a broader range of people, we decided to hold Mao Memorial meetings. These memorials would serve two purposes: one, to uphold the legacy that Mao had left and to defend and popularize the content of his leadership of the Chinese revolution and his contributions to the world revolution; and two, to clarify key questions about what had happened in China and the repercussions of this for the revolutionary struggle worldwide. We put a lot of work into creating public opinion around and building for these Memorials, which were held on the east and west coast, one in New York City and one in the Bay Area. I prepared and gave a speech entitled "The Loss in China and the Revolutionary Legacy of Mao Tsetung." This was a three-hour presentation, and it was followed by a question-and-answer session where people raised questions off of the talk and more generally questions they had about what had happened in China and why. Both the speech and the question-and-answer session were then published as a booklet, *The Loss in China and the Revolutionary Legacy of Mao Tsetung.*

These Memorials did fulfill to a significant degree the objectives we had for them. About twenty-five hundred people came to both events combined, and that, plus all the publicity we did around it and then the booklet that was published afterwards, had a major impact at that time, and did help many revolutionary-minded people to get at least a basic understanding of the significance of the issues and what had actually happened.

### Tell the Truth

Our objective was to enable people to understand the reality of what had happened. Some people seem to believe that if you understand reality, including what you might call the negative parts of reality, or the things that go against what you are trying to do, then you'll just get demoralized. But my feeling about that, and I think a more scientific approach to that, is that if you don't actually understand reality you will end up in a much worse place, much more demoralized by what are objectively negative developments and setbacks—and not only demoralized but disoriented, in a much more fundamental way. If there are negative turns in the struggle, or even monumental and world-historic setbacks—which is what had happened in China—the first thing you have to do is confront what has happened, analyze it, and if your analysis tells you that there has been such a setback, then that's what you have to accept. By "accept," I mean that you have to recognize that it's the reality that you're dealing with—I don't mean that you simply bow down and capitulate before this reality and give up trying to change the world.

But if the reality is that there have been negative developments and setbacks, you not only have to recognize that yourself, you have to tell people the truth about it. This doesn't mean that the goal of socialism and ultimately communism can't be achieved. But it drives home more fully that there can be not only great leaps forward, but also great setbacks along the path to that goal. Getting to where humanity needs to go in order to end this nightmare that most of humanity suffers every day is, to paraphrase Mao, a march of ten thousand miles. It is a twisting path, not a straight line forward, and it isn't a continuous ascent. As Mao put it: The future is bright, the road is tortuous. So you have to confront and continually deepen your understanding of this, and you have to tell people the truth about it in order for them to learn more deeply what the goal has to be and how, through all the twists and turns, advances and setbacks, we can finally arrive at that goal. So that's what we did. It may sound corny, but with that orientation, we set out to tell people the truth.

# Chapter Twenty-one

# *"A Fitting Welcome" for Deng Xiaoping*

The booklet from the Mao Memorial was barely published when we faced the question of defending Mao's legacy in practice as well as theory. After the coup and then the consolidation of a new revisionist, capitalist regime in China headed by Deng Xiaoping, the U.S. imperialists saw a big opening to further develop their relations with China, to more firmly bring China into the U.S. camp and open China up more fully to imperialist domination and exploitation. So a visit was arranged where Deng Xiaoping would come and hold meetings with the U.S. president at the time, Jimmy Carter.

## Confronting Deng

As Maoists, and in particular as Maoists within the U.S. itself, this was a political and ideological gauntlet that was being thrown down to us. We recognized that we had a responsibility to do something that would make a clear statement against this, and we decided to mobilize people from around the country to go to Washington, D.C. when Deng Xiaoping was there, to demonstrate and to create public opinion as much as we could, through the mainstream media but also through our own means—leaflets and publications of various kinds—to expose what had happened in China and what Deng Xiaoping represented, and to uphold the revolutionary banner of Mao.

So that's what we did.

Deng Xiaoping came in January 1979, and he was staying in the Blair House, which is near Lafayette Park and the White House. We had a rally in a church and then we left to go on the march through the streets of D.C. to politically confront Deng Xiaoping, to make as powerful a statement as we could in opposition to what he represented and to raise the banner of Mao. We marched with Red Books and banners upholding Mao and opposing Deng Xiaoping and the revisionist coup, and our main slogan—which I still remember ringing through the streets of D.C. as we marched—was: "Mao Tsetung Did Not Fail, Revolution Will Prevail!"

I remember very vividly people in the largely Black neighborhoods of D.C. coming out of their houses as we marched through, at first to see what was happening; but then—as they would hear the slogans we were chanting, and as they would see some of the banners with pictures of Mao and people marching while waving Red Books—a number of them ran back into their houses and came out with their own Red Books. Some joined the march, while many others lined the route of the march —a number of them were waving Red Books and others were shouting encouragement and in other ways indicating support for what we were doing. This was very inspiring and strengthened our resolve to stand up in the face of the revisionist coup in China and the way the U.S. was moving to further its support for the direction in which Deng was taking China.

As we began the march, it was already very clear that the authorities really didn't like this demonstration. And as we got to the area of Lafayette Park, the police unleashed a violent attack, beating as many people as they could, and finally succeeded in breaking up the march. They especially went after the women, brutally beating them; some were so disfigured from being hit with billy clubs and pummeled in the face that you could hardly recognize them, in some cases even for weeks afterward. Some people came very close to being permanently disabled or even killed. The assault the police unleashed was *extremely* vicious, and over eighty people in that demonstration, including myself, were arrested. I know some people who even to this day have kept the Red Book that they carried in that demonstration—their own blood was shed onto the Red Book, and they have proudly kept that as a blood-stained memento of the revolutionary and internationalist act of holding this demonstration, and upholding the revolutionary banner of Mao, in the face of these attacks.

While a number of us were arrested and taken to jail, some others who needed medical attention were driven around in paddy wagons for a long time before they were taken to the hospital. I and most of the people arrested with me spent the first night in jail handcuffed and chained outside our cells because we were continuing to chant revolutionary slogans and this pissed off the jailers. The men were held separately from the women but the lawyers who came forward to defend us told us inspiring stories about how the women continued to chant revolutionary slogans and shout from one cell to the other in Spanish, so the jailers couldn't understand exactly what they were saying, and how, in general, the women kept up their revolutionary spirit in the jail cells.

The Carter government, and the ruling class in general, was infuriated by this demonstration. Beyond the way the whole thing disrupted "business as usual" in the capital city, it *politically* disrupted what they were doing, it drew attention to the questions we were raising, and from a number of angles it politically embarrassed them. After all, here was this powerful demonstration against Deng Xiaoping—and other things happened around the same time, like two reporters from the *Revolutionary Worker* disrupting Deng's White House press conference by waving Red Books in his face and denouncing him as a revisionist—and this seized the spotlight, so to speak.

The demonstration, and the activities surrounding it, became an international incident. This was before the Internet and satellite news and all that kind of thing, but news of what we did went out over news services all over the world, and I later talked to people from many parts of the world for whom this demonstration was a very important and inspiring event. And that was part of what we were doing also—we were fulfilling our internationalist responsibility to let people know that, right in the U.S., there are people who uphold the banner of Mao and oppose what Deng Xiaoping represents and how he has taken China back to the hell of capitalism.

That's part of the reason why they unleashed this vicious police attack. Initially, they only charged us with misdemeanors; then they came back with heavier charges for a smaller number of us who were arrested—we were now charged with felonies, like assault on police officers. If we had been convicted and been given the maximum sentence for all of this, it would have amounted to over two hundred years in jail. In other words, they decided that in response to what we'd done they needed to come down with even more heavy political repression. So then, facing these heavy legal charges, there was a need to mount both a legal defense—but more importantly a political defense.

## Pranking the Parrots

Before getting into the seriousness of that, I want to briefly touch on something a little bit lighter—though with its own sharp edge. There was another group, the October League, which then turned itself into a party and called itself the Communist Party (Marxist-Leninist), or CP(M-L). They had gone right along with the coup in China and in their newspaper, *The Call*, they had put out all this stuff just parroting whatever was said by the revisionist leadership in China. The CP(M-L) leader, Mike Klonsky, had run right over to China and met with Hua Guo-feng, who nominally was the head of the government and nominally led the coup—though it was really Deng Xiaoping behind it—and there was a picture of Klonsky in the *Peking Review*, all dressed up and shaking hands with Hua Guo-feng. Some people in the movement at that time, like the *Guardian* newspaper, tried to turn things inside out and upside down and say that the reason that we didn't support the coup in China was because Klonsky got there first and got the mantle, so to speak, from Hua Guo-feng, and we were supposedly pissed off about that; and so, according to this distorted version of things, it was our competitiveness with the CP(M-L) that led us to take a position against the coup.

I have outlined in some detail the position that I held, and that others in leadership of the Party who weren't part of this Menshevik faction held, from the time of the coup in China; and I have summarized the basis for our position as well as the whole way we unfolded the struggle within the Party around this and why, in large part because of this Menshevik faction, it took us quite a period of time to get to where we could arrive at a final determination on this issue through a Central Committee meeting and then unite the whole Party around it. Those of us who held this position felt that what Klonsky had done, in rushing to embrace the coup, was disgusting—we were strongly inclined to oppose what had happened in China, and we recognized that Klonsky had just acted uncritically and unthinkingly, since there hadn't been any time to study and analyze the momentous events in China before he showed up in Peking and was shaking Hua Guo-feng's hand. But his visit is obviously not what motivated us to take the opposite position.

Anyway, we thought it would be good—it would make an important point, and also involve some fun—to ridicule the position Klonsky and the CP(M-L) had taken, and their basic approach to things. So we put out a phony issue of *The Call* which parroted and slightly, but only slightly, exaggerated the ridiculous positions that they were taking on China. For example, at the time we put out this parody of *The Call*, the Chinese revisionists were beginning to attempt to improve their relations with the Dalai Lama. And so in this *"Call"* we put out, we had an article which talked about a meeting between the Chinese leadership and the Dalai Lama and how there was so much emotion generated over the wonderful things that had been done by the Dalai Lama. The article said that, for this ceremony, they brought drums that had been made with human skin in Tibet under the rule of the Dalai Lama to celebrate the occasion. And this was referring to a very real fact of history—things of this kind had been done under the rule of the supposedly "benevolent" Lamas, including this Dalai Lama, and in writing this parody we made a point of referring to this reality and to the torment and the horrendous oppression and literal torture the masses of Tibetan people suffered under the rule of the Lamas.

Despite widespread misconceptions about this—due in large part to the "repackaging" of the Dalai Lama to make him appear as a worldly (or "other-worldly") wise man of peace and benevolence, and the promotion of this myth in the mainstream media—the truth is that, under the rule of these Lamas, the masses of people in Tibet were brutally exploited in conditions of feudal serfdom: they were denied health care and education and punished severely if they tried to get access to these things, with the flaying off of their skin a common punishment. And, of course, the oppression of women in that society was even more extreme. So, even as we were doing a parody of *The Call*, and inventing this scene involving the Chinese revisionists and the Dalai Lama, we pointed to the reality of what life had actually been like for the masses of Tibetan people under the rule of the Dalai Lama and his predecessors.

## The Battle in the Legal Arena

Returning to the heavy legal attacks that were coming down on us, I've said that political defense and political mobilization was the key thing in terms of defeating them. But it was also necessary, of course, to battle in the legal arena. I did an interview, for example, with a reporter from the *Washington Post*—which the *Washington Post* never ran, but which we published as part of a pamphlet.[33] At one point, this reporter said: "I guess you see this as a 'win-win' situation for you—if you get convicted, that will prove that the system is repressive; and if you get off, then that will be a victory for you."

I answered emphatically: "No, that is *not* the way we see it at all. This is an attack from the state, and we have to beat back and defeat this attack; in the course of that yes, of course, we will be exposing the system, and if we succeed in mobilizing masses of people and fighting in the legal arena and beating back this attack and defeating it, that doesn't prove that 'the system works,' it proves that we were able to prevail in a very intense battle against the system." So that's what we set out to do, and it required a lot of attention to the legal arena as well as to the political battle on the part of the Party in general and on my part in particular.

When the government came after us, they apparently believed that we either would just capitulate or else would act like crazy maniacs and fanatics whom nobody could understand or in any way identify with. And we proved that was not the case. But I think that, at the start, this attitude existed to a certain degree even among the lawyers who came forward to take up our defense—or at least they were a bit concerned about whether we would just be sort of "lunatic revolutionaries" or whatever. We were able to dispel that and to make clear to them that we took this very seriously and recognized that there was a need to apply correct tactics and have good sense in battling in the legal arena, even while sticking to and being guided by our larger principles.

A lot of this came down to breaking-the-ice kinds of things, even on a personal level. For example, one time I was talking to one of the lawyers about maybe getting together to go over the legal case and he said he was busy and couldn't do something that evening, and I asked, "Oh, where are you going?" He told me he was going to the Washington Bullets basketball game. And I said, "Great, I'm gonna be going to a few games myself while I'm here in D.C." So we started talking about basketball, and then he saw that I was a "regular human being," at the same

---

33. *Bob Avakian Speaks on the Mao Tsetung Defendants' Railroad and the Historic Battles Ahead*, RCP Publications, 1981.

time as I was clearly a revolutionary and a communist, and that I didn't conform to some sort of weird notion he may have had about revolutionaries and communists.

These were good-hearted liberal and progressive lawyers, but they still had these misconceptions, and of course some differences developed between us over legal strategy and tactics, which we had to do our best to struggle out in a good way. For example, at one point they wrote up a brief to present to the court as part of this case, and I read it over and wrote a lengthy critique of it. But I didn't just slam it—I pointed out what I thought were the good points in it but also the weaknesses and things that should be done differently. And here, of course, the legal training I'd gotten ever since I was a little kid, at the dinner table and in other ways—such as sitting in the courtroom and watching my dad argue some of his cases, and the whole way in which, directly and indirectly, so to speak, he had schooled me in a lot of the legal arena—came in handy and I was able to contribute through this critique and in other ways to developing and sharpening the legal strategy, as well as the overall political strategy.

## My Family Grows Closer

By this time, my relations with my parents had become closer again, but on an even better basis than they'd been before. There had been a gap that had opened between us when I'd become a radical and then a revolutionary and a communist. My parents never came to fully share my political and ideological outlook. My mother in particular remained very religious, although to a significant degree that expressed itself in her being a compassionate, generous person; and my father was somewhat religious also. But by this time they had developed a growing understanding of and respect for what I was trying to do.

They saw me as a person of integrity, who stuck to my principles and who had high ideals, as they put it—someone who was trying to change the world for the benefit of humanity—and they respected the fact that I stood up for that in the face of repression and attack, and that I stuck to it and had not given up in the face of difficulty. Having gone through the whole period of the '60s, and as a result of some struggle between us, they had become much more aware of the larger injustices in American society and many of the injustices the U.S. perpetrated around the world. And they were very sickened by this as well. So we'd grown closer again on this basis, through a process of development and some struggle, and even a period of a some estrangement between us. A little later, around 1980, I actually wrote a letter to my parents setting forth some important aspects of my principles as a communist and how I saw them applying to a number of different things, acknowledging that they didn't agree with all of this and that we had differences, but that I wanted to spell out for them how I viewed these things.[34]

Right after I was arrested in the demonstration against Deng Xiaoping, at the beginning of 1979, my father, who had been a judge for a number of years and was something of a public person, was contacted by the *Washington Post*, and asked for his comment on this. I think they expected they would be able to play on contradictions—believing that my father would distance himself, or even attack me. But, instead, he said that both he and my mother were proud of me. He didn't talk about the particular event—the demonstration that led to the arrest—but he spoke in a general way: "We're very proud of him for his principles and the way he's sticking to them." This meant a great deal to me personally, and it was also an important statement in a broader sense.

My dad also gave me some general legal advice about this case. He was incensed at the whole indictment. He commented many, many times: "This is the most ridiculous and outrageous thing I've ever seen —look at all these charges where you and others are accused of 'assault on an unidentified police officer.' I've never heard of such a thing—how can you defend yourself against a charge of assaulting an unknown, unidentified person?!" To him it represented the whole outrageous character of the indictment to begin with, coming on top of this assault that the police had launched against the demonstration, and he frequently talked to his friends and legal associates about this as an example of political prosecution and persecution.

I remember thinking very soon after I got arrested that he might be contacted. And I didn't want my parents to be surprised and caught off guard if they were asked for a statement. So, as soon as I was able to do so after being arrested, I sent a message through a lawyer to someone I trusted, asking them to contact my parents and let them know what had happened. But sometimes people would make crank calls to my parents, and sometimes people who claimed to be speaking on my behalf, but

---

34. This letter was actually published as a pamphlet, *Communists Are Rebels*.

were probably actually working for the government, would ask my parents all kinds of questions about me. As a result, my parents were understandably wary about phone calls from people they didn't know, and I was aware of that. I tried to figure out a way that I could let them know that this person was really calling on my behalf. Then I remembered one of my father's favorite stories, about when he was in law school in the Bay Area and had gone with his uncle in San Francisco to an open-air farmer's market, and there was this guy hawking tomatoes at a fruit and vegetable stand. He was saying: "Step right up and get your ripe tomatoes, the most beautiful tomatoes—fresh from the farm, great juicy, plump tomatoes." This guy was going on and on like that, and then he saw my uncle and my father gravitating toward this fruit and vegetable stand where he was doing this hawking; he was a friend of my father's uncle, and he didn't want them to be taken in, so he changed his spiel, to work in a warning that only they would understand: "Step right up," he said this time, "get your tomatoes; absolutely the best tomatoes in the world, 'dardun tapeh' brand—great tomatoes."

Well, in Armenian, "dardun tapeh" means: "take 'em home and throw 'em in the garbage." So this was his way of letting my father's uncle and my father know, "Don't buy these tomatoes; I gotta sell these tomatoes as if they're really great, but in fact they're terrible." So I sent this message to the person who was contacting my parents on my behalf: "When you call my parents, ask to speak to my father, say that you're calling on my behalf, and that this is not a 'dardun tapeh' call, and then he'll know that you really have talked to me and are calling on my behalf." And this worked very well.

### The Preliminary...Railroad

Before the trial, we had a preliminary hearing, and that was also a real lesson and another thing that outraged my parents and in particular my father, given his legal training and background. The preliminary hearing is supposed to determine whether the prosecution can establish "probable cause" that the defendant was engaged in an unlawful act and therefore has to stand trial for that offense. But, being aware that this had been a political demonstration, at the start of the hearing the judge felt obliged to say that it wasn't sufficient to show that the defendants were present at the demonstration—that would not be evidence of a crime, because demonstrating itself is legal, Constitutionally-protected activity

—it was necessary to show, under these circumstances, that there was probable cause that the defendants had engaged in *specific* unlawful acts. Otherwise, he was indicating, he would dismiss the charges.

Then, we went through a couple of days of hearings and the prosecution didn't have any concrete evidence or testimony that pointed to any specific acts committed by anyone—they couldn't identify particular people with specific acts. This went along with the whole approach of charging us with "assault on an unidentified police officer"; the frame-up nature of the whole thing was very clearly on display. So what was the judge going to do? Well, at the end of the hearing, after listening to all this and hearing absolutely no concrete evidence pointing to any defendant committing any specific act, the judge solemnly said: I have listened to the testimony and evidence, and I am satisfied that it has been established that each and every one of the defendants was present when unlawful acts were committed, and therefore I find probable cause to continue with prosecution.

In other words, after it had been shown that the prosecution couldn't meet the standard of proof that the judge had established at the beginning of the hearing, he simply threw out that standard and ruled for the prosecution anyway. It was clearer than ever that, while we could lose this battle through legal mistakes, we could not *win* this merely by mounting the best possible legal defense.

# Chapter Twenty-two

# *Re-Evaluation...*
# *and Leaping Forward*

## *Interrogating Ourselves*

Even as this struggle against the legal attacks was unfolding, we were continuing to grapple theoretically with the implications of the loss of China. When you go through a major turning point, including a major setback like this, it forces you to re-evaluate and look much more deeply into many things. The logic and dynamic and the momentum of something of this magnitude confronts you with the necessity to do this. I suppose you can decide not to take up the challenge of doing that. But if you continue to believe that communism is what is needed in the world, then there is a strong compulsion to do this.

Through the course of this whole struggle in China and the struggle within our Party about what stand to take on that, those of us who upheld revolution and opposed counter-revolution got a much deeper understanding of the importance of internationalism. And here's a real irony. Earlier I talked about how, when the "Gang of Four" were arrested and denounced, and I expressed my determination to oppose this, Leibel Bergman had angrily said to me: "Here you go again, now you're trying to tell the Chinese people what to do about their revolution and socialism in China—it's not your business, it's not our business," and so on.

Of course, I and others very strongly disagreed with this. First, as I said earlier, one way or another, whether you supported the coup or you opposed it—or even if you said "I have no position on that, it's up to the Chinese people"—you were taking a position. So that wasn't the issue, the issue was *what* position were you going to take. But I also pointed out that Mao had emphasized that, if in the future the revisionists came to power in China, the people of the world should oppose them and unite with the great majority of the Chinese people to overthrow this revisionism. It is not just that Mao said this and that we agreed with Mao —it is a matter of our internationalist responsibility to do this. And struggle around this deepened our appreciation and understanding of the importance of internationalism.

As I said, when you go through a struggle like this, you're confronted with the need not only to go more deeply into things having to do with that issue but also to look again at some other things, to dig into them more deeply and perhaps to re-evaluate them. And as we came to understand more fully how this Menshevik position within our party had represented a fully developed opportunist, reformist—and, in particular, a pragmatic and economist, narrow trade-unionist—orientation (sort of the CP "slightly better," but not really any better), we started looking at some of our own practice. We started questioning how *we* had been carrying out work in the working class and among the masses of people generally.

For those of us who weren't in the Menshevik faction, our objective had always been to take revolution, socialism and communism to the masses. But had the means through which we'd been seeking to do that been the most correct means? And had our policies been the most correct ones?

## Upholding Mao, Rediscovering Lenin

We had fought to uphold, as we put it, the revolutionary legacy of Mao Tsetung; and in going more deeply into that, it took us back to Lenin, in a new way and a deeper way. We began to appreciate in a fuller sense some of the key things that Lenin had brought forward and contributed to the communist movement, especially—and this was something that Mao had also given great emphasis to—the role of consciousness in the revolutionary struggle. Mao had talked about the conscious dynamic role of people in the revolutionary process, as opposed to a more mechanical and more economist approach of appealing to people on the basis of their more narrow and immediate interests, and as opposed to a sort of static notion that people could only be mobilized around what they already understood. Mao emphasized that people could take a tremendous amount of initiative on the basis of their consciousness being raised and that—understanding this in a materialist and not a religious sense—they could accomplish miracles on that basis.

With this perspective and impetus from Mao, we went back again to things like Lenin's key writings, including *What Is To Be Done?*, where he had emphasized the role and importance of consciousness in the revolutionary movement and, in opposition to the reformists and in particular the "economists" of his time, argued against the notion that the struggle of the working class should center and unfold around its immediate economic needs and interests. Lenin insisted that the economic struggle of the workers is important but *not* the heart and pivot of work to build a revolutionary movement among the proletariat. In *What Is To Be Done?* Lenin emphasized the crucial role of genuine, revolutionary class consciousness and how the workers could only develop this consciousness by having their attention centered on *all* the events going on in society and in the world, among all different classes, strata and groups, and by learning to evaluate these events from a communist standpoint and no other. Lenin emphasized that communists have to expose all the ways in which different issues and events in society affect these different classes and strata, and how in turn these classes and strata respond to them, in a fundamental sense, in accordance with their interests. Only this, he insisted, enables the workers to grasp the larger relations in society and their own role in leading a revolution to transform society; this could *not* be done by focusing their attention mainly on their immediate conditions and struggles.

*What Is To Be Done?* is one of the most misunderstood, and misrepresented, works in all of Marxism. It is often distorted in such a way as to make it appear that Lenin believed the masses of workers and other oppressed people were incapable of understanding reality and of changing it in accordance with their own interests, whereas what Lenin was grappling with was precisely the question of *how* the masses could do this; and Lenin's conclusion, founded in a profound grasp of the deep-seated contradictions within capitalism (and all societies divided into classes), and in particular the contradiction between those who carry out mental labor and those who carry out manual labor—his conclusion was that, in order to change society consciously in their own interests, the masses need the leadership of an advanced organization of revolutionaries, drawn from the proletariat itself but also from among intellectuals and other strata in society, who have taken up a scientific, Marxist understanding of reality and can fuse that with the struggle of the masses and develop a *revolutionary movement* on that basis. Going back to, and digging more deeply into, this fundamental reality and these fundamental principles brought to light by Lenin was crucial for our Party in confronting more fully the monumental challenges of building a revolutionary movement in a country like the U.S.

We also began a process we have continued, over the past 20 years and more, of going back to Lenin's writings about imperialism—his major work of analysis, *Imperialism, the Highest Stage of Capitalism,* and articles like "Imperialism and the Split in Socialism," where he talked about what he called the *parasitism of imperialism*: how a handful of imperialist countries were exploiting and plundering countries and people throughout what today we would call the Third World (the colonial and semi-colonial countries); how the spoils from the extreme exploitation and plunder in these countries enabled them to pass out a few crumbs to sections of the working class in the imperialist countries; and how this led to a split, where the more bourgeoisified sections of the working class in the imperialist countries were fattened, so to speak, on these crumbs and spoils of imperialism, whereas in the lower, deeper sections of the proletariat in the imperialist countries, people were still brutally exploited and oppressed and would much more gravitate toward a revolutionary line and the program of socialism and communism.

In going back to and studying that more deeply, we began to look again at the question of what sections of the working class we should base ourselves on as the main force for revolution. Where should we have our most bedrock foundation in carrying out revolutionary work? We recognized that we should work among all sections of the working class, and all strata of the people, but we began to recognize the particular importance of—and we began to grapple more deeply with—this emphasis of Lenin's on, as he put it, "going lower and deeper" in the proletariat in terms of the bedrock base for proletarian revolution.

## Revolutionary Defeatism vs. Reformist Patriotism

As I discussed earlier, we had been strengthened in our internationalism by the whole experience of the struggle against this Menshevik faction in our Party, a struggle focused around what stand to take toward the revisionist coup in China. And this internationalism was further deepened as we re-studied Lenin's emphasis on what he called "revolutionary defeatism" in the imperialist countries. Lenin had argued that in an imperialist country that was plundering large parts of the world, the proletarians had no interest in siding with "their own" ruling class in the wars it carried out in order to fortify and expand this plunder and exploitation and to contend with other imperialist powers. Instead, the proletariat had to have its consciousness raised and be mobilized to oppose these wars. Rather than bemoaning the weakening of its own ruling class, the proletariat had to be educated to *welcome* this and, in fact, to take advantage of it to build the struggle in a revolutionary direction. It had to take a stand, not with "its own" ruling class against the oppressed people of the world, but with the oppressed people of the world against "its own" ruling class—this was a crucial principle and dividing line between genuine socialism and communism, on the one hand, and opportunism on the other hand.

As I've mentioned before, along with its rampant pragmatism, the old Communist Party in the U.S. just fell completely into the cesspool of "patriotic Americanism" and American chauvinism and, especially from the 1930s on, never upheld the Leninist orientation of adopting a revolutionary defeatist position toward the international exploitation, plunder and wars carried out by the imperialist ruling class of the U.S. Even when the CP opposed certain wars waged by the U.S. government, they did so on the most narrow, reformist, lowest-common-denominator basis, and never on the basis of what Lenin had formulated as revolutionary defeatism.

As we dug more deeply into Leninism, we got a greatly strengthened understanding of the importance of internationalism in general and in particular of Lenin's statement that a communist does not approach the struggle from the point of view of "my country," but "my contribution to the international struggle of the proletariat and oppressed people of the world."

That crucial dividing line had particular importance at a time in which it seemed very possible and even probable that the U.S. was readying for global nuclear war with the Soviet Union. By the late 1970s we had become more clear about the contradictions between the U.S. imperialists and the camp that was under their leadership—the imperialist countries of Western Europe and Japan as well as other countries aligned with, or under the domination of, the U.S.—and, on the other side, Soviet social-imperialism and the countries in its bloc and within its camp. The contradictions between these two blocs were sharpening up, and the danger of war between them was becoming more acute. As the decade of the 1980s approached and then as we entered that decade, many people became more acutely aware of and concerned about, and began to mobilize against, the growing danger of world war. At the same time, the revolution in Nicaragua ousted the dictatorial regime of the Somozas, long backed by the U.S., and there was a developing movement in other parts of Central America, struggling against reactionary and highly repressive governments backed by the U.S. Things were beginning to intensify, and when Reagan became president, he came into office with a program both of attacking these struggles against U.S.-dominated regimes in Central America (and in other parts of the world as well), of reversing any gains these struggles had achieved, and of adopting a much more openly aggressive stance toward the Soviet Union itself.

### Preparing for "Rare Moments"

Another crucial insight that we got from going back to and getting more deeply into Lenin was how rarely revolutionary situations arise in the imperialist countries. In these countries you don't have a situation similar to many Third World countries, where revolutionaries can generally take up the armed struggle to oppose the regime right from the beginning of the revolutionary process. In many of these latter countries, the systems of transportation and communication and in general the infrastructures are much weaker, and the people are much more brutally oppressed and deeply impoverished all the time and thus more prepared to gravitate toward a revolutionary struggle when it is brought to them. This was one of the things we learned from Mao: Mao had drawn a clear distinction between the imperialist countries and the oppressed nations (what today we call Third World countries) where, because of the conditions outlined above, it was possible and, as he said, necessary to begin a revolutionary war, even on a small scale in the form of gue-rrilla war, right from the beginning, and then gradually build it up and win more and more of the country and eventually surround the reactionary ruling class in its citadels of power in the cities, and then seize those cities and win the revolution in the country as a whole. Mao had shown that this path has to be taken in countries like China and other countries that have similar economic and social conditions and forms of reactionary rule.

But again, Mao drew a distinction between that and in the imperialist countries, where most of the time you don't have a weakened system of rule and instead you have very highly developed systems of communication and transportation and the very highly concentrated power of the ruling class throughout the country, and where the conditions of the people are not always such that they're gravitating, in their great masses, toward a revolutionary struggle to overthrow the existing system of rule. In these countries it is only when a number of factors come together—resulting from both the objective development of a revolutionary crisis and the work of conscious revolutionaries—that you get a revolutionary situation.

Lenin talked about this in terms of what he called "revolutionary conjunctures," when all the contradictions of the system are heightened and come together in a concentrated way, and a revolutionary crisis develops. At that point, Lenin said, the developments and events of decades get concentrated in months, weeks and even days, and *if* the revolutionary party has prepared correctly all during those times when there wasn't a revolutionary situation, then it can seize on those rare moments when all these things come together in a revolutionary crisis, and it can lead masses of people—whose desire for radical change has been greatly heightened and who will gravitate in much greater numbers to a revolutionary struggle—to actually carry through the revolution. This distinction is crucial, between the two types of countries and the two roads, as we say—in third world countries, the road of "protracted people's war," as I've briefly characterized it; and in the imperialist countries, a road, or revolutionary process, marked by long periods of political work which then, when you get a revolutionary conjuncture, goes over to the all-out struggle for power.

With the coming together and heightening of the contradictions to create a revolutionary crisis and a revolutionary situation in an imperialist country, people who in "peaceful times," as Lenin put it, "allow themselves to be robbed," are more inclined to an all-out revolutionary struggle—they then see both the need for and the possibility of that—and the revolutionary vanguard must have the orientation, and must have developed the ability, to seize on such rare moments to lead a revolution. All that is concentrated in Lenin's characterization of a "conjunctural crisis," or the conjuncture of events leading to a revolutionary crisis.

On the basis of grasping this, we understood more deeply that the upsurge of the '60s may have passed, and the revolutionary opportunities that could perhaps have arisen out of that upsurge may not have been seized to the fullest, but that didn't mean that there would not again be another conjuncture of events where a revolutionary crisis would deepen and sharpen, and millions of people would be in a revolutionary mood, or seeking a revolutionary way out. Whether that came sooner or later, we had to prepare for such a conjuncture, for such a coming together and intensifying and magnifying of the contradictions of the system to a very acute stage where revolution would become possible.

## Tribune of the People

In returning to and digging more deeply into Lenin's emphasis, as set forth in *What Is To Be Done?*, on the importance of revolutionary consciousness and his focus on exposing the system and arousing people's revolutionary sentiments and raising their revolutionary consciousness, and in that way preparing them to wage a revolutionary struggle when things sharpened up, we came to see more clearly that one of the main expressions of that—as Lenin talked about, and as we felt had decisive application in the U.S. at that time—was the importance of a revolutionary press. This is what gave impetus to the founding of the *Revolutionary Worker* in 1979, and what has inspired its continued publication since that time and its ongoing use as a key instrument of the Party and a crucial resource for revolutionaries and more broadly for movements of opposition and resistance. This is grounded in the understanding that, as Lenin said, the goal of a communist is not to be a "trade union secretary" but a *tribune of the people*, enabling them to come to an understanding of the need, and the basis, for revolution, socialism, and ultimately communism. But this understanding is something which, as Lenin also pointed out, is constantly undermined by "the pull of spontaneity" and the influence of classes, strata and groups in society which are more inclined spontaneously toward reform, rather than revolution; and this communist understanding of being a "tribune of the people" is something that we have had to continually and repeatedly fight to maintain and uphold in its fullest sense.

We did not and do not see our newspaper as a supplement or "optional accessory" to our work—rather it must be the hub and pivot of everything we do. A little later I'll discuss more fully how we brought nearly 200 volunteers to Washington, D.C. to create public opinion as the trials of myself and others were about to open. When these volunteers came to D.C., they constantly used the newspaper—in fact, they took this saying that Mao had popularized during the Anti-Japanese war in China,[35] that the supplies of the People's Army basically amounted to millet and rifles, and adapted it to say that all the D.C. volunteers needed was a *Revolutionary Worker* and a peanut butter sandwich. In other words, their use of the newspaper wasn't off to the side of their political work, it was very central.

### Revolutionary May 1st, 1980

One of the main things we undertook during this period, as an expression of our deepening grasp of some of these crucial principles from Mao and from Lenin, was a year-long campaign we waged for May 1st, 1980. We had a rally on May Day 1979 in the Howard Theater in Washington, D.C., and there was a phone hookup with San Francisco, where there was a simultaneous May Day meeting and rally. I gave a speech at the rally in D.C., and at the end of the speech I announced the call for a mobilization of the working class on May Day 1980—with the goal of mobilizing ten thousand or more workers on that day, a working day, under the banner of a revolutionary May Day.

This was a bold initiative, something that hadn't been done in decades, if ever, in this country. Through the campaign for this May Day

---

35. The Anti-Japanese War was fought against the Japanese invasion and occupation of China in the 1930s and 1940s, and was spearheaded by the People's Liberation Army, led by the Communist Party of China. During this time the PLA pioneered a style of relying on the support of the masses (as expressed not only in volunteers for the PLA but also intelligence, material support, etc.) to counteract the superior firepower of the enemy; a hallmark of their style was simple living.

1980, revolution—and specifically communist revolution—was made a mass question and people very broadly were challenged to grapple with and commit to this. And, as we built for this, we made many important advances—taking crucial issues to important sections of the working class and carrying out a lot of revolutionary propaganda in the course of this campaign over a year. It also led to very intensifying conflict with the powers-that-be and to the assassination of one of our comrades, Damián García, which I will speak to in depth later.

About ten days before May Day, we held Red Flag-Internationale Day. We called on people throughout the country to raise or fly the Red Flag and to sing the communist anthem, "The Internationale," all at the same time; and to my understanding, about two thousand people actually did that. And then on May Day we mobilized several thousand people, mainly from the working class, and there were some key concentration points of this struggle—for example, in Los Angeles hundreds of people were mobilized in Revolutionary May Day and it was viciously attacked by the police, who obviously didn't like this kind of revolutionary expression coming from the proletariat.

On the other hand, although we mobilized thousands, we fell short of our goal of bringing out ten thousand or more, and we had put a lot of work into this. One of the things we had to confront was that, while we had begun to take up Lenin's writings on imperialism and its effects on the proletariat in the imperialist countries themselves, and his emphasis on going lower and deeper, into the bedrock, most exploited sections of the proletariat, we had not yet fully made that transformation and hadn't really raised our understanding of that to a strategic level. So, while there were some important accomplishments through this whole campaign around May Day 1980, and then on the day itself; while there were thousands of workers who rallied to the revolutionary, communist banner on that day, and some of them came from the lower and deeper sections of the proletariat; by and large we had not yet made the transformation to where we were focusing and basing ourselves mainly and most essentially among the lower and deeper sections of the proletariat. This is something we had to sum up out of this whole experience around May Day 1980, even while we sought to build on the positive things that *did* come forward through all the work around that and on the day itself.

## Keeping an Open Ear

As I mentioned earlier, even during the period when I was listening to country music, partly for political reasons—as part of our efforts to integrate with sections of the working class, and in particular white workers, in order to do political work and win them over to a socialist and communist position—I never stopped being drawn to the culture that I'd developed a love for as a youth, namely Black music and culture. And during the time when the case was going on in D.C., and I was spending a lot of time there, the first rap song came out that, as I recall, really "made it big." It was "Rapper's Delight" by the Sugar Hill Gang.

I remember that, when I heard first heard it, although the lyrics had a lot of macho crap and other nonsense, I still really liked the whole feel of it, and I remember saying to people, not just about this particular song but about rap more generally: "This is something new, it's gonna become big." A couple of years later I explored further the role of rap and its relation to the situation of Black people and the need for revolution, in an article for the *Revolutionary Worker* called "A Message on Hearing 'The Message'," about the rap song "The Message," by Grandmaster Flash and the Furious Five (this article was later published in the book *Reflections, Sketches and Provocations*).

Earlier I spoke about going to a concert by Jimmy Buffett and the Coral Reefer Band in the late 1970s, and the impact this had on me. Around the same time, I started listening to Bruce Springsteen, who was popular among, and gave expression to a kind of alienated and rebellious spirit among, a lot of white youth in general and in particular a lot of white working class youth. This was another thing that at the time strengthened my sense that just because you're going to integrate with sections of the working class, and in particular white workers, to spread the politics of socialism and communism among them, doesn't mean you have to gravitate toward the more conservative cultural expressions that are popular among some of them, and in particular the less politically advanced among them. We should be looking for the sparks of rebellion and working to fan and develop this into revolutionary sentiment and consciousness.

This was one of those times when, as the Chinese saying popularized by Mao put it, "the wind in the tower heralds the approaching storm." Some of these cultural expressions were like that wind in the tower. You had "punk" coming over from England, and people turned me on to The Clash. I was also into reggae, and especially loved Peter Tosh. We were trying to learn from all this and as Mao said, to "extol" what was positive in it. There was this incident where I was doing a radio interview and talking about punk, and this guy became very irate: "There you go, you communists, trying to claim credit for everything! You are talking as if you invented, or discovered, punk music." I just had to laugh, and I replied: "No, no, that's not it at all. All kinds of people bring forward many different things, and we do our best to learn from these things and push forward their positive aspects and the ways in which they can contribute to a progressive or revolutionary or even a communist culture."

## Boston Busing

So this was, in many respects, an exciting time. To make such a rupture with economism was very revivifying and very liberating for me and for our Party as a whole. Our whole practice changed enormously. At the same time, Mao also wrote that "there is no construction without destruction"—and as that applies to political and ideological line, it means that if you are going to go forward you have to really settle accounts very thoroughly with your mistakes. And generally this necessarily entails some painful reassessments of things you thought had been right.

To use Marx's phrase, we interrogated ourselves very thoroughly, because what we're about is very serious and very difficult and demands a very serious approach. One of the things that was extremely painful to me personally, as well as to the Party overall, was when we began to look back at our practice around the big upheaval over the school busing program that was instituted in Boston in the mid-1970s. The neighborhood in Boston into which Black students were being bused was a bastion of segregation, including in the schools, which were essentially all-white. In these conditions, white supremacist and fascistic sentiment was being mobilized among the white people to oppose this busing plan, but more than that to attack the Black people, the Black families, and even the Black students who were being bused in.

During this period, before the Revolutionary Communist Party was formed, we in the RU had taken the position of opposing busing plans of this kind. Our approach to this was very eclectic at best. In one aspect, our thinking was similar to a number of Black nationalist forces and some progressive-minded people who opposed busing plans of this kind because these plans were part of an overall policy that allowed the schools in the Black neighborhoods to further deteriorate rather than putting more funding into and building up those schools. But, at the same time, our position on this actually represented a narrow and ultimately reformist approach which sought in a certain sense to finesse some of these intense contradictions in a kind of economist way. For example, we raised the demand for "decent and equal education," which on the one hand could be part of a correct program, but in the actual circumstances objectively amounted to an avoidance of the central question of segregation. As we saw it, the ruling class was fanning antagonisms among different nationalities—and, of course, there was truth to that. But, in this situation, rather than grasping that the key to opposing that was to fight against segregation and in *that* context raise demands like "decent and equal education," we instead tried to maneuver our way around this by presenting a position that called for building up *all* the schools, and in particular strengthening the schools in the inner city.

We fell into thinking that if we carried forward work in the working class around what we soon came to call the "center of gravity" of the workers' economic needs and struggles, we could get them to unite on that basis, and in that context we could get the white workers to oppose discrimination and racism. What went along with that, when it came to these busing plans, was to oppose them and instead call for decent and equal education all the way around, as if we could somehow finesse the antagonisms that were being fanned with these busing programs.

The result was that we missed the essence of what was going on. The essence of it was the white supremacy that existed in the school systems and the racism that was being whipped up in opposition to the busing programs; and, whatever the shortcomings of the busing programs, and however much the ruling class may have been maneuvering and manipulating things to fan these antagonisms, the key thing that you had to do was to take a firm stand against the white supremacist and white chauvinist relations and outlooks and the forces that were being mobilized to attack Black people on that basis, and then *from that standpoint* you could sort out the other issues involved. But if you didn't make that the cutting edge and the key thing and the pivot of everything you were doing, you were bound to get it wrong—which we did. And this was very painful to me personally, especially looking back on it and seeing it more clearly, because a crucial part of how I came to be a revolutionary and ultimately a communist, and of what has sustained me in that, has been a deep hatred for white supremacy and the recognition that it is built into this system and can only be abolished and uprooted through a radical, thoroughgoing transformation of society.

And here's an important lesson. It is not that my hatred, or the hatred of my comrades, for white supremacy had diminished in the slightest. But when you're trying to determine how to implement a strategy to make revolution and transform all of society and how to bring forward the necessary forces to do that, you're confronted with the need to approach things differently than when you're just proceeding from your basic feelings about things. You have to develop and apply *line*, as we call it—an analysis of the reality you're confronting and how to transform it, of where you need to go and how you need to get there, and what forces you need to mobilize to do that. Of necessity, you have to address things on that level, if you're trying to lead a revolution and radically change all of society. And if you get off track on *that*, it can even override some of the deepest sentiments you have. So there you can see—in a negative way in this case—the importance of line. In that case our line was incorrect, and this was, in a negative way, so to speak, an illustration of the profound importance of whether your line is correct or incorrect.

At that time the RU was putting out *Revolution* as a monthly newspaper, and I happened to be in a leadership meeting of the RU when the newspaper came out which put forward our position in opposition to this busing plan. As I recall, the headline was something like "People Must Unite To Smash Boston Busing Plan." One of the comrades who was responsible for putting out the newspaper brought the newspaper, hot off the press, to this leadership meeting. I and the others there were horrified at this headline. Because, while we did have a wrong position on this, this is not the way we felt that our position should be expressed and put forward, this was not the stand we thought should be taken, let alone blared in the headline of *Revolution* newspaper.

We did try to move to correct this as quickly as we could, and one of the things that we did do was to make a point of searching out, uniting with and then popularizing, through our newspaper and in other ways, instances where people stood up against these white supremacist mobs, including instances where white people had stood up against them and moved to defend the Black students and others who were being attacked by these mobs. Still, our position was eclectic and essentially wrong. So even while the leadership of the RU would never have wanted to put out a headline with that kind of an emphasis in it, it was a sort of grotesque carrying further of a position that was fundamentally wrong. And this often happens, when you have a wrong position—sometimes people trying to implement that position will carry it to even greater extremes and more grotesque expressions, but even though that grotesque exaggeration is not actually your position, it still reflects the fact that your position is fundamentally and essentially wrong. And that was the case here.

It was only later, during the 1978-80 period, and as a result of this whole struggle with the Mensheviks within the RCP—and beyond them, the revisionist legacy we were breaking with—that we began to re-examine things, and to change the way we approached similar busing plans in other cities. In the late '70s, we published a self-criticism in *Revolution* (which at that time was coming out in magazine form) examining our errors around this and why we'd made them, trying to both learn more deeply ourselves through systematizing that self-criticism, but also to enable others to learn from our mistakes.

This is a method we've tried to apply as consistently as possible: when we come to recognize an error we've made, we not only criticize it within our own ranks, but also publicly discuss our understanding of our mistakes and why we made them, so that others can learn from them as well, and so that we can be accountable to the masses of people, whom we're seeking to lead in making revolution. As I said, to recognize that we had made errors of this kind, around a question of this decisive importance, was a very painful experience; but, when you make such errors, recognizing and acknowledging them is a crucial part of what goes into doing what you have to do in order to help bring into being a radically different kind of world.

This whole process of deep rethinking, so to speak, went on for a couple of years. And everything—the efforts at self-criticism, the theoretical ferment, as well as what we were learning from taking out a more straight-up revolutionary communist line—would be brought to bear as we took on the charges coming off the Deng demonstration. With so much at stake—including potentially very long prison sentences and the ability of our Party to function—this would be a real test: could we build the kind of defense we needed, and even use that battle to develop greater political and organizational strength, while continuing to unapologetically put forward our revolutionary aims?

# Chapter Twenty-three

# *Stop the Railroad!*

As a result of the demonstration against Deng, I was facing what could have amounted to over two hundred years in jail, and a dozen or so other comrades faced similar charges. What the government was doing in this case was typical: *they* launched this vicious attack on the demonstration, as they often do; then, in effect, they charged us with assaulting their billy clubs with our heads and bodies. So that's why we were facing all these years in jail.

As I've described, we recognized that it was important to battle this in the legal arena. But much more fundamentally, we had to build a political defense and take not just our legal case, but our case in the broader political and ideological sense, to the masses of people, in the D.C. area especially, but around the country as well. What I mean by "our case politically and ideologically" had to do with *why* were we there demonstrating, what was the importance of this, what were the issues involved, what did Mao represent, what did Deng Xiaoping represent, what did Jimmy Carter represent—and what was being developed between U.S. imperialism, as represented by its chief executive at the time, Jimmy Carter, and Chinese revisionism and capitalism as represented by Deng Xiaoping—and why was this important to the people in the U.S. and the people around the world?

## Turning D.C. Upside Down

As part of building this political and ideological as well as legal defense, the Party leadership decided to issue a call for people to volunteer to come to D.C., where the legal case was going to be centered, and to "turn D.C. upside down"—in other words, to take our case politically to the people throughout D.C. We saw a very real basis to do that— represented, for example, by how people had responded to the demonstration. We intended to create tremendous political awareness and political turmoil and to mobilize masses of people in support of us. We aimed to get two hundred people to come as volunteers, and this is what happened. People not in the Party, as well as some Party members, volunteered, and we'd gone to churches and progressive ministers and others in the communities in D.C., and they'd agreed to help with housing and with some of our logistical needs, so that people would have a place to stay and food to eat and would be able to fan out all over the city with our message.

It was clear that we were going to be able to have a major impact politically and in terms of mobilizing masses in the city; it was going to become a very hot issue—something that was not only talked about all over the place, but something around which people were going to be actively mobilized. Already, in our very initial work around this, we found among the masses of people in D.C. a deep reservoir of support for Mao, a basic recognition of what Mao represented and what the Chinese revolution had been all about, along with deep feelings of distrust and hatred for the government in the U.S. itself. Many people remembered things like Mao's statement in support of the Afro-American people when they rose up after Martin Luther King was assassinated, and in general they remembered Mao as a revolutionary leader whom they admired and looked to. It was clear that there was great potential for mobilizing people on this basis.

## Defending and Popularizing Revolutionary Leadership

During the same period when we were mobilizing people to come to D.C., we were also taking our revolutionary line to people more broadly. This attack on our Party and its leadership confronted us with a certain necessity, but we were seeking to turn that necessity into further advances. Because of the way the ruling class had responded to this demonstration, the way they'd brutally attacked it and then piled on legal charges, this drew more attention to this issue and also to our Party. So it was both a necessity and also an opportunity in a sense to turn this back against them, and to popularize more broadly our Party and its leadership.

Since I, along with some others, was facing these heavy charges, I undertook a major speaking tour and did a lot of things with media all over the country, everything from campus newspapers to progressive radio stations, to Tom Snyder's late night TV talk show, which at that time was fairly widely watched. The Tom Snyder show was a half hour program, and Snyder slotted me for 15 minutes and then he brought in this guy who I think had defected from the Soviet Union and was an anti-communist and did a routine where he'd dress up and act like the stereotype of a typical Soviet "apparatchnik." Apparently, Tom Snyder's plan was to have me on first and then this guy would come in and mock me by acting like a typical commie bureaucrat, as Tom Snyder saw it. But Snyder's problem was that the discussion with me wasn't anything like you'd have with a typical Soviet bureaucrat, so this other thing he did afterward really fell flat. But it was interesting, and it reflected how big an issue this was among a broad range of people that someone like Tom Snyder—even though he tried to turn it against us—felt that this would be something that there would be an audience for.

As part of this overall campaign by the Party, we produced literature, including posters with my picture on it, which were put up by Party comrades and many other people all over the country. Again, this was a form of taking on this battle in support of the "Mao Tsetung Defendants," but also of popularizing the Party and its leadership, an initiative to broadly propagate what our Party was about and what I represented as its leader.

## Confronting My – and Our – Responsibility

On a personal level, and I spoke to some of this in leadership meetings of the Party, this caused me to come to grips even more fully with the responsibility that I had as the Chairman of a Party that was taking on the responsibility of leading people to make revolution and to stand with people all over the world struggling for the same goal. You are confronted with the fact that you are putting yourself forward that way, and in a larger sense the Party collectively is putting you forward in that way and saying to people out there broadly: "This is the person who can lead this."

Thousands and thousands of posters were put up, and millions of people saw them, and a lot of people saw the Tom Snyder show, as well as seeing or hearing a number of local television and radio programs I was on and reading interviews I did in various college and mainstream newspapers. So the responsibility I had was driven home to me much more fully. Along with this, it made me much more acutely aware of the responsibility that the Party as a whole had—that this wasn't a "personal thing"—yes, I have this responsibility as the leader of the Party but it was a challenge to the Party *as a whole* to rise to the responsibilities we had. I got a much deeper sense of that.

And there were a lot of positive responses by people. People among the most exploited and oppressed sections of society—the basic masses, as we say—recognize that they need leaders. And they also recognize that there have been negative experiences with leaders, where many of them have been killed or jailed, and some of them have sold out or gone off track and ended up at least objectively betraying the cause. So this is a big question among the masses as well.

This whole experience of going on a speaking tour throughout the country and in other ways putting forward our Party, and myself as its leader, further drove home, too, that millions and millions of people in this society hate this system to the depths of their souls, if you want to put it that way. Even if they don't understand it in a fully developed, scientific way, they hate this system—they have first-hand experience with or have witnessed many of the crimes it commits, in the U.S. itself and around the world, and they have a very acute sense of what it is doing, every day, to them and people like them.

They want a way out of this, but they wonder: *Is* there a way out? And they agonize over whether there can there be leaders who won't sell out or won't just be crushed or killed. This would be raised to us when we'd go out to people and say, "Here is your leadership"—the Party collectively and myself as the leader of the Party—"We are ready to assume this responsibility of leadership." These questions would come back to us. And this greatly deepened my understanding of the great responsibility that was on us and, yes, was on me directly.

## Cult of the Personality

So, in the course of doing this, the question of "the cult of the personality" would come up. As communists who understand both that it is the masses of people who have to rise up and make revolution and transform society and, on the other hand, that in order to do that the masses need leadership that makes them conscious of the need and the possibility to do this, we have a different view of this than people who don't have this understanding. We have a different view of leadership. We understand in a deep and scientific way why people need leadership and what kind of leadership they need. So we also look at the role of individual leaders differently than the bourgeoisie does, certainly, and also differently than others who don't have a communist viewpoint and understanding.

We understand that there are people who, as a result of a combination of personal experiences and larger social experiences and larger events and influences in society and the world, come to embody the kind of leadership that the masses of people, and the politically advanced forces among them, need in order to make revolution. Now "cult of the personality" is a phrase that has been used to convey a negative meaning—the word "cult" implies a kind of religious sect—but there is a deeper question here. And, in a certain way, it has been important to take this on directly, and at times in a provocative way. I remember, for example, being challenged by someone interviewing me—I believe this was on a college radio station in Madison, Wisconsin—who asked insistently: "Is there a 'cult of the personality' developing around Bob Avakian?" And I replied: "I certainly hope so—we've been working very hard to create one." This was my provocative way of getting to the real point.

What is really involved here is the role of individual leaders, especially ones who do come to represent in a concentrated way the kind of leadership people need, people who are outstanding leaders, if you want to put it simply. Many people don't have a hard time recognizing that certain people come to play outstanding roles in various other areas of life—science, sports, the arts, and so on—but when it comes to the sphere of political leadership, this seems to be a much more sensitive and controversial issue. And the deeper question is this: what is the relationship between such leaders and broader groupings of people? This question came up repeatedly, in a number of different forms, and we went into it deeply and struggled over it with broad numbers of people. We said straight-up that when you do have individuals who are of a high caliber, capable of being both far-seeing and of having a profound grasp of practical questions, able to grapple on a high level with theory and to provide guidance for the struggle, not only in a more immediate but in a more strategic sense, this is a very good thing, not a bad thing. This is a strength for the people. This is a strength for a party. This is a strength for the revolution. This is a strength in terms of contributing to the international struggle. So this not something to be embarrassed about or ashamed about or defensive about, it is something to uphold and to popularize to people that we *do* have this kind of leadership and we *do* have an individual who can play this kind of a role, who is willing to take that responsibility and is able to do so. Especially confronted with the challenge of defending, and popularizing, our Party and its leadership, we struggled over this within the Party itself, at the same time as we took this out more broadly and struggled with progressive and radical people about this question: we deepened our own grasp of this, and a number of people beyond the party at least came to a better understanding of the issues involved, and many were won to be supportive of our position.

### A Broad Defense

In the course of this campaign, a number of intellectuals as well as people in the arts and others in various spheres of society were mobilized in support of the Mao Tsetung Defendants. And a number of them took the stand, with regard to myself and the role I was playing: "This is an important voice that should be part of the political discourse and part of the overall movement in society, this is someone people need to be aware of and engage with, and we cannot allow the government to silence his voice or keep him from being politically active." There were many people who supported me on that level, people with many different viewpoints—revolutionary-minded nationalists, people from among different movements based in the middle class, artists, academics and others. Not all of them agreed with us about the need for revolution, or for communism, or the need for a vanguard party, or the need for, or importance of, individual leaders who come forward within that overall context; but they recognized that it was very important that what our Party represented—and what I represented as the leader of the Party—be part of the political terrain and of political discourse. At various times, there have been statements signed, and ads run in publications like *The New York Times*, with a number of people expressing support on that level.

## Outrage in Carolina

As I said in the last chapter, during 1979 we made a decision to put out a newspaper on a weekly basis and not just a monthly publication. And, on May Day 1979, we launched the first issue of the *Revolutionary Worker*, which was a great advance for the communist movement in the U.S. and made a big contribution in terms of its internationalism. To paraphrase Lenin, the role of this newspaper, as the voice of the Party, was to put before all our communist convictions; to expose the outrages and injustices committed, in the U.S. itself and all over the world, by this system and those who rule it; to show how these are all rooted in the essential nature of this system; to examine how different classes and groups in society are affected by and respond to these events; and through all this to make clear the need for a revolution that would be based fundamentally on the exploited class in capitalist society, the proletariat, and would be led by its vanguard party, with the goal of advancing to communism together with the proletariat and oppressed people throughout the world.

One of the outrages we had taken up, through the newspaper and in other ways, took place in Chester, South Carolina, where a young Black man had been found lynched. It was widely understood that this was because he had been dating a white woman in the town, and there was a mass outpouring of protest against this lynching on the part of the Black community in particular in Chester, South Carolina.

While I was in the course of the nationwide speaking tour to build opposition to the attempt to railroad me and other Mao Tsetung Defendants, this lynching came to our attention. I felt, and other Party leaders agreed, that it was important for me to go there directly and express the Party's support in that way for the people rising up against this outrage. So we went into this small, rural town of Chester, South Carolina, for a meeting in a Black church there. The church was packed with hundreds of people, and someone who was part of our group did some agitation about this lynching and more generally what was going on in the country and then introduced me and explained that I was there to express the outrage of our Party over this lynching and our support for people rising up against this. And then I spoke.

Here I was in this church packed with Black people, many of whom were clearly religious, and I was trying to figure out the best way to express our Party's support for the protest but also to help people see this in the broader context of the whole system. So I said, "You know, I don't believe in your religion, but I do know something about your Bible. I know that Paul in the Bible says that once he saw through a glass darkly, but then he came to see more clearly." And then I went on to talk about how we have to see this lynching as an outrage in itself but also as part of the overall crimes of the system and how this shows us once again why we need a revolution to sweep away this whole system. After I'd spoken, the meeting continued, and then at the end, when we had to leave, people said, "Look, you can't just go off in your car by yourself, this is heavy Klan territory here." So we left with this long caravan of dozens of cars, which the people from the church had mobilized to accompany us, and they drove with us a long way, until we were far out of that county and away from that area. That experience has stayed with me, ever since then, in a very powerful way.

## The Political Context:
## Political Shocks, from Teheran to Greensboro

Shortly after this, the volunteers arrived in D.C., and when they first got there I gave a speech to them to provide overall orientation and direction, the title of which was: "Don't Be a Typical Commie—Be a Communist." It was all about how we should go out with our real, living revolutionary message—not in the stereotypical, dogmatic way that people often expect, but in a lively, living, non-dogmatic way. We should take this to people and bring them forward to support myself and the other Mao Tsetung Defendants on that basis.

During this same time, there were many highly charged events going on in the world. This was the period when the Iranian revolution had reached its high point, and driven the Shah of Iran out of the country. I remember a headline in the *Chicago Tribune* when the Shah was teetering on his throne, just before he fell. This headline declared: "He May Be a Despot, But He's *Our* Despot." That was basically the stand of the Carter administration and the U.S. ruling class, right until the fall of the Shah. The U.S. had put him in power through a CIA coup in 1953, and they maintained him in power for almost three decades. And they were still doing what they could to protect him at the end. Then, after the Shah could no longer maintain his rule in Iran, they brought him into the U.S., after having tried to get a few other countries to take him.

People in Iran suspected the Shah was being given refuge here to prepare a counter-revolution, and a group of Iranian students and youth then seized the U.S. embassy in Teheran. The Iranians occupying the embassy got hold of the records there and proved that many of the embassy employees were spies and CIA agents who were working to undermine and reverse the course of the Iranian revolution and to bring Iran more fully back under the domination of the U.S.

With these students and others occupying the U.S. embassy, Ted Koppel pronounced "America Held Hostage," and the occupation of the embassy became a big controversial issue in the U.S. There was a big uproar, and the ruling class in the U.S. worked to whip up all kinds of chauvinism toward the Iranian people, including Iranians living in the U.S., and to inflame reactionary sentiments among the American people about the Iranian revolution. This was happening at the same time as our case was getting ready to go to court and as we were working, through the efforts of the volunteers and in an all-around way, to build support for myself and the other Mao Tsetung Defendants and to promote and project the line and objectives of our Party broadly throughout society.

And, in the exact same period, there was this group called the Communist Workers Party (CWP)—which we didn't consider to be a communist party at all, but which was involved in a struggle against the Klan in North Carolina. At one point they held a rally, and a combination of Klansmen and Nazis came to the CWP rally and opened fire and killed five people in broad daylight. This was all part of the increasingly volatile situation within the U.S. at this time.

Shortly before this assassination, I had gone to North Carolina as part of the speaking tour, but when our people got to the meeting site to set things up for later that day, people who were obviously FBI agents and Klan types were running all over the place. Clearly, there was something brewing there—it really looked like there was going to be some sort of assault on the meeting. So that particular speech and meeting on that part of the tour was extremely intense, because we expected that at any moment we might be attacked. But we decided that we had to go ahead with it anyway and, at the last minute, as a tactical maneuver, we changed the site of the meeting; and in that way, as well as by bringing more people to protect the meeting and prevent an attack, we were able to successfully hold the meeting. But it was very clear that there was serious and sinister activity by the Klan and Nazis allied with them, and that the government was also involved in all this. So, when the CWP people were attacked and murdered, this was an outrage that fit in with the pattern that we'd seen.

The CWP mobilized people in response to this murder and had a rally and march in the area. And, despite our very sharp and deep differences with them, we recognized that we had to work together with them in the face of this kind of an attack, so we worked out the basis for doing so and joined with them, and others, in mobilizing people in response to this murderous attack.

### *"It's Not Our Embassy!"*

At the same time, we had to take a stand in support of the Iranian revolution. This was something I felt very strongly about, and I spoke about this to the volunteers in D.C. The leadership of our Party was firmly united that it was very important to work to win people away from the whole chauvinist hysteria and mob mentality that was being whipped up. Iranian students in the U.S. were being attacked. When we would go out to do revolutionary work in general, and particularly to talk with people and do agitation about what was happening in Iran, larger numbers of people would gather. Things would get extremely heated, and sometimes there would be physical attacks on our people. But we were very determined that we had to take this on and turn it around, even as we had this major campaign and battle that we had to wage around the case flowing out of the demonstration against Deng Xiaoping.

One of the things that struck me, in reading a number of reports and talking to comrades who were involved in this work, is that while there was this hysteria, mob mentality and chauvinism whipped up against the Iranian people and the Iranians who lived in the U.S., and it was very widespread—the government and the media had put a lot of effort into this—it was also very superficial. When we talked with people about the history of what the U.S. had done in Iran, the torture and oppression to which it had subjected the Iranian people for decades through putting the Shah of Iran in power and keeping him in power since 1953; when we showed why the Iranian people were so angry at the U.S., and how they were determined to fight against the domination of the U.S. in their country—we could puncture this hysteria and quickly things would begin to change. As is so often the case with people who are whipped up around reactionary shit by the ruling class, there wasn't any depth to it. People were largely acting out of ignorance and not understanding what was motivating the Iranian people, and what had been going on for decades in Iran—all of which had been hidden from people in the U.S.

Just as all these things were happening and the case of the Mao Tsetung Defendants was about ready to begin, we built for a mass rally that was held in the Howard Theater in Washington, D.C.. The theater was packed. I gave a speech at the rally. I talked about the overall political questions involved with the battle around the Mao Tsetung Defendants, beginning with why we'd had the demonstration in the first place, and the stakes of that. I went into what this attack represented—not just the police attack on the demonstration, but then the legal attack, the piling on of legal charges, the threat of hundreds of years in jail off of this and the outrage of the whole persecution that was embodied in this indictment and these legal proceedings. But I also talked about world events that were going on, and in particular what was happening in Iran.

We had worked closely with the many radical and revolutionary-minded students from Iran who were living and studying in various parts of the U.S. Ironically, they had been sent to the U.S. by the Shah. The Shah had this program to modernize enclaves of the Iranian economy, while the masses of people would be enmeshed and enslaved in deep poverty and oppression. So his government, working with the U.S. government, had financed a lot of these students to go to the U.S. to get training in things like engineering. But, especially because of the nature of the times, many of them had become radicalized—and by and large this was a secular anti-imperialist radicalism, rather than fundamentalist religious militancy. Many of them had become revolutionaries of one kind or another, and the communist and Maoist trend had a lot of initiative among these thousands of Iranian students. We continued to work closely with them and support them as the Iranian revolution developed, although some of them were beginning to go back to Iran to take part directly in the revolutionary upsurge there.

So when I gave this speech at the Howard Theater I talked about this and why it was important that we take a stand in support of the revolution in Iran and the Iranian students here who were coming under attack—it was, once again, a question of internationalism. It was our responsibility to oppose our own ruling class in trying to reinstitute and fasten down more tightly the domination and oppression of the Iranian people. And, as I put it in that speech: "It's not our embassy, we don't have an embassy, this is the embassy of the imperialist ruling class and we stand with the Iranian people."[36]

This was controversial even among people close to us and among our broader supporters. Some people felt that by taking this stand, in the midst of this whole attack on us, we would be taking on an even bigger burden and bringing down even further repression on ourselves. We recognized this danger but our position was, as I put it in that speech: "If we don't stand with the Iranian people, then we're not worth defending. If we don't uphold our internationalism and our communist principles, then we're not worth defending."

## Uniting Broadly...On the Basis of Principle

During this whole period we focused mainly on the case of the Mao Tsetung Defendants, and in particular on the way in which this involved a concentrated attack on me. And that was definitely correct. But we also took up other sharp attacks and big questions in the U.S. and internationally, and we linked them with the struggle against the attacks on us and with my defense in particular. These connections were strongly in evidence at the rally at the Howard Theater.

While I was the main speaker, there was a very broad array of people represented there from different political viewpoints who stood in solidarity with us in the face of this attack. For example, the last surviving "Scottsboro Boy"[37] was there and spoke, and there were people from

---

36. The RCP came out with a transcript of that part of the speech almost immediately after the rally, entitled "It's Not Our Embassy." Party members and supporters took this pamphlet out very broadly, generating controversy and through sharp struggle helping to repolarize the terms of debate in a more favorable way.

37. The Scottsboro Boys were nine young African-Americans who, in the kind of gross miscarriage of justice commonly directed against Black males in those days, especially in the South, were arrested and charged in 1931 with raping two white girls in Scottsboro, Alabama, were found guilty and were sentenced to death— except for one who was only thirteen years old and was sentenced to life imprisonment. It was only after a massive campaign against this racist injustice, in which the Communist Party and other progressive forces played a key part; only after many appeals and retrials; and only after years had gone by that all of the Scottsboro defendants were finally free from prison.

progressive religious groups and nationalist forces and others. This was the result of building a relationship of "unity-struggle-unity" with them. In other words, we built unity around the things we agreed on, and we continued to have struggle about larger strategic questions as we worked to deepen our unity on a principled basis. This was expressed very powerfully at that rally, and I know it had a powerful impact and effect.

We took this out very broadly, into many different spheres of society. When I was in different parts of the country, I would see posters of myself staring down at me from overpasses on the highway and from buildings. And, in the movie *Blues Brothers*, which came out at that time, in the first few minutes of that film, when Jake Blues (played by John Belushi) gets out of Joliet Prison and is picked up by his brother Elwood (Dan Aykroyd), they stop right near a bridge; and there in the background, for a brief moment, if you look carefully, you'll see one of those posters of me. This was another reflection of how broadly we were building this and how broadly this got expressed in various ways, even finding its way into the popular culture.

All this was coming to a head, a number of us were facing serious charges and possibly long years in prison; but, through all that, I and others in the leadership of the RCP never considered retreating in a political or ideological sense. We never considered toning down, but in fact more aggressively and boldly took out what we were all about. That was a key part of how we understood we had to build support in the face of attack, as well as being a crucial part of working toward our overall strategic objectives of revolution, socialism, and communism. To return again to one crucial aspect of this, we had to take a clear and firm stand around the Iranian revolution and the "hostage crisis," for two essential reasons. One, because it was a major event in the world and people needed to know about it and be won to the correct stand on it; and two, if we didn't maintain this kind of stand, then we were compromising not in a tactical way but in a fundamental way, compromising everything we were all about. So, for those reasons, we were determined that, from a strategic standpoint, we must not back down, or water down our stand, around Iran or around our basic principles and objectives in general. Nor did we do so in practice.

# Chapter Twenty-four

# *Under Attack*

## *Contending in the Media*

During this time, and particularly in the context of the speaking tour and things I was doing with the media around the country, I appeared on the Barry Farber radio show in New York. Farber was sort of a forerunner of Rush Limbaugh (and, from what I understand, is still on the air) and right from the start, he was very aggressive and nasty and it was very clear that he planned to use this as an occasion to launch a political attack on me.

At one point I was talking about imperialism and he interjected that a communist is someone who sees one person doing well and another person doing badly and can't imagine that there's not some sort of oppression involved. I shot back with, "And a stooge of the imperialists is someone who sees a vampire and sees someone else with puncture wounds in their neck and doesn't recognize the relationship between the two." Well, before long he threatened to turn off my mike. He kept attacking me for representing and upholding dictatorship—and then he'd turn around and threaten to kick me out of the studio! So I said, "Well, who's acting like a petty dictator now?" That was representative of a number of battles I had with more reactionary types. But I was also struck by the fact that, while there were some more enlightened and progressive people I encountered in the media who were interested in serious and substantive discussion, there were also more than a few liberals who themselves were quite virulent in their hatred for revolution and communism and quite ignorant about the actual principles of communism and the historical experience of countries like the Soviet Union and China, when they were socialist, and the role of leaders like Lenin and Mao.

During the time I was in Los Angeles, as a part of the speaking tour, the *L.A. Times* assigned a reporter named Bella Stumbo to not only attend the speech itself but to hang out and talk with me for a few days before the speech, and a few days after, and on that basis to write an article supposedly providing insight into what someone like myself, the head of a revolutionary communist party, was like and what life was like for me on a daily basis as well as in my more explicitly political role.

But then it turned out that at least on her part, and perhaps more generally on the part of the *L.A. Times*, this involved a significant aspect of a set-up. When she finally wrote what turned out to be a rather major and lengthy article, she attributed a statement to me that could have had the effect of making it sound as if I were threatening Jimmy Carter, who was the president at the time. I remember very vividly sitting in a meeting somewhere when somebody gave me the *L.A. Times* with this article in it, and I started reading it, and when I got to that part, I just about jumped out of my seat and exclaimed, "Shit, this is complete bullshit what she's done here, and this is clearly a serious attack!" And, in fact, even though this was a total distortion, the Secret Service picked up on it and tried to make something out of it—to use it as a basis to go after me—even though there was nothing to it.

We actually fought back by, number one, going into court and trying to prevent the government from acting on this basis, by showing that it was, in fact, a total distortion. And, although the judge wouldn't grant us this injunction, the fact that we took this initiative did have an impact. We also put pressure on the *L.A. Times*, threatening to sue them if they didn't print a retraction; and they did finally print a partial retraction, admitting that this was a distortion and in effect that there was no way that something I said could legitimately be interpreted as a threat against Jimmy Carter. We were able to derail this particular attack, but this gives you a sense of how they were moving against me and the Party, now in one way, now in another; while pushing ahead with these phony, politically motivated legal charges in D.C., they were utilizing this *L.A.*

*Times* distortion to come after me as well.

On the other side of the picture, we were beginning to demonstrate our potential to "turn D.C. upside down," as we had said in our call to the volunteers. Broad support was growing in our fight against the legal attack, and there was growing awareness of what our Party was about, and growing support for us on various levels. So, in this context, literally a few days before the mass rally at the Howard Theater, we went to court and the judge ruled in our favor and dismissed the charges. Part of the judge's ruling in dismissing the charges was that this case involved what is called "selective prosecution"—in other words, that there was an element of political persecution in these prosecutions. The government subsequently appealed that and later the charges were reinstated, but in the short run they had to back off as a result of the potential that was shown for us to mobilize support, and the ways in which the growth and breadth of support was beginning to indicate that there was going to be a significant political price to pay for continuing this attack right then.

## Tactical Retreat, Mounting Attacks

But even though they'd been forced in the short run to drop these charges, this was a tactical retreat and maneuver on their part, and it was clear that in an overall sense, they were continuing to mount attacks on our Party and on myself as its leader. There were more and more reports of threats coming from the government and from Nazis, Klansmen and similar types. We got threatening messages from Nazis in North Carolina, and this carried particularly heavy weight given what had happened there, both in terms of our experience with the speaking tour and more acutely with the CWP people. And there were a lot of comments coming from police and others like, "We should have killed that guy"— referring to me—"when we had him in our hands." And, although we were able to beat back the Secret Service attack flowing from the *L.A. Times* distortion, this also made very clear, from the whole way they went after that, that the government was not intending to just back off, in an overall sense, even if they had to retreat temporarily in the legal case in D.C. So these attacks were being mounted from many different directions, and the situation in an overall sense was intensifying then, even with the temporary dismissal of these charges in D.C.

This *L.A. Times* thing was a deliberate and gross distortion by the reporter. But once something utterly false like that gets planted and becomes part of the public record, so to speak, by being printed in a major newspaper like the *L.A. Times*, the government can come in on the basis of *that* and use that as a pretext for an attack. This is a pattern of attack they've used, not just against our Party, but more generally. It is very important to understand that, while you can't just ignore the mainstream bourgeois media, at the same time whatever dealings and encounters you have with them are a matter of class struggle, as we say. They represent the ruling class, and they're going to serve its interests in whatever way they can, even when they appear to be talking in a friendly way to you, and even if you find a few honest reporters here and there.

I remember way, way back in the days when we were in Richmond, this reporter for the *San Francisco Chronicle* wrote sympathetic articles about the movement, and he eventually had to quit because he came under such attack from the editors and publishers of the newspaper. People seeking to build a movement to change society will have to deal with this arena of the mainstream media—it's an important part of waging the struggle—but you have to understand that *that's* what you're doing: you're waging a struggle, and you can't let your guard down or think that this is a neutral arena.

Over many years as a political activist and then a revolutionary, I had seen this fact illustrated in many different ways, and then the experience with the *L.A. Times* drove this home much more profoundly. There was the interview I referred to with a *Washington Post* reporter who in effect tried to induce me to say: "Oh, yes, it's a 'win-win' situation for us, and if we get convicted that will be fine too, because that will prove that the system is oppressive"—which was not our orientation at all. And I remember even earlier, back in Berkeley in the late '60s, these reporters had come from *Fortune* magazine to write an article about the radicals in Berkeley, and someone I knew in the movement in Berkeley said, "I'm gonna be talking with these reporters from *Fortune* magazine, do you want to come along?" And I said sure.

So we were having breakfast and talking in an International House of Pancakes, and these *Fortune* reporters were acting as if they were all friendly and hip, and they started asking us about our views, and then at one point one of them said, "You know, one thing strikes me funny: don't you think it's kind of ironic that there are all these radical students and others from the middle class who go around calling the police 'pigs' when the police are really working class?" And I answered: "No, I don't think it's ironic at all—the police aren't working class, the police are part of the state apparatus that brutalizes and attacks people who oppose the system or people who are oppressed under the system. I've seen it myself many times—they are pigs." So then these *Fortune* reporters weren't really interested in talking to us so much any more, and I noticed that my comments never made it into the article when it was published.

So, through those and many other experiences, I had learned clearly about the role of this mainstream bourgeois media and the fact that dealing with them is a part of the struggle. You always have to be on your guard, as shown by this *L.A. Times* reporter who totally distorted what I was saying in a way that provided an opening for a further attack by the state.

## Help from the People

But it wasn't just attacks in the legal arena, it wasn't even just the trumped-up charges off the demonstration against Deng Xiaoping or this whole thing with the *L.A. Times* article. For example, during this period I went to Atlanta at one point to meet with people in the Party there, to do some political work together with them and to learn about how things were going there. Part of what I was doing was getting together with comrades there to sell the *Revolutionary Worker*, which the Party had just started publishing that year.

At one point I was staying in a motel with some other people just outside of Atlanta, and some of the comrades from the local area came over to meet with us in our motel rooms. Some of the comrades were Black and some of them were white, and apparently this infuriated the authorities—I'm not sure to this day if it was just local authorities or also agencies like the FBI that were involved. In any case, it turned out that this scene was a provocation to the pigs, who were preparing to mount an assault on us.

And it is very interesting how we found about this. At one point, one of the people who was in our room got thirsty and went out to the coke machine at the motel, and there was this housekeeper there, a young Black woman, who had positioned herself strategically so she couldn't be seen by all the cops who were gathering in the lobby. She motioned to this comrade to come over to where she was standing, and she told him: "Look, I don't know what's going on, but are you aware that all these cops are here and they're talking about your room?" She made very clear by what she said, and the way she said it, that it was likely that they were going to launch a physical assault on this room, even though we weren't doing anything but having a meeting talking about what kind of political work we were going to be doing—selling our newspaper and things like that.

I think it is interesting that the very thing that provoked the cops—the fact that we had Black people and white people together in this motel—along with the fact that they were mobilizing these police forces against us, was probably the very thing that made this housekeeper feel sympathetic to us and sense that we were probably people who were worth siding with, in the sense of letting us know that this attack was about ready to be mounted. In a real way she saved us from that attack, because we immediately packed up our things and left. We left in two cars and we were followed for miles before the cops finally decided to give it up.

We were never able to fully find out whether it was just a case of Black people and white people being together that in itself was a provocation to these racist police and authorities, or whether it was more a result of consciously directed surveillance on our Party, or some combination of the two—which seems the most likely, because as we did more investigation afterward, there were indications that people had been followed there in the first place. But this is another incident that indicates how the overall atmosphere was heating up. And I always think back with great affection about that housekeeper and how she saved us from what was clearly being prepared as a major assault; and who knows what we would have been subjected to if they'd come flying into the room with masses of police.

### Damián García

I spoke earlier about our efforts to build a revolutionary outpouring on May 1, 1980. As May Day 1980 approached, the repression against our Party and the people who were rallying around this vision intensified week by week, with arrests, jailings, beatings and threats. Finally, on April 22, one of our comrades, Damián García, was murdered while carrying out revolutionary work in a housing project by someone who declared, "You hate the government, I *am* the government, your flag is red, mine is red, white and blue," and who very shortly after that was himself mysteriously murdered (in what may well have been part of a cover-up).

This murder of Damián García was very clearly tied in with police agents, and it was very clear that it was an attack on our Party and on the May Day we were building for—and it was something else along with that. Not long before this, Damián García had been one of three people who had raised the red flag over the Alamo and denounced the imperialist conquest and domination that it represented. The war against Mexico and the theft of its land was a key part of the expansion of the system in the U.S. as it approached and then reached the imperialist stage at the end of the 19th century and the beginning of the 20th century. So Damián García, in a profound expression of opposition to this, had climbed to the top of the Alamo, unfurled a red flag, and read a denunciation of U.S. imperialism. And we always understood the murder of Damián García to be not only an attack on our Party in general and on our building for revolutionary May Day 1980 in particular, but also retaliation for that internationalist act.

The assassination of Damián García was a towering injustice and it had a profound effect on our Party and on many others including, I remember, a prisoner in Georgia who, upon learning about the murder of Damián García, wrote an extremely moving poem. Right after Damián García was murdered, I issued a statement on behalf of the Party, a portion of which I want to quote here:

> "To die in the causes for which the imperialists and reactionaries have and will on an even more monstrous scale enlist the people, or to give up living and to die a little death on your knees, or to consume oneself in futile attempts at self-indulgent escape; all this is miserable and disgraceful. But to devote your life, and even be willing to lay it down, to put an end to the system that spews all of this forth, to live and die for the cause of the international proletariat, to make revolution, transform society and advance mankind to the bright dawn of communism—this is truly a living, and a dying, that is full of meaning and inspiration for millions and hundreds of millions fighting for or awakening to the same goal all around the world. Such was the life and death of

Comrade Damián García, a fighter and martyr in the army of the international proletariat."

This statement was read at memorial meetings that were held all over the country shortly before May 1, 1980, and then a poster of Damián on top of the Alamo, red flag flying proudly, was put up around the country, with portions of that statement included.

# Chapter Twenty-five

# *Exile*

$J$ust to step back for a minute, this was a very wild and tumultuous period. I was leading the Party to re-examine a lot of what had been our guiding assumptions and to forge a new and much more revolutionary political line. We were taking this line out to the masses, and we were coming into very sharp conflict with the powers-that-be, and the Party in general and myself in particular were being more and more directly targeted.

In this situation, it was necessary and crucial for us to examine very carefully, deeply and from many different sides what was going on with the attacks on the Party and in particular on myself: not just what was represented by the legal case that had been mounted against us in the aftermath of the attack on the demonstration against Deng Xiaoping, but also the *L.A. Times* fabrication and distortions and the way that had been picked up by the Secret Service; the growing reports of death threats against me from various quarters, including from the police; the murder of Damián García; and then other things as well. We determined that it was necessary to make a tactical move in order to disrupt a dynamic that could be headed toward something very serious and perhaps even disastrous.

## Learning from the Experience of Lenny Bruce

Here, there was something to learn from the experience of Lenny Bruce, the comedian who in the early 1960s was continually harassed by the police and repeatedly arrested for using words like "fuck" and "shit" in his nightclub act—it seems unbelievable now, but that was the character of those times. And, as he was busted for this, time after time, his whole life and activity was caught up in defending himself around these various busts, and this seriously undermined and took away from what he was trying to do with his life's work. So, kind of analogously, besides the outright death threats and other things, we wanted to disrupt the dynamic where they were going to keep coming after me in particular, in one way after another, and where all of our efforts would have to be increasingly focused on dealing with just that, and it would take away from the broader revolutionary work we wanted and needed to do.

### A Tactical Maneuver, Not a Strategic Retreat

So, in 1981 I took the extreme but necessary step of going into exile and I applied for political refugee status in France. But this was not a *strategic* retreat—it was not, in other words, giving up on revolution in *any sense,* or giving up on the Party leading the revolutionary struggle in the U.S. or giving up on my own role in leading the Party in fulfilling its revolutionary responsibilities. This was a *tactical* move on our part to, as I said, disrupt this dynamic and this momentum of increasing attacks and mounting repression on the Party and on myself in particular, and to change the circumstances so that I could in fact continue to provide leadership to the Party in the decisive sense—in terms of ideological and political line.

### Applying for Refugee Status

The experience of applying for political refugee status in France, in 1981, was very interesting and revealing, and very intense. I didn't actually apply directly to the French government. The way the process worked was that you went to the UN High Commission on Refugees, which was in Paris, and you applied there for political refugee status. And if that commission of the UN granted you political refugee status, then the French government was supposed to grant you the rights that went with that, including the right to remain and be able to live and work in France.

When I went with my lawyer to the office of the UN High Commission in Paris, we went from one desk to another in the office with my application for political refugee status, and we were turned away at each one. They kept demanding to know, "Where are you from?" When I would answer, "the United States," I would be told, "We don't have a desk for the United States or North America, because the United States is a democratic country." In effect they were telling me— and finally one person in the office told me explicitly—that I couldn't even file my application for political refugee status because I came from the United States and there is no political repression in the United States. So here I am, arguing with the people in this UN Commission office about the real nature of U.S. society: how Black people and others are shot down and murdered by the police in the hundreds every year, how political demonstrations are attacked, such as the one that I took part in against Deng Xiaoping as well many other demonstrations against the Vietnam War and the protests that took place in the course of the civil rights and Black liberation movement, and so on. I kept exposing these things, and they just kept turning me away, sending me from one desk to another, and refusing to even accept my application to start the process.

Finally, my lawyer talked to someone that she knew in the office and they said, "Well, go talk to so-and-so—he'll probably accept your application." So we finally found this guy, and he did agree to sign the application so at least the process could be undertaken. But at the same time he said: "Oh, you're from the United States, and you're from the Revolutionary Communist Party in the USA? Well, you know, you'll have to go down to the prefecture of police, and they'll definitely want to talk to you. They might want to question you, they might even keep you for days questioning you." So, even though he was signing my application, he was obviously trying to scare me off at the same time. But finally, after hours and hours, we did get the application signed and filed and the process began.

The Party also began a process back in the U.S. where, through the channels of the Party and more broadly with people we worked with, or had contact with, we got all kinds of statements and evidentiary material documenting political repression of all kinds in the U.S. itself. I remember, for example, a very brief statement by Dr. Spock, who said, "I can testify personally that there is political repression in the United States." Our documents and evidentiary material included many things relating to the case that had arisen out of the attack on the demonstration against Deng Xiaoping, as well as many other examples of political repression directed against the Party and myself in particular. We had hundreds and hundreds of pages of documentation that we eventually submitted to the Commission—even though, as it turned out, they refused to read almost all of it.

## Adjusting to Exile

Going into exile had been a very difficult decision. This was a political decision and I felt, as did the rest of the Party leadership, that it was the right and necessary decision to make. Still, it was personally very difficult and a big dislocation. I left behind family and loved ones and many friends. I even had to leave behind my dog, a half German shepherd, half huskie named Dude that I'd raised from a pup.

I was also going to completely new and unfamiliar circumstances, and a different culture. On the one hand, I was excited, on a certain level —Paris, the city of lights, full of life and vibrancy and vitality, and more than that, a city that drew people from all over the world. I would have a chance to meet and be exposed to people from many different countries and cultures and hear about their experiences. And in fact that did happen—that was one of the very positive things about going there, and it deepened my understanding of what the imperialist system does to people all around the world, from Chile to Turkey to many places in Africa—throughout the Third World in particular, but also in other countries, including countries of Europe. I met people from countries in Latin America and elsewhere where the U.S. had pulled off coups and installed brutal dictatorships that tormented and tortured, and brutalized and murdered thousands and thousands of people. I talked to many Chilean refugees, for example, who gave vivid accounts of this.

A number of people I met, including refugees from other countries who had been in France for a while, helped me learn the ropes, as they say, and in various ways were supportive. And there had also been some political work done, in France and other parts of Europe, around the Mao Tsetung Defendants case, so that had laid a groundwork for some people to understand why I had to go into exile. All in all, I found a great deal of sympathy and support of various kinds when I arrived in Paris.

So those were positive and very important things. Yet the fact remained that, especially at first, it was a difficult thing to uproot myself and have to go into entirely new surroundings. Even though it was a very exciting city, I felt out of place in many small ways. For instance, I was determined when I went there that I was not going to be an ugly

American, trying to make everyone speak English. I was going to learn French, so I could converse with and get to know people there, and so I could read the newspapers and generally have a sense of what was going on. By reading the French newspaper *Le Monde*, for example, you could get more interesting news than you could from almost the entire mainstream bourgeois press in the U.S.

So I was determined to learn the language, but it took a while. I can remember riding on Le Metro, the subway in Paris—I'd see little children get on and they'd be talking, and I remember actually saying to myself at one point, "These French children are all *geniuses*, they all speak this French language that I'm having so much trouble learning!" And sometimes I'd be riding on the Metro with people who spoke English as well as French—I would hear other people talking, and it seemed so mysterious, so I thought what they were saying must be really heavy and substantial, and I'd ask the people I was with, "What are they talking about?" And they would dispel the mystery and awe by explaining that people were just carrying on mundane conversations about everyday humdrum things that weren't of very great importance in most cases. But to me this still often seemed mysterious and heavy, until I myself learned French well enough to understand what they were saying, and the mystery then dissolved.

## Getting into the Scene

At the same time I was trying to take in as much as I could of the culture of Paris and of France. It's very easy to get around in the city, because the Metro was not that expensive and you could hardly ever get lost. There was a Metro station within two blocks of almost anywhere you were in the city, and each station had a very good map showing what lines you would take to get to where you wanted to go—you just had to get on trains, and transferring was very easy. So that was a great thing. Also, at many, many Metro stops all over the city there would be people from all different parts of the world singing and doing other kinds of performances—as there are somewhat in the New York subway stations, but it's on a much bigger scale in Paris. It was just a great cultural experience—all this diversity from all over the world.

So that part was very exciting, although I do remember the first day I got on the Metro, I got sort of freaked out because periodically they have what they call *un controle*, where the police who work in the Metro gather in force and demand to see your *billet* (your ticket for the Metro), and this happened to be one of those times. They came up to me and I was trying to figure out what this was all about, and they just said, "bil-let...ticket, s'il vous plait," so I figured out that they wanted to see my ticket, and I did have one, so that turned out to be nothing. But other than that, and as I became more familiar with it, sometimes I would spend hours just riding around the city on the Metro, getting off and walking around different places and looking at the architecture and other things that were very different from the U.S., and listening to musical performances, taking in the scene there for a little while and then getting back on the Metro and riding to another stop to explore that area.

There was food at all different prices throughout the city—everything from little kiosks or stands to fancier restaurants—and, so far as I could afford it, I would seek out all different kinds of food. You could go to different parts of the city and find restaurants of all kinds—Moroccan, Greek, everything. But I also sought out things that felt familiar to me, even while I was trying to take in more and more of this new culture. For example, I right away discovered this weekly magazine called *Pariscope* that told you what was happening everywhere in the city during that week, including the schedule of the movie theaters. The movies made in the U.S. would arrive in Paris within a few months, and then you could go see them in English with French subtitles or you could see them in French, depending on how you wanted to take in the movie and what experience you wanted to have. But even after I learned French more, I would still mainly go see movies from the U.S. in English with French subtitles, because that was the language they were made in. There would not only be new movies, but there would also be what they called a "cycle"—a series of movies featuring one actor. There would be a theater that featured a week of movies with Marlon Brando or a week of movies with Dustin Hoffman. I remember first seeing *Lenny*, about Lenny Bruce, played by Dustin Hoffman, as part of a "Cycle Dustin Hoffman."

When I was traveling around on the Metro, I would also get out and walk around to discover where different treats could be had. I learned where the stand was with the best ice cream (or *glace*, as they say in French) and the stand with the best *frites*, or "French fries" as they are called in the U.S. Since I love waffles—I actually like to make waffles, but I love good waffles in any case—I discovered the one place in the city where a guy had a little stand selling waffles. And then I discovered to my horror a few months later that he'd moved, he wasn't there anymore. So I tracked him down and found him in another part of the city. These were some things that I did while I was learning the language and increasingly taking in the culture of France, while at the same time I was interacting with and learning from all people and cultures from all over the world.

### French Basketball, "The Deerhunter," and Doo-Wop

I also discovered French basketball leagues, although I was frustrated because they usually only played once a week. There was a team in Paris and teams in other cities, and each of these teams was allowed to have a certain number of players from other countries, which mainly meant Americans. Some people who either didn't quite make it into the NBA but had played in college in the U.S., or who had played a year or two in the NBA but didn't "stick," came over to Europe to play. I would go to as many games as I could, and sometimes I'd talk to some of the players after a game, particularly the ones who were from the U.S.

Also, people back in the U.S. sent me videotapes of basketball and other sports. When the NCAA basketball tournament would take place in March, I would get videotapes of this, but they would arrive about a week late, so I'd have to go through all these convoluted efforts to make sure that I didn't find out the results before I was able to play the videotapes (this was before satellite TV was widely available). So this involved a lot of complications, but still I managed to keep up, and that's how I found out about and first watched the Houston team that came to be called Phi Slamma Jamma, which I loved and about which I wrote an article that was included in the book *Reflections, Sketches and Provocations*. So that was another way I could keep up with things that were dear to my heart.

It was in France that I first saw the movie *The Deerhunter*. Culture, especially if it's done well technically and artistically, can have a very powerful impact in influencing people's thinking and in creating public opinion. And that was the case with *The Deerhunter*, a movie about Vietnam and American soldiers, which came out in the late '70s. I remember, for example, a story told to me by someone in the Party shortly after *The Deerhunter* came out. He was leafletting about something at this factory—not about *The Deerhunter* but some other politi-cal issue or event—and this young worker stopped and said, "I'm not gonna take your communist literature because I saw what you commu-nists did to our boys in Vietnam. I saw that movie, *The Deerhunter*."

*The Deerhunter* was a conscious and systematic attempt to take images that people had known from the Vietnam War and reverse them and reverse the meaning of them. For example, there was a famous image that people all over the world saw of this suspected Viet Cong member who had a pistol put to his head and was executed in the streets by a member of the political police of the Saigon regime. Well, *The Deerhunter* had this whole motif in it where one of the U.S. soldiers had kind of dropped out of things and was playing Russian roulette; and the scenes of Russian roulette in the movie were aimed at subtly and sort of subconsciously (or "subliminally," as they sometimes say) recalling but then *reversing the meaning* that had been conveyed by that pistol-to-the-head shooting of a Viet Cong suspect in real life in Saigon. The images of pistols-to-the-head became, in *The Deerhunter*, the tragedy of what happened to American soldiers in Vietnam, instead of the outrage of what the political police of the puppet regime installed by the U.S. was doing to people that they accused of being Viet Cong.

And there were other ways in which the meaning of things was reversed. For example, in the actual war in Vietnam, the Vietnamese in the liberation army who were captured by the U.S. side were put in these tiny "tiger cage" prisons and tortured there. But *The Deerhunter* reversed that and had the U.S. soldiers being put in tiger cages by the Viet Cong. This, again, was a very conscious attempt to reverse the meaning of things, and "reverse political verdicts"; and it was done in an artistically powerful way, because it was a very well-made and well-acted movie, designed to create reactionary public opinion in a big way around the Vietnam War.

Knowing this, I couldn't just go to this movie like any other movie, so I didn't go for quite a while when it was actually showing in the U.S., and then I had to go into exile. Finally, seeing that the movie was play-ing in France I said to myself, "It's time to go see *The Deerhunter*." And I discovered that indeed it *was* a very powerful and very reactionary movie, which played the political and ideological role that I have described here. And yet, at the end of this very long movie, I found myself saying, "Well, I'm ready for a few more hours of this," even though I knew "going in," and saw very clearly in watching the movie, what a reactionary statement it was making. I wanted more of the movie, even though I understood what it was doing and recognized how it was manipulating people's thinking and feelings, even somewhat unconsciously, as well as more overtly. I wasn't "taken in" by it—but I did feel the powerful pull of it, even while I was resisting it. So I learned something more about the powerful effect that art and culture can have, in this case in a very negative way.

One pull I did not try to resist, nor would I ever want to, was my continued love of doo-wop. There was a record store I discovered in Paris called the "Crocodisque." They had all kinds of records, including old doo-wop records I had lost or had to leave behind when I came to France, and other music from the '60s and '70s. I bought an album of songs by the Spaniels, a group I really liked and that a lot of people modeled themselves after when I was in high school.

And French radio sometimes played songs from the U.S. as well as music from France. One time, I was sitting in a room with someone, and we were talking while this French radio program was on in the background, and all of a sudden I jumped up and said, "Oh, my god!" And the person with me asked urgently: "What's the matter? What's the matter?" I said, "Nothing, this is just a really great song they're playing on the radio." It was the classic doo-wop song, "Speedoo," by the Cadillacs featuring Earl Carroll, with the famous opening line: "They often call me Speedoo, but my real name is Mr. Earl." I was just so excited to hear this song.

### Leading from Exile

When we made the decision for me to go into exile and apply for political refugee status, we did it with the understanding and the analysis that we had to and could find the ways for me to continue to give overall leadership to the Party. Now, it is important to understand that leading a communist party doesn't mean that you have a "hands-on" role in every particular thing that the party might be doing. First of all, it is impossible for any one individual to do that. But more essentially, the ability to lead involves learning about the work of the party in many diverse arenas and parts of the country, through reports and other ways in which information about the work and the thinking of party members is passed along and summed up and synthesized at various levels of the party. When I was living in the U.S., in my role as the Chairman of the RCP I wasn't trying to directly involve myself in every thing, even every *important* thing, that the Party was relating to. That would have been impossible—and not the correct method of leadership.

Even with regard to leading particular areas of work of an organization like the RCP, what is involved is learning about the key problems and contradictions that are arising in the work and helping people to address those questions and to put them in a larger, strategic context, through studying communist theory and the historical experience of the communist movement, as well as learning from the practice and ideas of others, and to be able, on that basis, to take initiative to solve problems and to move things forward, not only in relation to the more immediate objectives of that particular struggle but in relation to the strategic objectives of the party. In other words, as we say, leadership is essentially a matter of line and not a matter of tactical guidance.

And, although providing direction and forging specific tactics for a particular struggle can be an important aspect of leadership, that is not the most important aspect by far.

The essence of communist leadership is to enable people to continually raise their sights to the larger objectives of the struggle—revolution, socialism, and the final goal of communism worldwide—and, proceeding from that perspective and orientation, to grasp and act on the living link between those long-term strategic objectives and the work and struggles at any point in the process.

In order to provide that kind of leadership, it is necessary to study the historical experience of the communist movement, internationally as well as within particular countries, and to draw lessons from that. It is necessary to continually study communist theory and apply the essential principles and methods that are concentrated in that theory. And it also necessary to pay attention to and learn about what is going on in many different spheres, not just in the political sphere, but in the arts, the scientific realm and other fields of intellectual activity, and many other arenas of human endeavor. It is necessary to learn what people working in these various spheres are learning, what problems they are wrestling with, and so on. You have to look into social commentaries of various kinds, putting forward different viewpoints on important questions. You have to apply the scientific communist viewpoint and method of dialectical materialism to all these things, but you have to apply it in a living and creative, not a lifeless and dogmatic, way. In this way you can concentrate important lessons and insights that can be drawn from this rich diversity of experience and work to popularize this within the Party, and more broadly, so that people themselves can take this up and apply it concretely and take further initiative to themselves study these questions and apply this outlook and method.

Communist leadership involves the application of what Mao called "the mass line." It requires learning from the experience and the ideas of the people you are seeking to lead. However, it means not just "being a mirror" to the masses but instead applying the scientific viewpoint of communism to concentrate what is correct in their thinking, raising that to a higher level, and then returning *that* to the masses in the form of lines and policies, propagating these among the masses and uniting and persevering together with the masses to carry out these lines and poli-cies...in an endless process. The mass line can and must be carried out not only in the relations between the vanguard party and the masses but also within the party itself, on all levels. The mass line is not a recipe for tailing the masses, whether inside or outside the party, but a means for learning from and leading them—from the standpoint of, and toward the strategic objective of, communism.

All this is what is meant in saying that communist leadership is essentially a matter of leadership through line. The question we faced was finding the ways in which I could continue to do that in the new cir-cumstances that arose when I was forced into exile.

As part of that, and coming off the whole monumental struggle around what stand to take in the face of the revisionist coup and restora-tion of capitalism in China, we recognized the importance of not only going more deeply into Mao and Lenin and their development of com-munist theory, but also studying more deeply the history of the revolu-tionary movement and in particular the history of the international com-munist movement and of the Soviet Union and China as socialist coun-tries. So one of the first things I did, once I got settled somewhat in Paris, was to begin a fairly major study of the history of the international com-munist movement, beginning with the October Revolution in Russia, in 1917, and the first few years of the Communist International (the Third International), when it was led by Lenin, through the period of the next several decades when, in essence, the international communist move-ment was led by Stalin, until his death in 1953. My aim was to learn what was positive, what real contributions there were, but also what mistakes there were, both in analysis and strategy and—at least as importantly—in methodology and approach.

I read analysis and criticism of this period, or particular parts of it, from many different viewpoints: supporters of Trotsky, people who were social-democratic (reformist socialists) in their outlook but had made important analysis of the international communist movement, and people who were strident anti-communists, as well as people writing from a communist perspective, including those who had been part of the international communist movement and were themselves aiming to draw important lessons from a summation of this experience. I set out to learn from people with many different perspectives. My approach was, in a real sense, to look at this history anew, applying a critical approach to everything I was studying, even those things written by communists, while at the same time applying the fundamental outlook and methodology of communism to draw, from all this, the most essential lessons, positive and negative.

### Conquer the World!

Out of this study, I first wrote up some summations of what I thought were the main lessons—an outline summation of the history of the Third International, that is, the Communist International that was founded under the leadership of Lenin and then, after Lenin's death in 1924, was led by Stalin. Then, proceeding from that outline summation, and continuing to study and wrestle with the profound questions involved, over a period of a year or so, I developed my thinking into a talk called *Conquer the World: The International Proletariat Must and Will*, which was recorded and then transcribed and published in *Revolution* magazine.[38] *Conquer the World* was my attempt to further develop this critical summation, and in this talk I did not limit things to the experience of the international communist movement under the leadership of Lenin and then Stalin, but tried to take in the whole sweep of the communist movement from the time of Marx and Engels up through Mao.

*Conquer the World* was and is very controversial because, again, I

---

38. The weekly *Revolutionary Worker* had replaced the old monthly *Revolution* newspaper, and *Revolution* then became a magazine, which was published periodically.

tried to take a critical look at this whole experience. Marxism is a critical revolutionary scientific approach. It is not a dogma and not some kind of religion where you just blindly follow the leaders of the movement, no matter how great those leaders may actually be. So even with Marx, and Lenin and Mao, as well as Engels and in particular Stalin, I not only took account of and tried to sum up the main contributions they had made, but I also focused to a significant degree on what, with historical perspective, I felt could be and had to be recognized as short-comings in their outlook and approach to things—shortcomings which are hardly surprising because everyone, even the people who make the greatest innovations and the greatest contributions, in any sphere, are conditioned by their time and circumstances. In order to grasp—and, in a certain sense, to "unearth"—the most important lessons from this whole historical experience, it was necessary to take this kind of critical approach. And I am firmly convinced that, not only in this particular case but in general, this is the kind of approach and method that has to be applied.

As a funny side point, for a number of years I had been smoking a pipe and I found that, under the intense circumstances of the late '70s and early '80s, including this great change of going into exile, my smoking had increased. I was not only smoking a pipe, but smoking cigars, and then I started smoking cigarettes—and smoking them more and more. People were really starting to get on me, warning me about the serious dangers to my health. Plus my mouth hurt all the time and I started not being able to taste food. But I was still stubbornly continuing to smoke, while increasingly recognizing that people were right in telling me I should give up smoking.

But then one thing finally convinced me I really had to quit smoking. I was intensely working on writing up some things having to do with the outline of the history of the international communist movement, and I got to a certain point where I was stuck and couldn't figure out how to formulate something I wanted to say. So I thought, "I know what I need, I need to light up my pipe, that'll help me to relax a bit and be able to solve this problem." Now, there's a certain ritual you go through when you smoke a pipe. I had a metal pipe cleaner with which I'd scoop out the bowl of the pipe, and I had these other pipe cleaners I'd run through the pipe to clean out the stem of the pipe, and then I'd take the tobacco and put it in the bowl of the pipe, then take this metal instrument and tap the tobacco down and get the pipe all ready to smoke. I went through this whole routine, and then I grabbed my lighter and brought the pipe up to my mouth, so I could light it and begin smoking it...and that pipe banged into another pipe that I was already smoking! So I said: "That's it—it's time to quit smoking." And I did.

## War Clouds

During the early 1980s, and even before I left the U.S., there was a broad awareness, not only among communists but more broadly in society, of the growing danger of global nuclear war. The Reagan administration came in with this very bellicose posture and approach of trying to roll back gains that had been made by the Soviet Union through the 1970s, and Reagan took the explicit position that if it came to nuclear war, he wouldn't back down. In the RCP we had already begun to note some of these developments and the severe sharpening of the contradiction between the U.S. and the Soviet blocs, even in the latter part of the 1970s—such as Jimmy Carter's declaration that any move by an "outside force" (meaning, of course, the Soviet Union) in the Persian Gulf that threatened the interests of the United States would be treated as an act of war—and this further intensified in the 1980s.

I think that, since we were based in the U.S., in some ways our party was more keenly aware of this growing danger of world war than people from some other parts of the world. In the U.S., the ways in which the government was aggressively pushing out and confronting the Soviets in various places was constantly in the public eye, and there were things in the U.S. popular culture at that time—like the TV movie *The Day After*, about what would happen if there were a nuclear war and the U.S. were hit with a nuclear attack—which brought this sharply into the popular consciousness. With the U.S. being one of the two superpowers, the head of one of the two blocs of contending imperialists, the possibility of world war was pushed to the forefront, shall we say, more prominently and broadly in U.S. society. Some people from other parts of the world didn't see as acutely some of the changes that were being undertaken on the part of the U.S. in the international arena and some of the ways in which the contradiction between the two imperialist blocs was sharpening up. So we had some struggle with people over that, and it is still a contentious issue whether in fact the contradiction between these two imperialist blocs, one headed by the Soviet Union and the other by the U.S., really was the main thing shaping world events in the 1980s.

In fact, our Party had devoted a lot of attention to studying this whole question. In the 1980s, a book, *America In Decline*, was written by the Maoist political economist Raymond Lotta. It made a lot of concrete analysis of the development of the contradiction between the U.S. and Soviet blocs and the growing danger of war between them, as well as putting this in the broader framework of analysis of the contradictions of the imperialist system and its overall dynamics. I read drafts of this book and offered comments and suggestions. In this and other ways I was also devoting a lot of attention to the intensifying contradictions between the imperialist blocs, the growing danger of world war, and the truly monumental challenges this posed for the masses of people in the world and the communist movement.

But given that world war did not result from this—and this was a development we believed would in fact happen, if it weren't prevented by the advance of revolution in key parts of the world—it has been important for our Party to make some critical summation of this; and in the late 1990s the Party published "Notes on Political Economy," where we put forward our understanding of what had been correct in our analysis of developments toward world war, particularly in the 1980s, and what errors we had made, in particular methodological errors, which did not enable us to foresee the possibility of dramatic developments, other than world war or revolution, changing the course of world events in a profound way. Specifically, instead of world war, a very unexpected and almost unprecedented event happened: the momentum set in motion by Gorbachev led to the implosion of the Soviet Union and the end of its bloc. In summing this up, we continue to believe that there *was* a real danger of world war in the 1980s, and that the contradiction between the two imperialist blocs—headed by the two superpowers— was in fact the main contradiction shaping things in the world and was intensifying greatly. We were right to call attention to the danger of world war, even though there were ways in which we were somewhat mechanical about that. So, while upholding what was correct in our analysis and approach to this, we have had to sum up and draw important lessons from the mechanical tendencies we fell into.

## Learning To More Deeply Hate Imperialism

In thinking about this whole experience of exile, even though there have been some difficulties involved in this very dramatic change in circumstances, one of the most important and positive things about it has been the opportunity to learn more about many other societies. Having become a communist in the U.S. and having been part of the struggle in the U.S. for many years, I had learned a great deal about the terrible crimes that U.S. imperialism was carrying out not just in the U.S. but in many other parts of the world and the horrible suffering that the daily functioning of this system inflicted on billions of people all over the world. But going to another country, meeting people there from many different parts of the world and learning from them about the horrors that the imperialist system, and in particular the U.S., inflicted on people, deepened my understanding of the importance of internationalism. And this helped to strengthen our Party's firm commitment to and grounding in the communist stand of proletarian internationalism and approaching everything we do, as Lenin put it, not from the point of view of "our country," or the struggle in "our country" above all else, but from the point of view of our contribution to the world revolution.

# Chapter Twenty-six

# In Exile...
## And Leading Through Line

Since going into exile, I have paid attention to a number of different dimensions of the overall struggle for communism. I have continued leading the Party to develop lines and policies for key issues and struggles inside the U.S. itself *and* to grasp the relation between that and our strategic revolutionary objectives. I have also continued to devote attention to summing up and drawing lessons from the history of the international communist movement, and I've tried to learn as much as I could from the revolutionary struggle throughout the world, especially where that is led by communist, Maoist forces. This has occupied a great deal of my time and efforts, and this has been concretized and concentrated in various talks I've given that have been recorded and transcribed, and distributed inside the Party and sometimes published in the Party press.

### Democracy: Can't We Do Better Than That?

I have also written a number of books on major questions confronting the communist movement. In the mid-1980s, because it is such a big question in the U.S. but also more broadly in the world as a whole, I focused on the question of democracy. I wrote a book with the deliberately provocative title, *Democracy: Can't We Do Better than That?*, which put democracy in its historical context and analyzed the actual content of different kinds of democracy throughout history. I went back to ancient Greek and Roman societies, which were democracies for a small sliver of society but were founded on the enslavement and exploitation of the majority of the people in those societies, and I took that up to the present and showed how the "great democracy" of the U.S. is not some classless, pure democracy, but is a system of rule, and of democracy, that is also based on the exploitation and oppression of masses of people, not only in the U.S. but throughout the world. In other words, this is a democracy that is founded on and serves the capitalist and imperialist system and the ruling class that presides over and benefits from that system.

I took on a lot of the popular misconceptions and illusions about democracy and showed how, in fact, the vaunted "American democracy" has a definite social and class content—it is *bourgeois* democracy, and in fact a form of bourgeois dictatorship, an oppressive system of rule in the interests of the bourgeois ruling class and the capitalist system of exploitation. *Democracy: Can't We Do Better Than That?* showed that, in order to put an end to all systems and relations of oppression and exploitation, it is necessary to transcend all states—in other words, all dictatorships—and eventually get to a classless society where we would no longer need, and would have transcended, the institutions and formal structures of any kind of democracy, and where the people themselves would be able to handle their affairs collectively without the need for one part of society to exercise democracy in its ranks while it exercised dictatorship over the rest of society.

Of course, I cannot go into all the complexities of that here, but *Democracy: Can't We Do Better Than That?* examines, at some length, the complexities and contradictions of this question of democracy: why it is not possible to "perfect" bourgeois democracy so as to make it really serve the interests of the masses of people; how in socialist society, with the rule of the formerly exploited and oppressed masses of people, there will be a qualitatively different and far greater democracy for the great majority of society; and finally how, with the advance to communism and the abolition of class divisions and social inequalities, democracy will be surpassed and replaced with the free association of people, without the need for formal structures and institutions which are supposed to—but, in fact, in class-divided society cannot—protect one part of society from oppression at the hands of another part of society.

One of the main points I have emphasized in *Democracy: Can't We*

*Do Better than That?*, and in a number of other writings and talks, is that even progressive and somewhat radical-minded people often have a hard time getting beyond what Marx called "the narrow horizon of bourgeois right." In their thinking, as well as in the realities of how society functions, they are still trapped within the framework of what is in fact *bourgeois* democracy, a system of bourgeois rule—a bourgeois dictatorship, in which, yes, the people are allowed to vote in a country like the U.S., but all the politics and in fact all the affairs of society are dominated by a small class of people that rules on the basis of exploiting millions and millions of people inside the U.S. itself and billions of people around the world. So "democracy" continues to be a source of considerable illusion and confusion, and addressing and laying bare the realities of democracy in a country like the U.S., in its actual functioning and social content, remains extremely important.

## The "Crisis" of Marxism, the Rise of Religion

In the early 1980s, a little before *Democracy: Can't We Do Better Than That?*, I wrote a book called *For a Harvest of Dragons*. At that time, even before the Soviet Union collapsed, there was a lot of talk about how Marxism was in crisis. So I wrote this book to defend Marxism and communism, both as a theory and as a political movement, and also to sum up what I saw as some of the key aspects of Marxism and how they applied in the contemporary world, toward the end of the twentieth century.

Also in the 1980s, but particularly into the '90s, I took note of the growth and the significance of religious fundamentalism: not only Islamic fundamentalism and other kinds of fundamentalisms in the Third World, for example in India, where there has been a growth of Hindu fundamentalism, but also, very significantly, the growth of Christian fundamentalism in the U.S. itself and the whole fascist-like political program and ideological thrust that this religious fundamentalism has been associated with, particularly on the part of those influential and powerful figures in society who have been leading and promoting it, like Pat Robertson and Jerry Falwell—and now, of course, the president of the United States, George W. Bush. Bush, besides self-consciously taking on the swagger and smirk of a philistine know-nothing bully and promoting that as a model, is also deliberately promoting religious fundamentalism in all kinds of ways. He even refuses to acknowledge the reality that evolution is a well-established scientific fact. All this is part of his promotion of religious fundamentalism in the U.S. and what we, in our party, have very correctly labeled *Christian Fascism*.

Christian Fascism does not refer to Christianity in some general sense—there are people who take up Christianity from many different viewpoints, including people who are progressive and in many ways stand with the fight against oppression. Obviously, as a communist, I am an atheist and I don't agree with religious viewpoints of any kind, philosophically or ideologically, but there are many people who are religious with whom our Party works and seeks to strengthen unity. That is very different, however, from Christian fundamentalism and in particular its expression as an ideological and political force in society whose connections now reach right up to the highest levels of the ruling political structures, including the White House and House of Representatives Majority Leader Tom DeLay.

In the decade of the 1990s, I gave a number of talks and wrote several articles which spoke to the growing phenomenon, and danger, of religious fundamentalism, within the U.S. as well as in other parts of the world. I wrote *Preaching From a Pulpit of Bones*, a book which not only exposes the actual content and aims, and the hypocrisy, of people promoting Christian fundamentalism and "traditional values" in the U.S., but also the actual oppressive content of things like the Ten Commandments and the Bible overall, which upholds slavery and other atrocities, such as: the execution of homosexuals; the seizing and carrying off of women as prizes of war and their enslavement as concubines; the slaughter of other people who oppose your religion and seek to practice their own, with things like raping women and smashing in the heads of babies advocated as just punishment for such people; and the killing of children who rebel against their parents. *Preaching From a Pulpit of Bones* also includes a critique of various kinds of attempts to use the Bible for more progressive causes. While uniting with some of the sentiments, and many of the actions, of people who proceed from this perspective, I showed how in the final analysis the Bible *cannot* be a guide to liberation, it cannot be a guide to eliminating the injustices and outrages that many of these progressive religious people seek to struggle against and to abolish.

I have also devoted some attention to analyzing questions of military theory during this period. I gave a talk in the late 1980s called "Could

We Really Win?" which explored the contradictions involved in actually successfully carrying out a mass insurrection, of millions and millions of people, in a country like the U.S. at a future time when a revolutionary crisis had developed and masses of people were ready to move in that direction. Then, after the first war the U.S. waged against Iraq, I did an interview which went further into some of these questions, entitled *More on Could We Really Win?*

### Dictatorship, Democracy, Communism...Dissent

In the early 1990s, following up on *Democracy, Can't We Do Better Than That?*, I wrote a polemic called, "Democracy, More Than Ever We Can and Must Do Better Than That."[39] As a result of the collapse of the Soviet Union you had this phenomenon where in parts of Eastern Europe and the Soviet Union some people were pulling down statues of Lenin, and so on. In the face of this, certain people who had been part of the Maoist movement started tailing after bourgeois-democratic viewpoints and saying that we had to rethink the whole history of the communist movement and not just criticize certain errors, but essentially throw out altogether the experience of socialist society—and not only in the Soviet Union but in China as well. This was vastly different than what I had done in *Conquer the World*, where I had raised a number of sharp criticisms but had upheld the overall experience of socialism; this was an attempt to repudiate that and to argue instead for a more democratic—that is, *bourgeois*-democratic—approach to socialism. As I analyzed in polemicizing against this, it would amount to abandoning the cause of revolution and communism completely. So I wrote this polemic to lay bare the implications of this capitulation to capitalism in the form of advocating bourgeois democracy, and to follow up on some of the main themes and analyses I'd made in the book *Democracy, Can't We Do Better Than That?*

But while strongly rejecting, and sharply polemicizing and struggling against, the notion that we should basically adopt bourgeois democracy in the name of socialism and communism, I *have* tried to

---

39. This polemic, "Democracy: More Than Ever We Can and Must Do Better Than That," originally appeared in the magazine *A World To Win*, Issue 17, March 1992; it is now included in the second edition of the author's book *Phony Communism is Dead...Long Live Real Communism!*

draw lessons out of the experience of socialism in the Soviet Union and China—and, in particular, to recognize and emphasize the importance of *dissent* in socialist society. As I've put it, and as is expressed in our Party's new Programme, the dictatorship of the proletariat—the socialist state—should not only allow but should, in a real sense, encourage and foster dissent. This is part of developing socialism as a vital and vibrant society where people themselves are wrestling with and thrashing out all the big questions of affairs of state and the direction of society, within the framework of continuing on the socialist road. Even where people may not agree that we should continue on the socialist road, we should seek to learn from their dissent and criticism and should not seek to suppress it, so long as it doesn't take the form of an actual concrete organized attempt, once socialism has been achieved, to overthrow socialism and drag people back to capitalism. So this is one of the main questions I have been wrangling over and writing about, one of the main lessons that I, and the Party, are drawing from the experience of socialist society and more broadly the experience of the struggle to put an end to oppressive rule and oppressive relations among people.

I have also been focusing attention on how art and culture, work in the sciences, and more broadly work with ideas and work in the intellectual realm, have been approached in the history of the communist movement and socialist society, and the positive and negative lessons that we can draw from that. I have returned to the theme that Mao brought forward of letting a hundred flowers bloom in the arts and a hundred schools of thought contend in science, and I am trying to pursue further the contradictions involved in actually giving expression to that, both in building the revolutionary struggle and the vanguard party now, as well as in socialist society itself. How do you have a great deal of diversity and contention and clashing over different ideas, and different schools of expression and different forms, in the arts and sciences; and how do you unleash the creativity and initiative of people in these spheres and at the same time, in an overall sense, help lead and guide this to all serve the cause of uprooting oppression and exploitation and helping people both to know the world more fully and to transform it in a radical and fundamental way, in the interests of humanity as a whole, with all its diversity? How to do all this in a way that is full of vibrancy and vitality and critical and creative thinking and dissent and experimentation—and have this all contribute to the advance to communism?

Obviously, this is all *very* complex. Not only am I continuing to wrestle with this, and not only is this something which our Party is taking up, but it is something that communists everywhere have to take up and grapple with much more deeply and all-sidedly as we carry forward the revolutionary struggle. There is a great deal more to be explored and learned.

So these are some of the main questions I have been wrestling with and writing and talking about, not only to help the RCP itself develop its work, both in the realm of practice and in theory, but also to contribute whatever I can to the struggle internationally.

### Learning from Others

I have always taken that approach of reading very broadly. In studying the history of the international communist movement, I read summations not only by people who were within that tradition, but also people from a number of very different viewpoints. And I've learned more and more the importance of doing that. Again, I've taken up a principle that Mao brought forward: Marxism, as he put it, embraces but does not replace the arts and sciences and all the different fields of human endeavor. It is necessary to learn from many different people with many diverse viewpoints in all these different fields.

What Mao meant by saying Marxism *embraces* these various spheres is that the communist outlook and approach of dialectical materialism can and should be applied to all these different spheres. It is a comprehensive scientific viewpoint and method that can lead to grasping reality, in all its complexity and particularity, in the most thorough way. But an important part of applying that viewpoint and method is learning from many different people, including people who don't agree with or don't apply the communist outlook and method, in order to have the richest process and arrive at the fullest and best synthesis.

Obviously, in the sciences, in the arts, and in other spheres, many people who are not communists and don't apply the communist viewpoint and method have made important contributions and discovered important truths. That speaks to the "does not replace" aspect of what Mao is getting at. To really, correctly synthesize and embrace all this, as Mao said, is a great challenge, and it can only be done by applying the principle of learning from many others while applying the communist outlook and method to all this experience and all the truths that are discovered by many different people, in order to sift through all that and draw the greatest lessons out from it.

It is not easy to learn very broadly without losing your bearings; and it is not easy to hold on to the correct basic approach and method without getting dogmatic and mechanical about it and failing to learn everything you can from many different people with many diverse viewpoints and experiences. This is a real challenge, which requires the correct orientation, and hard work—in contrast to dogmatism, which, as Mao also emphasized, is the province of "lazy bones."

With all this in mind, in various talks and writings I have been exploring how this principle—"Marxism embraces but does not replace"—should be applied in our work now and in socialist society, when once again new socialist societies are brought into being.

### Madison, Jefferson, and Stalin

Stepping back for a minute on all this, and drawing from the title of a talk I gave in 1989, I've come to see this whole last period as the end of one stage of the proletarian revolution, and the beginning of another. The stage that's ended is the whole period that began with the First International, at the time of Marx and Engels, and then took three successive leaps with the Paris Commune in 1871, the October Revolution in Russia in 1917, and then the Great Proletarian Cultural Revolution in China. And now this historical period has ended with a situation where once again there are no socialist countries in the world and no Communist International.

But this has not led me to take the attitude that "we have nothing to show for all that." To the contrary, we have Marxism-Leninism-Maoism, which is the product of this whole period and which enables us to sum up that experience and move forward—which we have been doing. And there is also the regroupment of the Maoist parties into the Revolutionary Internationalist Movement (RIM) which has strengthened the struggles of these parties and has contributed to the future formation of a new Communist International.

At the same time, I see this new stage as one full of great challenge. With all their tremendous accomplishments, we can't just try to repeat the experience of past revolutions; we must do even better, and we can. And here again, it is important to return to the question of Stalin. A number of times in this memoir I've recalled our insistence on upholding the experience of the Soviet Union under Stalin, focusing on the ways in which the masses truly were making history under his leadership. But, over the years, we've continued to deepen our criticisms of Stalin's errors, while continuing to do this within an approach that is informed with an understanding of his accomplishments and contributions, as well as the enormous historical challenges he faced and the limitations of his times.

I won't go into all that here,[40] but to give a sense both of how I see Stalin and, by extension, this whole orientation towards the next stage of the proletarian revolution, let me make an analogy: Stalin is to the proletarian revolution and socialist society as Jefferson and Madison were to the bourgeois revolution and capitalist society.

Jefferson and Madison, of course, provided critical ideological and political leadership to the bourgeois revolution in the U.S. and then the writing of the Constitution and the establishment of the republic itself. At the same time, they both not only owned and traded in slaves—and the whole history of slavery remains one of the horrendous crimes of history, the extremely oppressive ramifications of which continue today —but they established the legal foundation and political structure that enshrined this ownership of human beings for another 85 years, until the Civil War. They were important representatives of the bourgeoisie and capitalist society, but at the same time there were significant ways in which, in theory and in practice, they applied and propagated things sharply in conflict with that.

For his part, Stalin represented a class, the proletariat, and a system of socialism whose goal is not simply replacing one set of exploitative and oppressive relations with another—which, after all, is the vision and mission of the capitalist class—but of abolishing all relations of exploitation and all oppressive divisions, throughout the world. And, especially in the early period of his leadership of the Soviet Union, the main and essential aspect of Stalin's role was to lead the workers and peasants of the Soviet Union on the road of transforming society to uproot exploitative and oppressive relations and to support the revolutionary struggle throughout the world toward the same goal. But, even during that time, and especially as the danger of military invasion of the

---

40. In this connection, see particularly "The End of a Stage — the Beginning of a New Stage," Issue 60, *Revolution* magazine.

Soviet Union by imperialist powers, and in particular Nazi Germany, grew acute and then became a reality, Stalin applied and propagated ideas and practices which increasingly ran counter to the nature and goals of the socialist revolution: tendencies to nationalism (which led to the subordination of and even suppression of other revolutions in the service of what Stalin perceived to be the state interests of the Soviet Union); Stalin's over-reliance on technology rather than people; his tendencies to mechanical and wooden (as opposed to dialectical) materialism; his heavy-handed dealing with dissent, particularly in the years immediately leading up to the Nazi invasion; and his increasing tendency to confuse and confound what Mao identified as two qualitatively different kinds of contradictions—those among the people, and those between the people and the enemy.

As Jefferson and Madison had a foot planted in the past, even in relation to the bourgeois revolution of their era; so did Stalin in relation to the era of proletarian revolution. We for our part need to do as Marx said —"let the dead bury their dead" and bring into being societies that much more fully and comprehensively correspond to the proletariat's emancipating outlook and interests and the overall direction in which it needs to take society, which include above all the abolition of all class divisions, the withering away of all states and repressive organs, the end of all oppressive social relations, and the transcendence of what Marx called the "enslaving subordination of the individual to the division of labor" and "the antithesis between mental and manual labor."

If the bourgeoisie and its political representatives can uphold people like Madison and Jefferson, then the proletariat and its vanguard forces can and should uphold Stalin, in an overall sense and with historical perspective. But because, unlike the bourgeoisie, we are aiming for the abolition of all relations of exploitation and oppression, everywhere in the world, we should not simply uphold Stalin—or even greater leaders of the proletariat and socialist society, such as Lenin and Mao—but more than that we should strive to learn from them, their great achievements and their shortcomings and mistakes, and to do even better.

## The Outcome of the Charges and the Refugee Status

My demand for political refugee status was eventually turned down, as we expected it would be. But it was important politically to raise that demand, to rally support for it, and to do exposure in the course of that of the actual nature of the U.S.—that, yes, there *is* a great deal of political repression in the U.S. In so doing, and through that whole process, we aimed to make it more difficult for the ruling class of the U.S., or any other country, to target and deliver a blow to our Party and to myself. So that was an important struggle to wage for those reasons, even though the demand was eventually turned down.

And even though the demand for political refugee status was turned down, in 1982 as a result of all the struggle that was waged to build support for myself and the other Mao Tsetung Defendants, and for my demand for political refugee status, the authorities in the U.S. were finally forced to back off the charges that resulted from the demonstration against Deng Xiaoping in 1979 and the police attack on that demonstration. The U.S. government was finally forced to come to a settlement which resulted in the charges being dismissed against myself, and none of the Mao Tsetung Defendants doing any jail time. And there is a very interesting and revealing story about that. It was a battle right down to the end, even in the final appearance in the courtroom. The other defendants had to appear for the final disposition of the case, but there had been an agreement that no one would have to do jail time. Well, as they were going through all the motions, defendant by defendant, at one point, when a Black defendant's case was being discussed, the federal prosecutor got up and started running out all this racist garbage about how this was a big Black man and he was scary and violent. At that point, one of the lawyers for the defendants got up and said, "Look, we have an agreement here, and if you do any more of this, the whole agreement's off and we're going to go to trial." So the prosecutor was forced to back down, and we were able to achieve a successful resolution of the whole case.

# Chapter Twenty-seven

# *Perseverance, and Inspiration*

## The Hardship of Exile

In many ways this period, beginning with exile in France in the early 1980s and up to the present, has been personally very difficult. I have had to be separated from family and loved ones and many friends. On the other hand, during this period, I have had the wonderful experience of finding a person who has been not only a close comrade but in the deepest sense a soulmate of mine, and that has made up for many things, even though there have been many painful experiences.

I was able to correspond with my parents, and we became closer in many ways. My father in particular, but also my mother, would read most everything I wrote—and not just read it because I wrote it, but actually think about it—and we would correspond about this; and in that and other ways we actually became closer over these years. Just shortly before she died, I had a chance to correspond with my mom, and talked about how I was trying to make a better world; and she responded that she was trying to do the same thing in her own way. Still, I was able to have very little contact with them because of the difficulty of these circumstances, and the same has been true with other people who had been close to me throughout much of my life.

Within the last few years, first my older sister, Marjorie, and then my mother and finally my father died. Of course, I felt a tremendous loss as

437

a result of this, and it was very painful that I was not able to be with them at the end or even to attend their funerals, although I did send messages at the time of their funerals. There is no way to truly express the kind of loss I felt as a result of this, because they had always been dear to me, even when we were somewhat estranged politically and there were a lot of strains in our relationship. Over the last period of time I became much closer to them, yet was physically separated from them almost entirely during this period—and then to have them die, and not to be able to be there, was very excruciating.

### *"Money Can Make Friendship End"*

In writing this memoir, I've come to reflect again on the many close friendships I've had. In some cases these relationships have ended when sharp political differences emerged; in others, they have deepened with battles fought and battles shared. In light of this, I thought about the great reggae artist Peter Tosh, and one of his last songs.

During the mid-1980s, Tosh came out with a wonderful album, *No Nuclear War*. The album's title song strikingly presented nuclear war as a concentrated horror, while at the same time driving home the point that life for the masses of people, worldwide, is already a horror. And there were a number of other very powerful works touching on struggles of the masses—he had an updated version of "Fight Against Apartheid" that connected to the inspiring uprising of the mid- and late 1980s in South Africa—as well as some rather deep ideological questions. But this album came out shortly after Tosh had been brutally murdered, in a really heartbreaking incident, and it prompted me to write to several of my closest comrades and friends:

> "I must confess that, especially in light of the brutal murder of Tosh—the robbing of such a powerful and beautiful voice against injustice—I am filled with an almost overwhelming feeling of sadness and anger every time I listen to this album—and yet, at the same time, a certain sense of triumph in the fact that the music does still go on. In particular, when I listened to Peter Tosh's song "Lessons in My Life"—with its lines about how people make you promises today and tomorrow they change their minds, and how you have to be careful of

your friends, because money can make friendship end
—I had a very hard time holding back tears....

"But what I think is most important to do is to take
up the challenge posed: Money can make friendship
end. Certainly I do not think that money, as such, will
cause us to turn our backs on what we have set out to
do and all the people who are—subjectively in some
cases already, but objectively in the case of millions and
millions of people—counting on us to do what we have
set out to do—to lead in doing this. I do not think we
will turn back from this, or be turned away from it,
because of things like money. But what about egos?
What about ways, petty as well as not-so-petty, in which
bourgeois relations and ideas permeate every pore of
society and encircle us on every side? Will we give in to
this? Those sugar-coated bullets are even more destructive than literal bullets, because when someone falls to
sugar-coated bullets it is demoralizing to the masses of
people beyond the loss of a particular person. Can we
resist these sugar-coated bullets, all the way through? I
believe we can. But we will have to struggle with each
other and help each other—and fundamentally rely on
that 'magic combination' of our ideology, MLM, and the
masses of people.

"In 'Lessons in My Life' Tosh poses this very sharply:
This song is very powerful: truly, hauntingly beautiful.
Like much of the album, it is powerful—and sweeping
—*in its simplicity*. And there is also a positive theme
within it, as voiced in the chorus: 'I'm a progressive
man, and I love progressive people; I'm an honest man,
and I love honest people...' This is, profoundly, a just
verdict on Tosh. We, of course, have differences with
him, in particular that he is (or was) religious and we
are against religion, ideologically. But he was one of
those of whom it must definitely be said that his religious convictions led him to stand, firmly, with the
oppressed of the world against the oppressors. And he
did so with sweep and power.

"We, with the most far-seeing and thoroughly liberating ideology there is, can learn from this 'fired man': We can rise where he rose, and take it still higher. Sadness to anger; anger to intensified revolutionary energy, fired with a profoundly realistic optimism: that is what should drive us forward and lift our spirit and sights.

"I'll leave you with that. Love, and a warm revolutionary embrace."

## Disappointment, Danger, and Going Forward

Over the years and now decades, I've experienced many disappointments. Beyond personal hardships and losses, there have been real, and even profound, losses in terms of the struggle for a whole different world and better future for humanity. There have been not only twists and turns but gigantic setbacks, like the loss of China as a socialist country and base area for the world revolution. This is something that I myself, our Party, and communists throughout the world have had to confront.

Of course, there are not only difficulties but also great dangers. The people who so viciously rule the world oppress and exploit people in the most ruthless and murderous way. These are not just words that get thrown around; those are words that hardly capture the reality of the suffering that people are put through—totally unnecessarily—under the domination of this system and the way it twists and distorts the relations among people and turns people into instruments either to be used for the amassing of wealth on the part of a relative handful, or else just to be thrown onto the scrap heap like so much useless material. And there is the crushing of human potential and spirit that goes along with that. None of that has lessened. The need to do away with all that—and, from a strategic point, the basis that exists to do away with all that—hasn't been eliminated, or even lessened, despite these setbacks and even real defeats.

When I reflect on all this, I think of a conversation I had with a friend when I was a teenager. He was a little older than me, and he was going to medical school. One day I asked him what he wanted to do when he got out of medical school, what kind of medicine he was going to practice. He answered that he wasn't going to practice a particular kind of medicine, he was going to go into cancer research because he wanted to help find a cure for cancer—he believed that was not only very important but was also possible, and he wanted to make whatever contribution he could to that.

It has been many decades since that time, and while some advances have been made in treating cancer, it's still a scourge. It hasn't yet been eliminated. A cure, to put it that way, hasn't been found. But that person has been working in this field all these years, and I would never say that his efforts have been wasted just because cancer is still here. The need to eliminate cancer, or find a cure for it, if you will, is as great as ever. And, if you take a scientific approach to disease, you know that it is within the realm of possibility to find the means to eliminate this scourge on humanity and that it is worth persevering in that effort.

The same applies to the question of uprooting, overturning, and abolishing these horrendous relations of exploitation, oppression, and plunder on which this system is based and on which it thrives, along with the wars that are waged, and the destruction and despoliation of the environment that is carried out, as a result of its workings and the actions of those who rule it. The need to eliminate this system and bring something much better into being is even more profound than the need to find a cure for cancer. And if you've taken up a scientific approach to investigating, learning about and changing reality, then you know that the means *can* be found to do that. There is a basis within the nature of the world as it is, within the nature and contradictions of this system of capitalism and imperialism, to overturn and uproot and finally eliminate this system and all the horrors it causes in the world. Where you fall short of that, you have to draw the lessons as fully as possible, you have to ground yourself even more deeply in the scientific approach to understanding and changing reality that is Marxism, apply it in a more creative and critical and living way, and work together and struggle together with others in order to both learn more and do more to change the world. All the experience I've been through and learned from has taught me much more deeply and shown me much more fully that it is both necessary and possible to do this, and that the best thing that I could do with my life is to make whatever contribution I can to this.

Even where there are terrible reversals and losses like what happened with China, this system will keep throwing up the need for revolution to abolish it and to bring into being a radically different and better world, a communist world. This need will continually be brought to the fore, over and over again. The conditions of the people and what they're put through will continually cry out for this change.

If you have had a chance to see the world as it really is, there are profoundly different roads you can take with your life. You can just get into the dog-eat-dog, and most likely get swallowed up by that while trying to get ahead in it. You can put your snout into the trough and try to scarf up as much as you can, while scrambling desperately to get more than others. Or you can try to do something that would change the whole direction of society and the whole way the world is. When you put those things alongside each other, which one has any meaning, which one really contributes to anything worthwhile? Your life is going to be about something—or it's going to be about nothing. And there is nothing greater your life can be about than contributing whatever you can to the revolutionary transformation of society and the world, to put an end to all systems and relations of oppression and exploitation and all the unnecessary suffering and destruction that goes along with them. I have learned that more and more deeply through all the twists and turns and even the great setbacks, as well as the great achievements, of the communist revolution so far, in what are really still its early stages historically.

## Being Sustained

And there *have* been great achievements, in what is actually the very brief and beginning experience of socialism and the advance toward communism. Whenever the masses in any part of the world rise up, even spontaneously, and especially when they do so with communist leadership, this is a source of tremendous inspiration and shows once again the potential for this whole revolutionary struggle and transformation of society and the world. This is a very powerful and sustaining thing when combined with an increasingly deepened grasp and application of the scientific outlook and method of communism.

As I spoke to earlier, since being forced into exile more than two decades ago, I have continued to give ideological and political leadership and direction to the RCP. I have studied and written extensively on profound problems and challenges confronting communists throughout the world in regrouping and carrying forward the revolutionary struggle in the face of truly devastating losses that have been experienced, above all the revisionist coup and capitalist restoration in China. I have continued

to dig into the experience of the proletarian revolution and of the socialist societies that were brought into being in the twentieth century, in the
Soviet Union and China, seeking to draw crucial lessons from both the
positive but also the negative aspects of all this, and focusing in particular on the questions: How can the masses of people truly become the
masters of society and of the state while at the same time advancing
toward the ultimate abolition of the state, together with the abolition of
all exploitative and oppressive divisions and social inequalities? And
what is the relationship between the masses of people and revolutionary
leadership in that process?

I have also focused attention on the monumental and unprecedented transformations that are going on throughout the world today
and their implications for the revolutionary struggle—in particular the
massive uprooting and migration of millions of peasants from the countryside to the urban areas each year throughout the Third World, with
the new situation emerging where half of the world's population now
lives in urban areas, with huge numbers of them in swelling shanty-
towns amidst tremendous poverty. I have continued to grapple with
social, political and ideological phenomena associated with these transformations, focusing particularly on the growing phenomenon of religious fundamentalism—not only Islamic fundamentalism in the Middle
East and other areas, but also Christian fundamentalism in the U.S. itself
—and the dangers and challenges this presents for the revolutionary
struggle to transform society, to bring true liberation and light and break
all chains of oppression—economic, social, political, ideological and
cultural.

I have written extensively and wrestled deeply—and continue to
wrestle—with questions having to do with the role of intellectuals and
artists and the creative process in relation to the larger interests of society, and the relation between collective and cooperative principles and
the interests of society as a whole, on the one hand, and the role and
rights of individuals and individual initiative, on the other hand.

In the context where our Party has undertaken the process of re-
writing our basic Programme, in line with changes that have occurred in
the world and important lessons we have been drawing in the more than
twenty years since our Party Programme was last written, I have led the
Party in breaking with serious errors, and a seriously flawed legacy of
the international communist movement, with regard to the question of

homosexuality. In the past, while we opposed discrimination against homosexuals, we regarded homosexuality as essentially a negative phenomenon which posed an obstacle to the ending of all oppression, and in particular we saw male homosexuality as something that contributed to the oppression of women. This is an erroneous and harmful position which we have not only changed but have set about deeply summing up and criticizing, not only within the Party but in published documents.[41]

Overall, I have continued to contribute whatever I can, and to lead the RCP in contributing the most it can, to the envisioning of, and the creation of, a whole new world, a communist world—a world of freely associating and cooperating human beings, a world in which the great majority of people, and ultimately all of humanity, would want to live and in which they would thrive, in ways never before possible or even imagined.

## Perseverance, and Inspiration

In recent years, just at the time when the rulers of the U.S. and other capitalists and imperialists were seizing on the reversal of the revolution in China and then the collapse of the Soviet Union to proclaim the ultimate triumph of the capitalist system, tremendous rebellions and protests have taken place, throughout the world and within the U.S. itself. In Los Angeles on a massive scale but also in Cincinnati and other cities, uprisings have taken place against outrageous acts of brutality and murder by the police. Through the work of our Party and others, a national coalition has been built against police brutality, and every year since 1996 there has been a National Day of Protest against police brutality, repression, and the criminalization of the youth, with thousands of people taking part in dozens of cities around the country. The battle around the right to abortion, as a key concentration of the fight against the oppression of women, has continued to rage, and is once again sharpening up. At the same time, the fight to eliminate discrimination against gays and lesbians in all spheres of society has taken new leaps. In recent years massive protests and battles have taken place against capitalist globalization and its devastating effects on people throughout the

---

41. This is discussed, and gone into in much greater detail and depth, in the new Programme of the Party and in a position paper, "On the Position on Homosexuality," available from RCP Publications.

world, particularly in the Third World, and on the environment. Our Party and Maoists in many other parts of the world have been increasingly involved in these movements and struggles.

Seizing on the events of September 11, 2001, the ruling class of the U.S. and its leading core have unleashed a juggernaut of war and repression, declaring a worldwide war to expand their global domination and exploitation in the name of "fighting terrorism," and instituting new levels of repression within the U.S. which are dangerous in themselves and represent precedent and potential for much greater and perhaps even unprecedented repression. All this has been met with increasingly massive resistance, in the U.S. itself and throughout the world, with tens of millions of people protesting against the war the U.S. was determined to launch against Iraq. I have characterized the juggernaut these imperialists have unleashed as "a cauldron of contradictions" and pointed to the fact that it holds the potential not only for great horrors and devastating setbacks for the resistance and revolutionary struggle of the masses of people throughout the world but at the same time the potential for great advances in this struggle—it holds the potential for these two extremes and everything in between.

This, of course, poses tremendous challenges for our Party and other Maoists throughout the world. One of the most important developments of the last twenty years is the fact that, in the aftermath of the tremendous loss in China, Maoists in different parts of the world, including the RCP in the U.S, have been able to regroup and unite together as an international movement, the Revolutionary Internationalist Movement (RIM). And in important parts of the world, Maoist parties, united in the RIM, are making crucial advances.

When I look at all this, I think again of my friend who decided to dedicate his life to ending cancer—and of the even greater need to put an end to the system of capitalism-imperialism and all the suffering and oppression this system embodies and enforces throughout the world. You see that there isn't anything more important that your life could be about, and whatever you end up contributing during the course of your lifetime is the most important and the most uplifting thing that you could possibly do. And yes, there are moments of great disappointment, but also moments of great joy as part of this. There is the joy that comes from seeing the ways in which people break free of constraints and rise up and begin to see the world as it really is and take up more consciously the struggle to change it. There is the joy of knowing that you are part of this whole process and contributing what you can to it. There is the joy of the camaraderie of being together with others in this struggle and knowing that it is something worthwhile, that it is not something petty and narrow that you are involved in but something uplifting. There is the joy of looking to the future and envisioning the goal that you are struggling for and seeing people come to even a beginning understanding of what that could mean, not just for themselves but for society, for humanity as a whole.

So this is what my life will continue to be devoted to, and this is what the ongoing story of my life will be about.

# About Bob Avakian

Bob Avakian is Chairman of the Revolutionary Communist Party, USA. A veteran of the Free Speech Movement and the revolutionary upsurges of the 1960s and early 1970s, he worked closely with the Black Panther Party. By the mid-1970s, he emerged as the foremost Maoist revolutionary in the United States. He has guided the RCP since its formation in 1975 and is a major leader of the international communist movement. Over the last twenty-five years, Avakian has produced a highly significant body of work, and he approaches Marxism as a living, developing science that must be constantly interrogating itself.

Avakian has penned the most comprehensive account of Mao's theoretical contributions to Marxism. He has been undertaking an ongoing examination of the experience of proletarian revolution in the twentieth century—its great achievements, in particular the profound lessons of the Cultural Revolution in China, as well as its setbacks, shortcomings, and mistakes. He has been addressing issues of revolutionary strategy in the U.S. and for the international movement. He has analyzed why revolution is not only necessary but also possible within the U.S. itself.

Through these and other critical investigations, Avakian has been bringing forward a vision of socialism and communism that breaks vital new ground for Marxism and the communist project. He has been deepening and enlarging the understanding of the tasks and contradictions bound up with the exercise of revolutionary authority and how the

447

masses can be unleashed to rule and transform society. In recent writings, he has been speaking to the indispensable role of dissent in socialist society—how it contributes to deeper knowledge of socialist society, the critical spirit that must permeate it, and the continuing struggle to transform socialist society towards communism. He has been drawing attention to the importance of the intellectual and cultural spheres in socialist society and in the revolutionary process overall, and he probes historic problems in the understanding and approach of the international communist movement. In works such as *Conquer the World—The International Proletariat Must and Will* and *Getting Over the Two Great Humps: Further Thoughts on Conquering the World*, he has been conceptualizing the international dimensions of communist revolution in ways that have far-reaching implications for the world struggle.

Avakian's writings are marked by great breadth—from discussions about religion and atheism and morality, to the limits of classical democracy, to basketball. It is often alleged that a vanguard party is incompatible with a searching, critical, and creative intellectual enterprise. Avakian gives the lie to this claim.

From his life experience and revolutionary perspective comes a profound sense of the struggles and sentiments among the masses of people; and he keeps his finger on the pulse of the movements of opposition in society more broadly. This is a revolutionary leader who has said about leadership: "if you don't have a poetic spirit—or at least a poetic side—it is very dangerous for you to lead a Marxist movement or be the leader of a socialist state."

Bob Avakian is the visionary leader of a Maoist vanguard party, the Revolutionary Communist Party, which has its sights on the revolutionary seizure of power and the radical transformation of society in the colossus that is late imperial America—all as part of a worldwide process of revolutionary struggle whose final aim is communism, a world without exploitative and oppressive relations and the corresponding political structures, institutions, and ideas and culture.

* * *

The author and Insight Press welcome readers' comments about this book. Correspondence should be addressed c/o Insight Press, 4064 N. Lincoln Ave. #264, Chicago, IL 60618. Additional information about this memoir and the author can be found at www.insight-press.com.

Several other websites contain further information and works by the author:

• **bobavakian.net**—contains various resources, including downloadable audio recordings of recent talks by and question-and-answer sessions with Bob Avakian.

• **rwor.org**—the official website of the *Revolutionary Worker/Obrero Revolucionario*, voice of the Revolutionary Communist Party, USA; includes an extensive collection of articles and other material written by Bob Avakian. The *Revolutionary Worker/Obrero Revolucionario* regularly publishes articles by Bob Avakian, and is published weekly in English and Spanish editions. For subscription information, write to RW/OR, Box 3486, Merchandise Mart, Chicago, IL 60654.

• **threeQvideo.com**—website of Three Q Productions, producer of the video *Revolution: Why It's Necessary, Why It's Possible, What It's All About*, a film of a 2003 talk by Bob Avakian. The video, in DVD or VHS format, can be ordered online.

Also by Bob Avakian